Retrospecta

38

● Studios   ▲ Advanced Studios   ■ Electives   ■ Events

Contents

Architecture is first and foremost the physical act of building. It has its own set of core values and competencies that form the foundation for ongoing explorations as architects address new social challenges, new techniques, and new technologies.

Retrospecta surveys the year's work and illuminates the spirit of our search not only by documenting a moment in time, but also connecting to the past and anticipating the future. Yale School of Architecture does not subscribe to one philosophy or methodology; rather, the constant in a Yale education is a commitment to pluralism. Deeply embedded is the responsibility to see a problem from multiple angles and resolve it.

This is a school bent on arming each new generation of architectural thinkers and makers with the intellectual, social, and critical skills to ask the right question of themselves, the profession, and the public. As we navigate today's complex landscape of design ideas and technologies, we are confronted with ever-more compelling questions. We welcome the challenge of the future confident that our approach does not insist on what to think, but on how to think.

The world within the walls of Rudolph Hall overflows with ideas, some hitherto unseen and others rediscovered. Retrospecta is not merely a collection of those ideas; it is a mirror to the culture of architecture as a whole. The exigent moments at Yale, captured in these pages, reflect a learning environment committed to nurturing the inner-life of creativity and a life-long journey toward excellence.

Robert A.M. Stern
Dean and J.M. Hoppin Professor of Architecture

Faculty Awards ↘

Peggy Deamer
Brunner Grant From The Center
For Architecture

Elihu Rubin
Rosenkranz Award

Turner Brooks
Sidonie Miskimin Clauss Prize
For Teaching Excellence In
The Humanities

Peter Eisenman
Topaz Medallion For Excellence In
Architectural Education

Adam Hopfner & George Knight
Professor King-Lui Wu
Teaching Award

Student Fellowships ↘

Karolina Maria Czeczek
William Wirt Winchester Travelling
Fellowship

Belinda Lee
David M. Schwarz Architectural
Services Good Times Award

Anne Ma
The Gertraud A. Wood Traveling
Fellowship

Andrew Sternad
The George Nelson Scholarship

Student Internships ↘

Kiana Hosseini
The David Schwarz Internship

Jean Chen
The Takenaka Internship

H.I. Feldman Prize Nominees ✳

Fall 2014
Dionysus Cho
Olen Snow Milholland
Mahdi Sabbagh &
Jonathan Feng Sun
Adam Ramsey Wagoner &
Raphael De La Fontaine
Julcsi Futo
Perry Wexelberg
Charlotte Algie

Spring 2015
Emau Vega
Benjamin Smith
Leah Abrams
Michael Cohen
Lauren Raab & Michael Miller
Stephanie Jazmines
Julcsi Futo & Karolina Czeczek
Apoorva Khanolkar
Alissa Chastain

The H.I. Feldman Prize Winner ⬟
Kara Marie Biczykowski

Student Medals And Prizes ↘

John Blakely Wolfe
The Moulton Andrus Award

Madhi Sabbagh
AIA Henry Adams Medal

Sarah Elaine Smith
AIA Henry Adams Certificate

Raphael De La Fontaine
The Alpha Rho Chi Medal

Maya Catherine Alexander
The Janet Cain Sielaff
Alumni Award

Eric Wycoff Rogers
The David Taylor Memorial Prize

Jonathan Feng Sun
The Parsons Medal

Dionysus Roy Cho
The Drawing Prize

Olen Snow Milholland
Gene Lewis Book Prize

Amy J. Su
The Sonia Albert Schimberg Prize

John Kleinschmidt
The Wendy Elizabeth
Blanning Prize

Emily Abruzzo
Critic

D. Michelle Addington
Hines Professor of Sustainable
Architectural Design

Victor Agran
Lecturer

John Apicella
Lecturer

Pier Vittorio Aureli
Louis I. Kahn Visiting Professor,
Spring Term

Sunil Bald
Associate Professor Adjunct

Thomas Beeby
Professor Adjunct and William
Henry Bishop Visiting Professor,
Spring Term

Anibal Bellomio
Lecturer

Andrew Benner
Critic

Deborah Berke
Professor Adjunct

Phillip G. Bernstein
Lecturer

Tatiana Bilbao
Louis I. Kahn Visiting Assistant
Professor, Spring Term

Rafael Birmann
Edward P. Bass Distinguished
Visiting Architecture Fellow,
Spring Term

John Blood
Critic

Kent C. Bloomer
Professor Adjunct

Kyle Bradley
Critic

Karla Britton
Lecturer

Miroslava Brooks
Critic

Turner Brooks
Professor Adjunct

Brennan Buck
Critic

Eric Buckley
Lecturer

Luke Bulman
Lecturer

Marta Caldeira
Critic

Aran Chadwick
Lecturer

Darin Curts
Instructor

Trattie Davies
Critic

Peggy Deamer
Assistant Dean and Professor

Peter de Bretteville
Critic

Hernan Diaz Alonso
Eero Saarinen Visiting Professor,
Spring Term

Keller Easterling
Professor

John C. Eberhart
Critic

Peter Eisenman
Charles Gwathmey Professor
in Practice

Alexander J. Felson
Assistant Professor

Martin J. Finio
Critic

Kurt W. Forster
Professor Emeritus (Visiting)

Bryan Fuermann
Lecturer

Mark Foster Gage
Assistant Dean and
Associate Professor

Alexander Garvin
Professor Adjunct

Martin D. Gehner
Professor Emeritus

Kenneth Gibble
Lecturer

Elizabeth Gray
Louis I. Kahn Visiting Assistant
Professor, Fall Term

Kevin D. Gray
Lecturer

Sean Griffiths
Eero Saarinen Visiting Professor,
Fall Term

Stephen Harby
Lecturer

Steven Harris
Professor Adjunct

Andrei Harwell
Critic

Robert Haughney
Lecturer

Kristin Hawkins
Lecturer

Dolores Hayden
Professor

Mimi Hoang
Critic

Charles Holland
Eero Saarinen Visiting Professor,
Fall Term

Adam Hopfner
Critic and Director of Jim Vlock
First-Year Building Project

Joyce Hsiang
Critic

Elijah Huge
Visiting Associate Professor

Nathan Hume
Critic

Sam Jacob
Eero Saarinen Visiting Professor,
Fall Term

John D. Jacobson
Associate Dean and
Professor Adjunct

Lawrence Jones
Lecturer

Yoko Kawai
Lecturer

George Knight
Critic

Alfred Kim Koetter
Instructor and Director of
Exhibitions

Leon Krier
Robert A.M. Stern Visiting
Professor, Spring Term

Amy Lelyveld
Critic

Jennifer W. Leung
Critic

M.J. Long
Critic

Greg Lynn
William B. and Charlotte Shepherd
Davenport Visiting Professor,
Spring Term

Niall McLaughlin
Norman R. Foster Visiting
Professor, Spring Term

Bimal Mendis
Assistant Dean and Assistant
Professor Adjunct

Edward Mitchell
Assistant Professor Adjunct

Kyoung Sun Moon
Associate Professor

Joeb Moore
Critic

Herbert S. Newman
Critic

Timothy Newton
Critic

Alan W. Organschi
Louis I. Kahn Visiting Assistant
Professor, Fall Term and Critic,
Spring Term

John Patkau
Norman R. Foster Visiting
Professor, Fall Term

Eeva-Liisa Pelkonen
Associate Professor

Miriam Peterson
Lecturer

Amrit Pilo
Instructor

Laura Pirie
Lecturer

Alan J. Plattus
Professor

Jeffrey Pollack
Instructor

Victoria Ponce de Leon
Lecturer

Alexander Purves
Professor Emeritus

Eero Puurunen
Lecturer

Craig Razza
Lecturer

Todd Reisz
Daniel Rose (1951) Visiting
Assistant Professor, Spring Term

Joshua Revkin
Instructor

Pierce Reynoldson
Lecturer

Kevin Rotheroe
Lecturer

Elihu Rubin
Assistant Professor

Evan Sabatelli
Instructor

Ryan Salvatore
Lecturer

Austin Samson
Critic

Joel Sanders
Professor Adjunct

Aniket Shahane
Critic

Daniel Sherer
Lecturer

Edward M. Stanley
Lecturer

Philip Steiner
Lecturer

Robert A.M. Stern
Dean and J.M. Hoppin Professor

Michael Szivos
Critic

Neil Thomas
Lecturer

Adam Trojanowski
Lecturer

Billie Tsien
William B. and Charlotte Shepherd
Davenport Visiting Professor,
Fall Term

Anthony Vidler
Vincent Scully Visiting Professor,
Spring Term

Annabel Wharton
Vincent Scully Visiting Professor,
Fall Term

Tod Williams
William B. and Charlotte Shepherd
Davenport Visiting Professor,
Fall Term

Carter Wiseman
Lecturer

M.Arch I, First Year, Class of 2017

● Caroline L. Acheatel
B.A. Univ. Pennsylvania 2012
Poway, CA
● Ava Amirahmadi
B.A. Columbia Univ. 2013
Kansas City, MO
● Elaina Diane Berkowitz
B.Des. Univ. Florida 2012
Seminole, FL
● John Lucas Zechariah Boyd
B.A.S. Carleton Univ. 2013
Toronto, Canada
● Graham Stuart Brindle
B.A.S. Univ. Waterloo 2011
Toronto, Canada
● Francesca Lena Carney
B.F.A. Savannah College
of Art & Design 2014
Bryn Mawr, PA
● Henry Wilson Carroll
B.S. Georgia Inst. of Technology 2010
Lakeside, MT
● Hsi-ning Anny Chang
B.F.A. Parsons School of Design 2012
Fremont, CA
● Nai Wee Chng
Bach. Royal College of Surgeons 1993
Singapore
● Dakota Anderson Cooley
B.F.A. Univ. Texas, Austin 2012
Houston, TX
● Robert Johannes Cornelissen
B.A.S. Univ. Auckland 2014
Auckland, New Zealand
● Ethan Fischer
B.A. Vassar College 2011
Brooklyn, NY
● Casey M. Furman
B.Des. Univ. Florida 2014
Oviedo, FL
● Rachel McKenzie Gamble
B.A. Clemson Univ. 2014
Elgin, SC
● Cathryn Alexandra Garcia-Menocal
B.F.A. Washington Univ., St. Louis 2012
Miami, FL
● Daniel Marcus Glick-Unterman
B.S. Univ. Michigan, Ann Arbor 2014
Evanston, IL
● Chad Andrew Greenlee
B.S. Ohio State Univ., Columbus 2014
Uniontown, OH
● Jacqueline Elizabeth Hall
B.A. New York Univ. 2012
Topsfield, MA
● Claudia Garrett Hardee
B.A. Univ. Texas, Austin 2013
Beatrice, AL
● Wesley Michael Hiatt
B.S. Ohio State Univ., Columbus 2013
Columbus, OH
● Robert M. Hon
B.F.A. Savannah College
of Art & Design 2014
Columbia, MO
● Yue Hou
B.A., B.S. Univ. Toronto 2013
Shijiazhuang, China
● Heung-Sum Cecilia Hui
B.A. Univ. Toronto 2011
Toronto, Canada
● Matthew Charles Kabala
B.A. Univ. California, Davis 2014
San Mateo, CA
● Samuel Redell King
B.A. Washington Univ., St. Louis 2012
Saint Louis, MO
● Alexander Oleg Kruhly
B.A. Univ. Pennsylvania 2013
Radnor, PA
● Aaryoun Lee
B.F.A. Rhode Island School of Design 2012
Tenafly, NJ
● Christopher Haiman Leung
B.S. Univ. College London 2010
Hong Kong
● Paul Jacob Lorenz
B.A. Univ. Wisconsin, Milwaukee 2006
Madison, WI
● Michael Loya
B.A. Columbia Univ. 2012
New York, NY

● Daniel S. Marty
B.S. Univ. Michigan, Ann Arbor 2013
Cincinnati, OH
● Stephen A McNamara
B.S. Ohio State Univ., Columbus 2014
Brewster, NY
● Tess Kathleen McNamara
B.A. Princeton Univ. 2012
New York, NY
● Laura Elizabeth Meade
B.S. Ohio State Univ., Columbus 2012
Columbus, OH
● Maxwell T. Mensching
B.A. Hobart & William Smith Colleges 2011
New Canaan, CT
● Rashidbek Muydinov
B.B.A. Tashkent State Tech Univ. 2007
New Haven, CT
● Elizabeth G Nadai
B.A. Yale Univ. 2010
Essex, MA
● Anna Alexandrovna Nasonova
B.A. Yale Univ. 2013
Voronezh, Russia
● Cecily Maria Ng
B.A. Univ. California, Berkeley 2012
San Francisco, CA
● Hannah L. Novack
B.A. Barnard College 2013
Saint Louis, MO
● Brittany Paige Olivari
B.S. Univ. Virginia 2012
Castine, ME
● Andrew Bryan Padron
B.Des. Univ. Florida 2012
Loxahatchee, FL
● Paul Lloyd Rasmussen
B.S. Brigham Young Univ. 2013
San Jose, CA
● Nasim Rowshanabadi
B.Arch. Bahai Institute for Higher Ed. 2011
Hamden, CT
● Benjamin Frank Rubenstein
B.S. Univ. Illinois, Urbana-Champaign 2013
Glencoe, IL
● James Schwartz
B.F.A. New York Univ. 2012
Old Westbury, NY
● Madison Sembler
B.F.A. Washington Univ., St. Louis 2012
Pinellas Park, FL
● Ilana R. Simhon
B.S. SUNY, Buffalo 2014
Plainview, NY
● Alexander Stagge
B.S. Ohio State Univ., Columbus 2014
Cincinnati, OH
● Georgia Mohr Todd
B.A. Colgate Univ. 2010
Charlottesville, VA
● Margaret Jau-ming Tsang
B.A. Yale Univ. 2011
Bethesda, MD
● Robert J. Yoos
B.S. SUNY, Buffalo 2014
Kings Park, N.Y
● Matthew Glen Zuckerman
B.A. Yale Univ. 2011
Mamaroneck, NY

M.Arch I, Second Year, Class of 2016

■ Lisa Ning Albaugh
B.S. United States Naval Academy 2006
Essex, CT
■ Mohammad Abdulatif Alothman
B.S. King Fahd Univ. of Petroleum and
Minerals 2008
Dhahran, Saudi Arabia
■ Luke Alan Anderson
B.S. Ohio State Univ., Columbus 2013
Cincinnati, OH
■ Jessica Flore Angel
B.S. École Polytechnique Fédérale
de Lausanne 2011
Paris, France
■ Li De Jack Bian
B.S. McGill Univ. 2013
Toronto, Canada
■ Dorian Ascher Booth
B.A. Univ. Pennsylvania 2012
Ogunquit, ME

■ Benjamin Stuart Harlan Bourgoin
B.A. Univ. Washington 2012
Lake Forest Park, WA
■ Ling Jun Chen
A.B. Princeton Univ. 2012
Huntsville, Canada
■ Tianhui Chen
B.A., B.F.A. Cornell Univ. 2013
Gaithersburg, MD
■ Andrew Eric Dadds
B.A.S. Univ. Waterloo 2012
Oakville, Canada
■ Shayari Hiranya De Silva
B.A. Yale Univ. 2011
Colombo, Sri Lanka
■ Jessica Lynn Elliott
B.Des. Univ. Florida 2013
Casselberry, FIL
■ Dov Feinmesser
B.A.S. Ryerson Univ. 2011
North York, Canada
■ Hugo Gregory Fenaux
B.S. Univ. Virginia 2012
Dillwyn, VA
■ Dante T.H. Furioso
B.A. Wesleyan Univ., 2007
Washington, D.C.
■ Anthony Vincent Gagliardi
B.S. Ohio State Univ., Columbus 2013
Parma, OH
■ Michelle Jennifer Gonzalez
B.S. Univ. Michigan, Ann Arbor 2013
West Orange, NJ
■ Michael Edward Harrison
B.S. Univ. Michigan, Ann Arbor 2013
Grosse Pointe Park, MI
■ Ting Ting Pearl Ho
B.S. Univ. Virginia 2011
Hong Kong
■ Seyedeh Kiana Hosseini
B.A. Tehran Univ. 2013
Karaj, Iran
■ Anne Lawren Householder
B.A.S. Univ. Illinois,
Urbana-Champaign 2013
Park Ridge, IL
■ Cynthia Hsu
B.A. Univ. California, San Diego 2012
Yorba Linda, CA
■ Samantha Leigh Jaff
B.A. Colby College 2011
Newton, MA
■ Lila Jiang Chen
B.S. McGill Univ. 2011
Panama City, Panama
■ Charles Anderson Kane
B.A. Clemson Univ. 2011
Lake Wylie, SC
■ Sarah Elizabeth Kasper
B.S. Univ. Illinois, Urbana-Champaign 2013
Crete, IL
■ James E. Kehl
B.S. Univ. Cincinnati 2010
Newark, OH
■ Nicolas Thornton Kemper
B.A. Yale Univ. 2011
Kansas City, MO
■ Eunhyung Kim
B.A.S. Univ. Waterloo 2012
Calgary, Canada
■ John Walker Kleinschmidt
B.A. Washington Univ., St. Louis 2008
Fort Atkinson, WI
■ Elizabeth Ann LeBlanc
B.A.S. Univ. Texas, Austin 2013
San Antonio, TX
■ Vittorio F. Lovato
B.S. Univ. Michigan, Ann Arbor 2012
Berkley, MI
■ Clarissa Astrid Luwia
B.Des. Univ. Sydney 2012
New South Wales, Australia
■ Anne Wing Yan Ma
B.A.S. Univ. Waterloo 2011
Toronto, Canada
■ Richard David Mandimika
B.A. Univ. Miami, Ohio 2012
Harare, Zimbabwe
■ Megan Elizabeth McDonough
B.S. Georgia Inst. of Technology 2013
Ambler, PA
■ Anna Meloyan
B.A. Univ. Calif., Los Angeles 2013
Glendale, CA

■ Seokim Min
B.S. Korea Advanced Inst. of Science
and Technology 2013
Seoul, Republic of Korea
■ Boris Morin-Defoy
B.S. McGill Univ. 2011
Montreal, Canada
■ Kristin Louise Nothwehr
B.A. Yale Univ. 2010
Brooklyn, NY
■ Justin David Oh
B.A.S. Ryerson Univ. 2013
Calgary, Canada
■ Xiaoyi Pu
B.S. McGill Univ. 2012
Beijing, China
■ Feng Qian
B.E. Southeast Univ., Nanjing 2013
Nanjing, China
■ Madelynn Christine Ringo
B.A. Univ. Kentucky, Lexington 2012
Bloomfield, KY
■ Luis Enrique Salas Porras
B.A. Rice Univ. 2011
Chihuahua, Mexico
■ Dima Ramzi Srouji
B.A. Kingston Univ. 2012
New Haven, CT
■ Katherine Rose Stege
B.E.D. Univ. Colorado, Boulder 2012
Leadville, CO
■ Andrew John Sternad
B.A. Washington Univ., St. Louis 2009
Norcross, GA
■ Winny Windasari Tan
B.A. Carnegie Mellon Univ. 2012
Singapore
■ You Zhi Eugene Tan
B.A. National Univ. Singapore 2012
Singapore
■ Caitlin Mory Thissen
B.S. Univ. Utah 2013
Salt Lake City, UT
■ Chengqi John Wan
B.S. Univ. College London 2013
Singapore
■ Shuo Wang
B.A.S. Univ. Waterloo 2013
Kitchener, Canada
■ Xinyi Wang
B.Arch. Tsinghua Univ. 2013
Beijing, China
■ Xiao Wu
B.S. Univ. Virginia 2012
Hangzhou, China

M.Arch I, Third Year, Class of 2015

▲ Leah Jaclyn Abrams
B.A. Univ. Pennsylvania 2011
Wall Township, NJ
▲ Maya Catherine Alexander
B.I.D. Louisiana State Univ.,
Baton Rouge 2007
Brooklyn, NY
▲ Elena Rachel Baranes
B.A. Boston Univ. 2011
Washington, D.C.
▲ Emily D. Bell
B.A. Colgate Univ. 2012
Southbury, CT
▲ Hiba Javed Bhatty
B.S. Univ. Illinois, Urbana-
Champaign 2011
Glenview, IL
▲ Kara Marie Biczykowski
B.S. Ohio State Univ., Columbus 2012
Amherst, OH
▲ Amanda Nicole Bridges
A.B. Harvard Univ. 2010
Villanova, PA
▲ Alissa Yen Chastain
B.A. Wellesley Coll. 2010
Lafayette, CA
▲ Dionysus Roy Cho B.A.S. Waterloo
Univ. 2011
Edmonton, Canada
▲ Stanley Minsoo Cho
B.A. Univ. California, Los Angeles 2001
Tujunga, CA
▲ Sungwoo Matthew Choi
B.A. Washington Univ., Missouri 2012
Gwangju, Republic of Korea

▲ Suhni Chung
B.S. Massachusetts Inst. of
 Technology 2009
Seoul, Republic of Korea

▲ Michael Robinson Cohen
A.B. Brown Univ. 2008
Chappaqua, NY

▲ Carl David Cornilsen
M.B.A, B.S. Univ. Michigan,
 Ann Arbor 2005①
Houghton, MI

▲ Thomas Aaron Day
B.F.A. Univ. Massachusetts, Amherst 2011
New Haven, CT

▲ Thomas Rush Friddle
B.A. Ball State Univ. 2012
Muncie, IN

▲ Tamrat Tesfaye Gebremichael
B.S. Univ. Virginia 2012
Alexandria, VA

▲ Bruce David Hancock
A.B. Princeton Univ. 2003
Costa Mesa, CA

▲ Kirk McFadden Henderson
B.A. Yale Univ. 2005
Washington, D.C.

▲ Zachary Dillon Huelsing
M.A. Eastern Illinois Univ. 2007
Chicago, IL

▲ Elisa Iturbe
M.E.M., B.A. Yale Univ. 2008②
Bonita, CA

▲ Tyson Jang
B.A. Boston College 2009
Seoul, Republic of Korea

▲ Haelee Jung
B.F.A. Seoul National Univ. 2009
Daejeon, Republic of Korea

▲ John-Thaddeus Keeley
A.B. Harvard Univ. 2007
Morristown, NJ

▲ Julie Kim
B.F.A. Cooper Union 2009
Port Washington, NY

▲ Peter K. Le
B.A. Amherst College 2010
Garden Grove, CA

▲ Belinda Lee
B.S. Washington Univ., Missouri 2012
New Haven, CT

▲ Hyeun Jason Lee
B.S. Ohio State Univ., Columbus 2011
Falls Church, VA

▲ Minu Lee
M.S. Seoul National Univ. 2012
Seoul, Republic of Korea

▲ Mun Hee Lee
B.A. Tufts Univ. 2010
Seoul, Republic of Korea

▲ Meghan Lewis
M.E.M., B.S. Washington Univ.,
 Missouri 2011②
Denver, CO

▲ Meghan Baker McAllister
B.A. Haverford Coll. 2010
Jenkintown, PA

▲ William Ross McClellan
B.Des. Univ. Florida 2012
Tallahassee, FL

▲ Henry Thomas Mezza
E.S. Ball State Univ. 2012
Arlington Heights, IL

▲ Michael Christopher Miller
B.S. Georgia Inst. of Technology 2012
Kennesaw, GA

▲ Nicholas Muraglia
B.A. Columbia Univ. 2008
Los Angeles, CA

▲ Phillip Josh Takeshi Nakamura
B.S. Univ. Utah 2012
Cottonwood Heights, UT

▲ Hui Zhen Ng
B.S. Univ. College London 2012
Singapore

▲ Daniel Huy Nguyen
B.A. Univ. California, Los Angeles 2011
Torrance, CA

▲ Junpei Okai
B.A. Univ. California, Los Angeles 2011
Murrieta, CA

▲ Alexander Osei-Bonsu
B.F.A. Univ. Oxford 2007
London, United Kingdom

▲ Jeannette Kittredge Penniman
B.A. Yale Univ. 2012
Essex, CT

▲ Tyler Benjamin Pertman
B.S. Univ. Alberta 2010
Edmonton, Canada

▲ Mark Wendell Peterson
M.B.A. Univ. Michigan, Ann Arbor
Brooklyn, NY

▲ Lauren Elizabeth Raab
B.S. Cornell Univ. 2011
Crown Point, IN

▲ Mahdi Sabbagh
B.A. Yale Univ. 2010
Jerusalem, Israel

▲ Robert K. Scott
B.S. Ohio State Univ., Columbus 2011
Columbus, OH

▲ Benjamin Lucas Smith
B.S. Georgia Inst. of Technology 2012
Hartford, WI

▲ Sarah Elaine Smith
B.S. Univ. Cincinnati 2010
Cincinnati, OH

▲ Melody J. Song
B.A. New York Univ. 2011
Seoul, Republic of Korea

▲ Amy J. Su
B.F.A. Rhode Island School of Design 2009
Portland, OR

▲ Jonathan Feng Sun
E.E. Univ. Toronto 2012
Ontario, Canada

▲ Zachary Adam Veach
B.A. Washington Univ. 2012
Teaneck, NJ

▲ Emau Vega
B.E.D. Texas A&M Univ.,
 College Station 2011
Waco, TX

▲ Perry S. Wexelberg
B.A. Univ. California, Santa Cruz 2008
El Cerrito, CA

▲ Matthew Hastings White
M.B.A., B.S. Washington Univ.,
 Missouri 2006①
Lake Forest, IL

▲ John Blakely Wolfe
B.S. Univ. Virginia 2009
Annandale, VA

▲ Ru-Shyan Yen
M.E.M., B.A. Wheaton Coll., Mass. 2008②
Pittsburgh, PA

▲ Sheena Shiyi Zhang
M.E.M., B.S. Univ. Georgia, Athens 2011②
Watkinsville, GA

M.Arch II, First Year, Class of 2016

● Jared Matthew Abraham
B.Arch. Univ. Oregon 2007
New Haven, CT

● Charlotte Leonie Algie
B.Arch. RMIT Univ. 2009
Hawthorn, Australia

● Daphne Binder
B.Arch. Cooper Union 2011
New Haven, CT

● Eunil Cho
B.Arch. Cooper Union 2010
Louisville, KY

● Shuangjing Hu
B.Arch. Tsinghua Univ. 2012
Changsha, China

● Roberto Jenkins
B.Arch. Pratt Institute 2013
Miami, FL

● Karl Elie Karam
DIPL Architectural Association 2013
Beirut, Lebanon

● Apoorva Gurunath Khanolkar
B.Arch. Univ. Mumbai 2013
Mumbai, India

● Jason Kurzweil
B.A. New Jersey Inst. of Technology 2011
Staten Island, NY

● Jingwen Li
B.Arch. Xian Jiaotong Univ. 2011
Changsha, China

● Jizhou Liu
B.Arch. Tsinghua Univ. 2013
Beijing, China

● Adil Mansure
B.Arch. Univ. Mumbai 2011
Toronto, Canada

● Abdulgader Samier Naseer
B.Arch. Univ. Miami 2014
Jeddah, Saudi Arabia

● Soo Young Park
B.Arch. Yonsei Univ. 2013
Seoul, South Korea

● Alicia Pozniak
B.A., B.Arch. Univ. Technology 2005
Alexandria, Australia

● Sofia Anja Singler
B.Arch. Univ. Cambridge 2013
Jyväskylä, Finland

● Isaac P Southard
B.Arch. Drexel Univ. 2011
Philadelphia, PA

● Mengshi Sun
B.Arch. Tsinghua Univ. 2014
Beijing, China

M.Arch II, Second Year, Class of 2015

■ Karolina Maria Czeczek
M.Arch. Cracow Univ. of Technology 2010
Krosno, Poland

■ Raphael de la Fontaine
B.Arch. Pratt Institute 2011
New Haven, CT

■ Julcsi Futo
B.Arch. Univ. of Applied Arts Vienna 2009
Brooklyn, NY

■ Elvira Hoxha
B.Arch. New Jersey Inst.
 of Technology 2013
Tirana, Albania

■ Stephanie Anne Arrienda Jazmines
B.Arch. Univ. Notre Dame, 2011
Glendale, CA

■ Amir A. Karimpour
B.Arch. Pratt Institute 2013
Moraga, CA

■ Read James Langworthy
B.Arch. Carnegie Mellon Univ. 2007
Seattle, WA

■ Mengran Li
B.Arch. Tsinghua Univ. 2012
Daqing, China

■ Yifan Li
M.Arch. Univ. Adelaide 2010
Chongqing, China

■ Kate Alexandra Lisi
B.Arch. Rensselaer Polytechnic
 Inst. 2013
Orange, CT

■ Laurence Peter Esmond Lumley
B.Arch. Univ. Cambridge 2011
London, United Kingdom

■ Daniel James Luster
B.Arch. Univ. Tennessee, Knoxville 2010
Philadelphia, PA

■ Peter Allen McInish
B.Arch. Auburn Univ. 2013
Dothan, AL

■ Olen Snow Milholland
B.Arch. Univ. Southern California 2009
Boise, ID

■ Katarzyna Magdalena Pozniak
B.Arch. Cornell Univ. 2013
Gdansk, Poland

■ Ian Stewart Spencer
B.S., B.Arch. Univ. Houston 2013
Spring Branch, TX

■ Adam Ramsey Wagoner
M.Arch. Kansas State Univ. 2009
McPherson, KS

■ Kin Tak Yu
B.A. Southern California Inst.
 of Architcture 2012
Hong Kong

■ Boyuan Zhang
B.Arch. Tsinghua Univ. 2013
Zhuhai, China

M.E.D., First Year, Class of 2016

● Geneva Morris
B.A. Loyola Univ., Illinois 2011
Chicago, IL

● Shivani Umesh Shedde
B.Arch. Univ. Mumbai 2012
Mumbai, India

● Preeti Murali Talwai
B.A. Univ. California, Berkeley 2013
Folson, CA

M.ED., Second Year, Class of 2015

■ Benyameen A B Y Ghareeb
B.Arch. 2008, M.Arch. 2009 Univ. Miami
Kuwait City, Kuwait

■ Eric D. Peterson
B.A. Hampshire Coll. 2010
New Haven, CT

■ Eric Wycoff Rogers
B.F.A. California Coll. of Arts
 and Crafts 2013
San Francisco, CA

■ Andrew David Ruff
B.Arch. Univ. Tennessee, Knoxville 2011
New Haven, CT

■ Brent Sturlaugson
B.Arch. Univ. Oregon 2008
Rapid City, SD

Ph. D., First Year

◎ Eugene Han
M.Arch. Art Center of College
 of Design 2005
London, England

Ph. D., Second Year

◎ Theodossios Issaias
M.Arch. Massachusetts Inst.
 of Technology 2011
Athens, Greece

◎ Skender Luarasi
M.Arch. Massachusetts Inst.
 of Technology 2005
Somerville, MA

Ph. D., Third Year

◎ Tim Steffen Altenhof
M.Arch. Acad. of Fine Arts Vienna 2009
Vienna, Austria

◎ Ioanna Angelidou
M.Arch. Columbia Univ. 2009
New York, NY

Ph. D., Fourth Year

◎ Anna Bokov
M.Arch. Harvard Univ. 2004
Calverton, NY

◎ Surry Schlabs
M.Arch. Yale Univ. 2003
New Haven, CT

Ph. D., Sixth Year

◎ Joseph Lawrence Clarke
M.Arch. Univ. Cincinnati 2006
New York, NY

◎ Kyle Andrew Dugdale
M.Arch. Harvard Univ. 2002
New Haven, CT

① Joint-degree program, M.B.A.,
 School of Management
② Joint-degree program, M.E.M.,
 School of Forestry and
 Environmental Studies

Retrospecta 38

Letter from the Editors

We believe that a true record of a year at YSOA is not a tidy catalog of final projects – it's messy. No single part of the school is separate from another. Events and coursework occur simultaneously to form a feedback loop, and this flurry of activity makes it impossible to experience everything in tandem.

The goal of Retrospecta 38 is not only to revisit and record, but also to make the entirety of the year accessible. Accordingly, this book brings the world of YSOA to life with intentional unruliness: studio projects mix with written abstracts, paintings comingle with plans, and lectures are scattered in between.

Retrospecta 38 is a chronological record made tangible — it opens with advanced studio lottery and closes with the summer Building Project and graduation. This book showcases final projects and transcribes reviews, but with equal rigor reveals the everyday. It remembers late nights in studio, Dean Stern's martini receptions, and chance epiphanies in Rudolph Hall's paprika-carpeted pits. Academic work pairs with these moments to generate the rhythm of content in this book. In short, this confluence of ideas and experiences tells the complete story of life at Yale School of Architecture.

We extend our gratitude to Yale School of Art's talented graphic design students, Laura Foxgrover and Moonsick Gang, who were instrumental in establishing the identity of Retrospecta 38 and worked tirelessly alongside us from the start.

Thank you to Dean Stern, who provided us with his keen eye and supportive criticism all year. Richard Kaplan of Allied Printing and Michael Bierut of Pentagram guided us through the complex world of publishing, while John Jacobson and Richard DeFlumeri worked with us to make our vision a reality. Retrospecta would not be possible without our generous donors or the support of our faculty. Finally, we'd like to thank Yale School of Architecture's students whose creative ambition both inspires and constitutes the content of this annual publication.

Cathryn Garcia-Menocal,
Wes Hiatt,
Laura Meade,
Maggie Tsang

Fall

1011a
First Year Design Studio
M.Arch. I

<u>Coordinator</u>
Joyce Hsiang {**JH**}

<u>Critics</u>
Brennan Buck {**BB**}, Peggy Deamer {**PD**}, Eeva-Liisa Pelkonen {**ELP**}, Michael Szivos {**MS**}

<u>Jurors</u>
Abby Hume {**AH**}, Alexander Purves {**AP**}, Alfie Koetter {**AK**}, Andrew Benner {**AB**}, Andrew Saunders {**AS**}, Angie Co {**AC**}, Annabel Wharton {**AW**}, Anya Bokov {**ABV**}, Ben Pell {**BP**}, Bryan Young {**BY**}, Dan Wood {**DW**}, Emily Abruzzo {**EA**}, Ilias Papageorgi {**IP**}, Irina Verona {**IV**}, Jennifer Leung {**JL**}, Jessica Barter {**JB**}, Julian Bonder {**JBo**}, Karen Fairbanks {**KF**}, Kate John Adler {**KJA**}, Keller Easterling {**KE**}, Kurt Forster {**KuF**}, Kutan Ayata {**KA**}, Kyle Dugdale {**KD**} Kyle Miller {**KM**}, Max Kuo {**MK**}, Michael Chen {**MC**}, Michelle Addington {**MA**}, Michelle Fornabadi {**MF**}, Mirka Brooks {**MB**}, Robert A. M. Stern {**RAMS**}, Sandra Arndt {**SA**}, Shane Neufeld {**SN**}, Shauna McManus {**SM**}, Sunil Bald {**SB**}, Surry Schlabs {**SS**}, Tim Altenhof {**TA**}, Trattie Davies {**TD**}, Turner Brooks {**TB**}

This studio is comprised of three projects that introduce the complexity of architectural design by engaging problems that are limited in scale but not in the issues they provoke. Experiential, social, and material concerns are introduced together with formal and conceptual issues. The projects, while related at a broad conceptual level, are designed to be independent and discrete to allow students to engage and explore a diverse range of architectural concepts and design methods. Projects sequentially increase in length, scale, and complexity demanding increasing development and resolution.

A Space for Learning ●
For the first project of the semester, students were asked to consider the relationship between interior and exterior, space and form, and issues of scale and habitation through the design and configuration—a study for one person. The private study is both a physical container of objects as well as an intellectual container of ideas. As constructed interior environment, it allows an individual to become immersed and lost in the spaces of her/his mind.

A Landscape for Learning ●●
The second project moves from site to exterior to interior. Students were asked to externalize and translate activities of organization, collection classification, and study from the confines of a discrete volumetric container to the design of a landscape for learning on a real site that engages the environment. The project is a public landscape and environmental education center on a prescribed 200,000 square foot site along New Haven's West River and expands in scope, embracing both the intimate scale of one person as well as the collective activities of larger groups.

An Institution for Learning ●●●
The final project is the design of a public library in Bushwick. This project is both typologically and site-specific, asking the students to simultaneously reinvent the public library as a cultural institution and engage a specific site and community. The library has always presented an allegory for a captivating humanist ideal. While the public library has functioned historically as a container of books, social center, and civic monument for a community, its role is continually recast within the shifting landscape of contemporary culture and new technology. Through the design of shared spaces, students were asked to examine, question, and reimagine the activities surrounding the library as a locus for social interaction. As a public building, students were asked to examine its integral connection to the site and its role as a piece of social and cultural infrastructure in relationship to broader programmatic and contextual forces.

Brennan Buck

ANNA NASONOVA

In the digital age, when almost any written resource can be accessed from any location through the Internet, the focus of libraries shifts from their books to spaces that they offer for public reading. The design proposes a centralized meeting space for the warehouse neighborhood, where roller gates hide exclusive activities of a disjointed community. A new type of a warehouse, open for everyone and accessible from every side, contains the most valuable library resource—public space. A public garden at the heart of the library leads to three ground level living rooms that provide different settings for informal social interactions. Pin-wheeled vertical expansion doesn't only frame and activate the volume of the garden, but also connects the informal separate pavilions with a more formal open reading room at the top level of the library. {●●●1}

> "<u>Your</u> <u>representations</u> <u>are</u> <u>machines</u> <u>of</u> <u>persuasion. When</u> <u>they</u> <u>lie, it's terrible!</u>"
> **Kurt Forster**

●**TB**: I think the section turns this building into something it's not. It ends up looking like a kind of Russian Constructivist, almost grinding building. ●**KuF**: It's almost scary how close this is to a real architectural project. You pull every stop you can to come across as a professional. Your representations are machines of persuasion. That's why when they lie, it's terrible! This is so powerful that you have to take measures, so to speak. And you take measures on the side of architecture. I compliment you, this is really a performance. The question is if we really want to see this piece. It's a piece of real persuasion. ●**JH**: On the outside there's a singularity to this, but in the section there's clearly multiple floors. What I like very much about the interior is these three angled triangles that we experience in the void. But when we're in the building, it's just a plan edge. So in general there's a one, two, three to this, but there's also a kind of oneness that I like. ●**AC**: I would like to commend you on the simplicity and resolution of this project. It's really believable as a building and really clear that at each level. The experience changes just from a few simple moves. I applaud that consistency. ●**BB**: I'm happy to see how you've been able to follow through with some of the logics that you established at the broader scale into things like floor material. It's nice to see that concepts have an implication even down to that level. It's a very clear project, but one that has an internal complexity that would make an exciting institution.

FRANCESCA CARNEY

The study is a space of quiet contemplation and appreciation. Designed for a collector of pens, the environment encases the user with the objects of their passion. Aspects of the pen are transformed into the overall form as well as the interior. The surfaces react to the procession towards the central working space by guiding and accepting the uncontrollable nature of ink. The ceiling begins to drip down to physically represent and imply ink moving around overhead. The ground shifts from a sullied surface at the entrance to a ramp which cleans one's tread to the destination at the center where ink again soils the ground. The experience is rhythmic and engages the user in the ritual of using ink. {●2}

> "<u>The</u> <u>subdivision</u> <u>of</u> <u>space</u> <u>is</u> <u>a</u> <u>dominant</u> <u>way</u> <u>of</u> <u>making</u> <u>space</u> <u>in</u> <u>our</u> <u>culture...but</u> <u>here</u> <u>there</u> <u>is</u> <u>kind</u> <u>of</u> <u>an</u> <u>infinity</u> <u>in</u> <u>putting</u> <u>things</u> <u>inside</u> <u>of</u> <u>other</u> <u>things.</u>"
> **Keller Easterling**

●**AP**: There is something wonderful about this pattern and the way it begins to develop its own vitality or its life—moving away from this sort of scarab piece. It's here in the building, but it's not quite there yet because it suddenly became a building. I think the mass is not very messy, I think if you want to introduce chaos you've got to let the ink do it so that there is an opportunity for something a little bit more random. I think if it hadn't become a building so quickly, it could have generated itself a bit longer. It could have been even better. ●**KE**: Its's a very strong move on the site to neutralize

the elevation and make it this kind of tumbling form. It's a strong choice given that it's about some kind of occupation with knowledge; but where do you start with that? I find it quite a difficult project, but there seems to be a very deliberate move, and that's a good sign. It's a bold choice and it's very deliberate. This is also a bold choice in that it's about concentricity, it's about nesting things inside of other things as a way of making space. The subdivision of space is a dominant way of making space in our culture, whether it's slicing this way or making partitions, but here there is kind of an infinity in putting things inside of other things that I really appreciate. It's a kind of endless space...are you in the stomach, are you in the esophagus?

CECILY NG

The Environmental Education Center along the West River in New Haven explores the analogy of a surface of water registering the impact of a dropped object as a way to consider how a building meets the ground. The landscape faces created through the insertion of the building organizes indoor and outdoor program. The uncanny relationship between building and landscape is heightened through materiality. The building is enclosed in a perforated metal skin that creates changing light effects during the day and night. Each adjacent facet is a different landscape material. {●●3}

●**SN**: In a sense, we're interested in the space around it—the disruption, the time. And then, what becomes the logic for how you make the space on the inside? The idea of time is as if it were an object, a meteor that hit the ground, or a spaceship that's landed softly. This threshold where you enter this stretch of ground to the moment you enter the building and see the set of stairs—what's that supposed to be like? That a tremendous moment when you've arrived at this monolith! There should be a logic to that passageway and how you move up the building and whether it does relate to landscape or is purely an autonomous thing within the object itself. ●**KA**: And there is a great example for you to look at on campus, right? The Beinecke Library. ●**MB**: I think it's a very elegant project actually. I like the proportions of the box and the disruption that it creates around it. If it went beyond what was given to you it would be way too much, right? And if it was just this little crinkle around, it wouldn't be much also. But right now, it's creating a really nice relationship between the disruption and the object. It's more than just what happens to the object, once you exactly figure out the landscape. ●**PD**: It's not that it needs to be brought in. It just needs to have a more provocative resonance, which really could be oppositional in a way. Frustrating, even.

Peggy Deamer

MAGGIE TSANG

If the main library is a civic icon and an institution, then the branch library is a hyper-local outpost that is familiar and safe—an extension of the home. This project reinterprets the library as a house or villa. Rather than the grand reading room or the tower of stacks, library visitors occupy the living room, the study, the garden, and the playroom. The entire building is lifted from the site to provide a provide a bookmobile park for the neighborhood. The reinterpretation of the library's programmatic spaces offer a place for individual reflection as well as gathering and encourages the Bushwick community to engage a typically austere public institution in a more casual and comfortable way. {●●●4}

> "<u>It's</u> <u>kind</u> <u>of</u> <u>a</u> <u>bouillabaisse</u> <u>of</u> <u>classic</u> <u>modern</u> <u>canon</u> <u>houses.</u>" **Andrew Saunders**

●**MK**: I just think in general there's an over-complication of the formal moves and the transformation of this cubic grid that you're establishing that is actually a bit mischievous in relation to how clear the section may be. Clearly, along the corridor, one side is more cellular and one side is more public. I'm curious how the cellular, domestic space connects into that grand, civic, egalitarian space. How do those mechanisms work systematically and serially in such a way that when you seclude yourself from the rest of the building

Infra Eco Logi Urbanism

Infra Eco Logi Urbanism assembled recent urban research and speculative design by the experimental Canadian architectural practice RVTR. Infra Eco Logi Urbanism undertook a study of the Great Lakes Megaregion using geographic, statistical, and cartographic analysis and proposed a rethinking of infrastructural systems in light of new mobility, renewable energy, and urban growth. Installed in the Yale Architecture Gallery in Fall 2014, the exhibition projected possible urban and architectural futures that envision new public domains.

Curator: RVTR

1

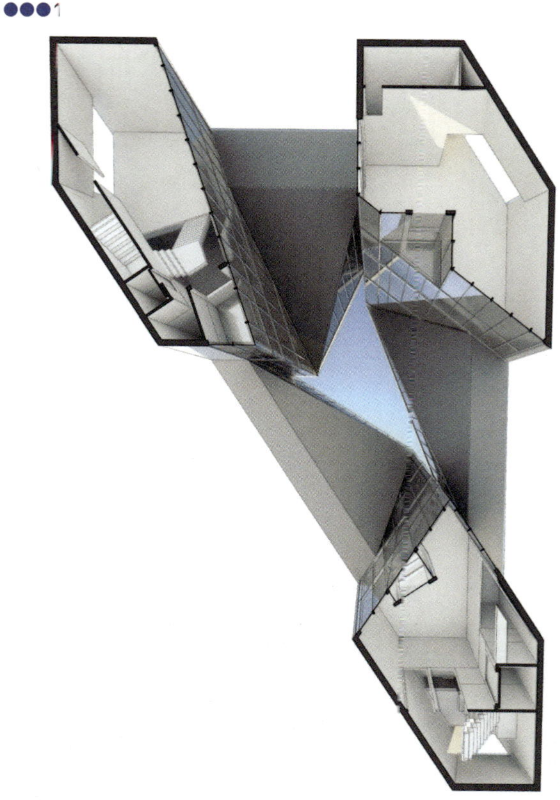

3

2

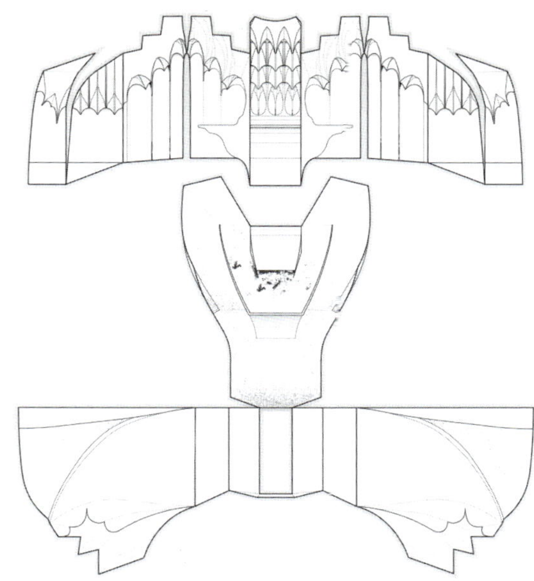

4

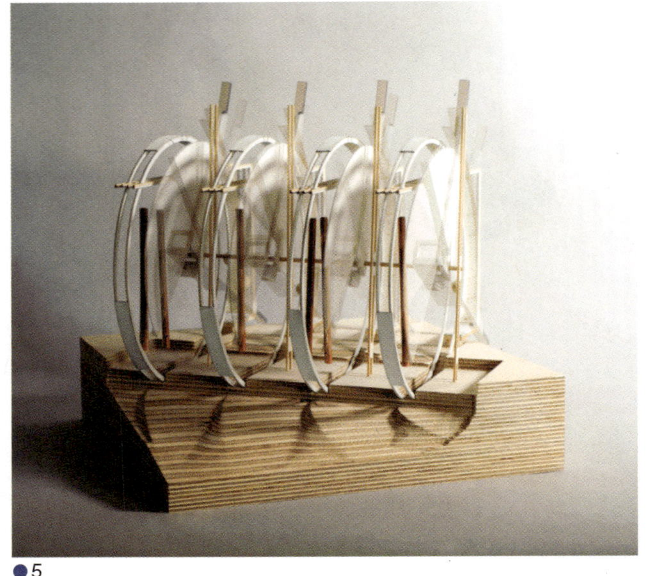

●5

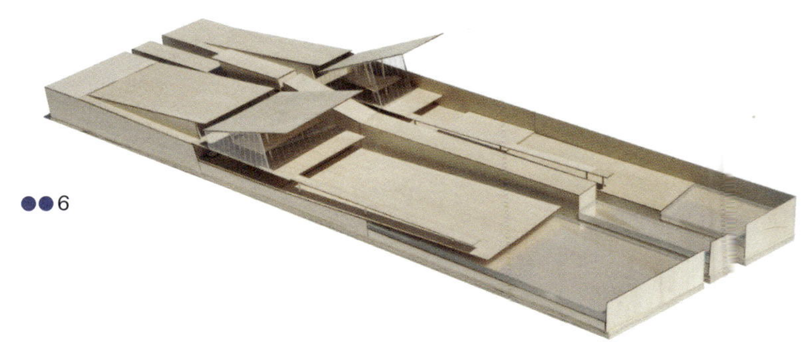

●●6

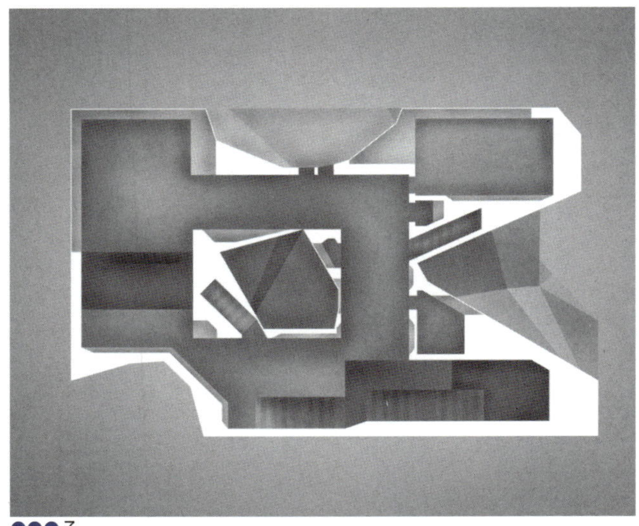

●●●7

●8

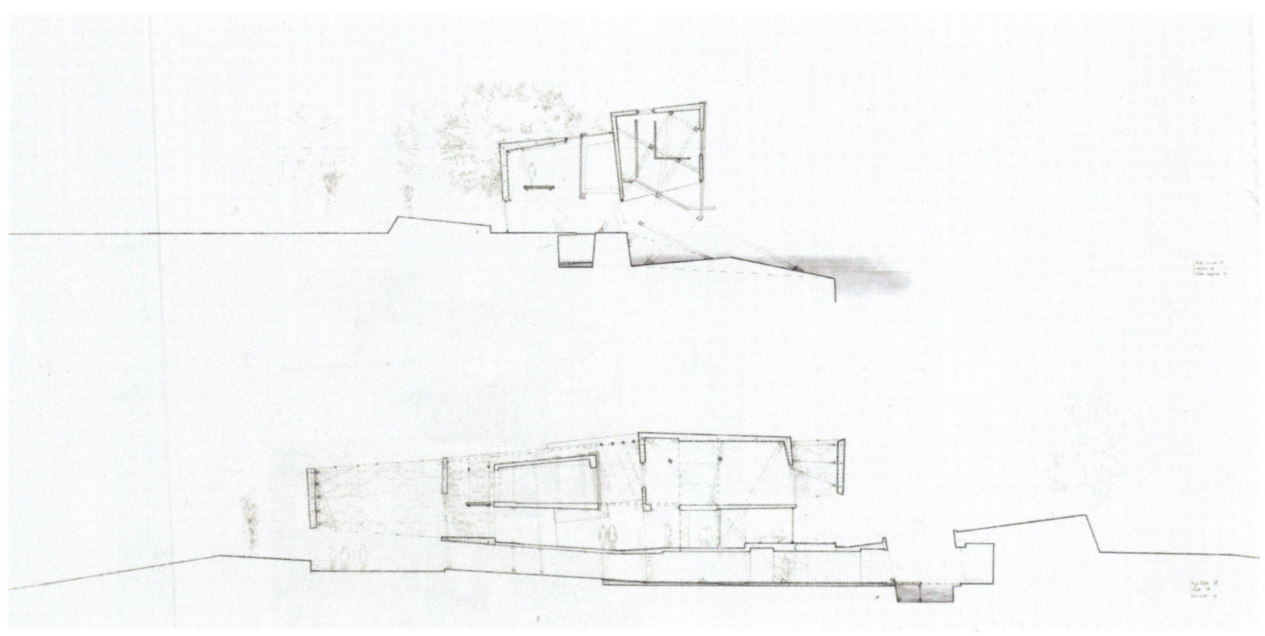

●●9

you always know how to let yourself out, in a way, both psychologically or programmatically? ●JL: First, the most domestic thing I've seen, which is just so bizarre, is the way that one of the facade looks like the Villa Stein. And I think that's a clue that it's not just a formal game, that's the industrial machine logic [and how] it meets the home—the way that it confounds the idea of domestic space. ●AS: It's kind of a bouillabaisse of classic modern canon houses. It's not really domestic, we're talking about the modern canon. ●PD: That can conjure different things, and the villa is really a villa in manner and not in a rough Bushwick way, and there's a problem there. But then I try to think about how to solve that problem. It just needs a fence around it. It needs to pretend that it's actually not in Bushwick. It needs to claim it's territory and say, "You know what, I'm in an ideal space."

GRAHAM BRINDLE

This instrument systematizes the interface between an inhabitant and a collection of cylindrical glass soil samples culled from peculiar landscapes. A structure of lenses, counter-weights, protractors and rotating plates allow for the measure of varying soil horizon depths and morphologies. A kinetic relationship develops between the inhabitant and the instrument as the system shifts, spins, and exaggerates the collector's manipulations. {●5}

"It has actually has this quality that it would be something that you'd find on a road to nowhere." Jessica Barter

●MS: I think the idea is amazing—the measured aspect of a tonal soil sample. It's become more apparatus than space. So by making it an array of four you've emphasized that fact. If you have one that can't be copied easily it would move toward a singular space. One way to make a space could be to have an apparatus and also design an observatory. ●SA: What if the spatial aspect is displayed as a mosaic of discarded soils—a residue that builds up to become something else, something you take control of. You could do this through erosion, retaining walls, or something that drives how discarded soil can build itself up. Then it becomes occupiable or something you walk through or experience in a way. This is so persuasive and the model is so beautiful. To me, I don't mind the apparatus. ●JB: Just exquisite. It's a really impressive resolution to have achieved in just two weeks. For me it really needs an enclosure—a subterranean occupation could be quite exciting, which you've started to allude to in the section. Actually, that would be better than an enclosure. It has actually this quality that it would be something that you'd find on a road to nowhere. You would come across it in a big field.

ROBERT YOOS

This project aims to mediate the abrupt juxtaposition of the bucolic landscape of the site with the adjacent commercial context and highway. By using the context as a generative tool, the major programmatic components of the project were placed in line with existing buildings and turn their backs to the street. In the interstitial zone between buildings, an artificial landscape pushes back on the commercial context creating an oscillation of land mass and building across the site. A corridor traverses this, which makes the inhabitant aware of the contextual mediation occurring on the site. The project aims to suspend the inhabitant within and deny the comprehension of the ground. At high tide, the built planes and axial corridor flood and destabilize the ground plane further. The architecture, in effect, blurs the distinction between the natural and the artificial by not only inverting the landscape with man-made construction, but also constantly fluctuating in water level throughout the day. {●●6}

"I think it's really important to consider this as an architect, because these buildings have lifespans." Kutan Ayata

●BB: It's an interesting perversion of contextualism—it's very difficult to get anybody to address the buildings across the street, then you do, and it's a completely arbitrary formal exercise to determine the width of these bars. Then it makes me wonder what these surfaces are. I can see the benefit and the abstract quality of these dimensions that aren't necessary to fit in but begin to be an arbitrary starting point that might have some uncertain relationship to its context. ●SN: The idea to insert this really straight line across as a way of experiencing this—I don't totally buy, but I think it's really the friction between these things sliding across different axes. It's the crossing of those worlds which makes this destabilizing happen, and I'm more curious about what it means to be between the abstraction of the context as it dives into the water. ●MB: These thinner pieces, which are really just berms, from the street look like buildings. But the buildings which are actually there seem to be just ground. So what looks like earth turns out to be program, and I really like that double reading. It goes back to your initial studies, and I really appreciate that. ●KA: It's always interesting to ask the question "What if?" when you're working on the immediate present. So, what if that context building just wasn't there? I think it's really important to consider this as an architect because these buildings have lifespans. So because of this, to explain a project completely in terms of its immediate context is kind of weak. Context might be a point from which you start, but to sustain an argument, you need to continue in different terms.

Joyce Hsiang

PAUL RASMUSSEN

This project proposes an evolution of a building type threatened by extinction in the digital age. While traditionally the library functioned as a repository, the future library must become a place of communal activity that provides a multiplicity of experiences and education. The exterior articulates an angular landscape inviting play and athletic activity. The interior is a series of interconnected library volumes envisioned as a mutation of the Beaux-Arts library ideal. Figural poché mediates the difference between faceted exterior and orthogonal interior, as well as establishes a third architectural force. The poche provides secluded spaces and houses library services. Breaks in the poché connect the athletic exterior and academic interior, prompting a mix of program and activities. {●●●7}

"How do you design an object to be misused?" Angie Co

●PD: The carving out that happens not within the poché but in the mass itself—as in what's carved out is exterior space—the rationale for that is just to make rhetorically explicit the idea of excising stuff; the once complete library is now not. But its inhabitation by athletes just seems accidental—it's like there's a mountain here, so let them climb. ●AC: What I find tricky is that parkour is an open-ended program and it necessarily takes place in an urban fabric, so I don't think people are going to go to a place that is made for it. There may be a value to it but you're getting into a difficult territory by saying that you're over-specifying a kind of design for something that is specifically improvisational on urban artefacts misused. So, how do you design an object to be misused? ●AW: This is like a skate park, and skating used to be something that was improvisational and done on the streets but now people love these parks.

CHRISTOPHER LEUNG

This project is a study designed for a photographer who seeks inspiration and reflection upon his personal collection of images. The physical picture as a two dimensional object holds immaterial and ephemeral qualities that prompt feeling and diverse interaction. This duality is amplified by the construction of space as an array of apertures that alter experience between interior and exterior. Emulating the process of photography, the rotating projection screen covers the study to develop a sense of anticipation as one approaches. As the screen rotates up, the photographer is presented with a myriad of directed openings that guides view in unexpected directions. Subsequently, the screen returns back to its original position to allow for a large scale projection and display of the photographer's work. The juxtaposition of framed pictures on the interior with background perspectives through the apertures gives a multi-layered range of visual experience where view supplants form through the disjunction of building skin and aperture. {●8}

"How do you translate a spherical representation of the world into a flat one?" Alfie Koetter

●AK: This is an abstract site with nothing else but cardinal directions. So, with a project like yours which is about framing a view outward, how are you resolving those decisions? If it is about what is happening between what your expectations are versus what it is you actually see, there should be some transformative process that happens that you can abstractly, on this non-site, say happens between outside and inside. ●AB: The difference between these frames is interesting too in that the project acts as an analogue for a kind of camera obscura, but there's also these things that look like bellows. I think there's a way that you can didactically demonstrate those things, but they're a little bit frozen at the moment. ●AK: The topic at hand, which is really interesting, is how do you translate what is a spherical representation of the world into a flat one—there is a transformation of reality when you take a photograph.

ANDREW PADRON

This project emphasizes the natural fluctuations within a tidal marsh by exaggerating its tendencies so that the building is an extension of the landscape network. The landscape is governed by erosion and sedimentation that reshape the shore and result in a series of edges that exist in either a state of flux or permanence. The project extends from this framework and manipulates the characteristics of edges and boundary. The constructed edges are deferential to the fluctuations in water so that the built landscape is an extension of the tidal marsh, that permeates around and underneath the building. This erodes program so that lowest levels are occupied by a vacated outdoor structure with the remaining program suspended and accumulated above or settled below. {●●●9}

"You're not from Columbia circa 1991 are you? For me this project is like Bernard Tschumi's wonderland." Dan Wood

●AB: You have this language that allows you to extend the elements past their programmatic limits, and you could reach out into the water and let people explore. I wish you would have engaged that. ●SS: You could do more, but I think it's stunning. You strike a nice balance between the serene and frenetic here, and perhaps if you did more marching into the you might have thrown off that equilibrium, it would have become too frenetic. ●DW: You're not from Columbia circa 1991 are you? For me this project is like Bernard Tschumi's wonderland. Every project from 1989–1992 was like this and it's so great to see this again! Complete lack of elevation, basswood taken to the extreme—it's great.

Eeva-Liisa Pelkonen

LAURA MEADE

Programmatic elements of this building are not distinct from each other. They are related and interlocked. Each penetrates into the other without residual space—the library is a fastened joint. A wedge is used as an architectural device that is mirrored and reiterated throughout the entire design; it can be seen at multiple scales. The neighborhood enters the building by wedging into its base and sliding beneath it. Two main functions of the space, studying and reading, cascade against and underneath each other to create the dynamic interior. The building's skin distorts its monumentality and brings humility to the streetscape. Along the sidewalk, the building engages with passersby and provides an outdoor living room—seating that wedges into the base of the building and introduces a human scale to the façade. {●●●10}

●MF: I have to say that it's a fantastic project. I really love the use of the wedge in multiple ways in terms of being formal, programmatic, and spatial.

I really love that, in this direction, the wedge acts as a device for scaling, like a projector. I just think it's such a great, hilarious moment when the Children's Section has the small-scale children's window size. You have the whole institution coming down to a very domestic scale. And this idea of scaling is done quite beautifully in the project. Both sides are registering this gesture. One side is treating that gesture as a cut, so that we see through, revealing the motion. This normalizes its scale. On the other side, I think there is something incredible going on. You have this mountain of books, but you don't read it as monumental, not only because of how the form is now flattened, but also because the façade is articulated to give us sporadic glimpses of the interior. It's really quite fascinating in terms of how you've moved us through these two devices, and how they work with the potential of the wedge on this site. ●JH: You put so much energy on the outside, which is really beautiful and elaborate, the way you deal with the geometry. That really wants to be the moment of tension in the middle between these two wedges. The only rectilinear moment in your project is so clear; it seems that transition wants to have the same dynamic quality. Then, it starts to really mold together.

LUCAS BOYD

Rather than design housing for a collection of objects, the project uses the basic principles of optics to make a transformative space through the social exchange of knowledge. In response to the lack of definition of site, this project seeks to abstract the most fundamental elements of architecture and representation. Through the projection of a Cartesian grid onto a surface within a vertical field, the ability to distinguish between column, wall, and roof is diminished. The system's woven quality produces the ghost of a figure that is at once occupiable and ambiguous. The distinction between figure and ground is blurred. The phantom of the internal figure disappears and reappears, while vertical members appear to change their profile. 〔●11〕

●JH: It's remarkable what extravagance and voluptuousness you get when you view all these rectilinear section profiles just by having them in one direction on the forty-five degree diagonal. That's really remarkable and it's one of those things that you don't really realize until you're spinning this thing around. You assume that it's a much more complex geometry. So it's wonderful to see how such a complex geometry can come from a straightforward series of minimal means and rules for how you generate this. To that end, your drawings are really beautiful, and I just wish we could understand more of that tension between just straight-up orthogonal, forty-five degree angle profiles, and the curvilinear. I get much more of a view of the curvilinear, and I see it more in the section. ●TD: For me there's something strange. I like the section cut a lot and how it seems to radically change as you move through to the point where it looks like you'd hit your head if you walked a certain way. What I wish or I wonder is, if you went there, would you really want to come out the way you came in? Like if your whole thing is about this optic play, it is best to have it be a loop? ●Lucas Boyd: It's funny because that was very intentional. ●ELP: You're forced to see the same thing in a different perspective. You see the same thing in a different way because you have to go out the same way you came in.

CASEY FURMAN

This intervention addresses the contradictory character of the site, namely, the switching of roles between the nature of the park and the industrial sprawl across the street. The "natural" side of the street is highly orchestrated, while the man-made side is haphazard and arbitrary. This project entertains the idea that "nature" is acting like architecture and buildings are acting like nature. This role-switch led to an exploration of the properties and consequences of inversion. The many edges of the site are nudged and manipulated using this method of inversion-as-negotiation, creating new zones that encourage the interaction of existing programs. 〔●●12〕

●ELP: This project demonstrates how hand drawing, at its best, is a way of gaining an intimacy with all the elements of architecture: the site, the tectonics and the program. The jury was stunned by the drawings and their ability to create texture, scale, and spatial depth with subtle changes of line weight, layering, and hatching. Instead of with a final set of presentation drawings, Casey worked consistently with one piece of paper as if constructing the building from ground up during a three week period. Appropriate to the assignment, natural elements were depicted with equal care and delicacy. The work by Macdonald and Salter from the 1980s provided an inspiration for how to endorse, through drawing, this intimate relationship between architecture and landscape.

Michael Szivos

PAUL LORENZ

The arboreal, authoritarian, ultimately brittle Dewey Decimal system is organized around categorization while the rhizomatic structure of text-to-text relationships within, for example, Amazon.com ultimately knows nothing about categories. Machine-learning forms predictions from the history of a visitor's interaction with the website's digital space. How can a library interact with a visitor without falling back on categories? In this proposal, the library gains the ability to reorganize itself constantly. Each volume of the library's entire collection can be transported through a network of Kuka KR-6 material handling robots. Any volume can be moved from one shelf location to any other shelf location. 〔●●●13〕

> "I would love to see the figure of the architect radicalized by this encounter. In other words, why confront the problem of the detail?" **Michael Chen**

●ELP: You talked so much about the system, but the space is created by the relationship between the floor plates and the tunnels that I want to touch. It's interesting that you didn't talk at all about how that space gets populated by people. ●MC: On one hand you're advocating for something that's clearly reductionist for the present and leading us to future. On the other hand, in this context, the product is offered from the relatively safe perspective of a conventional architectural project. So it has this exotic form—it could be a stem cell laboratory, whatever—but that notion of the future hasn't necessarily been anticipated in the mode of production or even the mode of evaluation. I would love to see the figure of the architect radicalized by this encounter. In other words, why confront the problem of the detail? Is the detail part of a set of circumstances that mitigate the encounter between body-space and machine-space? Is it about the stability of one system versus the corporeality of another? It's packaged in such a conventional manner, but we're asked to believe something so fantastical. There is something deeper, more essential to the that encounter between that big data system and the finite space of architecture.

ALEXANDER STAGGE

This project is a study for a collector of maps. The space used for storage and studying is defined by a boundary. An original rectangular volume is divided in two in order to house maps of contradictory border locations. The two volumes rotate away from one another to represent two different ideas about the edge. The wall one enters through into the spaces remains in its original placement to clearly show the movement. This wall is thickened by the rotation of the volumes and this thickness is used for entry and storage. The floor plates recede from the edge to allow a slight visual connection between the two spaces, while still blocking view of the other maps. The design is an investigation of political nature of maps. 〔●14〕

> "If you're in Juarez or in El Paso, you talk about the border more than you talk about Dallas or Mexico City." **Michael Szivos**

●JH: I like the form that's generated by this implication—there is an implication of that which is uncontested. The parts where there are lots of lines become quite impressive. But then how do you, without making twenty-five walls, create that sense of fluttering and tension along with the ambiguity of how you define a border? ●MS: The quality and the amount of models and speed with which you produce is great, but I think you might have played it safe. That oscillating cube is supposed to read as the radical politics between two volumes. It should be all over the place. The cubes are circumstantial. They're like a country, but the border is the cut point. If you're in Juarez or in El Paso, you talk about the border more than you talk about Dallas, Texas or Mexico City. The politics are a part of that, it makes the cut hyper important…it's neither here nor there if you stop oscillating. You might have carved that space so much that it would have become readily apparent that that apartness is a circumstance of these things. In an odd way, it might start to produce nooks and crannies. ●JH: You set it up that it would be a sectional view too. If you drew a line through it, it's constantly changing. I'm looking for something in the space thats a non-discrete boundary, but then the architecture itself is clearly defined. What would be an ambiguous border architecturally? The movement throughout that threshold is a fascinating complication.

MAXWELL MENSCHING

The goal of this project was to create a piece of architecture capable of teaching visitors about nature through both sight and sound simultaneously. The mirrored nature walk is shaped specifically to amplify the natural sounds of the most densely wooded areas surrounding the site. The walkway continuously transforms along its length, morphing from convex to concave and rising above and below grade. The changes in shape and height are finely tuned to literally "reflect" and amplify specific natural sounds of the surrounding environment to the visitor while simultaneously blocking and suppressing unwanted noise from nearby traffic. The end of the nature walk culminates in a small complex which is comprised of a center for environment learning, a scenic café, a boat launch, and an outdoor amphitheater. The mirrored façade of the learning center aims to act as an active camouflage in that the building becomes a mere reflection of its scenic surroundings. 〔●●15〕

> "I'm looking at your amphitheater which, in plan, is a really interesting moment when the snake swallows the rat." **Ben Pell**

●BP: Which came first, the pavilion or the path? I wonder if you could have accomplished all the things you just said without producing a discrete volume. I'm looking at your amphitheater which, in plan, is a really interesting moment when the snake swallows the rat. I can imagine along that path a set of direct relationships instead of reflected relationships. You could have made other spaces that address other parts of the program. It allows you to do the very thing you've been trying to avoid, which is make a piece of architecture that suppresses nature. ●RAMS: That box could have a been a cup-like wall, such as some of your other volumes, which wou d allow you to have viewing platforms out of doors, blocking the sound from Boston Post Road and allow you to experience the landscape at a different elevation from what you can get in the park generally because the park is basically a flat wetland. The path is great, but the delivery at the end with that big, black tar roof is wrong. One can never say it's wrong, but it's wrong. ●BB: The first two times that I visit the building, I would love it. The third time, I would be cursing you. ●RAMS: That implies that you would come back! ●SB: The one thing I'm a little bit skeptical of, always, is quantifying nature—being able to attribute certain measurable aspects to an environment which is always changing and always unpredictable. These spaces have things that are understood socially and culturally. Context is something that is much more of an expansive notion. I think that will allow you to think about how this space is used in a way that is more than just amplifying an experience that you think you can measure.

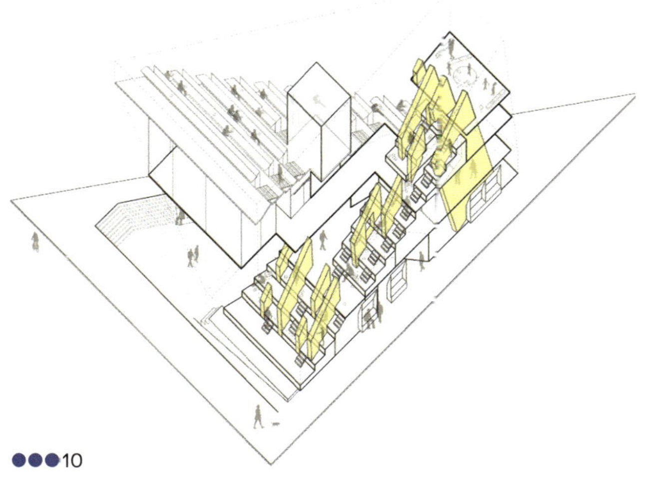

●●●10

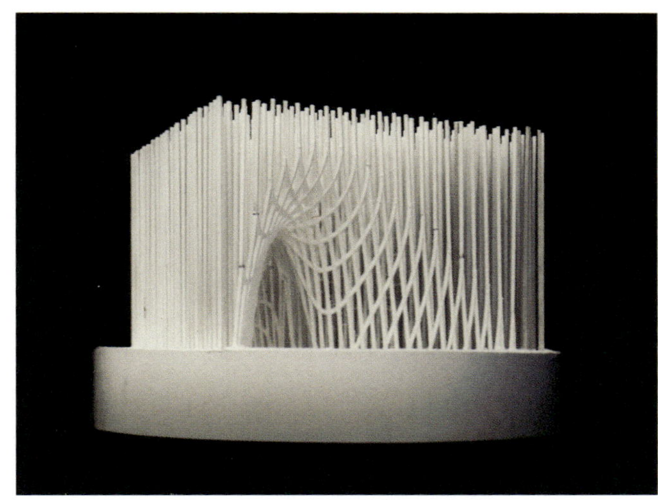

●11

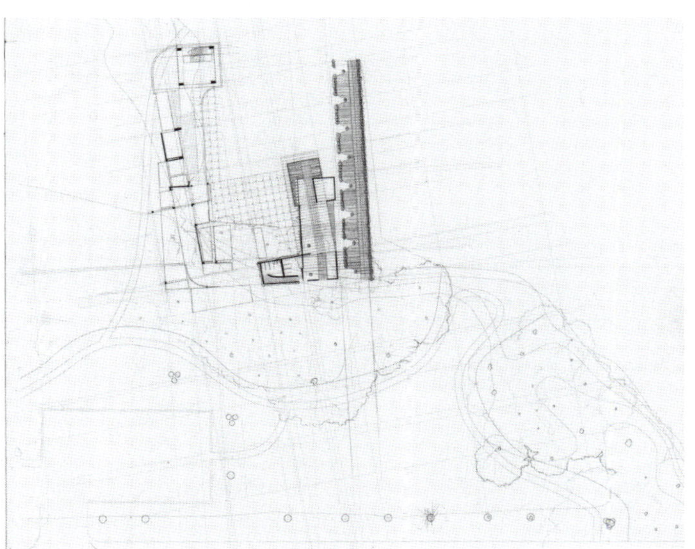

●●12

●●●13

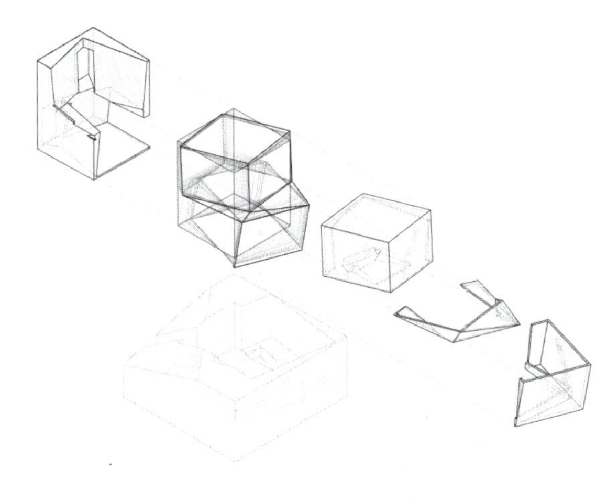

●14

●●15

Formal Analysis
Peter Eisenman, Miroslava Brooks

This course studies the object of architecture—canonical buildings in the history of architecture—not through the lens of reaction and nostalgia but through a filter of contemporary thought. The emphasis is on learning how to see and to think architecture by a method that can be loosely called "formal analysis." The analyses move through history and conclude with diagrammatic models of Palladian villas that invite multiple readings through conditions of adjacency, overlap, or superposition.

An architect must learn to see beyond the fact of perception. An architect must see as an expert. This expertise implies two things. First, being able to see, as a form of close reading, the not present—the unseen. Second, and more importantly, an architect is a maker, not just a reader. In order to make what contains "what cannot be seen," one has to know what that is, i.e. in order to make what can be close read, one has to know first how to close read. This is a class about that kind of learning. And its first and most basic form of close reading is formal analysis.

Alberti: San Sebastiano {■1–2}
Palladio: Villa Foscari {■3}
Borromini: Sant'Ivo and San Carlo alle
　　Quatro Fontane {■4}
Competition Drawings {■5–7}

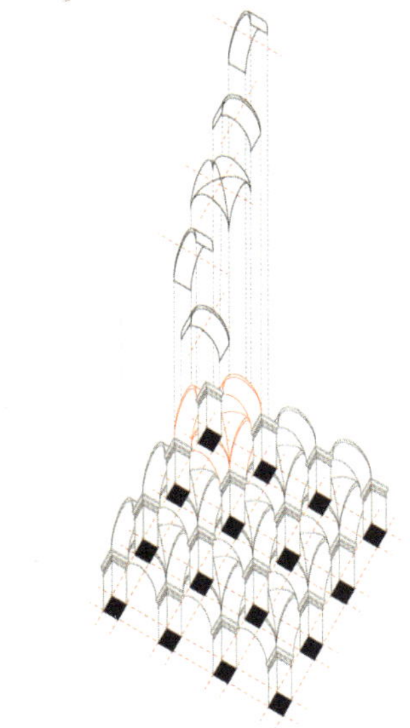

■ 1. Tess McNamara

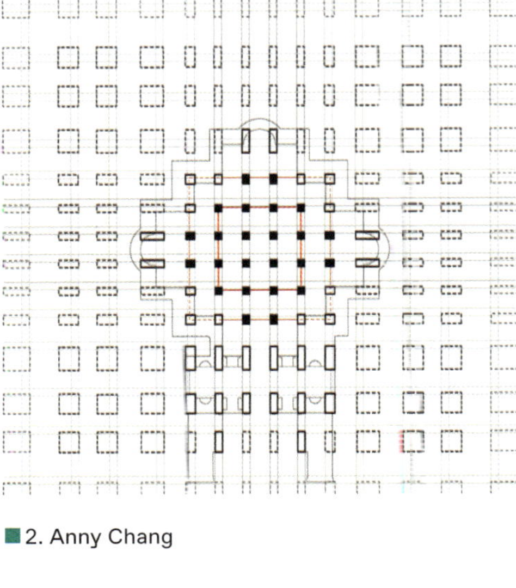

■ 2. Anny Chang

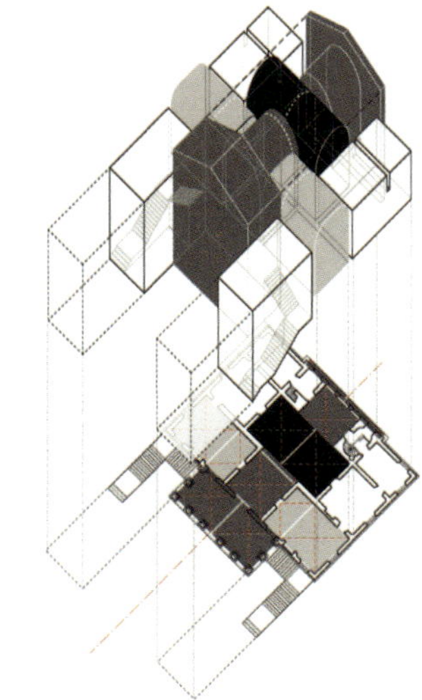

■ 3. Anna Nasonova

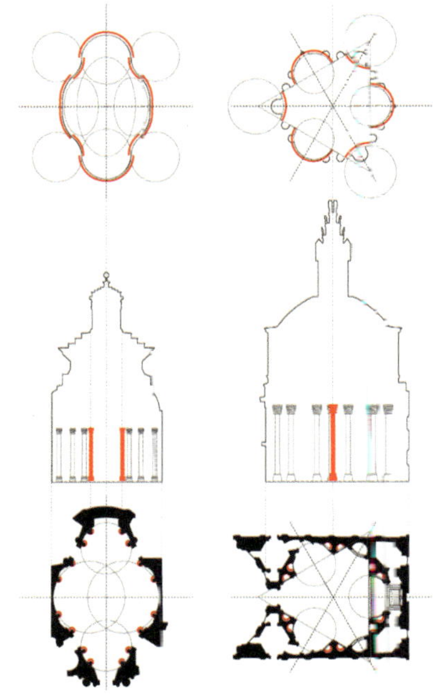

■ 4. Chris Leung

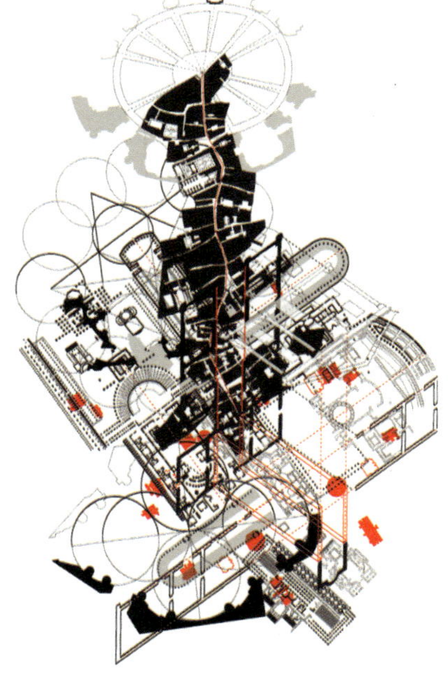

■ 5. Dakota Cooley

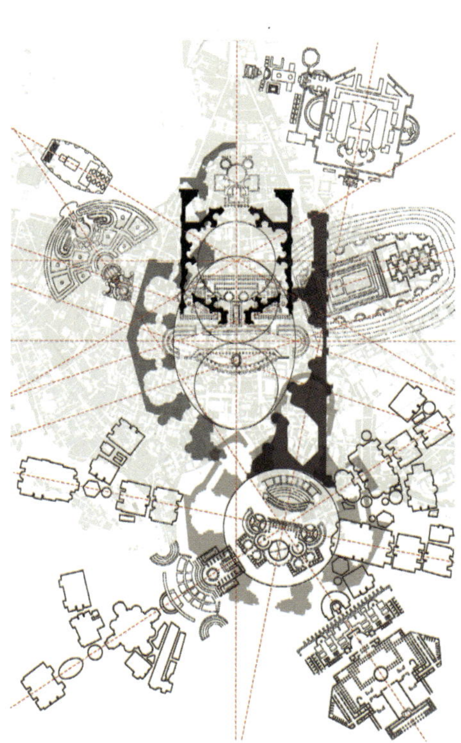

■ 6. Hannah Novack

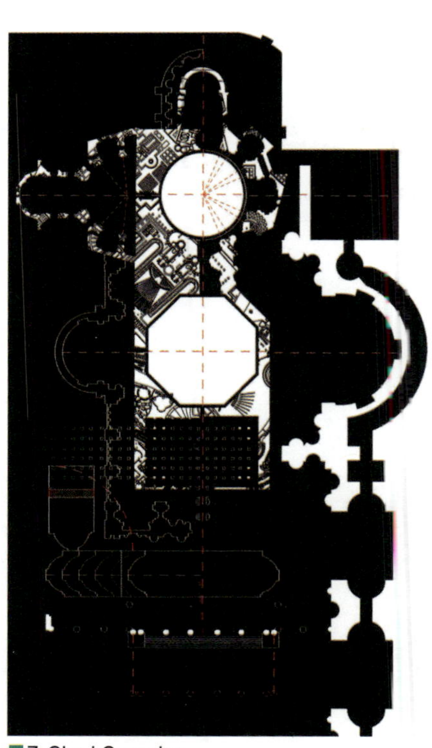

■ 7. Chad Greenlee

1015a
Visualization II
Sunil Bald &
Kent Bloomer

This course investigates drawing as a means of
architectural communication and as a generative
instrument of formal, spatial, and tectonic discovery. Principles of two- and three-dimensional geometry are extensively studied through a series of
exercises that employ freehand and constructive
techniques. Students work fluidly between manual
drawing, computer drawing, and material construction. All exercises are designed to enhance the ability to visualize architectural form and volume three-
dimensionally, understand its structural foundations,
and provide tools that reinforce and inform the
design process. (■1–3)

■1. Robert Yoos

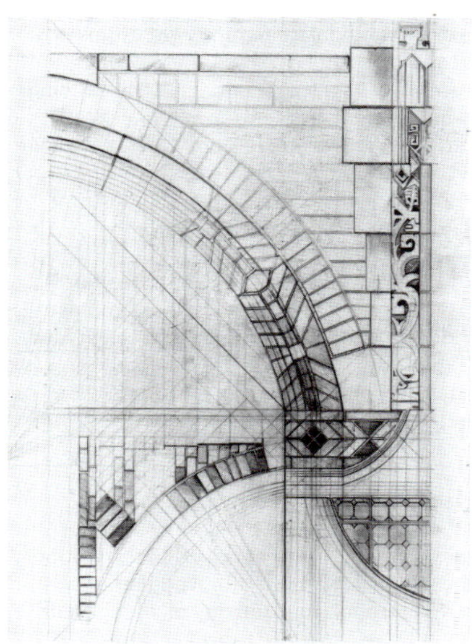

■2. Nasim Rowshanabadi

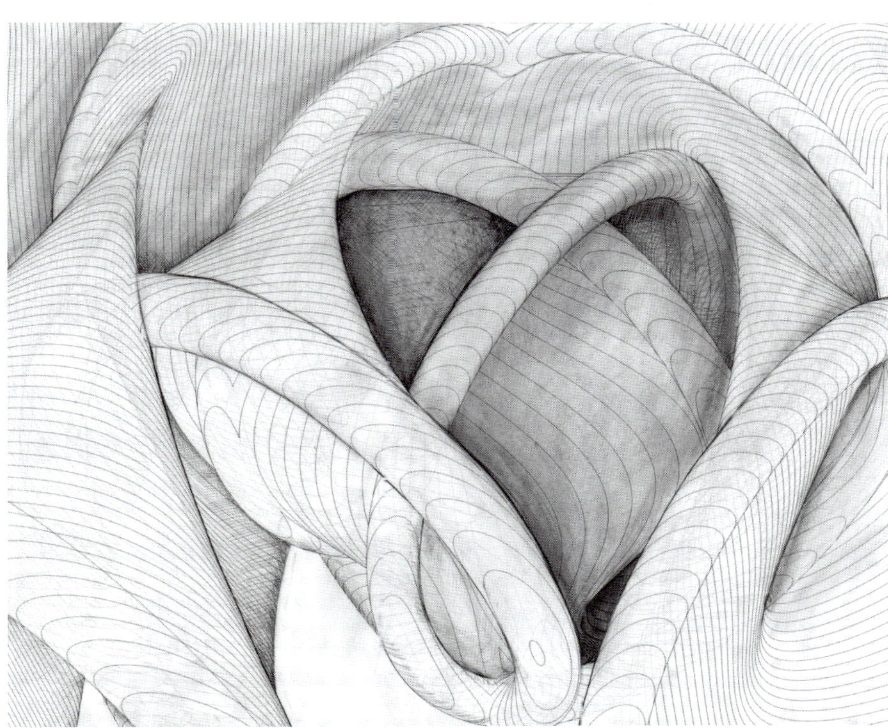

■3. Dakota Cooley

Second Year Design Studio
M.Arch. I

Coordinator
Mark Foster Gage {**MFG**}

Critics
Emily Abruzzo {**EA**}, Peter de Bretteville {**PDB**}, Martin Finio {**MF**}, Mimi Hoang {**MH**}

Jurors
Andrew Bernheimer {**AB**}, Stella Betts {**SB**}, Eric Bunge {**EB**}, Christy Cheng {**CC**}, Joseph Clarke {**JC**}, Peggy Deamer {**PD**}, Melissa Delvecchio {**MD**}, Mark Gardner {**MG**}, Peter Gluck {**PG**}, Louise Harpman {**LH**}, Andrea Kahn {**AK**}, Tessa Kelly {**TK**}, Nicole Koltick {**NK**}, David Levin {**DL**}, Ali Rahim {**AR**}, Lyn Rice {**LR**}, Rob Rogers {**RR**}, Tomas Rossant {**TR**}, Andrew Saunders {**AS**}, Robert A. M. Stern {**RAMS**}, Kyle Stover {**KS**}, Marilyn Jordan Taylor {**MT**}, Quang Truong {**QT**}, Marion Weiss {**MW**}, Beth Whitaker {**BW**}

Architecture from Scratch: Designing a School for Design

Architecture is in a state of uncertainty. The interconnecting capacities of the computer have rendered quaint the possibility of any form of global architectural consensus. Instead, architecture today operates in a more exploratory vein—one where monolithic "styles" and "movements" give way to much more experimental and individualized pursuits. Fueling this further is the emergence of vast, new creative tools at our individual disposal—from new and smarter materials, to software that gives access to entirely new languages of form, to methods of fabrication that make the building of anything nearly possible. We are in an era of discovery and exploration, not in terms of physical territories as much as disciplinary and technological possibilities. The conjunction of these currents places architecture in a unique position, simultaneously in need of progressive vision but increasingly desperate for the disciplinary fundamentals that lead to actual buildings. Learning this discipline requires conventions that must be actually understood in order to propose true and significant advances. Students will learn architecture as a discipline with many means of exploration, but will need to balance experimentation and speculation with a reasonable level of realism that results in a constructible building by the end of the semester.

The program is a new building for the University of Pennsylvania School of Architecture, which will include related disciplines all united under the rubric of "PennDesign." This is, perhaps surprisingly, a rather rare problem—the design of an architecture school specifically for a program of architecture. Only a handful of such buildings have been built in recent history including our own Art and Architecture Building {now Rudolph Hall} at Yale, along with architecture school buildings at Harvard, Ohio State, Florida State International University, The University of Houston, Penn State, and the existing University of Pennsylvania School of Architecture—Meyerson Hall. Not all of these have been success stories, and Meyerson Hall is perhaps the most in need of replacement, containing, as it does, an impenetrable core, indecipherable levels, a lack of daylight and no visible relationship between aspects of the programs. Addressing such a problem will not only allow us to address the aforementioned topics, but is also timed to align with Yale's own Department of Architecture's 100 year anniversary in 2016. It is a problematic task to absorb the momentum of two millennia of architecture's inherited conventions, technologies and associated lore, while simultaneously looking towards an increasingly unpredictable future charged with technological advances around every corner. Students walk a fine line by designing a building type with which they are intimately familiar—a purpose-built architecture school—one that, through its very design, suggests a pedagogical stance on nothing less than the future of the profession and the built environment.

Emily Abruzzo

JACK BIAN

This project is about the layering of three different architectural languages to produce a productive conceptual, programmatic, and experiential feedback. The street level is a "world of poché" about excavation and specificity. It is revealed through the process of discovery. The ground level is about openness, serenity, and exchange. It is inspired by the modernist language of large universal space created with two horizontal data, and is conceived as an extension of the landscape and continuation of the campus quad. The third level is about porosity, carving, and the articulation of specific characters for rooms that have a dialogue with their intended uses. The carving away process allows light to travel through the bottom two levels. {●1–2}

> "If two layers come apart, like bread, you still know they come from the same loaf."
> Joseph Clarke

●**RAMS:** I don't think you did yourself a service when you described your three layers as a history sandwich—something you could order at the Book Trader across the street. Your idea of contemporary architecture might be a little off-base, because it is almost indistinguishable from what is below. You're trying to make the building illustrative of art historical ideas, but it could be more illustrative of what makes up an architecture school. All of you should be doomed to occupy the buildings you design! There are no windows! ●**LH:** Different students use different tools to study projects. We're seeing a new set of drawings from you. One of the things that would be interesting is a really clear diagram. The historical overlay doesn't work for me. I see heavy and carved, and I have a middle section that is light, and finally I have a top hat. To me it would be interesting to see how that thought process played out and how it's made. ●**JC:** If two layers come apart, like bread, you still know they come from the same loaf. I would want to see the part to whole relationship articulated further. Right now, I just a field of parts wrapped with a totalizing skin. But the premise of the project as a podium with something floating on it is strong. ●**PD:** Urbanistically, I think it works incredibly well. We're getting picky about how you articulated this, but you are the first to actually say that we can enter at the street and that is a certain function of this school. I think all of those moves are really beautiful.

CHENGQI JOHN WAN

An architecture school building should be a teacher of the discipline. This scheme examines modes of interpretative conservationism in the crafting of a new building for the teaching of architecture. The building is a mirror of the profession at large; it structures the sense of chaos and pluralism that is the only certainty in today's world. Named for the Blanche-Levy Quadrangle of the building's site, the formal language and motifs of existing monumental Collegiate Gothic buildings are recomposed into a new school for design. This system of architectural collage grants the building not an absolute object-type form, but the freedom to iterate, grow and evolve as the needs of the School change over time. Spaces of gathering, intimacy, creativity and exchange are built into the composition of spaces, culminating in a ring of studios that crown the building, symbolic of the sanctity of the act of architectural creation. {●3–4}

●**AS:** You end up with a classic courtyard *parti*. It's a fuzzy courtyard. We're seeing a return of classical *partis* because there is no other way to deal with that much information so you make the classical *parti* and then there are some weird asymmetries within that and some nuance. It's interesting to me because it seems like the death of the *parti*, which is a contemporary, modern notion. It's interesting to see the innovation of the *parti*, once you don't focus there, and you become the editor of fringe work. If we follow that trajectory, we'll all become basilica designers. The radicality comes from its ambiguous figure, odd collage. ●**MT:** Or sentimentality. ●**AS:** Do you think he's sentimental? I think it's an accident. ●**AR:** I'm completely divided. I feel shortchanged by your

project. I'm uncomfortable. It feels reactionary, but you haven't stated it. On the one hand, some of these images are really incredible. On the other hand, when I really think about what you are doing, it leaves me anxious. It's sampling or it's more than that, because the object remains the same. The windows are an actual miniaturization of the building. You've got pitched roofs and rotundas. It's definitely trying to argue a particular aesthetic that's coming out of an accumulation and intersection of existing objects. ●**LR:** Is it a cynical project? There is potential to strip away all the historic references. You get the joke because you made the joke. Which buildings would you select, why, and what are the performative characteristics and how do you pair them with the program of an architecture school? How did each space in the program get paired with its historic reference? The danger is making the project "Greatest Hits", but maybe, through editing, you bring together the ones that are working and remove the rest. Then you have a project that's not just a critique.

EUGENE TAN

The first rule of this architecture school is: there are no artificial lights. You come at sunrise and leave when it gets dark. The second rule of this architecture school is: students are not assigned desks. They move from space to space, desk to desk, performing different tasks. This movement will therefore be governed by changes in light and shadow. These rules are a critique of current architecture education and stem from an interest in "time" as it applies to architecture students. The building's conceptual diagram takes the form of a mat with different roofs that modulate natural light differently. Because the site is not large enough to accommodate the program on a single floor, half the building folds upwards, which creates a tower where roofs are treated as windows. Each roof type has a unique structural logic that gives spaces legibility and depth, while shadow studies inform locations for specific programs. {●5–6}

●**RAMS:** It's too difficult to penetrate your drawings. They're very accomplished as graphics, but one doesn't feel an understanding of this. Also, you can't reinvent an architecture school—that was not your assignment. UPenn has an architecture school and they seem to know what they're doing. You can help them do it better. That's what an architect does—not tell them to do it some other way. Certainly you don't go in and tell them to go out of business, which is the premise of your argument. ●**PD:** They've been asked to think about what a contemporary architectural education is. You can think through the ideology of all-nighters. This building closes down at sunset and that's something that could be provocative when thinking about education. ●**AB:** There's a lot of contradictory things going on right now. One, I think this project is a lot simpler than it looks. It's a mat and a tower, and, in those terms, it's successful. It's like an architectural Millennium Falcon—a kitbashed set of pieces. ●**RAMS:** If there is no artificial lighting, how does one go to a bathroom, which has no windows or other lighting? There is a difference between an idea and the realization of that idea, and architecture is the realization of people's ideals. ●**TR:** You're only championing one issue, which is how much time we spend working. If your thesis is to really improve from the perspective of the user, there are so many more things to dig into and come up with an architectural response that makes lives better, which is the business of architecture.

Peter de Bretteville

CAITLIN THISSEN

Staying true to the project brief for the proposed "new" and "improved" University of Pennsylvania School of Architecture, spaces were measured in terms of the tools, equipment, and seating used to facilitate internal activity and interaction. The movements of occupants and provision of services establish a field of activity, unhindered by vertical, inner partitions. The building envelope expands and contracts as a result of interior demands. Thus, the form grows from a system of relationships facilitating human mobility, without distinct nodes or large,

1

2

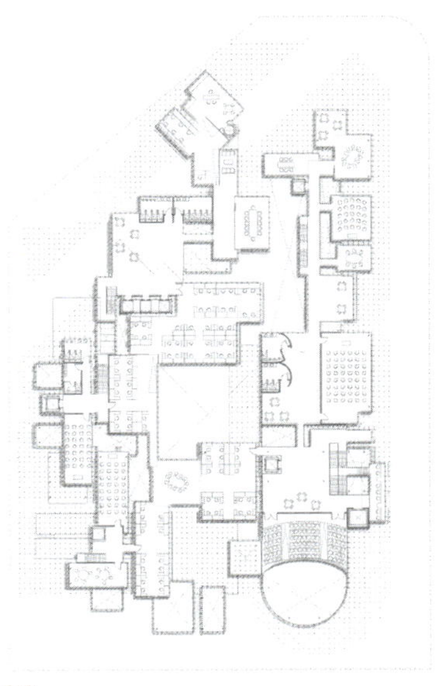

3

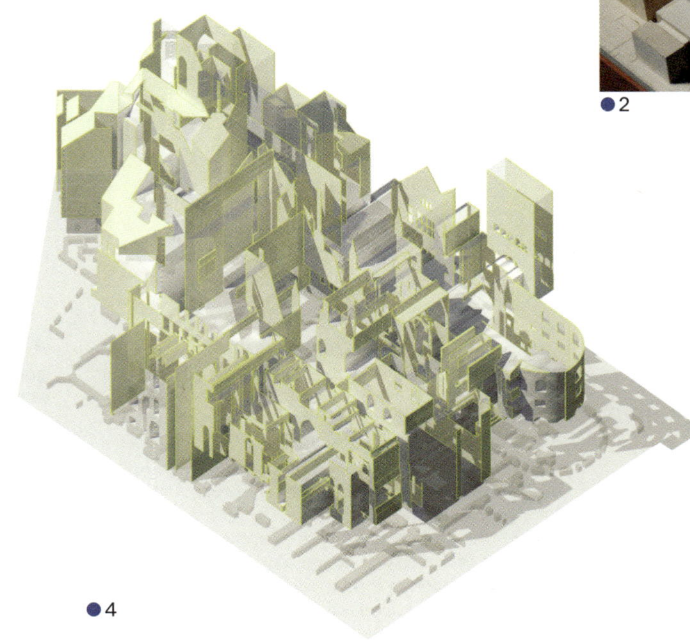

4

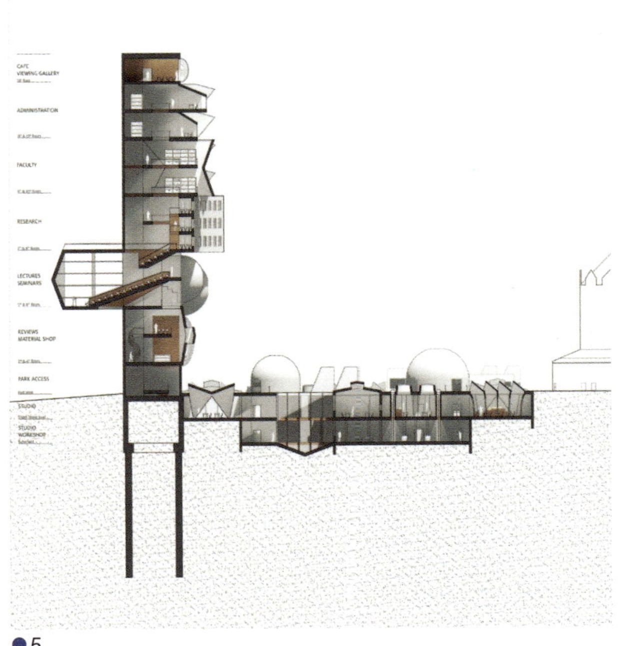

5

6

●7

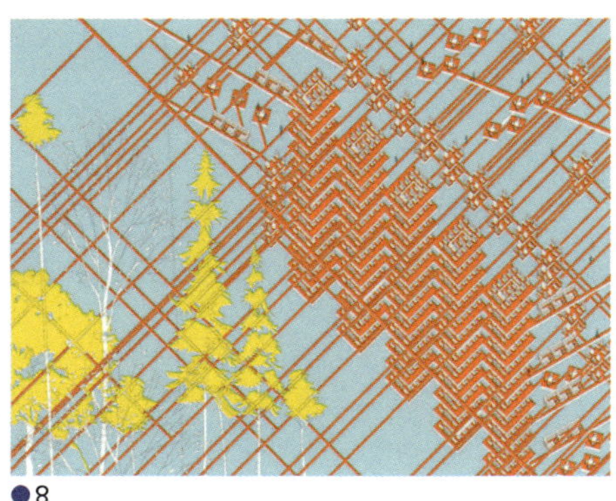

●8

●9

●10

●11

singular, and centralizing spatial gestures, ultimately allowing the occupant complete freedom of movement and expression. {●7–8}

"I hope you do, because this logic brings about things that are fabulously illogical."
Peggy Deamer

●PD: I think it's totally cool. The absolute logic *ad absurdum* is great, and it gets to be absurd. So any question about size results in a logical outcome. The logic made you do it! My question is, do you do this with irony? I hope you do, because this logic brings about things that are fabulously illogical. ●TR: I think you need to avail yourself to the thing that would allow you to denature the banality of this modular stacking, which is a response to context. You've only made a few things even slightly specific, and doing that more might make this building less machine like. ●LH: You're starting to understand that these are two systems, and in optics, when you overlay two systems, you get a *moiré*. There is a third thing, which I don't think you're getting yet. Somehow you're suggesting that this third system should happen but it isn't there. ●AB: There's no definition of enclosure at all, and that's really the beauty of this scheme. It would be something if you foregrounded that in your narrative. This is really an unenclosed building. If an attitude of a dematerialization of the envelope was more explicitly studied, then all of a sudden all these systems might start to come together. ●KS: I think this rigor of foregrounding all these elements that are usually secondary is wonderful. I think that you've accepted the brutality of this with comedy is great, and sometimes it seems that's how you have to deal with complex problems like this.

ANDREW STERNAD

Penn's reinvigorated School of Design aims to attract international recognition, yet also responds to local site forces. On the skyline, the building is an iconic pure volume that marks the entry to old campus. At ground level, the building is carved away to create sheltered spaces for public interaction. The prominent corner site demands a building perceived in the round, and each face becomes a front: to the street on two sides; to the ornate and historic Fisher Library to the south; and to the leafy inner quad to the west. Internally, double-height studio floors alternate in section with compressed levels for classrooms, offices, and casual gathering, referencing the interaction of served and service spaces in Kahn's Richardson Labs across campus. Circulation embedded in the facade—visible as diagonal voids from the outside—links review spaces, activating the perimeter with informal encounters. Courtyards and light wells cut down into the exterior plaza provide glimpses into fabrication spaces below and showcase designs-in-progress to the public and passersby. {●9–10}

●BW: You seem very in control of what you're doing, so you probably hit the program right on the money. It seems like you're taking advantage of all of that underground space on the first level and that's how you're freeing up square footage. But it's funny. You would think, with it being so tall, that it would seem too monumental or isolated. But you've done a remarkable job with negotiating the section. ●CC: I think it was a smart move to put that space underground. But at the same time, I think you didn't really challenge yourself. I wish the auditorium was broken in the same way. Why can't the auditorium be part of that sequence? ●AS: I intended for it to be read as part of the ground. ●MH: I think your project is relentless in all the good ways. You were relentless with the idea of the pinwheel, the studio spaces, and the circulation. The stairs are really interesting because the very end and the very top are always linking the double-height spaces, but then there are always two to another floor. So I think relentless is sometimes very good if you manage to play with the ideas in multiple ways, multiple scales, and in multiple elements. Given the articulation of that envelope and the small footprint of your building, do you need the articulation of the ceiling and the distinctions on the inside? ●BW: That is a small footprint. I like

it. It is overwhelming how highly overdone it is. It's great. Everywhere you turn there will be walls of fins and double height spaces. It's already singing. The ceiling grid is kind of odd. It has an architectural association that may be temporary. You're mixing your grids and your tectonic associations. All that is interesting.

SAMANTHA JAFF

This project is about in-between space. A school of architecture on such a large university campus must cater to the specific spatial needs of architecture students, but it must also invite and inspire collaboration with students from other schools and departments within the University. This establishes the basic diagram for the project: a large central core of open studio space, with other program (administrative offices, classrooms, auditoriums, and computer labs) pushed to volumes around the periphery that flex in response to the campus context. The void space created between the studio and outer volumes serves as the connective tissue of the building, as students and faculty must pass through it to move between the other programs. The multi-story interstitial zone hosts vertical circulation and informal break-out spaces for lounging, collaboration, and pin-ups. {●11–12}

"If the in-between space is more like glue or gum on the bottom of your shoe, what is it sticking to?" Mimi Hoang

●BW: I think you need a variety of spaces if you're going to live in a building 24/7 for four years. You have a particular kind of rigor. I think you've got this gooey space between that is super playful. ●BW: Everybody feels that they have to do their plans and their sections before they can get to the more inventive drawings. But frankly, sometimes you need to start there. I would imagine that you would have a series of models or axons that would diagrammatically describe the three big moves in the buildings, which are the perimeter volumes, the studio spaces, and then these little rooms and

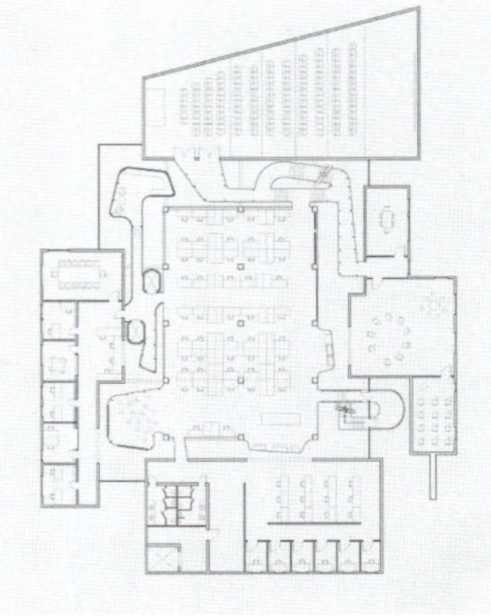

14

13

16

15

spaces that are floating. ●MD: I think it's better for the gooey stuff to be inside the box. ●MH: Does that box need its own articulation? I feel like the outer crust and the articulation of those barnacles on the outside is a leftover. At some point, you hit on this idea of the in-between space, which I agree is far more appealing. As a result, when you get to the final, you have this architecture, a glass box, and this stuff. It's probably too many ideas. If the in-between space is more like glue or gum on the bottom of your shoe, what is it sticking to? Can it be more a binding agent in between the studio spaces and the stuff on the outside? If you look in the plan, the way it sticks to the studio and outside space is always through one point. Can you force that engagement a little bit more? ●JC: Presumably, many of these barnacles will have their own skin. I think this is a really cool model, and I would love to see a rendering where we can see the individual skins of the barnacles. I'm so seduced by this model.

Martin Finio

CHARLES KANE

The University of Pennsylvania's design school holds a prominent site on the main quad and acts as the gateway between the city and the university. In contrast to this siting, the design program is characterized by insularity. Contact with the larger university, other disciplines, and the town rarely occurs. To compound this, PennDesign's multiple degree programs have remained relatively disconnected. This building threads together PennDesign's programs with the university and the city. Urbanistically, this linear building buckles at the center to address the opposing grids of the city and the university. On the interior, the studios inhabit two main floors, which serve as the field in which classrooms and offices hang. This creates sectional diversity and allows for visual connections between programs. The exterior of the building echoes the heaviness of Frank Furness' neighboring Fischer Fine Arts Library with

deep apertures, and contrasts it with large openings that expose review, exhibit, and studio spaces. {●13–14}

●MD: It's a nice nod to your neighbor.
●LR: This rendering implies a paper thinness.
●CK: That carries throughout the whole building so that there is an ambiguity of thickness and thinness. ●LR: That ambiguity is interesting but it's also perhaps the most dangerous part.
●MT: I love the diagram and the idealized section. It says a lot about particularity and then flowing into a shared center, which is at the essence of what we mean when we say "building the discourse". What seems not at all resolved is this piece, which I think you read correctly, that at least for the moment, we'd like to have equal entries. Really the campus entry is about the social connection of the school and the relationship to the university. But I find the colonnade there not particularly effective.
●AS: I think it's really nice the way you define these thresholds but then, at certain points, you decide to violate those thresholds so these major places start to spill out. I think you can play the same game on the other side, which doesn't seem to have the same level of sophistication.

BORIS MORIN-DEFOY

This project for a design school for the University of Pennsylvania started with the aspiration of creating overlap and interchange between the city, student body, faculty, and architecture students. At site level, the project acts as a bridge between the urban fabric and the campus. Following a study of paths of natural travel on the site, these trails have been carved out of the mass of the project. People are then redirected through the central void of the school without having to penetrate the envelope of the building. Internally, the school unfolds as two systems of platforms that cycle around the central void connected by double helix ramps. The platforms always overlap in order to create visual connections between the different spaces and generate a dialogue between the two cycles. On the same

level, the platforms are connected by a band of programmed bridges that act as gathering spaces for collaborative work. {●15–16}

"I wonder if you could have little versions of your building inside your building."
Mark Foster Gage

●MFG: Your skin is doing a lot of work. To have it do everything is probably not the best strategy. I'm reminded of Frank's Novartis building, which is really glassy—so glassy that he had to design these sun umbrellas for people to work there. So it's almost a language of architecture within a language of architecture, and I wonder if you could have little versions of your building inside your building that would provide relief from the relentlessness and vastness of the building skin. ●RR: I don't know if it wants to be of the same language. These rooms are all terrible. I know where your focus is, but if this is the big, universal thing, then how do you do the sub-occupancy within it? There are a lot of things that don't just live in the super-umbrella that are actually opportunities. ●MW: I want to applaud you on a very poetic, productive narrative, expression, and form that seems, in very many ways, could work very well. But I want to talk about space for a minute. The failure of your scheme resides in these drawings. If I were to look at your drawings without seeing these forms I would think "a little glib". And not glib enough to not leverage the amoeba form that's been voided by the paramecium and the tension between. So here's a at the Novartis question—whether you need a layer within a layer.

KRISTIN NOTHWEHR

This project is derived from the conceit that the program of the architecture school must accommodate two separate but complementary constituencies—students and faculty. Like any educational institution, the architecture school is dependent upon the integration of both groups; however the highly iterative and affective nature of design labor creates a unique requirement for individualized spaces. The

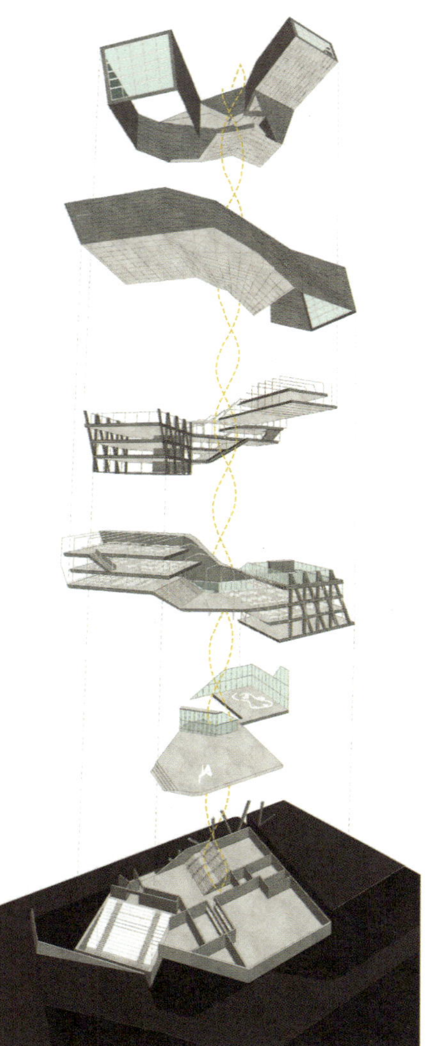

●18

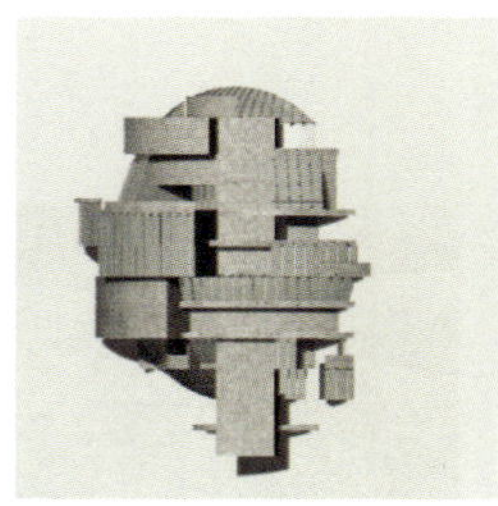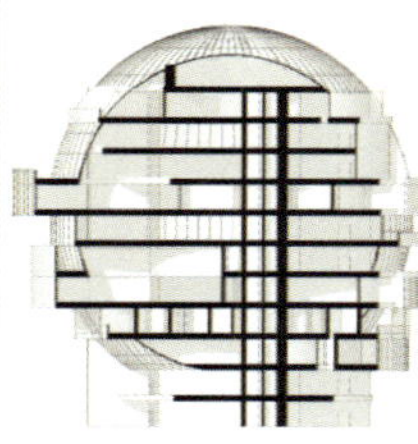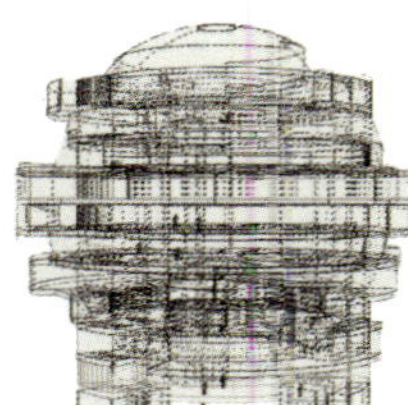

●19

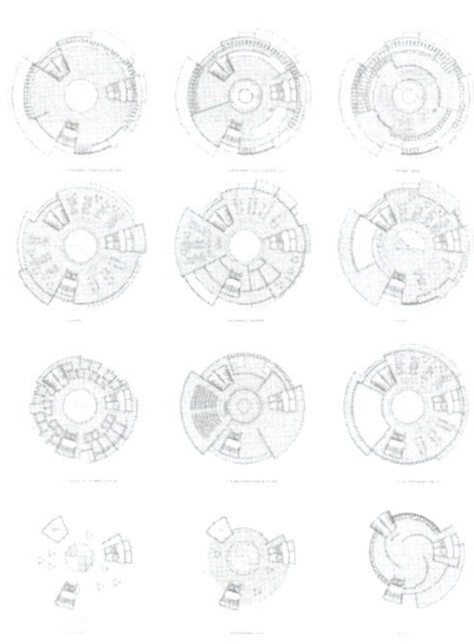

●20

●21

●17

building's form emerges as two individual volumes that take on the identity of the students and the institution, respectively. While each mass is physically distinct, they are dependent on one another for structure and support. On the interior, the interstices between the intertwining volumes create public spaces for display, exhibition, and collaboration. The result is an irreducible composition of defined parts. {●17–18}

●RR: What's the greatest benefit pedagogically, programmatically, socially of the separation? ●Kristin Nothwehr: It's not about just going to class, but about inhabiting the space. We take it over when the faculty is not here, and we have our own rituals that take place within. On a day like today, we are presenting ourselves very differently than we do on a day-to-day basis in the studio. It's important to be able to claim a space that is your own. ●AK: For you, the studio is distinct from the institution, which is funny because I have always thought of it as part of the institution. How are you thinking about, not just the skin of the building to the outside world, but the skins that exist between you and me. I'm the institution and you're the studio. How do we negotiate? ●Kristin Nothwehr: We're very friendly. ●EB: Why should the struggle between us and you be externalized to the whole world and reified in the form? I don't know if we should support this very formal and rigid articulation. ●MW: If we missed your narrative all together, I would see two interlocking forms—one that starts at the bottom with an ocular view of one side of the city and another that looks back at the campus. To me, the narrative is much more interesting that way. I'm going to take away the dichotomy you created between students and faculty because it may have gotten you somewhere, but then you can move on. I think the urban moves you create from the outside are way more important for you to get your arms around in terms of what it's producing than what the inside is doing.

Mark Foster Gage

ANNA MELOYAN

The University Of Pennsylvania School Of Architecture projects its identity from the exterior. Autonomous in its spherical volume, it is fundamentally confined and presents fortitude and speculation in its totality. Anchored by three cores, the building rises from a reflective study grotto at its base to a domed, grand library at its apex. A single focal point within the centrifugal void organizes the building—the review space. A tripartite review platform operates mechanically between studio floors to allow for a dynamic educational experience. For a larger review or event, the platform joins as one plane and transforms the atrium into an auditorium. Studio and classroom spaces radiate around this activated center and are also wrapped by outdoor terraces for individual contemplation or gathering. The pure and simple geometry of the building allows for both uniform and diverse spaces as well as discrete and continuous spaces for a variety of pedagogical events. {●19–20}

> "We can't help but think of Boullé or even George Lucas." Peggy Deamer

●PD: How important is the spherical aspect of this? We can't help but think of Boullé or even George Lucas, so I'm curious why you don't mention the symbolic side, but also formally because this doesn't seem to be really attended to. ●LH: You essentially have an atrium building, so what is at stake in the spherical nature of it? Do you position yourself alongside social theory like the Foucault's Panopticon? Do you think there is anything at stake in the radial arrangement? We know why a planetarium would be this shape, but not necessarily an architecture school. ●RAMS: I would have hoped the Dean's office was in the center—something I think would be a brilliant solution to many of the problems in architectural education. But if the center is a review space, the pragmatics

of this don't quite work because you don't have enough space for all of it. It's very deterministic. There's also a very machine-like quality, but you haven't said a word about why it looks the way it does. I think you haven't been very honest about your sources and you might as well be—Boullé, Ledoux, and Russian Constructivism. ●PDB: The plans suggest something that's very problematic, and that is the absolute being of this thing as radial on every floor. It's not a Russian Constructivist building at all in plan because there is no dynamism or collision. There is not enough internal tension casting some doubt into it to move it away from being such a self-referential thing. ●RAMS: It has romance!

DORIAN BOOTH

Conceived as simultaneously discrete yet inextricably entwined volumes, this proposal for a new PennDesign building creates space between the heavy, poché rooms of classical architecture and the light, open floorplate of modern architecture. At the building's core, three volumes pierce through the floor plates, legible on the exterior only, as they puncture the thickened outer wall to become entries. As the exterior walls erode for light to penetrate the building, the floorplates are exposed, yet the inner volumes remain hidden. The building flickers between revealing and concealing form. Materials and textures spill out from one space to the next. Exterior becomes interior as the rusticated concrete of the outer walls fold into the building and carve out cavernous space within the solid central volumes. Pure formal and visual legibility is eschewed in favor of an illusory ambiguity, where the building is slowly revealed through time and recurrent inhabitation. {●21–22}

●AS: I am super excited about this project because there's not an automatic deployment of material throughout. That's certainly a huge crisis in this generation whether it's parametrics or grids. It's fascinating that you are intentionally calling into question certain thresholds and boundaries.

● 22

● 23

● 24

● 25

● 26

This is one of the better entrances I've seen today because it seems that the interior is amplified and starts to crawl out so that the interior is on the exterior. ● **AR:** If you have a monolith, and you erode it to get your objects, that's interesting, but does it still remain a monolith? An external form that is seriously developed into something massive gives you the reading you want. It's interesting when the pattern blows up in scale and becomes a window. In a monolith, would that actually happen? Those moments, particularly at the base, are eroding. You have objects within objects, which I completely understand, but is the erosion participating in your discourse? What is the tension between eroding the monolith and moments where you actually cut out and are able to slip in? ● **Dorian Booth:** The tension lies in the ambiguity between those two conditions. There is a sense of connection but it's not quite fully formulated. ● **AS:** What about the ground? This is a contemporary project. It's about the object and the monolith, and there's a resistance to figure-ground blurring, yet you have to deal with ground in some way and it seems absent. You can't just put this thing on the ground. ● **MT:** Richard Serra just puts these things on the ground ● **MFG:** Most things in the world are just put on the ground. Every time I'm on a jury with Thom Mayne, all he ever says is "You have to interrogate the ground plane."

JUSTIN OH

Though light and airy, the tree coverage on this particular site is substantial. Ultimately the tree canopy is composed of individual leaves—small and meaningless when single, but vast and significant when multiplied in numbers. The unit of a tree canopy is a leaf. The unit of a sandcastle is a grain of sand. What is the unit of an architecture school? Aggregation of a simple 5' x 5' x 12' frame provides the University of Pennsylvania's School of Architecture with a unique appearance from all four sides of entry. The boundaries of the building are ambiguous. It is unclear where the building begins and where it ends. The large bulk of the 120,000 square foot program is mitigated by this logic and is consistent inside and

outside of the building. The structure, exterior, interior, floorplates, systems, lighting, enclosure—factors that typically have their own expression, dimensions, and color—here, are all unified to speak the same architectural language. [● 23–24]

● **LR:** This is a fantastic presentation. The representation is really some of the best I've seen. The question that is on everyone's mind is one of authorship. What are your thoughts in relation to this and precedents? ● **Justin Oh:** There are some obvious similarities. It didn't always look this way. This was a result of five different permutations that looked at different materials that could form a simple idea of stacking blocks to create a greater atmospheric effect. ● **MFG:** I would also say that Sol LeWitt existed far before Sou Fujimoto, and the grid in architecture goes back to someone like Durand. I don't think this has to be directly tied to one person. Certainly Eisenman did this at the Wexner Center. ● **AR:** Yes, but used differently. Sou Fujimoto's premise is the same premise. I really like that you take the part and array it in three dimensions to produce atmosphere and effect. At pavilion scale, the effect is clear. When the sun is setting, it looks fantastic. When you are actually able to inhabit the piece itself, do you lose that condition? ● **AS:** If you really did the structural analysis of this, you'd find that there would be major parts that would need reinforcement and other areas that don't need any. So if you want to take the Sol LeWitt approach, you would completely over-structure the ones on the periphery in order to make them the same as the ones in the middle. ● **MT:** This is beautiful as a piece of an extremely thick skin, but we don't have the opportunity to see the potential of air distribution systems, solid walls, diaphragms and shear walls. They might add to the vocabulary, or they might allow you to keep this nature of the trellis form that you are building because you've accounted for the structure in another way.

Mimi Hoang

XINYI WANG

The project is at the site of the current PennDesign building at the northeast corner of the campus quad. The diagonal road cutting the quad stretches ten blocks and links several open spaces in the city. The new building proposes an open plaza at the north end of the site and creates a node for the diagonal path. The building is a pile of five courtyard strips that are coordinated with each other and create a variety of spaces. The façade of the building creates a half-tone screen between the interior and exterior of the building. [● 25–26]

> "You make this in a way that feels like an inside joke." Eric Bunge

● **BW:** The way you're dealing with the site and the ground plan is really brilliant. The volume is a raised condition and yet it doesn't feel like a building on *pilotis*. Somehow, it is integrated into the ground plane and yet it's open with just the right amount of separation. ● **MD:** It does a really nice job of negotiating between wanting to read as an object building, but still having something that feels like it's realistic. There are views out of those spaces. There is light coming into those spaces. And then the sort of division in the ribbons gives it a nice sense of scale and rhythm. I think you're creating some really vibrant, interesting spaces. ● **EB:** The strongest part of the project is this interior court. There is an interesting idea in the perimeter increasing until it sometimes touches. That's a funny moment. I wonder if the split personality is important. Reinforcing that hermetic idea of the architectural discipline—you make this in a way that feels like an inside joke. ● **SK:** The scenario for me is that the liveliness of the interior world and the thinness or thickness of the envelope. You're hiding architecture as nothing more than a façade that you'd run into in an urban environment.

●27

●29

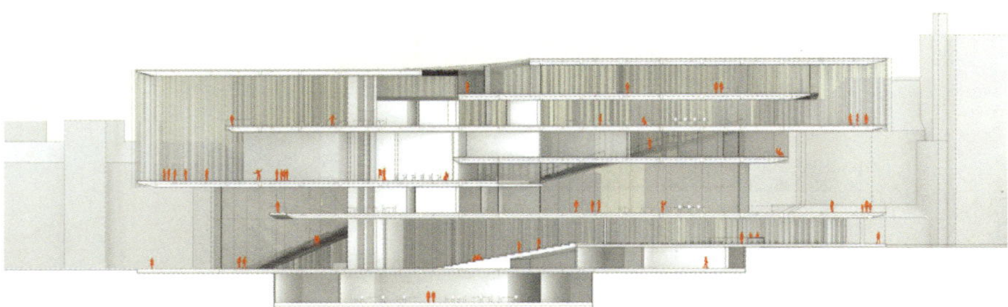

●28

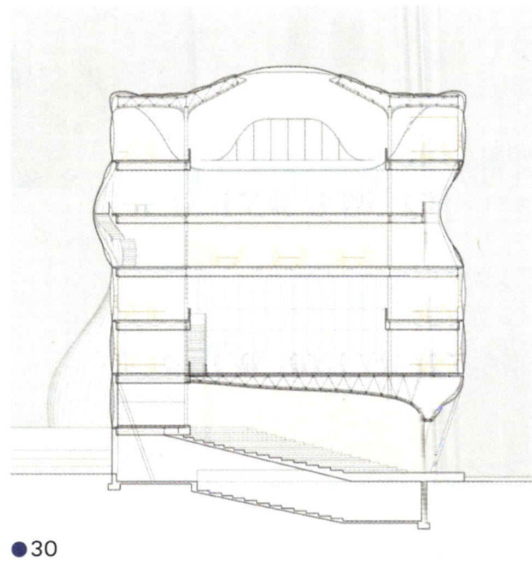

●30

KATIE STEGE

Situated on a prominent corner of campus, PennDesign draws from ideas of pedagogy and site context to organize form and program. An overarching parallelogram plan allows the school to hold a façade both on the urban street and on the campus quad. This creates a courtyard that frames the existing library and maximizes PennDesign's exposure to the major pedestrian thoroughfare that cuts a diagonal through the site. The building embodies the idea of "path," scaling from large, interdisciplinary campus connections down to the individual in transit. A corrugated façade directs views and mitigates sun as one travels through the school. Alternating full and half floor plates create a series of single, double, and triple-height spaces, which establish visual connections between some programs and maintain privacy for others. Designed to serve as a hub on campus, Penn Design creates academic and urban connections at a variety of scales. {●27–28}

●RR: You could be more expressive with the circulation if that's at the core of your idea. Be generous with that, and acknowledge that you're going to take up more space and enable the circulation to not only exist at the perimeter, but to invade as is suggested by the diagram. ●RAMS: Your parallelogram massing is one of the few relatively sympathetic buildings on the site. It's maybe a bit too big, but the way you honor the diagonal corner is very good. ●MW: This is a very good section. By the way, the section doesn't make me think about your building, which has some spiral logic. The site extrusion—the parallelogram—I like very much. You've done something strong. You've made a point, literally and figuratively, about holding that urban edge as a signal. And you've created a face that isn't shoved up against this building, which is so unfortunate, but is opened up to this landscape, which is so fortuitous. And you've actually pulled back here so that this extraordinary façade is given some breathing room. So you've produced some things that have nothing to do with your stair sequence. You produced something better.

●EB: Perhaps one way to achieve these exchanges and continuity is to let the stair liberate itself from the edge at some points and maybe cross through. So it's no longer about an envelope that's connected with the stair. Niemeyer's Biennale pavilion in Sao Paolo also takes the continuous ribbon at an urban scale and incorporates the circulation as an extension and can to enter the deep plan with the circulation rather than merely hug the pavilion adjacent to it. ●RAMS: That is a building to move through. This is not a building to move through.

ANDREW DADDS

The project's massing takes on a radial form stemming from the center of the quad, the sides of which are cut by a long diagonal pathway and an adjacent building. Studio spaces are partitioned into smaller milieus, arrayed around the perimeter of the building, and clinging to an inflated façade system. Glass windows interrupt the ETFE façade, allow for clear views and ventilation for the students, and spiral around the envelope in a corkscrew formation. The perimeter studios are stitched together through programmatic bridges that distort and inflect themselves on the façade. The bridges provide enclosed classrooms and research spaces, the tops of which provide places of spontaneity in the form of unprogrammed collective space. Individual studio spaces are subjected to collective bridges to promote contraction and serendipity. {●29–30}

●EB: It's funny that the cross section reveals the collective, but the long section reveals the individual more. The cross section actually only works a couple of times because there really are very few of these connectors where people can congregate. In a way, it's a courtyard plan with a south, and I wonder what your take on architectural education is because there are a lot of individual, compartmentalized spaces for learning and fewer opportunities to work together. It would become much more three-dimensional if it felt like a thickened facade. A hive would have many layers or have a lot more buzzing and activity. To me it's more of a monastery. ●Andrew Dadds: The space encourages you to take more chances and avoid doing what's beside you or being concerned with what going on in front of you. People are encouraged to be weird. ●MW: It's a didactic point that you've made. You've created an intimacy and there's a one-to-one relationship with the window. It has a lot to do with how the student gets natural light and how the larger world interacts with their individual work. You should look at SANAA's building at Novartis. It is the most maligned building by the people who work on campus. It has slender office areas and very few connecting areas. They dislike the necessary act of passage and the lack of depth they have in their work areas. They hate the extent of light that they are overwhelmed with. When there's somebody in their office, they're seen all the time and there's not enough room; so the narrowness is both beautiful and inflexible.

Introduction to Planning and Development
Alexander Garvin

This course demonstrates the ways in which financial and political feasibility determine the design of buildings and the character of the built environment. Students propose projects and then adjust them to the conflicting interests of financial institutions, real estate developers, civic organizations, community groups, public officials, and the widest variety of participants in the planning process. Subjects covered include housing, commercial development, zoning, historic preservation, parks and public open space, suburban subdivisions, and comprehensive plans.

JULIE ANDRESS, WILSON CARROLL, SAMANTHA JAFF

The site includes two eighteen-story residential towers that are bridged by a ground floor lobby and entry space. The towers are positioned such that the distance between them allows sunlight to filter into both buildings, and their orientation creates privacy by ensuring that residents' views are not directed towards one another's residence. The two towers also offer different views for different units. The roof of the lobby allows a private garden terrace for residents. There are two types of residential units: micro-units and lofts. Both unit types are prefabricated off-site, which reduces construction cost and time significantly. The project has 12,560 square feet of rentable retail space. The retailers represent significant market opportunities, since similar services do not currently exist near the site. They also cater to the student and young professional population. ⟨■1⟩

WILSON CARROLL, GRAHAM BRINDLE, SUSAN SHUO WANG, RYAN WITHALL

The Metropolitan Waterfront Alliance aims to reestablish New York's waterways as the city's greatest natural asset by making them accessible, clean, and inviting, as well as drivers of economic activity. In Long Island City, we envision a continuous, publicly accessible promenade along the East River that will connect the Gantry Plaza State Park to the South with the Queensbridge Park Greenway to the North. The main objective of the Metropolitan Waterfront Alliance's rezoning proposal is to ensure the success and preservation of this future waterfront park. To finance the purchase and initial operation of this new park, the city will issue tax-free municipal bonds. In order to maintain the waterfront park, the MWA is proposing a Business Improvement District comprised of local property owners, merchants and civic leaders. A cultural hub will activate the waterfront area, while a public pier will provide commuter links to Manhattan via water taxi. ⟨■2⟩

EMRE CILEM, CASEY FURMAN, NICOLAS KEMPER, ANDREW STERNAD

Our team took the position of the Partnership for New York City, a pro-development business association, to propose a new central business district for Long Island City, Queens, New York. A future transit hub at Sunnyside Rail Yard generates and sustains the new center, with street improvements along the boulevard linking to the East River waterfront and tidal basin. Along the water, a new light rail line and expanded ferry service connect to surrounding boroughs. Long Island City: a basin, a boulevard, and a business district at the center of a new New York. ⟨■3⟩

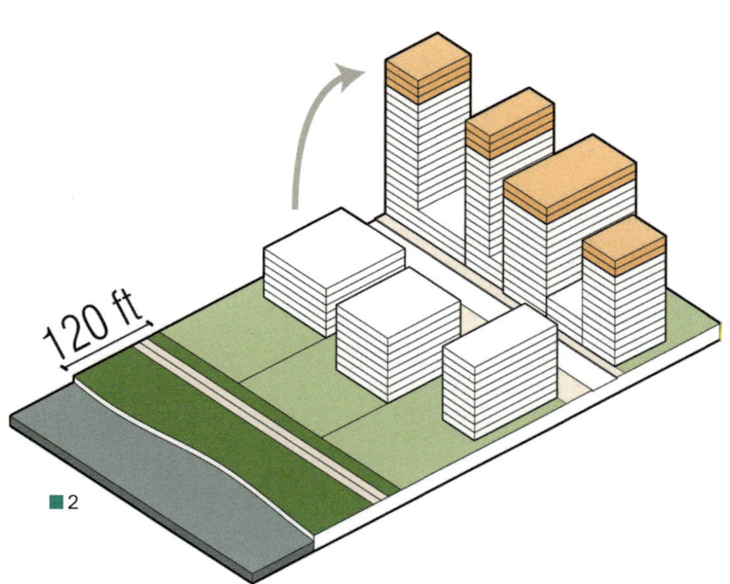

1211a
Drawing and Architectural Form
Victor Agran

This course examines the historical and theoretical development of descriptive geometry and perspective through the practice of rigorous constructed architectural drawings. The methods and concepts studied serve as a foundation for the development of drawings that interrogate the relationship between a drawing's production and its conceptual objectives. Ultimately, the goal is to engage in a larger dialogue about the practice of drawing and spatial inquiry. {■1–3}

3021a
Architectural Theory 1750-1968
Marta Caldeira

SAMANTHA JAFF

Stelae and the Sublime
In order to fully understand the romantic sublime of Edmund Burke, we must define its contemporary form through the examination of a present expression. An investigation of the use of repetition, silence, and abstraction at Peter Eisenman's Memorial to the Murdered Jews of Europe will enable contemporary viewers to evaluate Burke's treatise in the context of devices and emotions associated with the sublime throughout its evolution. While the elements that evoke the sublime at Eisenman's Memorial clearly have their roots in romanticism, their implications in the larger contemporary cultural context are rather different. A denied predisposition of the spectator, combined with the disorientation, isolation, and unease that visitors experience inside the field of *stelae* enable the evocation of contemporary feelings of the sublime that are romantic in lineage, but that retain new meaning and relevance in the context of digital technology and a collective trauma of mass human destruction post-1945.

MICHELLE CHEN

The New Architecture: Organicism Within the Mechanical Order
Gropius is not alone in his belief of an architecture that could be more socially responsive by technological means. Like him, Le Corbusier also perceives engineering and architecture as "two things firmly allied, sequential, the one in full flower, the other in painful regression." Both Le Corbusier and Walter Gropius share the preoccupation for an architectural agenda that embraces scientific ingenuity as a means to rejuvenate people's lives and livelihood. Nevertheless, to take into scope both Gropius and Le Corbusier's means of argument through the lens of Theodore Adorno and Max Horkheimer's *Dialectic of Enlightenment*, what is perhaps revealed is a subtle subversion to the scientific argument. While the architects argue for a new architecture that incorporates scientific rationale, biological origins, and embodiment of reason; the indestructible identity of logic and the notion of "progress" created may ultimately be what stifles architecture from any further experimentation and adaptation to future change. Reason, as given by Adorno and Horkheimer, is a myth consummate. Unerring and absolute, it is no longer reflective of a natural condition since there is no genuine room for error. Stripped of any potential to change, this architecture of reason can only adhere to its prescribed methods of creation and can only exist in perfection within this ideological framework. It may very well not stand up to the real test of time, life, and use.

■1. Sarah Kasper

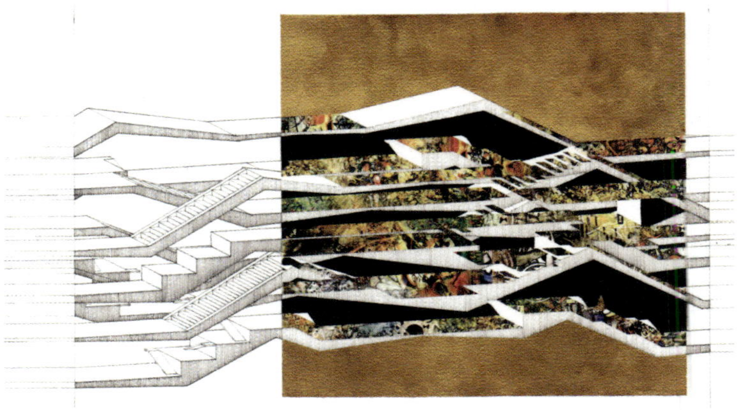
■2. Kiana Hosseini

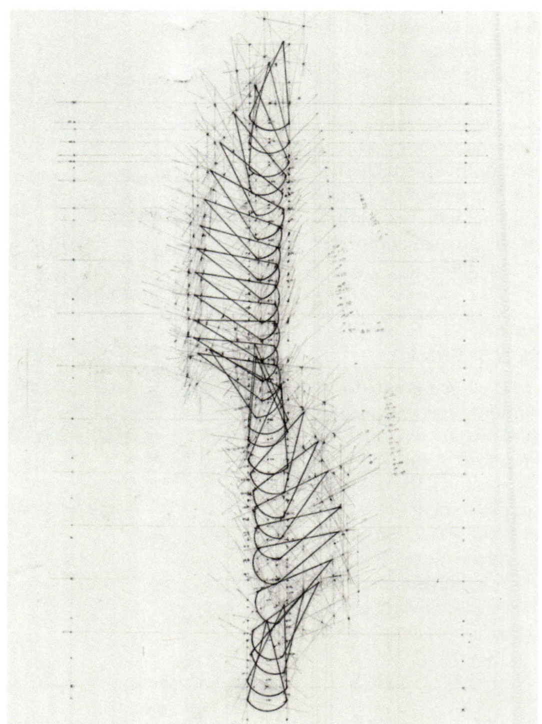
■3. Justin Oh

Once More With Feeling

FAT Architecture:
Sean Griffiths, Charles Holland, Sam Jacob
{Eero Saarinen Visiting Professors}

The point is that architecture is, on one hand, representation, but it is a "thing" as well. It is both fiction and the material and the spatial product of that fiction. It is culturally and materially constructed. Given that position, we argue that architecture's representational quality—its cultural project—could also be its real project that affects the world.

These kinds of things were important because they began to talk about fundamental issues, which we think are architectural: things like class, like vanity, like meaning, like lifestyle, and, perhaps most importantly, taste, which was embedded in our name: Fashion, Architecture, Taste. And so I suppose it is kind of fitting that one of the last acts FAT performed was to build a mound in the heart of the British Pavilion. It is a mound which is an anchor with the Neolithic barrows, the ancient landscapes of X, an anchor of the demolished slums being heaped into the new, optimistic future of housing estates. It is a mound for the past and future of British architecture, but it is also a burial mound for ourselves right in the heart of the Giardini.

Scarce Means, Alternative Uses

Lisa Gray & Alan Organschi
{Louis I. Kahn Visiting Assistant Professors}

O **Lisa Gray**: Alan and I knew that the act of building is how our ideas would best play out. Maybe that is part of the DNA here at Yale. We do believe that building is the medium through which architectural ideas are most forcefully and unforgivingly expressed. So we knew we wanted to work with material to manipulate and gain facility over architecture's special tools. We explored material processes and impacts like texture, surface, form, space, light, scale, contrast, environmental analysis, fabrication, production, and site among many others.
O **Alan Organschi**: When I look at that relationship of material to the body and translate those ideas through industrial design and sculpture to produce things that are outside typical architectural experimentation—for example, planes and boat hulls. There is an important notion about how you limit your approach and work. Charles Eames said that design is the sum of all constraints. That idea is one of the few effective keys to the design problem: the ability of the designer to recognize as many of the constraints as possible and his willingness and enthusiasm to work within these constraints. Constraints of price and size, strength and balance, surface and time—each problem has its own peculiar list. Does design obey laws?

Custom Crafted
Components
Kevin Rotheroe

This historically grounded, hands-on, project-based seminar requires individual aesthetic expression via the crafting of tangible, original, intimately scaled architectural elements. Exploration and experimentation with unusual combinations and sequences of analog and digital representation are encouraged by way of challenging preconception and expanding the spectrum of aesthetic expression. Selected iterations are developed into designs for specific building components and contexts. Relationships among creative liberty, craft, and manufacturing are explored via prototyping custom components using materials, means, and methods that are reasonable in contemporary professional practice. [1–3]

■ 1. Andrew Sternad

■ 2. Minu Lee

■ 3. Kin Tak Yu

179

Yale Academy for Andean Studies

Tod Williams & Billie Tsien

Critics
Tod Williams {**TW**} and Billie Tsien {**BT**}
William B. and Charlotte Shepherd
Davenport Visiting Professors

Instructor
Andrew Benner {**AB**}

Jurors
Sandra Barclay {**SB**}, Tatiana Bilbao {**TB**},
Jean Pierre Crousse {**JPC**}, Martin Finio {**MF**}, Joel
Sanders {**JS**}, Annabelle Selldorf {**AS**},
Karen Stein {**KS**}, Phillip Ryan {**PR**}, Robert A. M.
Stern {**RAMS**}

Yale University has a long and complex connection to Peru, forged with Professor Hiram Bingham's arrival at Machu Picchu in 1911. This initiated a regular series of expeditions and scholarly visits to Cuzco and the Sacred Valley that continue to this day. However, during Bingham's initial forays, he removed most of the significant artifacts found at the site and took them on loan to New Haven for further study. After a protracted period of negotiation, the objects were repatriated, beginning in 2007 and completed in 2012. They are now housed in a new facility, the UNCAAS-Yale International Center for the Study of Machu Picchu and Incan Culture at Casa Concha.

Building on this legacy and the recent turn to cooperative engagement, our project will pursue the establishment of an academy in Cuzco to support research on contemporary Peruvian and Andean socio-economic issues while also sponsoring educational exchange with the local community. Our program will consist of three elements: a small facility for visiting scholars and students, a training program for teachers, and a school for local youth. There will be spaces for interaction and dialogue, classrooms for instruction, and workshops for exploration. The academy will launch with a mandate to find topics that build on local know-how and wisdom and connect that with expertise from the wider world. A primary subject will be refinement of vernacular farming practices in collaboration with the Yale Sustainable Food Project. Another will be research connecting regional weaving techniques with algorithmic coding and computer literacy.

The studio traveled to Peru, visiting Lima, Cuzco, Machu Picchu, and the Sacred Valley. This allowed us to track the deep section of Peru's landscape, from coastal shoals to Andean terraces and down to the edge of the Amazonian cloud forests. We seek an understanding of the cultural and building practices that follow these shifts. We focus on Cuzco in particular as the site for our academy and as a locus for connecting the ancient and latent order of the city with its contemporary urban concerns and opportunities.

We are interested in using this project to reflect on and test the potential of temporal experience as a source of architectural inspiration. We will explore the capacity of our designs to show the simultaneity of the natural, the archaic, and contemporary in Cuzco. This is a city and community with historical depth and grounding that is in the throes of economic and social change. This means that there is also at stake a question of cultural identity and the extent to which architecture can be used to embody or cultivate character for a place and its people relative to the confluence of global trade and tourism.

OLEN MILHOLLAND ✳

Two separate worlds, one lifted towards and open to the sky and one embedded into and rooted to the earth are linked through light and water. Set above everyday life, a serene volume devoted to higher learning consists of serialized programmatic spaces arranged around courtyards fostering a communal and introspective academic setting. Each space provides specialized ways to work and study in various fields pertaining to the Andean culture, thus creating a modern cabinet of curiosities based on the country's history. Open to above, the spaces get light and views from the sky. Sealed off from the city, only the courtyards open to the surroundings to remind the scholars of their purpose. The ground level seamlessly integrates into the city fabric creating a new public garden plaza protected and shaped by the upper world. Light and rain pour down through choreographed voids above to create moments of brightness and downpour. This feeds the pools and gardens that weave their way throughout the public promenade. A curated selection of new works and historical objects are housed in the walls and vitrines that both support the world above and bring light down illuminating the articles on display. (▲1–4)

> "I would say it's not alien enough."
> **Joel Sanders**

▲**MF:** It's a beautifully rendered project. There's a clarity about the way you presented the project, although my peeve is that I don't think architects should use adjectives to describe their spaces. The box is not a "serene" box. Allow it to be what it is. ▲**JS:** One of the conundrums in such a small building is how you differentiate these communities who inhabit this small floor area. What I think is ingenious is the clarity with which you not only separate the community of scholars, but also cleverly use the section and the idea of courtyards and light to allow them to spatially overlap even if they are not necessarily interacting face-to-face. That's really the great strength of your project. As much as I appreciate what is almost like inhabiting archaeology at ground level, it is a public space. I wonder how other people feel about it. I worry do you need signage. Do I need to hire Michael Bierut to come in and tell me where to go? I also feel that this should be a linear sequence as opposed to a centralized sequence. I would have thought the carved architecture—I understand why it belongs to the plinth—but if you are creating a levitating project that's a minimalist, modernist aesthetic, then I'm troubled by the disconnect, and I question why the programs would want to be isolated. There's a beautiful relationship to the courtyard, but I wish there could be greater continuity. ▲**TB:** I appreciate the public space. This is a great thing for the city. You are giving something to the community. I think the surprise space and the problematic part that you see—all of the meandering—I see the richness because Cuzco is like that. The community would appreciate a space that is not an open plaza. ▲**RAMS:** I think part of the problem is this big floating La Tourette-like mass. Maybe if it came down like a wall or an arcade, it would have a better relationship to the street. Why does it have to have a flat roof in a city where there is no flat roof? You could subject yourself to the discipline of the size and volume that is characteristic of the place, and push it as far as possible. This is a piece of modern architecture sailing in—an alien visitor is not necessarily welcome. ▲**JS:** I would say it's not alien enough.

▲2

▲3

▲4

THOMAS DAY

It is a mass. It is a mass whose presence is verified through inhabitation. It is a place where the study of Andean culture is sheltered and nurtured. Architecture is often thought of as parts which together form a whole.

The center for Andean Studies in Cuzco, Peru works against a series of parts through the carving away from a mass which is the site and building form. The project is at once a divide within the ancient city of Cuzco and a link for the inhabitants to their cultural past. It offers a place for them to synthesize their own history through a learning center and exhibition space. Within the building, what could be traditionally understood as service spaces are now interwoven with public spaces and programs resisting rigid divisions between public and private until they must divide.

The façade is an extension of this carving that reads as a homogeneous wrapper punctuated by large apertures and smaller ones that create a play between filigree and form. In a bustling city where old meets new, the project offers a garden for repose and reflection. Through the garden, we enter into the building internalizing the city through study and development. {▲5–8}

"It's a great scheme. Stop talking about it." Martin Finio

▲AS: Conceptually, that's a contradiction: the wall as an object. ▲KS: I think the contradiction is the idea of the wall as a wrapper. As soon as you talk about stone as a wrapper, I just think ,"really?" One of the things that you try to do is play on the massive nature of this, but then you are treating it like a wrapper, which seems to be antithetical to your concept of inhabiting the wall. ▲AS: It's a definition issue. You have to distinguish between perimeter and inhabited wall. ▲TD: There's definitely a different treatment in the way this wall articulates certain spaces and this wall encloses a volume. ▲MF: I think the more you talk, the more I think of the wall as built-in. I love your plans. If you didn't say a word, then I would look at these plans and enjoy the small spaces and large spaces and the relationship between them. It feels like a convincing place to be. But you set the terms, and from midterm until now, the wall is still as confused as it was. ▲JPC: I would say maybe you don't realize that the most important part of your project is not the wall, but the making of an exterior space, like a sunken patio. When I see these plans and imagine the space you are creating and the relationship between the wall and the void, I recognize plenty of Incan spatial strategies that make me think that your project is much better than just the materiality and the walls. The void in a city like Cuzco where it's not cold and not hot and it rains a bit—imagine if the rain fell in and created an ambiguity or a duality between the interior and exterior. That is enormously powerful. At some point I asked you to describe the functionality, but at some point, I disconnected because it doesn't matter. It's the duality that makes it. ▲TB: Going back to the polemic of the wall, the solidity of these spaces and the thickness of the wall and the sensation of being in a space with these thick walls—this is the great thing. The thing that is bothering me, again, is the wrapping and the skin. ▲TD: If I wasn't going to use the word wall, it would be about creating tighter, more enclosed, more tactile experience within this series of spaces. ▲MF: It's a great scheme. Stop talking about it. ▲KS: Or at least don't try to hang on.

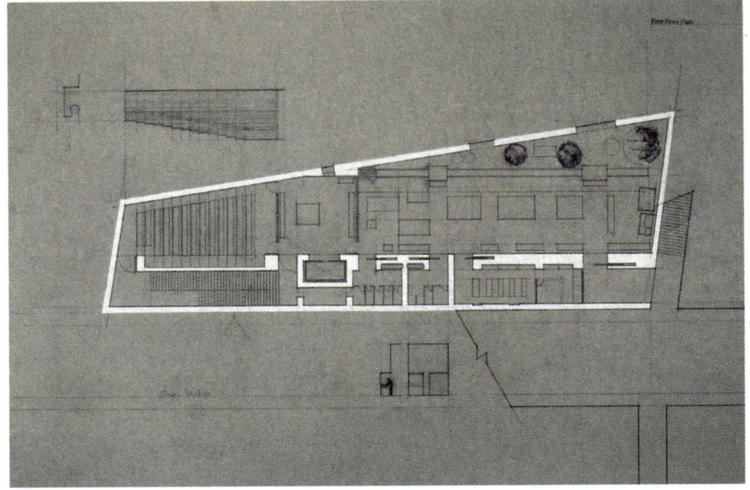

▲5

▲6

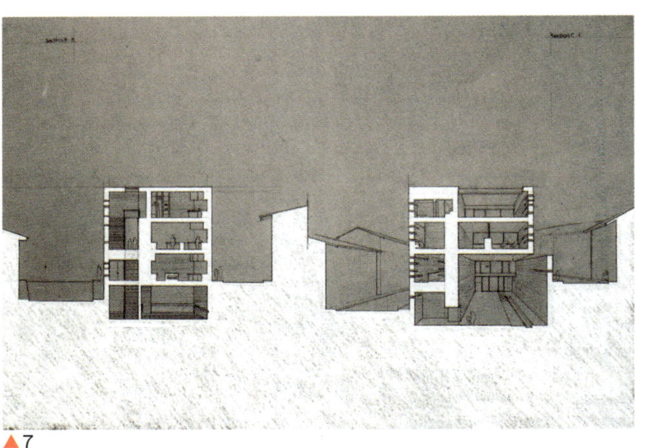

▲7

▲8

DANIEL LUSTER

With the starting point of the solid and massive character of the historic and colonial city of Cuzco, this project establishes a continuity with that language as a singular, porous building block that clarifies a complex program through a series of three courtyards. Reserved and largely monolithic in its exterior representation to the city, the building is an interior world rich with qualities of material and light that develops a dialogue between the realms of the public and of the private. Leveraging the two dominant architectural devices of the historic city—the arcade and the courtyard—creates a tension between these two realms. It is at once extremely private and extremely public. This mass, which fills the bounds of the urban site, is eroded by three courtyards that organize and give light to the three groups of people who inhabit the building—the public, the scholars, and the students—while the large public courtyard is intersected by a public promenade of two arcades that cut through the building, linking it with the historic center and with the neighborhood to the East. [▲ 9–12]

> There's been a tension between one gesture of directionality and moving this way in relationship to the street.
Jean Pierre Crousse

▲ **JPC:** I think this ceiling is very beautiful. You can see it in the section. ▲ **JS:** All of us should be so lucky that when people critique our projects, that the first thing they talk about is so fine-tuned as the relationship to the window. Needless to say, this is a beautiful project and incredibly well resolved. I also applaud the way the courtyard and the vertical section are differentiating identities. But I have more of a question. There's been a tension between one gesture—in your building and others—of directionality and moving this way in relationship to the street. The façade suggests a horizontal movement through the city, but at the end of the day, the building can be open and yet introverted and centralized. As much as I like the individualized identities, I wish you could have found a way to allow some sort of cross through, not only to connect on one level, but on all three courtyards. ▲ **JPC:** I think the quality of light inside the building could be amazing. You are drawing light through the building. You don't need anything else. ▲ **RAMS:** This scheme is even more troubled by the overscaled quality. Look at the corner: so monumental like a 1960 Boston City Hall. And the blank wall—it's always a problem when you have a hill going down and people are getting more and more cut off from the datum of the inside. That's a physical and painful condition—at least I was taught that when I was a student. ▲ **TW:** I will say that I'm thrilled with the work. Interestingly enough, when we stayed in Cuzco, we stayed in a hotel with a little courtyard. The problem—and this has been a problem all day long—is that the project is set in an extremely sensitive city. In every place, you have taken on the tools, but tools still are too powerful. It's the hammer. But that will happen. I applaud the bravery, and I actually think the breaking down of the scale is very good.

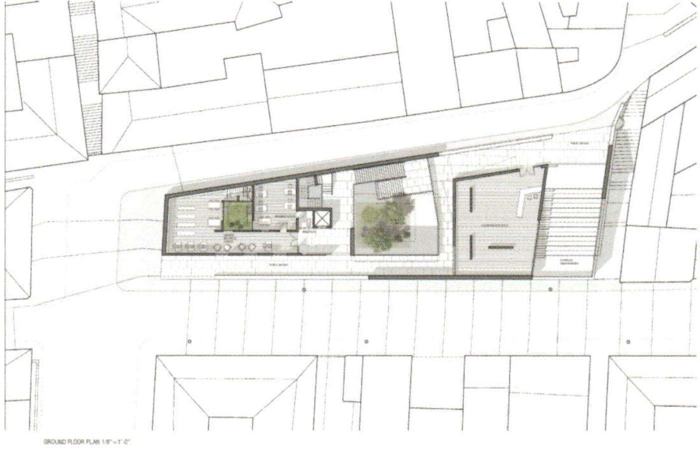

▲ 9

▲ 10

▲ 11

▲ 12

ELVIRA HOXHA

Influenced by both the porosity and the walls of vernacular Andean architecture, this building introduces passageways that welcome the public. Elements recalling the traditional balconies of Cuzco mediate these passageways and stitch the massing together.

Cuzco is a host of many elements that are unique to the culture and location: long and narrow streets, facades masked by colonial elements above Inka stone foundations, courtyards visible only from small openings on the streets that, and, more importantly, the flow of movement and activities that animate the city. This delicate balance between the public and private realms inspired me to design a building that blends within the existing, multilayered urban fabric, while evoking the same energy through the articulation of an inner courtyard.

Cuzco has been shaped in many ways for over seven centuries; this has led to the historical anthology that is the modern day city. Throughout all this change and evolution, Cuzco has very much remained an inviting city that is porous in nature. The city was originally built over the Kancha city blocks and later altered by the colonial interior courtyard typology. Cuzco offers the dichotomy of hiding the interior of the blocks, but remaining accessible to the public at varying degrees. The proposed scheme builds upon this contrast by collaging various activities within the building and calls for a permeable *parti* that organizes the occupants' flow, while welcoming the public and the pedestrians to explore the inner articulated courtyard. ▲11–14

"It's a strange building. It seems like a building that could have only arisen out of this particular site and with these particular conditions." **Martin Finio**

▲ **MF**: It's a strange building. I mean that in a good way. It seems like a building that could have only arisen out of this particular site and with these particular conditions. I'm conflicted about this wall on the street side. It does some really wonderful things, but I don't know if it's enough. The way that these other, smaller buildings separate and have an autonomy and then collect and become singular—I like this ambiguity between being a compound of buildings and one building and never quite resolving itself. ▲**AS**: I look at the photographs that you have shown us, and I totally appreciate how you have views that inspire some kind of thinking about space. I feel what you've tried to do is juxtapose an institutional character and a private experience. You are doing something that hasn't been done, which is to address people from the place coming together with people who are not from the place. As an attitude, I very much appreciate that because you are trying to say, somehow or another, that they have to overlap and become one. ▲ **JPC**: There are colonial walls from convents that are exactly that kind of wall—massive and very high. It's correct to do it in an institutional building. You are taking the convention of convents as institutional buildings and not dwellings. I don't know if it's redundant to do another street inside. To do a hidden street is a very interesting challenge. You are creating this gap of a quiet and safe street. I'm wondering what happens in this street while you are walking. I would have appreciated more transparency. ▲ **JPC**: Another interesting thing is these balconies. They are a transition between interior and exterior, but for me that's not where the transition begins. ▲ **AS**: When you look at those balconies, they are not just balconies. ▲ **JPC**: There is an opportunity to see this hidden space. It could be nice to rediscover this hidden space from different levels. ▲ **MF**: The potential of the middle world is very powerful. ▲ **JS**: I find this project very strange. It seems to me that, in addition to the public street, there are two buildings or three programmatic identities that, in a very beautiful way, bring back and recapitulate the scale of the domestic fabric around it. And then the logic of the giant wall comes from another precedent and operates at another scale that gives it a public legibility. I want to have a more precise understanding of the identity of the pieces and how they interrelate.

▲ 11

▲ 12

▲ 13

▲ 14

Inner Worlds
Brennan Buck

The vast majority of people who occupy buildings experience them without much conscious thought, yet these precognitive, affective modes of experience go largely unexamined within our discipline today. This blind spot is abetted by two primary critiques—first, that affect is vague, unspeakable, and therefore nondiscursive and, second, that affect, amplified by the residue of architectural phenomenology, is inherently essentializing and conservative. However, both of these arguments are undermined by an "Affective Turn" in other fields. Over the past two decades, developments in philosophy, sociology, and neuroscience have redefined affect as a state or capacity beyond the individual and capable of influencing not only our moods, but also our ideas and our collective culture. This seminar examines contemporary ideas of what Nigel Thrift calls the 'spatialities of feeling," the nonrepresentational yet potentially political impact of the built environment. The majority of the course focuses on readings and discussion before shifting to studies of existing spaces conducted through hybridization and subtle transformation.

CHENGQI JOHN WAN

What grants architecture its character? This study contrasts the treatment of space, surface and color in two large public buildings that demonstrate opposing principles of articulation: Oscar Niemeyer's Ciccillo Matarazzo Pavilion in São Paulo and Grand Central Terminal in New York. To demonstrate interchangeability, the spaces are inverted in pursuit of the other's spatial affect, while restrained historicism grants the Matarazzo Pavilion added layers of information that refer to the grandeur of the Beaux-Arts school and draw the viewer's attention away from abstracted form. [■1]

JAMES KEHL

This study explores the affective possibilities of two different spaces through the exchange of material and surface properties. By transforming one space's color, pattern, and texture into the other's—a radically different experience is created out of the same structure. These transformations substantiate the central role that materiality and affect play in our experience of architecture. The British Art Center and the School of Management were chosen for the formal similarity of key elements as well as their drastically different characters. On one hand, the BAC exudes stasis, domesticity, warmth, and maturity. The SOM building expresses transparency, movement, fluidity, and corporatism. [■2]

JESSICA ANGEL

This project investigates the affect of two spaces of "high culture". On the one hand there is Versailles and its highly decorated rooms, ornamented by a superimposition of frames. On the other side of the spectrum, I picked a typical contemporary Japanese home, characterized by its white walls and intersecting rectangular volumes. Transferring the intrinsic qualities of one space onto the other creates hybrid affects. [■3]

■1

■2

■3

Universals
Keller Easterling

The seminar explores the pleasures, perils, and potential productivity of architecture's love affair with, or faith in, systems of standards. From the belief that the proper combinations of geometry would actually generate transcendence in ecclesiastical architecture, to the various adoptions of a neoclassical language for the redemption of buildings or cities, to the modular systems that would allow modernism to rewrite the world, to the hidden mysteries of ISO's {International Organization for Standardization} supposedly rationalizing decisions, episodes in the alchemy of standards feature many architectural disciples. This seminar studies the ways in which the desire for standards has created isomorphic aesthetic regimes as well as productive renovations of construction and assembly. The seminar also explores the more expansive organs of decision-making that overwhelm and dictate to the architectural discipline, trumping the internal theories of design society with universal standards of much more consequence. While the seminar revisits familiar architectural theory, it also visits some less-familiar episodes such as Eiffel's prefabricated cathedrals designed for distant French colonies, the origin of Sweets Catalog, the context of Konrad Wachsmann's modular systems, or ISO's control over everything from credit card thickness to construction industry protocols.

DANTE FURIOSO

The contrast between the world of building presented by the Home Depot and modernist projects for universal standards are not opposed, but rather manifest distinct notions of the universal. Analyzing universal concepts of the home, distinct notions of brand, the universality of the color orange, the concept of "worlds," and the poignancy of the "Homer Bucket," this paper attempts to precisely delineate The Home Depot's ideology by arguing that the nostalgic building materials offered by the store serve as images or stand-ins for what we remember was once the real thing. A home constructed with products purchased at the Home Depot becomes a substructure of standardized parts, clad in the consumer choice for images of the symbolic signs of American vernacular architecture. The building materials, such as framing members and sheet goods are dictated by industry standards; and everything else, that which covers the standardized materials and fills up the space created, acts as a sign or image for consumption through which the consumer builds his identity, reinforces his nationality or assimilates, by entering the self-contained universal world that is the Home Depot.

PEARL HO

Like Mondrian's starry sky, Aldo van Eyck's constellation of playgrounds in postwar Amsterdam marked the beginnings of place. Each playground can at first be viewed as a particle, yet they are particularized down into the play elements with care and detail in each object. These particles are particular. For van Eyck, the play equipment is the elementary, yet each playground itself cannot be reduced. Therefore, the universal is monistic in that a playground is a single reality as a unified whole. The universals are unbounded with each child who plays at one playground and brings the world of play he has learned home with him. The playgrounds are not static constructions. They were never fixed. They tinkle with Klee's return to child-like imagery. They are Mackian, with their vitality and life requiring human contact to be revealed. They are even Miesian with their social aims and tension between the spatial and physical object. The playground was a rediscovery of the essential that brought light to the original and elementary forces present both in the subject and object. The human figure was no longer the privileged figure. It was no longer about the figure, but about the ground. In order to highlight the elemental, van Eyck played with Ground.

The Liquid Threshold Between Order and Chaos
Neil Thomas & Aran Chadwick

This seminar explores the design of complex three-dimensional structural systems. Through discussions on existing projects, including some of the instructors' own, and also modeling and testing new systems to destruction, both physically and digitally {using tools such as Karamba 3D}, the seminar intends to foster a deeper intuitive understanding of structures. At what point do you know a structure is at its limit? {■1–3}

■ 1. Ben Bourgoin and Justin Oh

■ 2. Madelynn Ringo, Jonathan Sun, and Ian Spencer

■3. Luke Anderson, Raphael de la Fontaine, and Hugo Fenaux

Once More with Feeling
FAT Architecture

<u>Critics</u>
FAT Architecture: Sam Jacob {**SJ**},
Sean Griffiths {**SG**}, Charles Holland {**CH**}
Eero Saarinen Visiting Professors

<u>Instructor</u>
Jennifer Leung {**JL**}

<u>Jurors</u>
Tim Altenhof {**TA**}, Peter Eisenman {**PE**},
Florian Idenburg {**FI**}, Jimenez Lai {**JL**}, Skender
Luarasi {**SL**}, Ariane Lourie Harrison {**ALH**}
Mitch McEwen {**MM**}, Joan Ockman {**JO**}, Robert
A.M. Stern {**RAMS**} Annabel Wharton {**AW**},
Ellis Woodman {**EW**}

The 2014 FAT studio at Yale was the practice's last joint work. As such, the studio engaged in a little revisionist history and based the starting point on the work of FAT, its methods, techniques, influences, and philosophy.

The studio examined the philosophical and historical underpinnings of key examples of London architecture {Soane, Hawksmoor, Wren, Stirling, The Smithsons/Independent Group, Archigram} and conducted detailed analysis of their formal, spatial, and technological characteristics. The studio also investigated the implications of copying, sampling, superimposition, repetition, re-scaling found in these examples.

In the beginning of the semester, students were given one of FAT's projects. Each student redrew this in plan, elevation, and section and made a model in order to gain an understanding of, and familiarity with, the project in question. Following this exercise, students were asked to produce an investigative and speculative piece of work that unraveled the techniques, references, and tactics of their assigned project from their own point of view. They explored the architectural, artistic and cultural references involved, but also brought something of themselves to the process. They were tasked as translators, psychoanalysts, detectives, and architectural historians in the production of this piece. The idea was not to merely faithfully reproduce the narrative of the project, but rather that to speculate on other possible narratives, stories, sources, and possibilities as a psychoanalyst or detective would in their attempts to diagnose a condition or solve a crime. The outcome of this process was a beautifully produced, multi-media mind map {like a detective's mind map} of the process as they saw it.

The site for the final studio project was Nine Elms/Vauxhall Embankment in London, one of the largest sites currently in development and the new home of the American Embassy as well as the refurbished Battersea Power Station {with associated projects by Gehry, Foster and many more}. Following a week-long studio trip to London, students used their "Mind Map" of a FAT project as a starting point to develop three physical architectural models to be sited in Vauxhall. These were intended to be formal studies, exploring the possibilities of re-writing FAT projects through the criteria the students had developed themselves. Emphasis was on the transformative design process displayed by the students on the original reference. The students also developed a program for their sites. After midterm, students chose one of the on-site studies or a combination of all three, to create a parti, which provided the basis of an architectural proposition on the site. Overall, we intended for the studio to explore what we might call the psychology of FAT's work, to both refer to the office's body of work, but also to develop techniques and design approaches that extend the original language.

KARA BICZYKOWSKI ✳⬠

Vauxhall is currently one of London's larger sites being developed as the city looks to the future. Various influential projects in the area include the construction of the new American Embassy and the refurbishment of the Battersea Power Station.

The proposed hotel functions both as a gateway for both embassy employees arriving for short periods of time and long term immigrants. The idiosyncratic clash of a non-denominational prayer hall for immigrants and a hotel for embassy and event guests is a new type. The scale of Vauxhall becomes an issue, as surrounding built work does not relate to a human scale. The hotel uses a telescoping technique to slowly introduce visitors into the site after crossing the Thames River, and it gradually grows in size to blend into its neighboring context.

The hotel's organization provides a hotel lobby/lounge, prayer hall, wedding hall, funeral hall, party venue, and more. This organization is structured as a typical Latin cross plan; however, rooms are stacked above the "aisles" next to a "nave" where two transepts then slice through the hotel, which creates atriums for sunlight. The ground level can transform into a colonnaded Mosque prayer hall or remain divided for small intimate gatherings. The "nave" ends in a space devoted specifically for any religious event. The tectonic assemblage of volumetric components create opportunities for light to enter indirectly through various colored glass. This also provides privacy and a stronger sense of community for guests and visitors. {▲1–4}

> "Hey man, why don't you make it a diptych?" **Peter Eisenman**

▲ **MF:** The model is absolutely amazing. ▲ **PE:** I find something very disappointing about the relationship of the building to your research. The research took a very diptych format, which is two halves that are sutured together. It's a very clear format. Fabulous. Then you come to this damn symmetrical thing and I say, "Hey man, why don't you make it a diptych?" What I'm disappointed about is you didn't see the difference: you produce this classical thing. You produce what seems to be a very mundane organization of a building. ▲ **MW:** That sort of happened with the introduction of the cathedral. I have a hard time with the way you oriented the chapel. You realized you were achieving something amazing with the glass effect. You saw something in these volumes, and then in the colors. Then you went for a program that would justify that. ▲ **FI:** With the symmetry sneaking in. ▲ **CH:** I don't have a problem with the symmetry. It's a normal building that you've ended up with; it's definitely less weird than the model. In a strange way though, it's less controlled than the model and perhaps less unique. The tropes and the elements creeping in there seem to be more thoroughly absorbed into some sort of volumetric and spatial exercise in the model. To describe it is extremely interesting, but they perhaps don't come across so compellingly. ▲ **JL:** I'm completely enamored by the project. You begin to think about it in terms of the extrusions. Considering the properties of geometry, it's kind of easy to be thinking about the distribution of differences. In the act of symmetry, can considering that 50/50 be a way to be thinking about proportion? If we were to say, "Let's be fair to all elements." The abrupt change between the two glass shapes would have been really interesting. ▲ **EW:** One of the striking things that connects these images is that they're both awkward perspectives. That horizon line in the middle is literally in the middle. They're opposites too. It's all about an expression of distance—the vanishing point is naturally far away. When I look at your plan, it's clear that there is a point where you would stand, and this perspectival arrangement would be organized in front of you. ▲ **MM:** There is so much rigor in this project, and it's so compelling. It's very clear how the representational logic developed from the initial study. It gets you so far that you really develop the extrusion to get these effects that are beyond mass. They're about a light, and they're about these kinds of voyeuristic relationships. I kind of wish you were talking about the project in terms of reinventing the hotel atrium. There's a lot of bold potential, it's a pretty major feat.

▲1

▲2

▲3

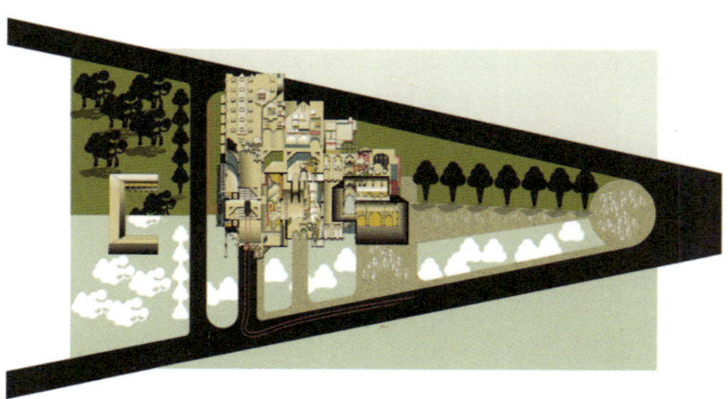

▲4

NICHOLAS MURAGLIA

On January 16th, 2013, a helicopter crashed into the St. George Wharf Tower, plunging into the rush hour traffic of the major transportation hub below. The fifty-story tower, shrouded in thick London fog, and so new that it had not yet been entered into the GPS database, was completely invisible to the pilot. Chaos followed the crash; the Cartesian digital grid which had been trusted to provide an absolute, clear, and stable mapping of reality had suddenly become the violent, destabilizing force which caused the collapse of all rational order in the city.

The proposal for a Dementia Village extends this temporary suspension of faith in the rationality of the city by engaging with the supposedly neutral framework of urban life which silently structures our experience of the world. The project plays with the subconscious operations of the grid by using it not as a rational, neutral tool for orientation and objective stability, but instead as a means through which an unstable, irrational dream-state consciousness is accessed. In the dream-state logic of the Dementia Village, memory of the rational order of the city is recollected in fragments and conflations which don't adhere to the original rules of the waking state references; the city grid is rotated and thickened into an array of incomplete open houses lifted off the ground, inhabited by the dementia patients. Shared amenities and medical services are housed in monumental objects whose readings hover between universal platonic primitives and recombinations of specific historic reference.

The project is a simulacrum of a city which drifts between urban, architectural, and paper spaces, between symbolic representation and tautological flatness. It flirts with a seductive metaphysical dream-state and a self-referential sarcastic awareness of its own illusion through misbehaving shadows and representational contradictions. (▲ 5–8)

> "It's a kind of moment where the rational suddenly becomes wild and irrational."
> **Joan Ockman**

▲ **MM:** This is very New York. It's as if even your language is wanting to read as *Delirious New York* and demented. ▲ **JO:** It's *Delirious New York* plus Rossi's *Analogous City*—a very perfect marriage of two totally different systems. I'm leaving aside the question of whether such a place would make somebody who is not totally demented yet become immediately demented by accelerating the process. The delirium you're producing with this process of disorientation plus this scale or shifting causes this beautiful wedding of Rem and Rossi. It's astonishing. ▲ **MM:** I really like the implication of this ghostly plinth. I'm not sure why, in the model, there is this monolithic object that is repeated to signify the house. I don't understand that, but when it's operating here, and you've attempted to redraw and rethink the block in a demented way, then we see it becoming a ghostly rain. So then we have to rethink the background and everything on the rest of the page. Then the figure/ground becomes something that could be reread into the project. I want to see more of that developed. I don't know if it would be better in section or what, but the idea of that is really fascinating. ▲ **CH:** I'm interested in the discussion of the frame, because it is broken at the bottom. The grid suggests a continuity beyond the frame. Your grid is quite contained, and it suggests a fragmentary extension of the nine-square grid. Is that deliberate? It seems highly ambiguous. It suggests a physical perimeter to the site that is then bridged by the road, but it also plays a conceptual game with the frame. Do you see that as some kind of physical barricade, and does that relate to the programs? ▲ **JO:** There is another grid: a repetition of house frames. We see the big house frame also as a giant framing object within the square...The whole question of rationality is a hard project. How we see anything as becoming ambiguous by this grid play is difficult, even when thinking about your stripes in relation to Loos and Josephine Baker. It's a kind of moment where the rational suddenly becomes wild and irrational. ▲ **CH:** Insanely irrational. The grid should be in plan—an infinite recression of grids. ▲ **MM:** In a way, he's asking us to rethink the plinth in terms of dementia, right? As if every time we try to separate the ground, we're acknowledging our own dementia in the city.

▲ 5

▲ 6

▲ 7

▲ 8

MICHAEL MILLER

This collection of work pursues an investigation of the partial control of meaning, positioning of work within history, constructing the critical joke, and the discipline of copying. The project proposes an unlikely marriage of a banking headquarters, social housing, and luxury condos. These programs exist in a singular form—a mimicked Battersea power station that reates a metaphor of 21st century financial power against 19th and 20th century industrial power.

The façade explores a new version of a classic discipline that translates two-dimensional drawing into three-dimensional architectural surface through tone. Using alphas and digital stamps, the façade overlays Gothic, domestic, industrial and corporate symbols and illustrates the interrelated complexity of real estate and the contest for space, power, and urban life in contemporary London.

A mind map of FAT's work, in the form of a chess set of art, architecture, and literary influences, reconstructed and remixed FAT into semi-accidental encounters. What if chess characters took the form of Thomas Pynchon, Doge's Palace, and Jasper Johns and could come together to make something else entirely? How about Piranesi, Soane, Gandy, Giles Gilbert Scott, Portman, and Rudolph? [▲9–12]

"<u>As a social theorist, you're kind of D+. But as an architect you might be interesting.</u>" **Robert A.M. Stern**

▲**JO:** There is something very astute about making the floor plates of this hotel housing larger than the floor plates of the oligarch housing because, as investment in apartments goes, they're often empty. So you're saving the space. That's a smart move. ▲**RAMS:** If this is social housing, count me in. ▲**PE:** You sound like me when you're doing that. ▲**RAMS:** You mean being an architect? As a social theorist, you're kind of D+. But as an architect you might be interesting. You could put something inside something, and that is not an unknown strategy. But I think you need to be paying a little more attention to privacy and other factors. ▲**AW:** I don't know if this is something you've learned in the studio, but it's certainly something that we haven't seen in the other projects, which is a real texture. All the forms that we've seen have a flat façade, and I love the kind of forms that you've built in these facades that look very Venetian. They're already so activated. ▲**JO:** The textural quality also relates to the strategy of moves that overlap with each other. I think one can see very clearly from the strategy of the chessboard overlaying the plan. For me, where it gets lost is in describing these blunt oppositions between the people who live in the apartment and the bankers. And it's a very binary relationship where we know there is a space for protest. But your chessboard suggests there are many more operations there. I think it would be interesting to go back to that idea. Maybe there is not just a cut, but more nuance in a strategic relationship. ▲**MM:** It seems like there is so much concern about value in terms of currency and stacking these programs. It seems like you want to position yourself in relation to these questions. I don't know if you're setting form as a Trojan horse. You're using these tools as a recognizable signifier as a way to introduce something completely different programmatically. So, in a way, I like to think that it's a critique of the position of the architect. Often, we do the inverse. ▲**TA:** What is so compelling is the ambiguity of the state of construction and destruction. If Piranesi were to draw any of the ruins in the state of decay, he would always draw bits and pieces of nature reconquering and reoccupying that piece of architecture that is falling into oblivion, thus revealing all the hidden structures that are usually concealed. All of your drawings signify this, which makes it ever more ambiguous and so powerful. ▲**MM:** It seems like you have another method of drawing the ruin over there that is more compelling. I live in Detroit, so I am in the capital of this investigation that you're taking on. And ruin means more in terms of glazing if it's going to be reduced to a façade game. When the windows are gone, you read these structures as ruin. What you're doing is much meatier.

▲9

▲10

▲11

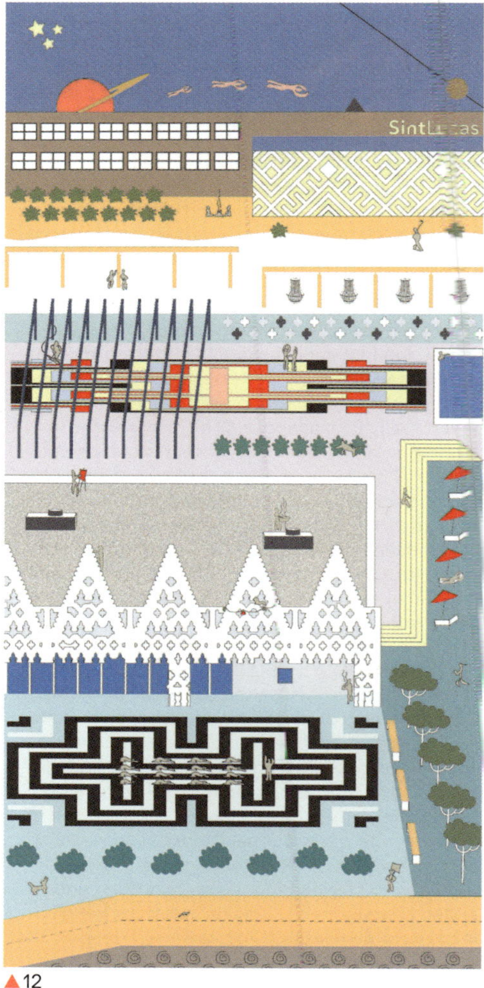

▲12

Composition
Peter de Bretteville

This seminar, consisting of weekly exercises, addresses issues of architectural composition and form. Leaving aside demands of program and site in order to concentrate on formal relationships at multiple scales, these exercises are intended to establish proficiency with "the language of architecture" as well encourage confidence in personal, formal proclivities. The goal is not only formal and compositional dexterity, but also developing eyes that can see the organizational paradigms at work in any piece of architecture.

JARED ABRAHAM

These compositions aim to study the effect of formal operations on canonized building typologies. The exercise begins with a standard building type (i.e. tower, courtyard, linear building, etc). Operations such as shearing, shifting, adding, subtracting and rotating are then used to yield transformed formal variants. Using a sequential method, three to five operations were combined to create new interpretations of type. The result is a series of entirely new forms which retain some memory of their parent type while establishing new variety and formal complexity. (■1)

AMY SU

These studies from *Project One: Form and Assembly* demonstrate various strategies in creating formal compositions. Each set of iterative models is generated by a repeated action on the same set of objects addressing concepts such as subtractive/additive, inward/outward, and open perimeter/bounded perimeter. (■2)

KATIE STEGE

This study, part of a series from *Project One: Form and Assembly*, used regulating proportions and subtractive operations to explore the relationship between original and perceived geometries. Three whole cubes, placed in a line, formed the starting point for the series; this final study used regulating lines and subtractive processes to manipulate the original cubes, blurring the boundaries between them while creating the suggestion of an altogether different geometric base. (■3)

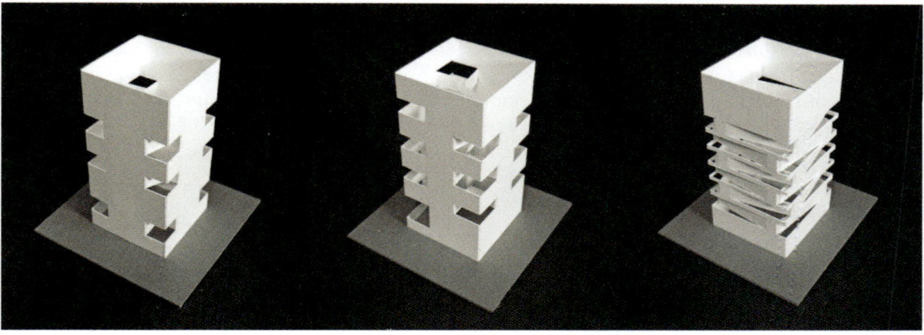

■1

■2

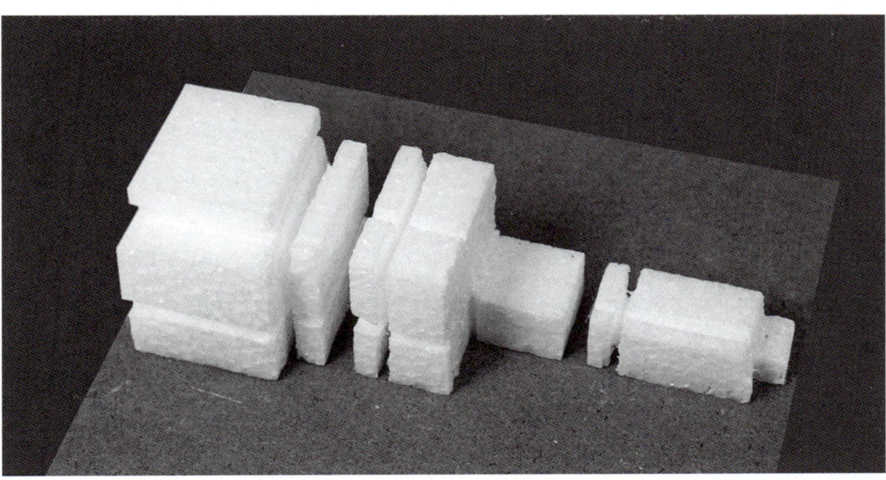

■3

3262a
Jerusalem
Annabel Wharton

Venerated by the world's three dominant monotheistic faiths, Jerusalem is a city whose religious and political importance has made it the focus of spiritual and military conflict from biblical to modern times. Its struggles are global, not local, in their implications. Jerusalem's urban order presents a model for understanding the built-in contentiousness of cities elsewhere. This seminar investigates the contribution of Jerusalem's physical topography and its built fabric to the city's agonistics. In addition to primary sources {e.g. Josephus, Eusebius, Margery Kempe} and theoretical texts {e.g. Eliade, Deleuze, Foucault, Augé}, the city is investigated through its representation in film {Gitai, Gibson} and digital media {e.g., Assassin's Creed and Second Life}. Student projects treat a particular historical site in the city as if in preparation for restoration, reconstruction, or removal, addressing the question, "How will this intervention make a belligerent city less so?"

MAHDI SABBAGH
The Sa'eed al-Husseini House
The Sa'eed al-Husseini House stands at the end of an elongated garden lawn. Upon entering the property through a modest front gate, one is greeted with a procession of coniferous trees at the end of which the house's white and pink stone façade appears. A freestanding house with a front garden is atypical in Jerusalem.

The plan is "U" shaped. The rooms on the ground floor are organized around two spaces: the main East-West hall and the backyard. The three-meter hall connects the north-facing bedrooms, the central radio room, and two other bedrooms. The house was built to serve members of a single family. The backyard breaks the symmetry in the plan and ties the guest salon, kitchen, and bathroom in the west-wing to the rest of the house. A wide staircase, also on the west-wing, leads to the second floor. All bedrooms face either the backyard or the front garden. The spacious hall is analogous to the communal courtyard plan wherein family members lived in rooms that connected only through the courtyard. Like a courtyard, the hall is used as a gathering point. It is south-facing thus well-lit and appears to be used today as a living and dining area.

The Husseini House can thus be understood as an expression of the communal aspects of courtyard living, combined with a modern type. It is an outward looking house with a clear front and back, a modern configuration.

LAURENCE LUMLEY
The Via Dolorosa in Jerusalem
This is the peculiar nature of the Via Dolorosa: that it is a site that seems to be all about being somewhere else. The actual site is obscured, either through the projection of spiritual exercise, the textual creation of an imaginary historical location in place of the real one, or the non-place of the tourist experience. This is in direct tension with the simultaneous importance of the physicality of the street and the sites of the Stations, of the stones and the ground, and with the everyday working life of the city. The experiences of the tourist and the pilgrim are thus close in the sense that they both are caught in the tension between physical locatedness and un-presentness. The Via Dolorosa is a site in which the entanglements of the sacred and the everyday, the historical and the eschatological, the physical and the spiritual are at their most extreme. Such binaries are not merely opposed, but rather form together a 'reciprocal field' of relations in space that become twisted and distorted over time. It is such places in which there is the greatest overlap and intertwining of this field that are most likely to experience sudden violence. These are the flashpoints of Jerusalem, with the Via Dolorosa one of the foremost among them.

DAPHNE BINDER
Ha-Shabbat Square
From Israel's establishment in 1948 until the present time, Ha-Shabbat Square is the repeated site of conflict between Jerusalem's ultra-orthodox community and secular state authority. Originally an unknown traffic intersection not intended for public demonstrations, the reasoning behind the square's selection as a space of protest becomes evident when examining its space and location within the city. Its vicinity to emergent Jewish religious neighborhoods outside the old city walls made it a central site to this developing periphery. As such, the intersection accommodated a range of social and religious institutions as well as commercial activities. Yet the square was also identified as a point of vulnerability, unbound and unprotected. It threatened the religious community's gated courtyards and fortified row houses, indicative of their growing desire for isolation from their secular neighbors. Due to the square's proximity to the 1949 border between Israel and Jordan, the Israeli military asserted their control over adjacent buildings and moved through the site regularly, including on holy days, exacerbating the concerns of the religious communities. The ensuing protests over the violation of Jewish law took place on a site that had become equally valuable to both religious and secular sides, highlighting the growing divide between them.

RAPHAEL DE LA FONTAINE
Division Through Collective Infrastructure
In Jerusalem, nothing is more important than control over space. Therefore, the city has developed a long tradition in which spatial products and infrastructure have come to serve as means for control and power. These tools have allowed for expansion, contraction, division, and reconstruction of space. This study identifies the modern light rail as a contemporary example to an eternal conflict over space in Jerusalem. An analysis of the Jerusalem Light Rail explains how the train both symbolizes and induces violence. It alludes to the train's role in a larger, politically charged Israeli-Palestinian conflict. Furthermore, it suggests that the extensive infrastructural project is primarily used to secure and contain a population, rather than meet the transportation needs of Jerusalem citizens. While the infrastructure attempts to mask its violence through an architectural aesthetic and script, the physical violence it attracts brings to light its true disposition. Despite the nature of the train as an object of free movement, forward thinking, and connectivity; the Jerusalem Light Rail appears to reflect the eternal battle for space and power in the holy land.

3261a
Pedagogy and Place
Robert A.M. Stern

Preparatory to the Spring 2016 exhibition celebrating the School's one-hundredth anniversary, this research-based seminar examined the relationship between significant architectural pedagogies and the architectural buildings designed to accommodate them. Students were asked to document examples from the early 19th century to the present, combining class presentations, written texts, and graphic analyses that formed the basis of display panels to become part of the exhibit. Lectures provided a historical overview of the topic as well as a detailed history of the Yale School of Architecture.

NICOLAS KEMPER
École des Beaux-Arts
The École cannot be understood as a single homogenous institution. It was a hybrid between an organic, fragmented system—the ateliers where students worked were located in rented space in the neighborhoods surrounding it—and a centralized one with absolutist roots, for not the École, but the Academy, rewarded *The Grand Prix*, established by Colbert to put the reins of taste in the hands of the King and, through the prize, create a hierarchical system by which the state adjudicated the good in architecture. Navigated by a series of skilled educators, the tension between the centralizing absolutism of the academy and the meritocratic reality of its scattered parts helped drive the École. For instance, Julien-David Le Roy {1724–1803} shepherded the École through the revolution by proving their architecture relevant to the principles of the Republic. Yet there was no Julien-David Le Roy in the protests of 1968, when the government replied to protesting students not by adjusting and proving its continued relevance, but instead breaking up the École into eight Unités Pédagogiques, essentially fragmenting those contradictory forces which the school had once contained. None of them would approach the prominence of the École.

ROSS McCLELLAN
Kent State University
The architecture program at Kent State formally began in 1947 as one of a number of new areas of study introduced during the large influx of students under the GI Bill. Beginning as a two-year course of study in the Department of Industrial Arts, the program grew rapidly under the guidance of Joseph F. Morbito, who founded the department and served as its director for thirty years. In 1962, the department earned NAAB accreditation for its five-year degree in architecture, and by 1967 found its first permanent home in Taylor Hall, where it still resides today. The program outgrew the spaces in Taylor Hall long ago and, out of necessity, currently divides its 800 students among three buildings across campus. In the Fall of 2016, under Dean Douglas Steidl, FAIA, the College of Architecture and Environmental Design will find a new home in the Design Loft by Weiss/Manfredi. This project will house over 100,000 square feet of space and will mark the first time in over thirty years that the entire program has been housed in a single building.

SHAYARI DE SILVA
Illinois Institute of Technology
The College of Architecture at the Illinois Institute of Technology is an almost singular instance in which a lone figure plays a definitive role in delineating the greater campus master plan, designing the architecture school and crafting its pedagogy. That figure is of course Mies Van der Rohe who, in 1938, upon the request of Henry Heald took over as chair of the Department of Architecture at the Armour Institute of Technology {to be renamed the Illinois Institute of Technology in 1940, when the school merged with the Lewis Institute}. That same year, Mies was charged with designing a master plan for the new campus. He designed twenty of the twenty-two buildings on the campus, symbolizing "a new urban form and a language of openness and movement."[1] Crown Hall, which housed the architecture and design programs, was completed in 1956, and is easily the finest building on the campus. Crown Hall's rational, controlled expression of structure and material were very much in keeping with Mies' pedagogical goals for the school. Mies began drafting a curriculum before leaving Germany, essentially decreeing that students would first learn to draw, then master the use of building materials, and finally learn the fundamental principles of construction before undertaking building design. The incisive programmatic clarity of Crown Hall in the 1950s is instructive in its correspondence to a set of pedagogical ideals in a particular era.

[1] Phyllis Lambert, Introduction, Mies in America, ed. Phyllis Lambert, p. 196

3265b
Architecture and Urbanism of Modern Japan: Destruction, Continuation, and Creation
Yoko Kawai

This course examines how design philosophies and methodologies were developed in Japanese architecture during the 130-year period from the Meiji Restoration until the postmodern era. Special attention was paid to the process of urbanization through repeated destructions and the forming of cultural identity through mutual interactions with the West, both of which worked as major forces that shaped architectural developments. Highlighted

September 11th, 2014

Suspending Modernity: The Architecture of Franco Albini {George Morris Woodruff, Class of 1857 Memorial Lecture}

Kay Bea Jones

This has been a conundrum for me throughout my work: it is not hard for me to see how, between Kahn's new monumentality and Albini's magical abstraction, we find similar responses to post-ideological modernism. Both architects were very active during a period of late modernism with clear criticisms of the problems of ubiquity and of the one-size-fits-all International Style critique. Land speculation, mass marketing, mass consumption: all of these things were entirely changing the environments in which they worked. Both of the architects taught while they practiced. They were involved in the discussions of their time. They showed a great deal of reverence for human culture instead of an easier, nostalgic idea of tradition—a tradition that was very carefully defined and critically assessed, but, above all, constantly changing. They introduced a new reverence for the site, the context, the city, the human experience, and the integrity of materials—always with innovation, where tradition and modernity were no longer perceived in opposition. Both architects, albeit from different cultures, came to the same conclusion: situated modernism.

October 9th, 2014

Radical Cities: Across Latin America in Search of a New Architecture {Brendan Gill Lecture}

Justin McGuirk

Latin America has a long history of testing radical ideas in city-making. Mexico City is an example: it was a city of one million people in 1940, on its way to becoming a city of fifteen million people by 1980, and over twenty million today. Mario Pani designed housing for 100,000 people. It is the largest housing estate of its kind in Latin America—this is where the Corbusian idea of the city is taken to its conclusion. No housing estate in Europe was built at this scale, and my argument is that the Corbusian idea of the city gets built on the scale of the New World in Latin America. Latin America is also where the modernist idea of utopia goes to die. By the 1970s, governments realized they could not build megablocks fast or cheaply enough to keep up with urbanization. Gradually, from 1979 onwards, they decided not to because of a new liberal politics trickling down from the north: The Washington Consensus. It argues that the free market should take over this question of free housing. Architects get removed from this equation and it becomes more of a social issue—they get replaced by economists and social policy makers. A kind of *laissez-faire* urban politics took hold, and the result was an absolute explosion of slums through the '80s and '90s—effectively, the segregation of cities into formal and informal.

architects include Chuta Ito, Goichi Takeda, Frank Lloyd Wright, Kameki Tsuchiura, Sutemi Horiguchi, Kunio Maekawa, Kenzo Tange, Arata Isozaki, Fumihiko Maki, Kisho Kurokawa, Kazuo Shinohara, Tadao Ando, and Mirei Shigemori. Historical photos and excerpts from films are used to better understand context.

PHILLIP NAKAMURA

Shinsekai

This paper relates the architecture of Shinsekai, an early 20th century amusement district in Osaka, to the changing nature of urban life in modern Japan. Unlike the "modern" buildings built by the first generation of professional architects in Japan, Shinsekai, literally "New World," was an urban development at the border of the feudal city and the planned Osaka metropolis. Although Osaka's urban design in the early 20th century focused upon infrastructure, most notably roads, Shinsekai offered western architecture as entertainment and included the Tsuutenkaku, modeled after the Eiffel Tower, and Luna Park, a reference to Coney Island. Through this quotation of the West, Shinsekai's architecture framed modernity through a lens of *taisho romansu*, manufactured nostalgia for the modern world seen during the Taisho era (1912-1926). The conflation of these different images of Paris and Coney Island, among others, manifested a new international culture in interwar Japan as modern architecture. Despite this, Shinsekai emulated the Western world solely through its appearance. Its spatial planning within the Osaka metropolis reveals adherence not to the modern planning, but feudal entertainment quarters and the traditional spatial phenomena of *oku*, or deep space. Ultimately, Shinsekai offers an alternate narrative of modern architecture in Japan as amusement, and certainly as a "new world" for Japan—operating as fragments of the Western world and as a stage for the modern spectacle of the city.

CYNTHIA HSU

Isozaki Arata: Fragmentation and Ruin in Post-modern Japan

Although a collaborator and contemporary of the Metabolists, Isozaki Arata's vision of the future ran counter to the modern perception of linear progress, carrying a distinctly pessimistic tone with undercurrents of morbidity, irony, and skepticism. At the height of his career, two reoccurring themes of fragmentation and ruin distinguished Isozaki among his contemporaries. While post-war Japan made an unprecedented leap forward as one of the world's most powerful economies, Japan's unique identity rapidly receded behind modern spectacle. Isozaki feared the nation was chasing after progress that would ultimately turn out to be a myth. Rejecting the role of architecture as part of society's "commercial catalogue," Isozaki attempted to establish architecture as conceptually independent but able to communicate an image of the nation by discovering power through metaphor. His controversial design of Tsukuba Center announced an alternate, schizophrenic reality, forcing architecture to become an instigator of cultural debate. Isozaki's fixation on the subject of "ruin" reveals how it is uniquely defined in the context of Japanese urbanism. Traumatized by the destruction of nuclear bombings and natural disasters, the romantic ruins of the West held no resonance with realities of entire cities leveled in a single moment.

WINNY TAN

Evolution to Devolution of Capsule Architecture in Japan

In addition to providing Japan with a newfound identity and symbol for post-war resurgence, Metabolism introduced a new architectural type—Capsule Architecture—which, together with the development of pre-fabrication construction methods, led to the integration of industrial products for domestic consumption that is still very much applicable to Japan's home construction industry today. Subsequently, this new experimentation on micro-living led to the invention of Capsule Hotels and the proliferation of One-Room-Mansions as clear direct tangible descendants of the first Capsule Architecture, and thus of the Metabolism movement. But perhaps the greatest legacy of the movement lies in the acculturation of pre-resurgence mindset of a liberation towards individuality, towards free movement,

and independence to filter own information, which not only sets out the potential for mass mobility and rapid expansion, but more importantly preempted the housing industry for Japan's current atomized domestic state. As such, in the short decade between the formation and declaration of the Metabolism group at the 1960 Tokyo World Design Conference, and the 1970 Osaka World Exposition, which effectively marked its apotheosis and end, the achievements of the small Metabolist team was no small feat.

4214a
Built Environments and the Politics of Place
Dolores Hayden

Call it the built environment, the vernacular, everyday architecture, or the cultural landscape; the material world of built and natural places is intricately bound up with social and political life. This research seminar explored research methods and sources for writing the history of the built environment, such as maps, aerial and ground photographs, planning documents, landscape analysis, and GIS. The course included readings from history, geography, anthropology, and architecture as well as readings on narrative and graphic strategies for representing spaces and places.

MAYA ALEXANDER

The Orleans Parish School Board

Between 1951 and 1959 the Orleans Parish School Board built twenty-nine new schools. This was the first building campaign by the city in nearly fifty years and the student population was in dire need of updated facilities. The schools that were built at the turn of the century were for a much smaller and whiter student population and these new schools were meant to ease this growth. Despite the 1954 ruling of Brown vs. Board of Education, nearly all of these schools constructed were for either black or white students. However, many of the schools built for these seemingly neglected and undervalued students did showcase highly innovative architectural and ideological principals. Today, only one of these neighborhood schools still stands. Although the growth and development of the post-war era was not unique to New Orleans, the city became the preeminent leader in the architecture of schools. Leading this movement were two young newcomers to New Orleans, Jacqueline Leonhard and Charles Colbert. Their entry into the school system and local architectural community began in 1947 as a news reporter and an assistant professor of architecture respectively; within four years they would have risen to two of the most powerful positions in the Orleans Parish School Board (OPSB).

JONATHAN SUN

Graffiti City 1971

The emergence of graffiti culture in New York did not happen by accident, and it did not happen overnight. Through the lens of Kevin Lynch's *Image of the City*, the growth and establishment of the graffiti community can be understood as its own urban structure, taking advantage of New York's existing infrastructure—namely, its subway system. Graffiti City—the urban structure of the graffiti community as it is referred to in this paper—can be defined by Lynch's elements of the city: path, edge, district, node, and landmark. New York's path—its subway system—provided the perfect structure for the development of all the elements of graffiti city, in terms of growth, networking, and place-making. In this sense, the establishment of graffiti city shows how an existing urban environment creates opportunity for other urban environments to form.

GENEVA MORRIS

The Rise of Kitchenette Apartments in Chicago's Black Belt, 1940–1960

Prompted by changing household compositions and an affordability crisis, there is an increased

interest in micro-apartments within the conversations of housing development. This renewed interest in small-space living prompts questions and attention to historical models of small-space living. In between the boarding house of the late 19th and early 20th centuries and the micro-apartment of today is an often-overlooked housing type—the kitchenette apartment. First appearing in Chicago in 1916, kitchenette apartments featured "Pullman kitchens" and a "Murphy in-a-door bed" to conserve space appearing as a model of efficiency and modernity, much like today's micro-apartment unit. However, during the second wave of migration of African-American families to the industrial north, this small-space living concept was co-opted and corrupted as a way for landlords to capitalize on increasing demand for housing and the spatial and economic restrictions imposed by government-sanctioned policies of segregation in cities like Chicago. Kitchenette apartments in the Black Belt of Chicago were cut from an older house or larger apartment, long since abandoned by Chicago's wealthy whites, and converted into multiple make-shift apartments with entire families living in a space better suited for a single person. With in-depth archival research and an analysis of literary texts by Chicago author's Richard Wright and Gwendolyn Brooks who wrote extensively about the experiences of living in a kitchenette apartment, this paper details how spatial realities such as the kitchenette apartment exist at the apex of larger social movements such as urbanism, segregation, and economic (arguably capitalist) forces at work in housing. The kitchenette apartment emphasizes inadequacies in building management and maintenance, but also in its design principle to provide the smallest space possible for a person, a family, and a community. In this way, kitchenette apartments were less modern and efficient, but instead were seen by their largely black residents as the material embodiment of the oppressive conditions of segregation in the mid-20th century American city.

Case Studies in Architectural Criticism
Carter Wiseman

This seminar concentrates on issues that influence the way modern buildings and their architects are perceived by critics, scholars, and the public. The careers of such architects as Frank Lloyd Wright, Eero Saarinen, Louis Kahn, Philip Johnson, Robert Venturi, and Frank Gehry provide a framework for the examination of how patronage, fashion, social change, theory, finance, and politics affect the place of prominent designers and their work in the historical record. Readings include such critics as Catherine Bauer, Alan Colquhoun, Henry-Russell Hitchcock, Ada Louise Huxtable, William Jordy, Rem Koolhaas, Lewis Mumford, Colin Rowe, Vincent Scully, and Manfredo Tafuri. Responding to lectures by the instructor and visitors, students develop criteria for judging architectural quality {program, site, "message," details, etc.}, and then apply those criteria in three brief analytical papers that build toward a 2,500-word research paper investigating the elements that contributed to the "success," "failure," or "reevaluation" of an individual building, an architect's career, or a body of architectural work.

IAN SPENCER

Something Borrowed, Something Blue
I miss Norman Foster. Like any millennial viewer of *Mad Men*, I have a tendency to contrive a nostalgia for a zeitgeist I wasn't a part of—"Beatle-mania," say, or the moon landing, thin neckties, and boozy lunch breaks. And like any good student of architecture in the digital age, I have a similar nostalgia for the complexity of vintage High-Tech. It was therefore with great disappointment that I beheld the Yale School of Management building. Gone is the sensitivity to and proliferation of tectonic connections; here to stay is the pastiche of modernist tropes cloaked in a heavy-handed Yale blue. Edward P. Evans Hall seems to be an exercise in half-measures, as though everything is said with quotation marks: it isn't symbolic, it's "symbolic." It insists on symmetry, only to ashamedly sneak its {barely} asymmetrical plan past the unsuspecting eye. The seminar rooms, which form six blue—rather, Yale blue—tubes, reduce surrounding spaces to over-sized hallways {indeed the building seems to be mostly hallway}. The building isn't simple; it's simplistic, although the project hardly begs for complex problem solving. Still, for my money {$1000 per square foot, to be exact}, a little subtlety goes a long way.

WINNY TAN

Meyerson Hall: Let's Tear it Down Already
For a building whose primary purpose is unquestionably to inspire its students, University of Pennsylvania's School of Design is a colossal disappointment. Never have I been to a building more depressing and hated by its occupants than Meyerson Hall. Completed in 1967 as part of Penn's Master plan for a new Fine Arts building, one of the oldest architecture programs in the United States moved into Martin, Stewart, Nobel & Class's brick-clad bunker of a building. Since then, in the attempt to freshen its dark and gloomy interior, the building has gone through numerous cosmetic alterations whose frequency has plateaued into a perpetual state in recent years. But with a building burdened by unwieldy spaces and awkward circulation, there really isn't much that can be done except to tear it down and start anew a proposal second-year Yale architecture students are currently exploring and PennDesign students ironically anticipating.

SOFIA SINGLER

One Boston Place
From afar, the façades of One Boston Place {Pietro Belluschi, 1970} proclaim a bold structural-expressionist manifesto, but closer inspection reveals that the bold coal-grey mass is, in fact, composed of svelte metal fins that express a delicate, nearly feminine, grace that striates the elevation into a fine composition of thin verticals. The fins make One Boston Place a refined *étude* in degrees of exposure and disguise. Looking straight ahead, one sees directly into the offices—but take a step or two in a different direction, and the views become obstructed. The tower engages the city-dweller in a gentle game of peek-a-boo. At dawn and dusk, the façades attain an amber blush; at night, the building petrifies into a satisfyingly uniform black mass. The inky profiles of the elegant fins flow to the street like velvet stage curtains, allowing for the filigree detailing of the Old State House to bask in the spotlight. The genius of One Boston Place is that it constructs a functional framework for business and routine with lucidity, but tints it with a splash of grandeur. It makes no attempt to boast or complicate its character, but avoids embarrassed meekness and insecure lethargy. The everyday and extraordinary need not be mutually exclusive.

Architectural Speculation in a Black Market: Carbon Economics and Building Technology
Lisa Gray and Alan Organschi

This seminar traces the story of carbon, a chemical element essential to the form and function of the contemporary built environment and a photosynthetic building block in the growth of forests and the formation of the fossil energy sources that fuel current building production and operation. As levels of atmospheric carbon climb past sustainable thresholds, its role as a dangerous pollutant has become a focus of climate science and environmental policy. Until very recently efforts to mitigate anthropogenic climate change through technological refinements within the building sector have centered on reductions in energy consumption in building operation. Today, however, the economic management of carbon pathways through the entire building lifecycle has become a topic of scientific scrutiny and assessment, a driver in the development of new construction technologies, and an impetus to reshape our buildings and cities. {■ 1–4}

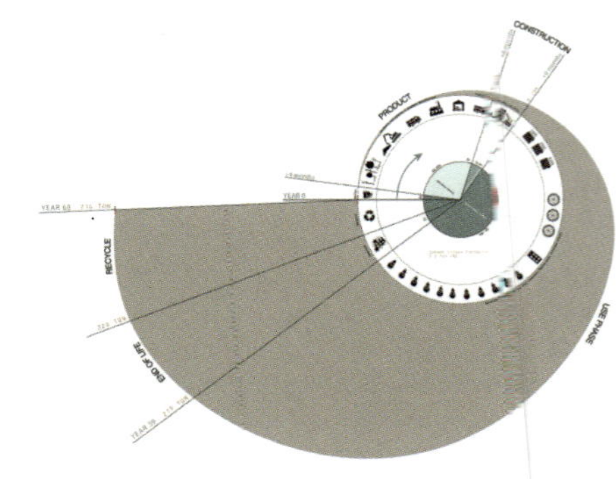

3. Jessica Angel

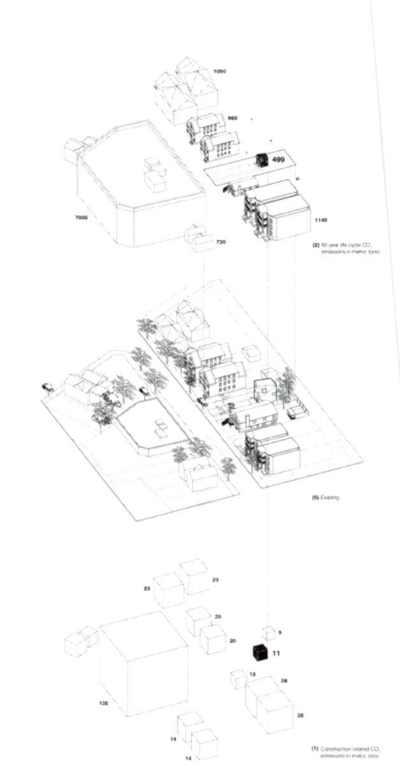

4. Justin Oh

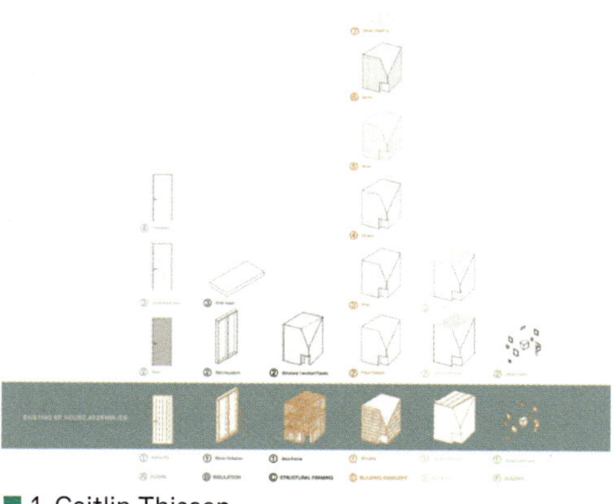

1. Caitlin Thissen

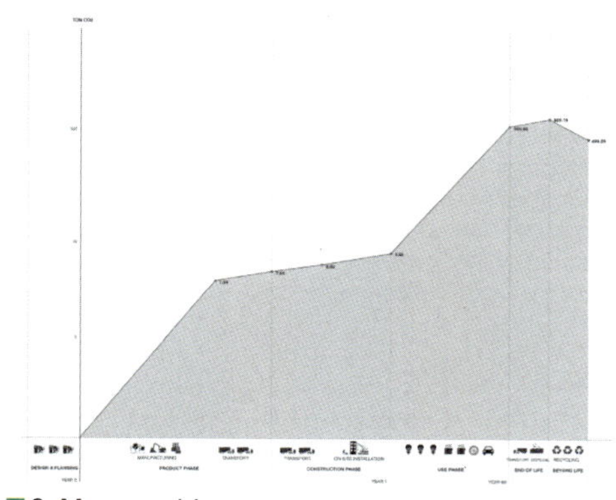

2. Mengran Li

Material + Force = Form
John Patkau

<u>Critics</u>
John Patkau {**JP**}
Norman R. Foster Visiting Professor

<u>Instructor</u>
Timothy Newton {**TN**}

<u>Jurors</u>
Michelle Addington {**MA**}, Cynthia Davidson {**CD**}, Alexander Felson {**AF**}, Kurt Forster {**KuF**}, Kenneth Frampton {**KFr**}, Dana Getman {**DG**}, Lisa Gray {**LG**}, Pekka Heikkinen {**PH**}, Joeb Moore {**JM**}, Alan Organschi {**AO**}, Surry Schlabs {**SS**}, Mark Simon {**MS**}

This studio investigated the essential and formative contribution that material issues bring to an understanding of architecture. We focused on architecture as the spatial and formal outcome of a process of material construction. To quote Rafael Moneo from his discussion of the origin of architectural form in the work of Antoni Gaudi, we focused on how "the invention of form coincides with the invention of the building process."[1] We considered the potential experiential characteristics of materials; the structural characteristics of materials and the implication of configuration on the structural characteristics of materials; the material dimensions of energy use and distribution, and the logistics of construction and how tools and techniques, from tower crane to digital printer, affect building form; for while a work of architecture can be broad, multivalent, and even self-contradictory in its cultural engagement, it is nevertheless highly specific in its material resolution. Musical instruments embody a direct connection between material form, force, and performance. Although typically more singular in their performance parameters than buildings, the direct expressive character of musical instruments provides a wonderfully demonstrative example for architecture. The Yale Collection of Musical Instruments comprises nearly one thousand objects including instruments, accessories, and related items, the majority of which document the Western European and American art music traditions. A growing minority represent the cultures and traditions of Asia, Africa and South America. A significant number of the instruments have been restored and are maintained in excellent playing condition, allowing for their use in performances, demonstrations, lectures and tours.

Presently, only 10% of the collection is displayed due to the space limitations of the current facility. To make the larger collection accessible to both the Yale community and the broader public, a new museum facility is planned. The site is to be located between College Street, Temple Street, Wall Street and Elm Street. The project began with an analysis of the block within which an open space plan and building site for the new museum was proposed. The constructional possibilities of different materials were subsequently investigated, especially in regard to the spatial and structural potential they offer. To experience buildings and structures in which material inquiry has been truly generative, in which issues of material construction have contributed both enduring value and meaningful invention, we traveled to Stuttgart, Bregenz and Zurich. We visited a variety of projects, large and small, by architects and engineers including UNStudio, Frei Otto, Peter Zumthor, Le Corbusier, Shigeru Ban, and Christian Kerez. We also visited the Achim Menges Institute for Computational Design and the Institute for Lightweight Structures founded by Frei Otto at the University of Stuttgart, and the Gramazio & Kohler digital fabrications lab at the ETH Zurich.

[1] José Rafael Moneo in his speech of acceptance as a full member at the Real Academia de Bellas Artes de San Fernando in Madrid, dated January 2005 and titled "Sobre el concepto de arbitrariedad en arquitectura."

DIONYSUS CHO ✳

WAVE Museum is a proposal which seeks to redesign Yale's Collection of Musical Instruments from a depository into a museum.

The first step reorganizes the block with a new master plan to densify and enliven the street edges. The northeast corner is redeveloped to continue the length of pedestrian-friendly restaurants and shops along the street, while the southeast corner makes way for larger Yale development. The swath of parking, which occupies the center along with flanking buildings, has been excised to make room for the heart of this proposal.

The rolling field, playing off the campus green, not only serves as a continuation of the park, but, as it rises gently, houses a performance space underneath the green roof hill which terminates in the swell of an amphitheater. The flowing wave along the hill, which switches from façade to roof, shields the collections within while revealing, at moments, the folds and swirls of circulation. The roof has been developed parametrically to allow for an easily buildable, ruled surface with gradually shifting structural fins—shaping itself to the volumes within and alongside the hill beneath.

WAVE organizes the program in two strips. The main galleries are in the larger northern wave, with administration and back of house on the south, separated by the hill between. Continuing the Cross Campus fields into the site, WAVE takes the form of both landscape and building, and draws people across the greens with the lyrical grace of the instruments and sounds housed within. [▲1–4]

"What's wrong with a cute little building?"
Mark Simon

▲ **RAMS:** I always end up liking your work, even though it drives me crazy. I think this answers a lot of the problems about how you terminate the axis, and how you might shape the landscape. I think you have some thought about how to display the musical instruments inside and not have the circulation get in the way. However, I don't know where these seductive views happen in your model, because you are very good at editing non-verbally. You've taken out everything that could clutter this up—it's the old Eero Saarinen problem. You make a beautiful shell and then stuff two auditoriums in, and then it is suddenly not a beautiful shell anymore. If you could just build this and then have animals grazing under the shelter of the roof, then it would be great. But if you would close it in with glass and fill it in with stuff, I don't know. ▲ **LG:** I think it's a very simple scheme, and urbanistically it's really working. I have some questions about the scale of the building in relationship to everything around it, particularly in elevation. I feel as though the long bar is a good museum solution, because you're allowed to invent a solution for how you display the instruments. You're allowed to invent where and if they're played, and where to place a little bit of service stuff. Essentially, you've come up with a landscape that responds to the problem of cross campus where the landscape, I hope, is really subtly shaped to become a gentle roof form. It creates an amphitheater that itself is held along the northern edge by a bar building. Does the set of solutions need to be that big? It's potentially a very subtle solution, but by pumping it up into this massive thing, you weaken it. ▲ **MS:** If the curvy part were half its size, it would be a lot more effective. ▲ **AO:** I disagree with both of you. I actually think then it would be just a cute little building. ▲ **MS:** What's wrong with a cute little building? ▲ **AO:** I think there's stuff here that you're hiding, which is always a problem in these buildings. I would embrace it rather than edit and make the nice views that you already know are under your control. That is what starts to justify a building like this for me. ▲ **AF:** The landscape is bulging up and the roof is coming down. There are captured spaces in between that start to create this inside/outside relationship. These sculptural moves are expressed in the way you are organizing your staircase and the flow into the building. It really transforms the identity of that central square, or I imagine it could. There are a lot of interesting plays on scale and organicism.

▲1

▲2

▲3

▲4

ROBERT SCOTT

This project proposes not only a new museum for the Yale Collection of Musical Instruments, but a new center for the School of Music. Inspired by the quadrangles which define Yale's campus, the Musical Instrument Museum lies opposite the Sterling Library. It's pulled back from the street to create a forecourt, pulling visitors into the porous inner courtyard. The collection occupies the entire second floor and portions of the first. The museum is conceived as a continuous ring of spaces. At times, this ring pulls away from the outer edges of the building to allow for performance rooms, offices, and circulation, and at times swells to create grand spaces for exhibition. The surfaces of the exhibition spaces are clad in perforated, foamed aluminum, and the interiors of the performance spaces envelope the musician in rich, wood panels. [▲ 5–8]

> 'If you have that, then you have accepted that our culture—the only culture I know of on Earth—has no ceilings." **Kurt Forster**

▲ **AO:** You've found a bunch of devices for creating density and thickness, and I wonder if you've tested it. It seems like a vestige of an earlier, more reductive, diagrammatic process. So you have a really sophisticated, incredibly clear system whereby you understand where the program goes, how it works, and how you flip it. I think the presentation was great. I'm worried about how locked-in it feels. I feel like the problem is not the development, but that it reduces too much granulation or particularity to all the surfaces so you lose that really clear reversal of figure to ground and ground to figure. Could you imagine that this is a really taut surface on the inside and more responsive on the exterior? It's losing its center, not to be too classical about it. ▲ **JM:** I'm going to agree. I think your presentation and the way you take us though the diagramming and the explanation is incredibly provocative and elegant. But you're doing yourself a disservice in the way you are representing the project. You are the one who set up that the real power is not the figure, or the objects. ▲ **KuF:** One might well wonder which way you would need to go to *reculer ou avancer.* You must go back to go forward. You put all your stuff in the representation of the single monumental space, whereas the whole thing is made up of so many other spaces whose character is entirely left to our imagination. If you have a space of these qualities, which alludes to what we have across the street, then you cannot have a ceiling made of Belgian waffles simply hung in here. If you have that, then you have accepted that our culture—the only culture I know of on Earth—has no ceilings. It is of a fundamentally different nature from everything else. Even the carpet is more of a manifestation of built reality than the ceilings. ▲ **AO:** I think it's interesting that you went to Bregenz and the Kunsthaus where Zumthor is saying that it will only be orthogonal and every line matches, and that's a really minimalist technique that's really fascinating to see. ▲ **MS:** I agree with Alan. You need to simplify. You have too many concepts, and it's already really strong, but if you simplify it'll be even stronger. ▲ **SS:** I want to echo what some of the others have said. The comment that you have ignored the ceiling plane relates to the fact that all of the operations that you perform here are done in plan. Your emphasis on the courtyards is terrific. I'm totally sympathetic to that. Yale is a campus of courtyards.

▲ 5

▲ 6

▲ 7

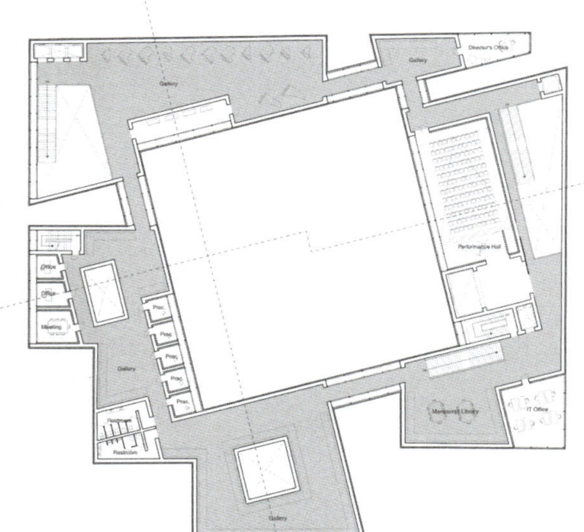

▲ 8

RU-SHYAN YEN

The idea that museums are not simply warehouses for objects, but vehicles that transport visitors to exotic places and cultures is the inspiration behind this design for Yale University's new Museum for Musical Instruments.

As objects with the capability to emit sound, instruments in particular have a transformative effect on museum visitors. Many of the instruments in Yale's collection are still functional and played regularly. The size, dimensions, lighting strategy, and acoustic qualities of each exhibition room of this museum were designed to fit the instruments they contain.

The museum's position on the southeast corner of the block completes the Yale School of Music quadrangle, and creates an inner courtyard for students to meet, relax, study, and play. The front façade faces the New Haven Green and adds renewed identity to the Music School while restoring Yale University's original ties to the town center.

Constructed of compressed earth blocks—a form of brick made primarily from soil—the museum uses an ancient construction technique to create a building with a low-environmental impact but high-performance functionality. The thick walls of the museum provide thermal and acoustic mass that regulate temperature, humidity, and sound. The instruments housed within are protected from the elements and unwanted background noises without added technology or energy. The modular nature of the bricks makes construction easy while providing opportunities for texture, color, and light variability. {▲ 9–12}

"It's an intricate puzzle box that has multiple solutions, maps, and overlays in terms of how one would not curate an exhibition, but curate a building."
Michelle Addington

▲ **MS:** This is great, I don't know where to start. ▲ **KFR:** I think it's a beautifully presented scheme, and I think the way you talk about the different *mises-en-scene* for different kinds of music is all very impressive. There is something running through the whole studio that is very curious. One is this question of a public building and how you enter and circulate through it. If I understood correctly, there's some concert space, but exactly what the visitor would do after coming through the entrance to get to that concert space is a bit opaque to me. What kind of journey would that be? The second point is you have this analysis—an expansion of the brief and a taxonomy of bits and pieces—but when it actually comes to making a museum, there's a drive to preempt the curator completely. It's as if it's not good enough to design a building that can be used by the society in a very creative way. You occupy the entire space. ▲ **MA:** I would argue it's an intricate puzzle box that has multiple solutions, maps, and overlays in terms of how one would not curate an exhibition, but curate a building. ▲ **KFR:** It's definitely that. You've curated a building. But is that the role of the architect? ▲ **LG:** Does that bring up a larger studio-wide question about how an architecture studio solves a museum program? Because current thinking on museum programming is flexible space—less hand-of-the-architect, more hand-of-the-curator. And here's a very curated experience—an architectural series of spaces. I agree they seem to have an 18th or 19th century classification obsession. I think there's a strange, old-fashioned approach that you use to generate a series of absolutely amazing spaces which are interlocking with each other. Is it a museum or something else? What if we didn't call it a museum? What if we called it a new performance space? It has so much promise as an architectural experience. So, bravo. ▲ **SS:** This is less interesting to me as a series of performance spaces, but more as a sequence of symbolically oriented or allegorically oriented spaces that contribute to a really rich, experiential narrative. It positions the building—whether it's a museum or a classroom—as a teaching tool.

▲ 9

▲ 10

▲ 11

▲ 12

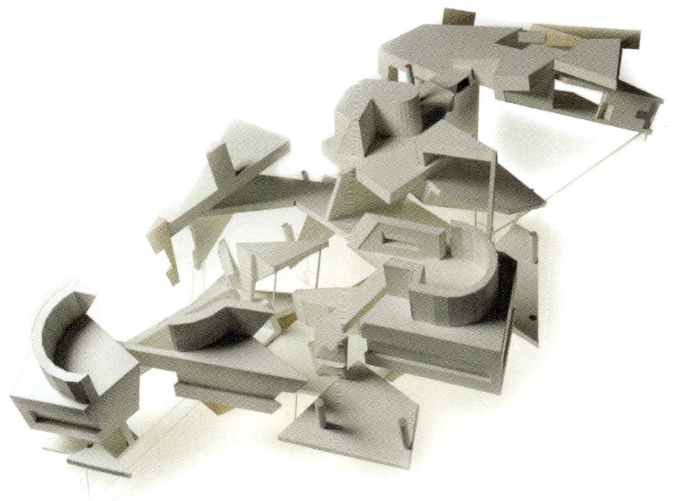

■1

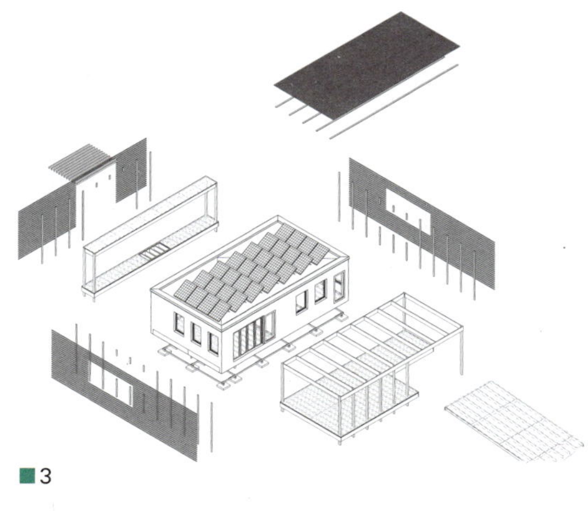

■3

■2

■4

1239a
Theory Through Objects
Mark Foster Gage

Since Alberti, architecture has been differentiated from building through its relationship to concepts, theories, and various strains of philosophy. Recent trends in the discipline, however, place these ideas in locations other than the final architectural "object." Instead, they are lodged in processes—through diagrams and mappings or scholarly intellectual practices distant from the actual act of design. Although this trajectory leaves the discipline of architecture fortified with informed intellectual content, it is left with few mechanisms that allow it to actually be manifested within the primary product of our discipline—form. This seminar reverses this process by using the design of actual forms and objects as a means to directly engage emerging developments in architectural theory and philosophy.

Ideas addressed include object-oriented ontology, strange realism, alien phenomenology, aesthetic causality, and other subsets both from and tangential to the speculative realism movement. As a background to this pursuit, students also study moments in recent architectural history when architectural theory, typically emerging from metaphysical philosophy, had a direct and tangible influence on the design of form.

LOVATO

Building from Harmon's interpretation of Lovecraft's method of writing, this object attempts to produce a hybridization of forms only alluding to its sense of the whole. Organized around a series of false privileged views and materials, image and form unite these fragments by merging distorted idiosyncratic parts. In effect, the image of the Venturi House or the forms of the Villa Savoye and the Farnsworth House, which begin to emerge from particular viewings, only reveal an alternate fragment, exposing the gaps between perception and reality {architecture and representation}. This linkage is therefore simultaneously fusing and scattering its qualities, constantly denying a coherent understanding. {■1}

2232a
Solar Decathlon
Michelle Addington

This seminar/workshop continued the second phase of development of Yale University's entry for the 2015 Solar Decathlon. In regard to the design/build aspect, schematic design is finalized and carried into design development. Special topics throughout the term focused on alternative energy systems, unconventional environmental technologies and systems, and enclosure/material systems. Students were broken into teams to research and design different systems, but all students contributed to the overall design development of the house.

THE Y-HOUSE

The Y-House construction consists of two simultaneous phases: the main shell assembly, the assembly of the mechanincal core, the exterior screen system, and the solar panel racking system. These specialized systems are plugged into the prefabricated shell of the house. The house will then be shipped to Irvine, California for finalizing touches and the two week competition in October 2015. A driving concept in the design of the Y-House prototype was to consider it as a social space. The frontal ramp draws the visitor directly into the main living spaces. Likewise, the activity within the house is meant to spill out into the exte-rior porch. The space covered by the trellis is exactly the same square footage as the interior space—the house doubles in size while still maintaining a minimal heating and cooling load. The team was committed to the idea that the house might minimize these loads through the design itself, relying less on technologies and more on natural ventilation and natural daylighting. Emphasis on shifting the activity to the outside was therefore both a social consideration as well as an energy-efficient decision. Team members include: Kate McMillan, Thaddeus Lee, Pablo Ponce de Leon, Robert Loweth, Edward Wang, Madeline Landon, Victoria Ereskina, Elizabeth Qi, Lori Kaufman, Sijia Yang. {■2–4}

1

2

3

3257a

Techno-Sensations: Architecture, Technology, and the Body
Joel Sanders

Since the Enlightenment, the introduction of new technologies has expanded the capacity of the human senses: audiovisual devices from the camera obscura to iPhones have enhanced the eye and ear while infrastructures like plumbing and HVAC have catered to the needs of the flesh. This class considers the architectural consequences of these technological developments and their impact on our sensory experience of space. Looking at this subject from a sociohistorical perspective, the course considers how a series of technical milestones transformed architecture and the human sensorium from the Enlightenment to the Digital Age. Topics include the symbiotic relationship between optics and the development of the camera obscura, the panorama, and the panopticon; the impact of cinema and television on the modernist window; the impact of plumbing and climate control on domestic hygiene; the birth of modern acoustics as a response to metropolitan noise; the influence of listening devices on the modern workplace; and the impact of two generations of digital devices—desktop computers and mobile handheld devices—on human interaction in public and private space. After charting these historical developments, students speculate about the future: how can architects harness new technologies to craft immersive multisensory environments that engage sight, hearing, and touch?

KIERAN BRENNAN HINTON
Rudolph Hall
I'm interested in how a space speaks for the cultural values and ideologies that produced it. The

Art and Architecture building at Yale, designed by Paul Rudolph, is not a traditional modernist space. It is a complex building that speaks about the trajectory of modernism and its continued impact on the human body. The interior and exterior walls of the building repel touch as well as subtly decorate or ornament the space. This is a contrast which perpetuates and subverts modernist ideologies by adorning the hyper-masculine concrete structure. I spent hours studying and exploring the stairwells of Rudolph's building. In my paintings, I'm not critiquing Rudolph's design, but meditating on his desire to have people rest and wait in these spots of transition and movement. The paintings are made by scraping away layers of paint to expose the texture of the surface, which I see as an investigation into what is physiologically buried inside the walls of a building and beneath the skin of our bodies. [1–3]

NICHOLAS MURAGLIA

The Garden Toilet: Reframing the Aesthetics of Abjection Through Landscape
We are dependent on the cleansing technologies of plumbing fixtures to participate in the realm of culture which perceives our wretched bodily waste as a threat to normative social practice. Yet a range of cultural forces, from institutionalized shame to the spaces of Modern architecture, work together to conceal the existence of these technologies and reinforce their apartness from the culture of everyday life. This apartness is reinforced by the illusion of a complete disconnect of the bathroom experience from landscape; the aesthetics of modern plumbing and "green" architecture frame the shameful abjection of the toilet in opposition to the purifying goodness of the garden which stages the recovery of Edenic nature as the sole source of redemption for our polluting bodies. The Japanese garden-toilet provides an alternative model, which reframes the bathroom experience as one that has sociocultural value by reconnecting defecation to multi-sensory pleasure and landscape both directly and digitally. A comparison with Modernist bathrooms reveals the conflicting psychocultural

associations inherited from the Western service-core toilet and the Japanese tradition of "night soil". The toilet, far from being a neutral fixture, actively structures our ideas about the abject body through an intertwining of aesthetics, technology, and landscape.

CHARLES KANE, JOHN KLEINSCHMIDT, ELIZABETH LEBLANC

Cloud-Watching From the Cubicle: An Answer to the Tyranny of the Gridding Ceiling
The gridded, acoustical tile ceiling is standard fare in post-war modernist offices. All environmental controls are consolidated into one coordinated system that promises to hush office chatter, heat and cool the air, and lend work surfaces an even, gentle glow. In practice, the open office ceiling yields a flat, generic quality of sound, heats the warmest part of the room in the winter, and blows superfluous cold air in the summer to compensate for unnecessarily bright lights. In the name of modular flexibility, the gridded acoustical ceiling is taken for granted and has produced an incredible sameness of light, temperature, and sound—absolute rigidity from absolute flexibility. As designers address the changing nature of the contemporary workspace, they must expand their field of view to include the ceiling as a malleable surface that can define space and meaningfully shape the acoustical qualities of that space. We propose a challenge to the accepted model of interior space. This proposal is a provocation, one solution out of many possible solutions to this pressing question. Lighting, heating and cooling, sound attenuation, and seating are all reconsidered.

The Unreason of the Modern: The Transformation of the Sacred
Peter Eisenman

Critics
Peter Eisenman {PE}
Charles Gwathmey Professor in Practice

Instructor
Miroslava Brooks {MB}

Jurors
Ioanna Angelidou {IA}, Anya Bokov {AB}, Harry Cobb {HC}, Peggy Deamer {PD}, Sean Griffiths {SG}, Sam Jacob {SJ}, Margaret McCurry {MM}, Caroline O'Donnell {CO}, Ingeborg Rocker {IR}, Robert A. M. Stern {RAMS}, Stanley Tigerman {ST}, Anthony Vidler {TV}, Ellis Woodman {EW}, Guido Zuliani {GZ}

With the rise of Christianity, Neo-platonism had the greatest influence on theological thought, since it emphasized a realm of immaterial ideas and transcendental truths over the phenomenological world of senses and materialistic functions. St. Augustine {354–430}, one of the most influential theologians of Western Christianity, equated Plato's higher realm of eternal truths with the realm of God, separating it from the sinful realm of humans. One could argue that this conceptual separation created a hierarchical view of the world—a potential space defined by a dualistic practice: secular and sacred. With the advent of modern science, the invention of perspective in the 15th century and the development of the Cartesian coordinate system by Descartes in 1637, the hierarchical universe of post-medieval times was conceptualized as a mathematically precise and uniform space—Alberti's homogeneous space. In light of this, it is possible that the rational subject of the humanist enlightenment may have inadvertently covered up other spatial possibilities and their representations. The aim of the studio is to activate what may have been concealed by the Enlightenment project of reason. It does so first by looking back to the pre-Enlightenment era of sacred architecture, more specifically to the Christian churches. Second, the studio exercise is a Catholic church in New Haven, chosen because it represents supposedly the most obvious and stable iconography of the modern era. When examining the history of Western sacred architecture, several issues persist in relation to conceptualizing sacred space: ① The dialectical relationship between sacred and profane. ② Liturgy {or ritualistic practice} and its relationship to form. ③ The evolution from heterogeneous {hierarchical} space of the medieval times—pre-enlightenment, to the homogeneous {uniform} space of modernity. ④ The role of images and symbols in the communication of meaning.

The aim of the studio was to produce a critical project in architecture, which falls both inside and outside the enlightenment project of reason. The studio questioned the term "sacred" and what it means today. It is not to be confused with the idea of "religious" in architecture. The concept of sacred deals with the term "ineffable" or "unspeakable," which can be argued offers the possibility of dialectical resolution of sacred and profane through architectural conception of space. The studio challenged the typological characteristics of sacred space within the discipline, through precedent analysis, and the autonomy of the sacred object within the context of today and of the contemporary city. But above all, the student's goal was to add something to the discipline of architecture. It is important to point out that the church is only an avatar to help arrive at an understanding of the nature of the discipline. Close reading helped to define a methodological approach to the studio, and students were asked to rethink prior definitions of space formation and raise questions regarding its internal representation.

RAPHAEL DE LA FONTAINE ✳ & ADAM WAGONER

The original mission of the Catholic Church was to negotiate and unite dispersed Christian cultures. The church would capture and manipulate existing public space in order to become present within a community. Space and sanctity became inextricably linked. The Roman basilica developed into the archetype for a public building. This project critiques the church by reversing this process. The mat building surrounds sacred spaces, recaptures the church, and consequently reveals the interdependence between the church and the public.

The site negotiates between the idealistic plan of New Haven's nine-square grid {itself derived from the proportions of Solomon's Temple} and the contextual, non-linear boundaries of Wooster Square. Since the site has not revealed an attitude towards the neighborhood, it is ripe for a mat building—a homogenous structure that is equipped with a rational, internal organization for growth. Sacred space is produced by interrupting this rational homogeneity. Traditionally, church architecture juxtaposes a figural mass against a homogenous context. This project reinterprets the same basilica in the same fashion— irrational heterogeneous space interrupts the highly rational mat building. The mat building creates a clear structure from which to subtract the irrational, figural space of the church. {▲1–4}

"It's the only church I've ever described as a sausage." **Sean Griffiths**

▲**Adam Wagoner**: We were critiquing the idea of a figural church that reaches out and grabs the public space by covering it with a homogenous building form. ▲**RAMS**: I don't like that. ▲**HC**: I love it. ▲**RAMS**: Harry would love it, and I don't. What are you taking away from the sacred project? ▲**SG**: Given that you're carving out these sacred places from the mat, and there's a strong distinction between them, it would have been better if these spaces were typologically more recognizable as church spaces. I was thinking of James Stirling. It's the only church I've ever described as a sausage. ▲**PE**: Suppose their idea was to make it weaker. ▲**GZ**: But it's not weaker. It's borderline picturesque. ▲**Adam Wagoner**: What's wrong with that? ▲**RAMS**: Oh, you can never get picturesque here! ▲**CO**: The way you set up the argument in the beginning is really important. It's the public, normative city against the sacred city, which itself has a different logic. If public/normative is represented by the grid, then the sacred is off the grid. The church is doing its own thing. It has its own fabric and is therefore an object. That's picturesque. It's about looking at something on an oblique rather than straight on. It's about a sequence of events that happen one after the other. So, yes, it's absolutely picturesque. You shouldn't say it's intuitive, you should ask yourself, "What is the logic of the picturesque, and how can I play those two ideas against each other?" I think it's great; it's a really strong political project. The church is being consumed by the secular—there is no object of the church anymore. It is a consequence of the public. I would like you to calibrate those two against each other a bit more to understand how the void of the public space can start to tell you, formally, how to arrange the object/void of the church underneath. This is the kind of project that can talk about formal moves and legibility through architecture, but then it gets so far that we are able to talk about lots of other things. ▲**RAMS**: I find the problem to be a brilliantly interesting phenomenal question. But where you really trip yourself is when you get practical. ▲**PD**: I completely agree with the positive reading of this. It's the first project I believe could actually exist in New Haven. The premise is really interesting, because it brings up context in every possible way that a spatial mat building can. But I do think that the issue of the picturesque is problematic. What you're saying is that you can absolutely see the figure as a space. The space itself, when the figures are clear, can be an icon. Great. But then the issue arises when I can't recognize them. They're too varied. They're too manipulated. When it becomes picturesque as opposed to iconic, it is a problem. I think it's fabulous. I just think you're too interested in complexity right at the moment when we just can't take it because it's already asking a lot of us to look at the space as an icon.

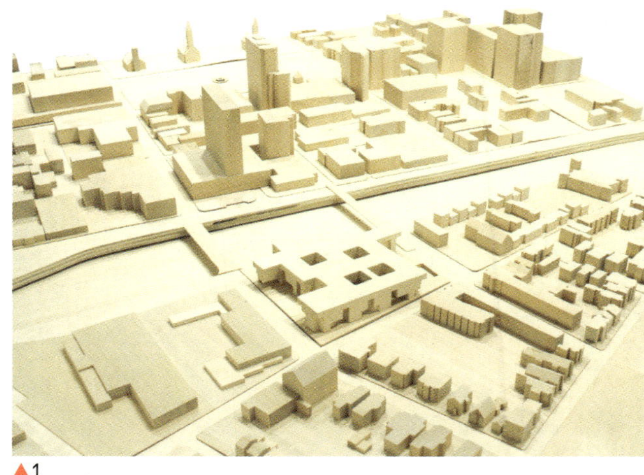

▲1

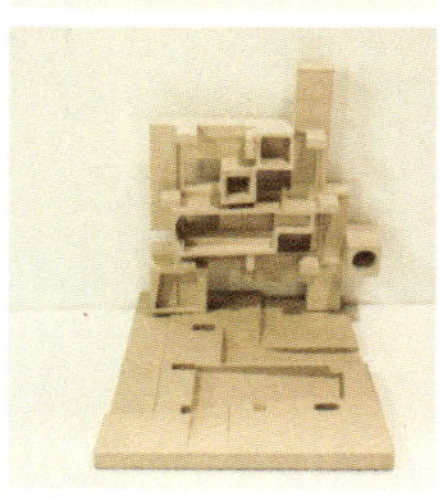

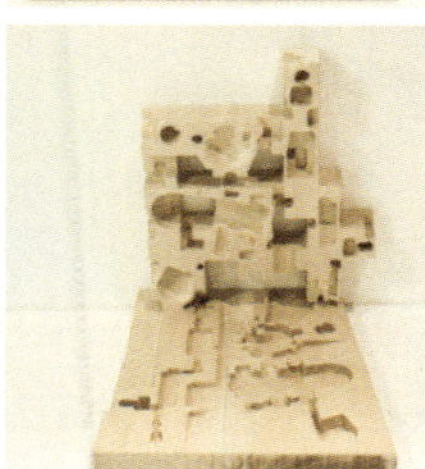

▲2

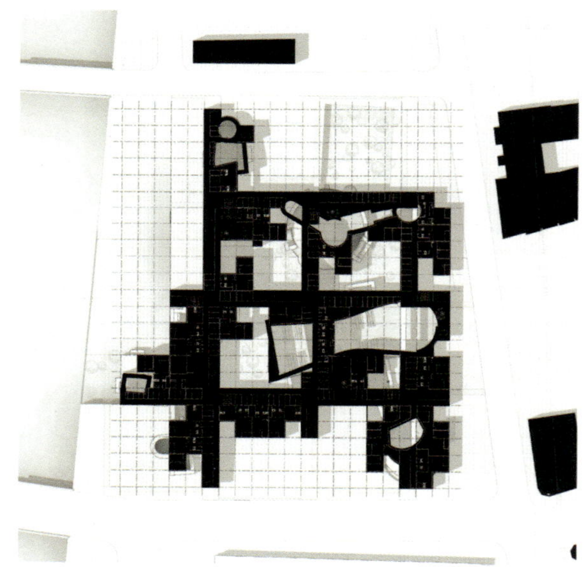

▲3

▲4

LAUREN RAAB & HUI ZHEN NG

This project constructs a paradoxical and iconic sacred space by using a church cloister enclosure scheme. Our scheme achieves a resonance of difference by juxtaposing the cloister against New Haven's urban fabric, itself embedded with object-buildings. Through the investigation of context, type, and iconicity, the project questions how religious spaces might exist in a contemporary setting, specifically in the city of New Haven. Currently, existing railway tracks form a depression on the ground that physically separates two adjacent street networks—the New Haven nine square grid and the Wooster Square grid. Using the church cloister type, the scheme bridges this gap by enclosing the immediate urban block. The otherwise isolated State Street train station is repositioned as the connection between the two neighborhoods. While enclosures typically disconnect the space of the interior from the forces of the exterior, the courtyard invites the movement of the trains to become part of the event of the cloister. This dramatic gesture results in a cloister without a ground. In a city dominated by object-buildings, the void of the cloister appears out of context. Both the erosion of the existing fabric and the displacement of the cloister within the urban infrastructure create a resonance of difference—an effect that creates iconicity. A private chapel sits within the cloister at the exact and only point where the sacred and the profane. (▲5–8)

> "Simplicity is the hardest thing to do in architecture. That's why architecture students always have angles in their plans." **Sean Griffiths**

▲ **HC:** In a way, you're juxtaposing the most private aspect of the church with the most public aspect of the city: the infrastructure. ▲ **PE:** Trying to bring the train into the project is an interesting idea. It's activating this gap, because the gap is real. There's hardly any connection between the two. When you move across, you know you're moving into another world. Whether you would do it with a monastery is another question. Why would you try to bridge a gap with a monastery? ▲ **HC:** It's more than just bridging a gap with a monastery, the monastery is building a frame for the public bridge. I would argue that it justifies the monastery. You need that frame, otherwise you're just crossing the path. ▲ **SG:** The monastery almost becomes a piece of public theater. You've got people using the cloister, which is visible, but inaccessible. The question about the shifted grid is the major one. That seems extremely contrived. It seems to undermine the programmatic and conceptual frame of your very brave, extremely simple proposal. Simplicity is the hardest thing to do in architecture. That's why architecture students always have angles in their plans. They're under the misapprehension that it makes their buildings more interesting, and it doesn't. ▲ **PE:** What difference does it make if you remove the shift? What happens to the project then? ▲ **SG:** It's a sort of distraction, isn't it? It detracts from the beautiful simplicity. It's a very nicely proportioned project. ▲ **HC:** This project would not work if one of the lower parts of the center bridge were merely under the upper one. This skew is very important. ▲ **PE:** Sean's saying that the skew has no meaning. ▲ **HC:** But it does. ▲ **SG:** It seems to me that the geometry is arbitrary. ▲ **HC:** It acknowledges the difference between the streets' alignments. ▲ **EW:** I agree that the twist is a distraction. You're making a gateway between these two distances, and the violence is lacking. ▲ **PD:** Don't you think that, without the twist, it mythologizes the monastery? The bridge says that the monastery is only secondary and participating in a larger urban scheme. You don't ask as many questions about it as a space-maker, although it's opening the space in an odd way. ▲ **SJ:** It dramatizes the city by framing it. Then it's the way in which that space, which would have been imaginary, internal and cloistered, is actually a frame of the real world. Not ideal. How do you dramatize the ideal versus the un-ideal? I can see that the strategy is really about making that internal space the point where you see this friction between those two very different worlds.be even stronger. ▲ **SS:** The comment that you have ignored the ceiling plane relates to the fact that all of the operations performed here are done in plan. Your emphasis on the courtyards is terrific.

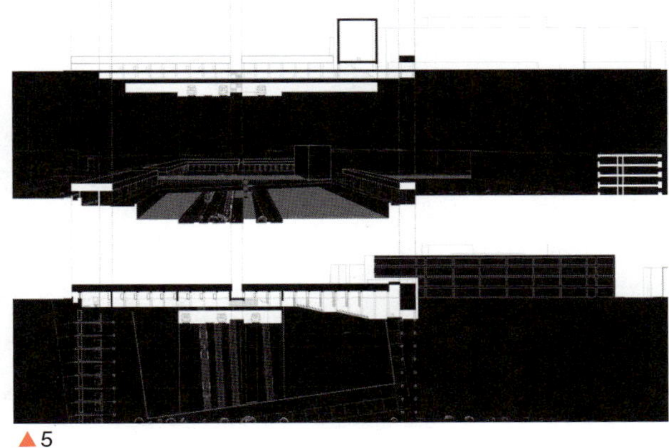

▲ 5

▲ 6

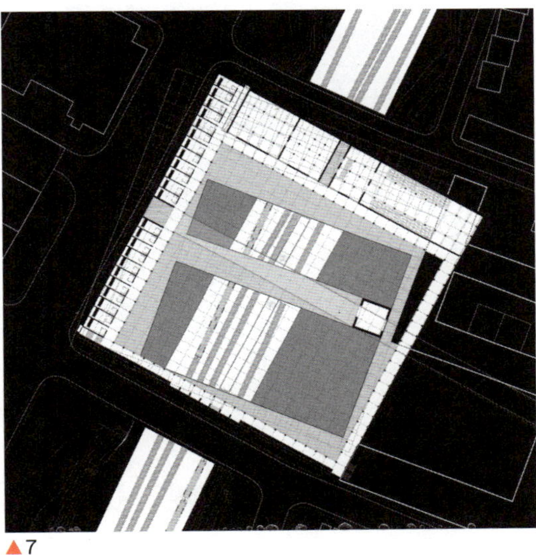

▲ 7

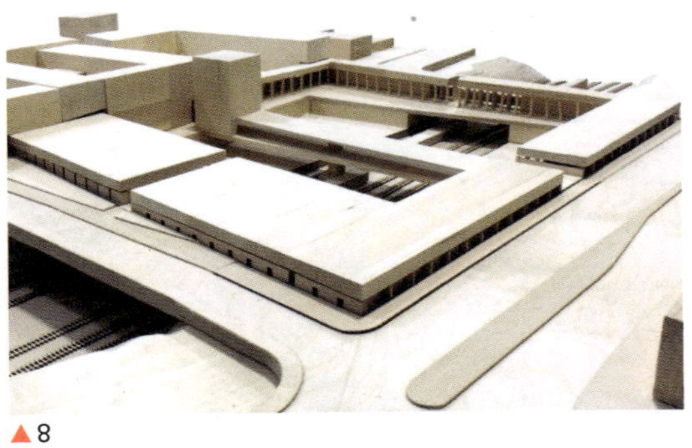

▲ 8

Timber Innovation District
Lisa Gray & Alan Organschi

Critics
Lisa Gray {**LG**} and Alan Organschi {**AO**}
Louis I. Kahn Visiting Assistant Professors

Jurors
Peggy Deamer {**PD**}, Kyle Dugdale {**KD**}, Alex Felson {**AF**}, Pekka Heikkinen {**PH**}, Hauke Jungjohann {**HJ**}, Yoko Kawai {**YK**}, Tim Love {**TL**}, Joeb Moore {**JM**}, John Patkau {**JP**}, Eero Puurunen {**EP**}, Milton Puryear {**MP**}, Susan Rodriguez {**SR**}, Surry Schlabs {**SS**}

The Kahn Studio explored the potential of new timber technologies and contemporary high performance wood architecture in an experimental timber district in and around Ball Island on the Mill River in New Haven, Connecticut. Through the design of four urban building types and their associated structural morphologies, students test the capacity of an ancient building material to produce beautiful and innovative architecture in the contemporary city.

The studio addressed the detailed design of individual buildings, but in the spirit of Louis Kahn, undertook that architectural and technical work within the framework of urban culture, building, and infrastructural context. Students worked individually or in pairs to develop one of four building types {and their associated structural morphologies and enclosure systems}. Each building type was tested and deployed as an architectural solution in an urban site within a shared plan for a mixed industrial/residential zone: Live-work housing {mid-high rise repetitive span}, Manufacturing/recreational facility {long span}, Vehicular and service infrastructure {dynamic high loading}, Commercial office and market space for local food distribution {open flexible structure}.

A study trip during travel week examined two specific "cultures" of timber building design that are today connected through a shared manufacturing base and economic and political union. Both Finland and Austria have experienced a recent resurgence in wood design and architecture, fueled by ample forest resources and silvacultural infrastructure, as well as robust traditions in building with wood. Today, Finnish and Austrian architects, engineers, and researchers work at the forefront of new "mass" timber technologies. They are charting an alternative course in the design of dense urban building and infrastructure that is reinforced through methods of embodied energy, emissions analysis, and measures that seek to mitigate global environmental impacts of the building sector. Finland's innovative wood design culture is rooted in the soil of 20th century Finnish Independence—a conscious effort by the national government to build a political and industrial apparatus at mid-century that was geared to develop new value-added manufacturing products wrought from its vast natural material resources. Today, the region around Helsinki and Jyvaskyla is a locus of sustainable building and urban development. Austria's contemporary boom in new timber technology and sustainable architectural design is founded in the country's tradition of timber construction and culture of wood craftsmanship. Vorarlberg, a province in the nation's western edge that borders Germany, is home to innovative wood architecture and state-of-the-art producers who today export mass timber construction products and techniques throughout Europe, Asia, and the Americas.

PERRY WEXELBERG ✳

This Timber Market Hall uses contemporary timber manufacturing technologies to express wood as a monolithic material. The structural assembly system is a series of large, cantilevering box beams made of laminated timber trusses and cross-laminated timber panels. This allows for a thickened plan of deep wooden coffers supported on a field of hollow timber pylons. This material expression proposes a new vision for urban wood buildings in contrast to the typical use of wood in stick frame construction.

The Market Hall creates a large, new public space that connects the Fairhaven neighborhood to the waterfront and to the Timber Innovation District. The open plan of the first floor creates an uninterrupted connection from the Market Hall to the waterfront and allows for views of the Mill River Bridge and power plant. The second level is a grocery store accessed by a landscape stair that provides bleachers for the existing soccer field. Above this, there is a housing tower containing apartments which open onto the roof garden and provide the residents with exterior yards for gardening and private recreation. A series of clerestory windows are set in the roof garden planting beds, allowing light to penetrate down to the market hall below. ▲ 1–4

> "This civic scale is kind of the reverse for what you'd expect of a Whole Foods."
> **Joeb Moore**

▲ **TL:** I think the underside of your model is fantastic, and the idea that you're bringing borrowed light down to this market hall and getting a roof that's thick enough so that you can actually occupy it is a beautiful idea. I'll say again what I said at the midterm—you distract yourself by taking on the high-rise tower and slab where there's lots of units, and working out housing units is far from the questions we're asking about structural solutions. If you would have just dealt with the column system all semester, I think you would have come to a point of real invention. ▲ **JP:** This is a very satisfying and handsome thing—it doesn't really need any justification beyond that. You know, the Whole Foods on the roof, from a marketing standpoint, is not going to happen. They want to be on the ground. So, is there a way, without changing anything, to simply reprogram this so that it would be more convincing? ▲ **JM:** I think John's comment isn't just about the supermarket being on the second floor. It's the carving away of those spaces which makes on that second floor plan a grid in which no supermarket would work. The distance you'd have to travel from the eggs to the lettuce is just not going to happen. But I think there's a curious inversion where you've monumentalized the height. This civic scale is kind of the reverse for what you'd expect of a Whole Foods. ▲ **EP:** One thing about the slab that everybody likes is the tower, because otherwise in the urban context it's just another big box store that's strangely in this place. ▲ **SR:** I think the intersection between the housing and the horizontal plane should be a void or a public space. That maybe would energize the relationship between all the components. If you calibrated its scale to match what's across the street, you would have had the same scale but one that's been totally reinvented with this different paradigm for housing. It could have been these kind of loft units, or something to infiltrate this plinth zone. Right now it's sort of stratified—you're on the ground or you're not. ▲ **TL:** There's a question of iconography in your building. If it's just a thick roof with big legs that come down, it reads as a civic structure. It would be very interesting and enigmatic seeing a glimpse of this thing down the street far away as a kind of icon. It's also a nice first cousin to the power plant that's across the channel. But as soon as you make it a mixed-use building, it has a whole different set of associations, and it loses its ability to communicate its civicness as an icon.

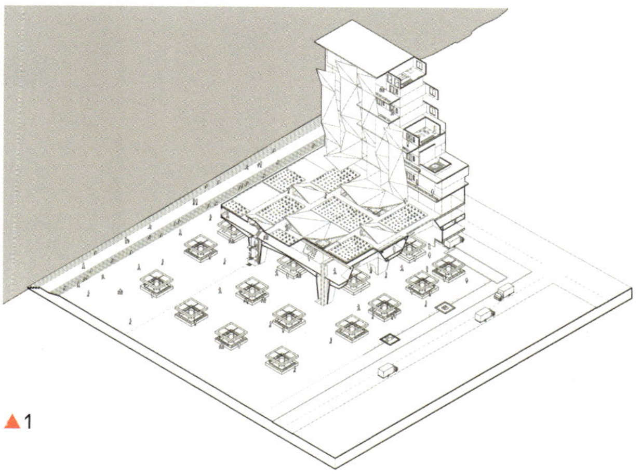

▲ 1

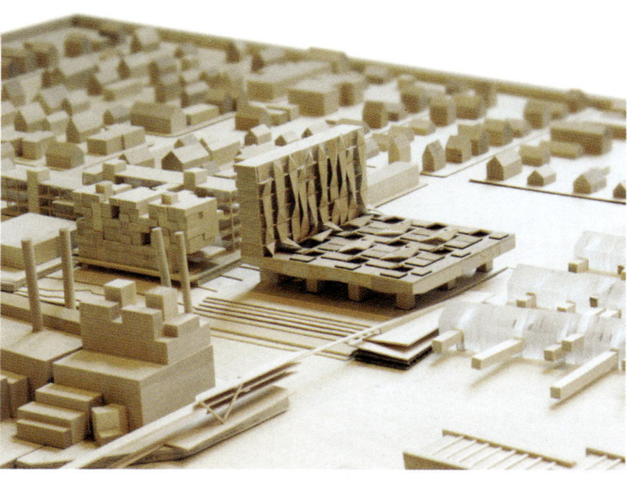

▲ 2

▲ 3

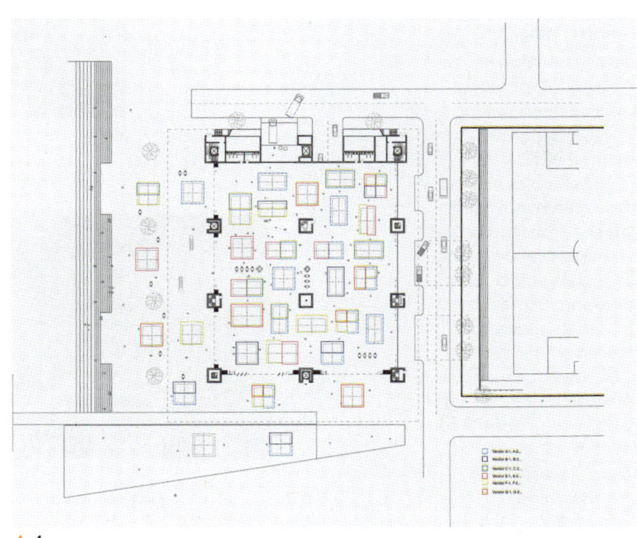

▲ 4

MENGRAN LI

The overall configuration of this project aims to celebrate a potential public architecture of the forest industry on the New Haven Mill River site, while remedying this site's wetland ecology within the flood zone. By creating a large-scale expressive timber structure formed in undulating and arching long-span glue-laminated timbers, the project accommodates a variety of programs for material receiving, processing, manufacturing, storage, and transport, as well as multi-story offices and research/design sectors along the riverside, education and exhibition spaces, and a street-front supply market under the cantilever. The original inspiration was derived from Glulam precedents by Alvar Aalto and others during the studio's trip in Europe. As a result, the giant, bent Glulam members, which delaminate to touch the ground and laminate as arches to support the roof, demonstrate the potential of long-span contemporary timber construction. The big canopy captures both rainwater and daylight through its topography and apertures, collecting ambient north light for the factory halls and stronger south sunlight for the freight rail track platforms in between. Meanwhile, skylights and passages pierce the canopy to introduce daylight and circulation into the building. Toward the river is a wetland park for the workers and public that contains a series of storm water catchment basins and pedestrian paths that weave nature with the built environment. (▲ 5–8)

> "We've been talking about cathedrals, but factories have become kind of secular cathedrals now to be reinhabited or remembered." **Surry Schlabs**

▲ **JM:** Because of how you've set it up, you pose the question of how or which direction this sectional model should be read—longitudinally or transversely. I think it has potential both ways. I have to compliment you on the feel of the model and how it's so demonstrative. You didn't just illustrate or represent the structure. You built the lamination. You built the clerestory. You built the skylight, and it's incredibly precise and really strong conceptually. I also admire the pragmatism. This is something you could really think of building and even finding funding for it. ▲ **SR:** You know, this is so colossal and beautiful, why not make it a landscape too? You could create this amazing park on its roofscape—not that you have to walk on every inch of it—but I think it would be quite spectacular to engage it in that way, and it would make it more than just a factory. I wish you would have shared what inspired or brought you to this place, because it seems almost like a cathedral with the way the light works. The project is about the roof and what's happening above and below it. ▲ **JM:** It's interesting that this is an arcuated system instead of a trabeated system, which is most typical of wood frames. You're arguing for arcuated, which is where we're getting the cathedral reading. It's obvious you've looked at Miralles and Gaudi, and I think that's fantastic as a proof of concept—that the ways in which wood could be digitally manipulated are not limited to the ways that we think wood should be used. ▲ **SS:** I would have loved to have seen a section model built the other way because what I find most fascinating about this, being in New Haven's Mill River District and being a reinvention of a factory building, is its relationship historically and in terms of memory to the sawtooth factory type. We've been talking about cathedrals, but factories have become kind of secular cathedrals now to be reinhabited or remembered. ▲ **AF:** It's quite a spectacular project, and I like the character it has from the waterfront. You know, one of the things you see from the bridge is this wonderful roofscape. The only real problem with it occupying a lot of space is that street side is not a place you want to stroll along. So, for this neighborhood, to develop as a friendly place is challenging. ▲ **JP:** What I wondered when I looked at the model is what the order of the structure was. The roof structure comes all the way down through this other building, apparently not even connected to it, and touches the ground. Yet, it appears that there is no place where this structure supports the roof. What baffles me is why you need it in the first place. There could be an order of the structure where you have a primary structure supporting the building and a kind of lighter roof floating above.

▲ 5

▲ 6

▲ 7

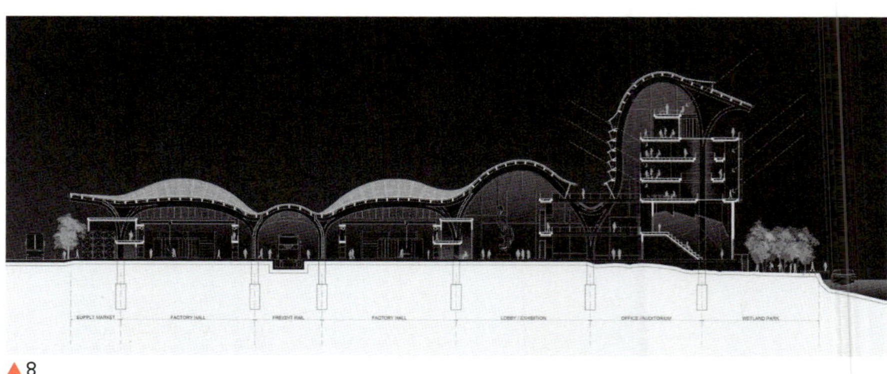

▲ 8

Manipulating Models

Annabel J. Wharton
{Vincent Scully Visiting Professor of Architectural History}

Models are manipulated, acted upon, and fashioned, obviously.
Less obviously, at least beyond this sanctuary of models,
is that models also fashion, manipulate, and act upon the
world. Insofar as their weakness or strength can be defined
by their relationship to analogues, when we are talking about
specifically architectural models, we can think very much in
terms of their power lying in relationship to their prototype.
A strong model acts as a dominant subject that determines
its weak object. An architect's model, for example, may be
expected to work as an archetype for the building to be
constructed. Joan Smalls, the supermodel, makes clothes
look fabulous, though she makes women feel ungainly. There
are also, of course, weak model agents: weak models act like
copies, and a copy is always subordinate to its archetypes.
This is the nature of copies.

A model of a car might be cited as an example of a weak
model. Is this distinction I have made between weak models
and strong models relatively clear to everyone? Of course
it shouldn't be, because model agents, in contrast to most
human and chemical or business agents, exert their agency in
part by oscillating between their weak and strong potentials.

A Deliberate Architecture

Billie Tsien & Tod Williams
{William B. and Charlotte Davenport Visiting Professors}

○ **Student**: The question of the Folk Art Museum is: was the
future of that not anticipative enough? Was it too precious,
or so fantastic for its anticipated use? ○ **Tod Williams**: I look
back, and I'm—this is a parent who has lost a child.
○ **Billie Tsien**: It's not too precious. ○ **Tod Williams**: You
cannot help but wonder how you contributed to that, and we
did. Done. I can list five or six things that would still not make
the building different. It would go anyway, because MoMA did
not want it there. We thought we were making connections,
and we actually sent our drawings to Taniguchi. In the end, he
lined up a floor—with ours!—quietly, without telling MoMA. I
thought we were anticipating the future, but we did a bunch
of other things that did not anticipate the future. We really
thought it would last, and that was probably silly, but we did
contribute to it very simply. I thought we could put an air
barrier in so we could not have a vestibule in the building. To
what extent did I think running an air barrier over a single set
of doors, which I thought would bring us closer to the street,
would bring people to the street without a vestibule? That
would have helped. I realized it did not do a good enough job.
I can give other examples, one after another, but I do not think
that brought the building down. The building is gone. And we
are responsible. Someone else is too.

BENJAMIN SMITH

Over the last fifty years, the American home has become a place of consumption and self-expression. The Mill River Co-op reincorporates a place of production back into the home. These spaces generate revenue and extend the function of the dwelling space. Mill River Co-op breaks down the work- ive separation that is a result of current zoning practices and reactivates the urban environment. Rather than becoming inactive during periods of neglect, the co-op transforms multiple times throughout the course of the day and alternates between domestic and productive functions.

Mill River Co-op mediates between two scales: the domestic scale and the manufacturing scale. Manufacturing takes place in the large, translucent shed structures which run parallel to the river. Dwelling takes place in the smaller, wooden bars which run perpendicular to the river. These two programs are woven together. At the intersection, the two create a hybrid space. Supplies are delivered on the south end of each shed and move north along the river. Residents arrive from the mews, which run down the center of the complex and receive either a view to the street or a view to the waterfront. Mill River Co-op provides multiple housing options. One can build either a single-family or a loft model according to lifestyle needs. (▲ 9–12)

▲ TL: A similar model to this is a collective in Somerville, Massachusetts called the Artisan's Asylum. It's a 40,000 square foot fabrication space where you can either own an actual space there or be a member, sort of like a gym, and use the facilities. I can see the residential owners that belong to each collective having free access, but then generating income by selling memberships to each of the fabrication shops. That might be a way to bring some realism to the co-op idea.
▲ JP: The challenge is that it's got an incredibly evocative formal character. The transition workspaces are seductive, but the places where people live are not so much. You know, those tubes are pretty singular in their character, which doesn't give you a sense of the spatial variety that the overall project has. ▲ JM: I was concerned we would fall back on this kind of trope of a residential extrusion. The model actually operates in a way where you're not sure if you're dealing with the industrial or residential, and that's what charges it for me. In the territories I deal with—suburbia, residential—it raises questions and ways of living that could be very fascinating. A powerful precedent is Donald Judd's own warehouse and house in Marfa. It's meant to be lived in, literally. Sometimes it might have these large scale entertainment dinner parties, and other times it would be used for production of his large-scale works. ▲ HJ: I was once planning a hotel in Helsinki's harbor, and it was a big cross. One of the main issues we had to deal with was privacy between the wings. If you have all these bars, and they're next to each other, it doesn't solve the privacy between them. ▲ TR: Maybe you could have one wall open and one wall closed, just like the Charleston, South Carolina house type to solve your privacy issues.
▲ JM: I think a really interesting problem is the issue of privacy because we deal with the non-private constantly in urban contexts. You think of something like The Standard, which has its own mythologies around it now concerning the body and public space. These are really important questions, and this is an amazing project for that. ▲ SR: So I'm curious about the toggling—what's on at night and what's on in the day—and how that informs this. Somehow I was surprised that you actually live in the bars. You're living in this thing, and then all of a sudden the lights go out. The success of this is at times it will be all on. Its strength is when the whole thing becomes aglow. That is a hard thing to control because it is so nuanced.

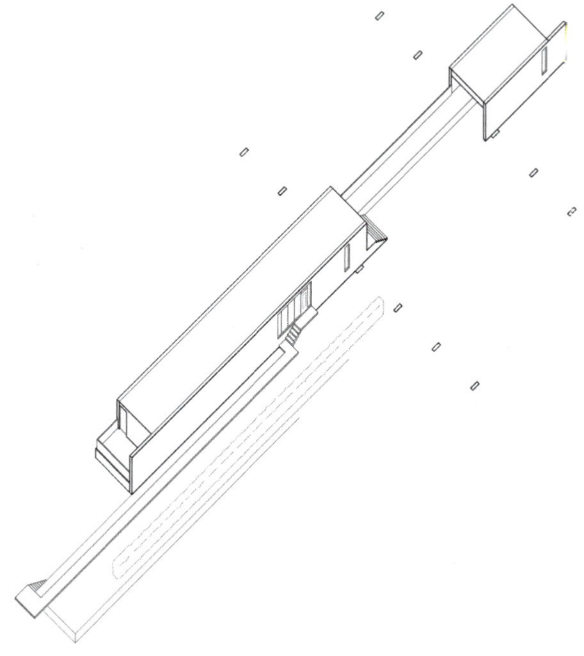

▲ 9

▲ 10

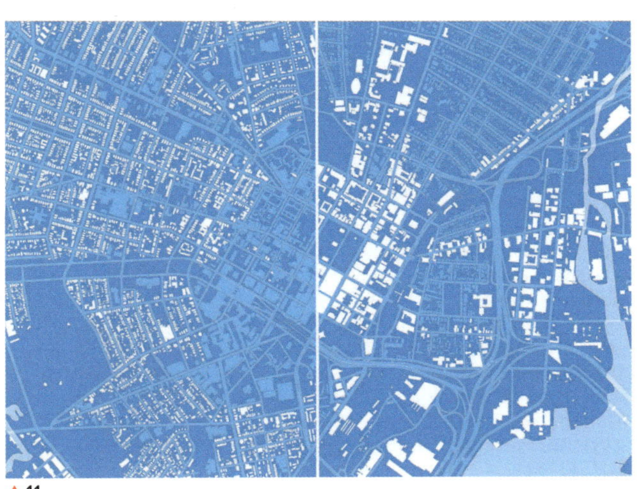

▲ 11

▲ 12

AMY SU

The intersection of Mill and Chapel Streets serves as a marker for the entire Timber Innovation District. To capture people's attention, the site contains a twelve-story tower as well as a six-story slab building, which are linked by a publicly accessed plinth. Both buildings consist primarily of live-work spaces with additional commercial spaces at street level. Here, the idea of live-work spaces is reimagined and varied to create a diverse community of people. There are three types of living arrangements. First is co-living, which consists of minimal private units {dorm-style rooms} and maximum shared spaces—kitchens, dining, social, and work areas. The second type of living arrangement is co-working—larger private units that include private bathrooms and kitchens, and shared work areas. The last are live-work units—entirely private apartment units with personal work spaces. A mix of the three types of living units are organized within a CLT tray system. Three levels of living units are stacked between two CLT super trays, interconnected by shared circulation spaces including stairs that bring people up to the second and third stories. The living units themselves are prefabricated CLT boxes set into place on site. The buildings made up of prefabricated parts and a repeated structural system allows for efficiency in the construction process while the diverse combinations of living units provide space for a redefined model for living and working. {▲13–16}

"Experiments have proven that more than six people living in a cohousing situation becomes a social problem that leads to revolutions." **Tim Love**

▲ **TL**: How many people live in a community? It's a funny scale relative to dormitory suites on the one hand, where experiments have proven that more than six people living in a cohousing situation becomes a social problem that leads to revolutions. It's not enough people that you can be anonymous—it's a very particular scale that requires rules of order. You know, who's cleaning the toilet? Who's making sure the food is thrown out? As a sociological proposition, it's one that theorists say to stay away from—more than six and less than one hundred. I think your answer would be that architecture could solve that, and we all admire the spaces, but this project is so fundamentally based on a kind of vertical neighborhood logic that it requires a bit more lifestyle engineering.
▲ **JM**: I think it's an incredibly nuanced and rich system when you look inside. You've set it up so that each floor plate has a different community or cohousing, but what if you were to think of these as being two or three levels and a family lives in them and the shared spaces between them are sort of flex spaces? Building more social possibilities into this without being too rigid about it would be good. You could have any range of people—large family, small family, or just a group of people that want to live and work together. ▲ **KD**: I wonder if the scope for taking the next step is the question of orientation. So now that you have the model, and you have a sense of how spaces might be arranged within each piece. Does a north facing unit want to be the same dimension as a south facing one? If not, you might break away from the symmetry of the plan. And can you take advantage of views in one direction or another? ▲ **JP**: It's very unusual to see this three-story frame into which modules are inserted. It takes you back to Habitat 67 and all sorts of things, but if you think about wood and the scale and varieties that are possible with wood construction, what we have here is big and medium scale but no small scale. So, I wonder if there's another scenario where the structure within the three-story cell is actually the smallest scale—stud frame construction—where you can create an incredible variety. The division between each of those cells could be increased. Certainly wood doesn't limit you to this, and it may be possible to develop considerable variation within this structure.
▲ **PH**: You were in the CLT factory, and I think the point is that the units in the factory can be done quite economically. Timber is light enough to be lifted up. If it was concrete it would be too heavy. If it were steel it would be too expensive for housing. So I would think this would be a way to make housing better, and I would maybe not think about the cohousing part of it.

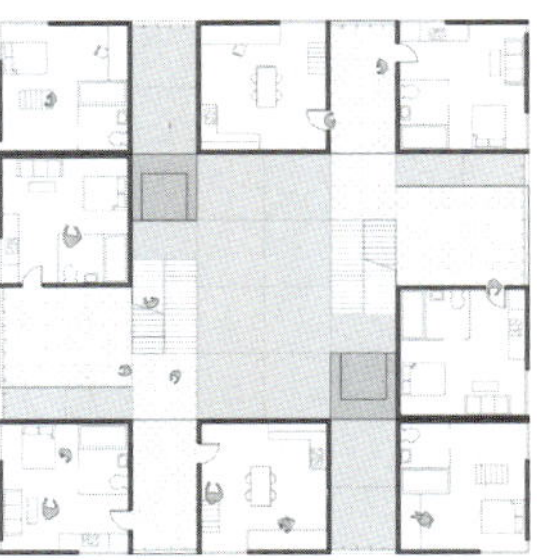

▲13

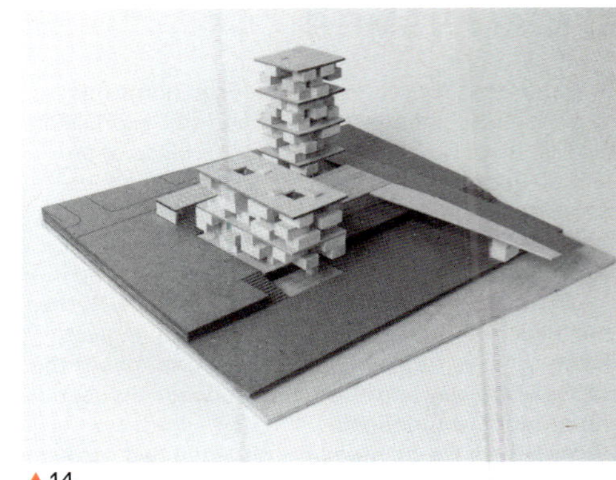

▲14

▲15

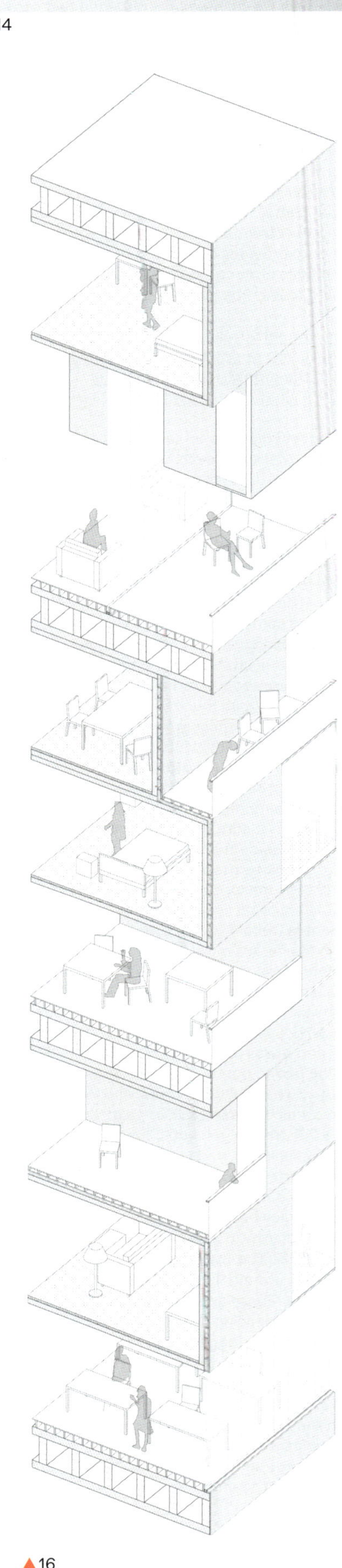

▲16

3263a
Models
Annabel Wharton

Models are now ubiquitous: scientific models, business models, supermodels, toy models. Their powers, whether they are diagnostic, cultural, or ludic, are commonly acknowledged. In contrast, architectural models, though they have always been central to the human understanding and production of built spaces, have traditionally been treated as passively subordinate to the structures that they precede or reproduce. This seminar attempts to revise such assumptions. In the first part of the course, the sources of the power of models in general are probed through theoretical readings. In part two, the political, ethical, and practical effects of architectural models are explored by means of specific historical examples (e.g., an 18th century olive wood model of the Holy Sepulchre, a 20th century urban model of Rome, a 21st century digital model from *Assassin's Creed*). Model theory and the history of models support an understanding of models as significant architectural agents. Student projects analyze the history and form of one physical or digital model with two primary objectives: establishing its agency and identifying its implications for a theory of architectural models.

SKENDER LUARASI

The Model-Object, The Model-Space, and The Digital

The digital has provoked an existential crisis of the traditional model. It is hard for the architect in a digital environment to point out and say: "This is my model." Instead of one model, or image of a model, there are multiple variations and model instantiations. A question that has become rather proverbial in any digital design studio emerges: Where do you stop? How do you select the best model or model instantiation? In this paper, however, I am more interested in the obverse: where does one start? How does one begin the model in a digital environment? How does one determine or judge whether, at any one moment, what one has in the screen is a model or a mere blobby scribble? Is a line or spline a model? Is a line extruded into a surface a model? Is a planar surface extruded into a solid a model? How is a thing on the screen more or less of a model than any other thing in the screen? My claim is that, once in the grasp of an architectural modeling program, absolutely everything that appears on the computer screen, a vague graphic gesture as well as the most complex three dimensional representation of a building, is minimally a model.

OLEN MILHOLLAND

Vincent de Rijk: Architecture's Most Famous Model Maker

Vincent de Rijk is one of the best-known model makers in the world of architecture today, but he occupies a strange territory within it. In a culture currently based heavily on digital fabrication and the study model, he revives the historical tradition of craftsmen who utilized skills in other fields and media in the creation of physical architectural models. Trained as an industrial designer, he is the leading artist in the medium of cast resin applied towards model making, as he developed many of the techniques himself. The capacity of these processes to create models with strong material and affective qualities give him a particular status among model makers. The series of models that de Rijk made for OMA since the late 1980s helped shape both the firm's image and its notion of space. In an office so closely tied to the disposable blue foam model produced by the hundreds, de Rijk's models stand as the antithesis: singular precious art objects worth saving. While he is not an architect, nor was he trained to be one, his work shapes the outcome of many of the world's preeminent buildings as much as many leading practitioners.

4236a
Poets' Landscapes
Dolores Hayden

This course was an introduction to techniques poets have used to ground their work in the landscapes and buildings of American towns and cities, including Chicago, New York City, and Los Angeles. Attention was given to poems from a national automotive landscape as well as narrative poems about cities. Writing exercises included short essays and exercises in various poetic forms; readings from the works of Dickinson, Frost, Bishop, Lowell, Wilbur, Dickey, Pinsky, Cervantes, and Merrill.

NATALIE PUNZAK

Elizabeth Bishop: Questions of Loss, Discovery, and Travel

Elizabeth Bishop was a prolific 20th century American poet, known for her illustrative, introspective works on travel and landscapes. Three of her poems, "One Art," "The Map," and "Questions of Travel," all explore the meaning of place on varying scales in specific, focused contexts, while subtly engaging the reader in a philosophical discussion or reflection on what it means to be alive. Her method is consistent—she uses a primary structural device to connect with an explicit theme—and her tools in these respective poems are the structured villanelle to emphasize loss through repetition on growing scales, the metaphor of mapmaking as an art which mirrors poetry, and the question as a method of engaging the reader's own voice in thoughtful reflection. Tactfully, she tackles concepts like overcoming loss, defining the role of the artist, and exploring the significance of travel in these poems. She provides a guide and a lens for a reader to interpret her art, but ultimately empowers us with the freedom to travel through her works and emerge with our own opinions and reflections.

SHUANGJING HU

On Robert Pinksy's Personal Approach to Ordinary Urban Poetry

Robert Pinsky's poems "The Day Dreamers" and "House Hour" are the first and the third pieces of the series of poems *City Elegies*, which covers a wide range of urban aspects. The poet's cultural background of Long Branch, New Jersey and the general history of change in American cities define his personal angle and interest in ordinary small things in his poems. By selecting frames of both the artificial and natural landscapes in the city and skillfully arranging them into stanzas varying in scale and distance as well as incorporating diversified kinds of sensations—sight, sound, touch, taste and smell— the poet establishes the city from his individual view in both first person narratives. By carefully depicting architectural details and everyday life, he displays the image of the ordinary things whose own beauty and importance is easily ignored by people. He handles the macro world with micro perspectives as a provincial with a broad view of society. This stance, together with his acute sense of changes in the city which can be seen from the feeling of nostalgia and loss in the poems, shapes these two provocative city elegies.

ISABELLA KLITZ

Calvocoressi's Circus Fire

In her 2005 poem *Circus Fire, 1944*, Gabrielle Calvocoressi fictionalizes graphic accounts of the Ringling Brothers and Barnum and Bailey circus fire that transpired sixty-one years earlier. The places, people, and moments in time related to the fire all have objective boundaries. In a poem about a circus tent, the intangibles are physicalized as well. Calvocoressi provides different axes on which to visualize space: the placement of word on page, the rhythm in which the words are read, the time frame in which the poem is presented, the range of characters addressed, and the landscape within which the poem resides. Each *stanza*, or room in Italian, builds on the skeletal frame through which Calvocoressi means for the reader to digest the horrors of the fire.

4216a
Globalization Space
Keller Easterling

This lecture course researches global infrastructures as a medium of transnational polity. Lectures visit the networks of trade, communication, tourism, labor, air, rail, highway, oil, hydrology, finance, and activism. Case studies travel around the world to, for instance, free trade zones in Dubai, IT campuses in South Asia, high-speed rail in Saudi Arabia, cable/satellite networks in Africa, highways in India, a resort in the DPRK, golf courses in China, oil-financed development in Sudan, and automated ports. These investigations begin in transnational territory where new infrastructure consortia operate in parallel to or in partnership with nations. Not only an atlas or survey of physical networks and shared protocols, the course also considers their pervasive and long-term effects on polity and culture. Infrastructures may constitute a de facto parliament of global decision making or an intensely spatial extra statecraft.

SUSAN SHUO WANG

Geopolitics of Web and Sea: A Case Study of Huawei and the Emergence of Information and Communication Technology

In 1987, Huawei was founded by one man, Ren Zhengfei, in the southern Chinese city of Shenzhen to produce switches that connected individual organizations' telephone systems to public networks. In less than twenty years, it has become the world's largest Information and Communication Technology (ICT) company creating equipment, systems, and devices that enable broadband access and telecommunication in an age of globalized information. Huawei's corporate footprint and spatial impact are investigated through its narratives and territorialization—the company's physical infrastructure, as well as its own stories of rags-to-riches success, espionage, and political intrigue. The near instantaneity with which we communicate belies that fact that modern communication is supported by physical networks. A new geopolitic emerges based on one's access to and relevance in this infrastructure. With its massive spatial implications, access to communication is a new form of power.

JORGE LOPEZ

Mexico City's New Airport

A new airport for Mexico City is essential. The current airport is saturated and thus limits development of the city (and country). Nonetheless, the handling of the project by the government reveals its true story. Despite being critical infrastructure, its branding tries to give an image of a new Mexico, an open and stable nation—a country part of the newly denominated MINT (Mexico, Indonesia, Nigeria, Turkey) economic group, one of the next economic developing powers. The reality in the country is quite different. After two years of government under Peña Nieto (marking the return of the PRI, the political party which ruled Mexico for seventy years, to the federal government), a series of structural reforms achieved through bipartisan support gave an image of a better country, an economy on the rise. Recent series of events show the true disposition of the government—one that is still run under corruption and impunity.

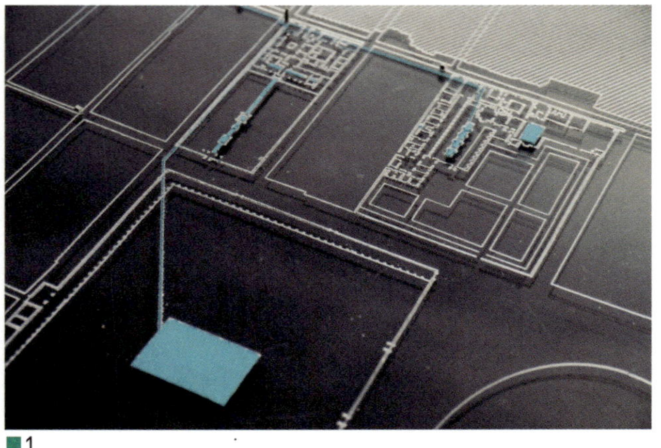

■1

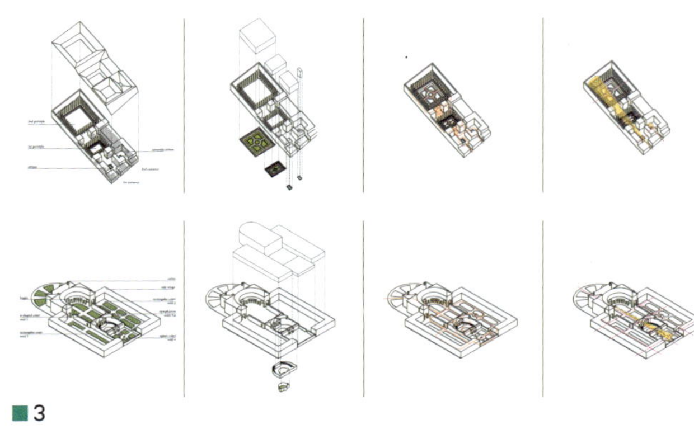

■3

■2

■4

4222a

History of Landscape Architecture: Antiquity to 1700 in Western Europe
Bryan Fuermann

This course presents an introductory survey of the history of gardens and the interrelationship of architecture and landscape architecture in Western Europe from antiquity to 1700, focusing primarily on Italy. The course examined the evolution of several key elements in landscape design: architectural and garden typologies; the boundaries between inside and outside; issues of topography and geography; various uses of water; organization of plant materials; and matters of garden decoration. Specific gardens or representations of landscape in each of the four periods under discussion—Ancient Roman; medieval; early and late Renaissance; and Baroque—were examined and situated within their own cultural context. Throughout the seminar, comparisons of historical material with contemporary landscape design were made.

HAELEE JUNG & MELODY SONG

Water features in gardens often form one continuous narrative. Even the smallest and most private water feature could be understood as part of a larger irrigation system. Pompeii is the perfect example of this; where water came in from one source and was distributed into different parts of town, taking various forms both in public and private realms, such as fountains, pools, baths, and euripas, entertaining the eyes and ears of its citizens. While some of the closer integrations of water and life in ancient Rome are lost in the course of history, Pompeiian use of water remains as an infinite source of inspiration to architects and designers. ⟨■1⟩

PETER McINISH

The gardens of 18th century France, under the *Ancien Régime*, were primarily concerned with the vista, its capacity to communicate power, and its perspectival relationship to Cartesian notions of geometry. This diptych diagrams the topography of court gardener Andre Le Nôtre's landscape at Vaux-le-Vicomte in two ways: as built and as perceived. By manipulating the rise and fall of the land with militarized precision and by reversing the classical methodology of surveyors, Le Nôtre produced distortions in the viewer's understanding of the ground plane and the placement of the horizon. This oscillation between idealized and literal construction is mapped analytically in the diptych, where reality is gauged against the privileged perspective of the Châteaux, and where, in part, the pleasure of the garden is one of uncovering novel deceptions. ⟨■2⟩

JULCSI FUTO

This chart captures the evolution of the relationship between voids in the landscape, such as sunken gardens and pools, and voids in the building volume, such as peristyle gardens, atriums, and courtyards through four projects ranging from Roman Antiquity through Italian Renaissance to an early 20th century Arts and Crafts building. The illustrations show the increasing autonomy of landscape voids as they move out from the building volume, emphasizing the connection between building and landscape. There is a progression from Pompeian introverted buildings, where the peristyle garden is surrounded by the building, to a Renaissance Villa, where sunken gardens are released from the building while still maintaining an inward focus, to a complete detachment of sunken gardens and pools ⟨that echo the building's form⟩ in a 20th century mansion, extending defined, architectural space into the landscape. The relationships of landscape voids and building voids are analyzed in four different categories. A figure-ground drawing shows the building and landscape elements and their relationship to each other. The Void drawing shows the relative position of the two types of voids ⟨superimposed or detached⟩. A circulation diagram shows the entry sequence of each building and what type of motion the landscape voids imply ⟨linear or circumferential⟩. Finally, the Axes diagram shows the main axes along which both types of voids are laid out and shows what kind of visual connection the voids allow for. ⟨■3⟩

STEPHANIE JAZMINES

This book provides a brief overview of the different types of funerary architecture and landscapes that have been used and designed over the past few centuries. The first five types were originally identified using Douglas Keister's book, *Forever Dixie: A Field Guide to Southern Cemeteries and Their Residents*. The last five types were labels I had assigned based on current trends, as well as historical precedent. For each of these types, an example is provided that is either concurrent with the initial development of the type or a contemporary project that has been projected onto. While the examples are either in the United States or Europe, ancient precedent must also be taken into account. Thinking of the tombs in Pompeii or ancient Egypt as a starting point, the series of types can be read as a progression reflecting the changing attitudes and beliefs of man towards death and its aestheticization. ⟨■4⟩

China Studio
Alan Plattus

Critic
Alan Plattus {AP}

Instructor
Andrei Harwell {AH}

Jurors
Forth Bagley {FB}, Ila Berman {IB}, Peter de Brette-
ville {PDB}, Hua Xiahong {HX}, Charles Holland {CH},
David Kooris {DK}, Liu Jian {LJ}, Edward Mitchell
{EM}, Gary McDonogh {GM}, Dennis Pieprz {DP},
Robert AM Stern {RAMS}, Sun Chenguang {SC},
Ben Wood {BW}

This studio is the fifteenth year of the Yale School of Architecture China Studio, and the fourth year of the collaboration between Yale and Tsinghua University School of Architecture in Beijing. With this studio, we also continued an investigation of urban development and redevelopment in the historic and contemporary Chinese capital city, with a particular emphasis on models of sustainable mixed-use and neighborhood development, in part funded by a grant from the Yale School of Architecture's Hines Fund. Over the first three years the China Studio studied the impact of preservation, infill, and new development on three sites along the historic North-South axis of Beijing, moving from the center outward to the urban periphery.

This year's studio inaugurates a new line of investigation along the development corridor that has recently been created by the high speed commuter rail connection from Beijing to the port city of Tianjin. Tianjin has been an important port city and center of trade since the Sui Dynasty {589-670} when the Grand Canal connected Beijing and Tianjin to Suzhou and Hangzhou in the south. In 1860, at the end of the Second Opium War, Tianjin became a Treaty Port and was opened to foreign trade, which fueled rapid development. More recently, it was granted special administrative and economic status as a National Central City, along with Beijing, Shanghai, Guangzhou and Chongqing, and is already the fifth largest city in China after those megacities. In 2009, the so-called Binhai New Area was established as an economic development zone along the lines of Pudong in Shanghai and Shenzhen, creating a new center east of the historic center and in relation to the port area along the Bohai Sea. This area will have its own master planned CBD, being built from scratch in a bend of the Hai River. Already 258 Fortune 500 companies have established offices there and development is projected to include over nine million square meters on a 2,500 hectare site.

The site for this year's studio is a 170 hectare industrial site along the Hai River just to the west of the new CBD and flanked by the high speed rail corridor connecting to the South Station in Beijing with almost fifty pairs of trains a day travelling at speeds of 330 kph and making the roughly 120 km trip in around thirty minutes. The focus of the studio is to understand the potential consequences for urban form and function of the corridor created by the high speed rail connection and current planning and urban design strategies and to propose critical models for future sustainable development in relation to that corridor. The studio also researched various linear structuring models that have been developed over time, including historic urban axes such as the North-South axis of Beijing itself, modernist linear cities, and contemporary corridor and trail-based planning. Strategies developed will be tested at the scale of the site and specific architectural projects within the site.

As in past studios, Yale students travelled to China, toured the site and other projects in and around Tianjin and Beijing, met with local planning officials, and, most importantly, collaborated with their counterparts, graduate students at Tsinghua University, to develop preliminary site analysis and design concepts. This interaction continued throughout the term via video conferencing, and Tsinghua students and faculty were been invited to participate in final reviews at Yale.

MAHDI SABBAGH
& JONATHAN SUN ✳

The Campus Ward of the Hai River Master Plan takes the existing industrial fabric of the site and reconfigures it in a series of individual courtyards. Each courtyard is framed by a different combination of building types and programs. The courtyards are formed by combining existing and proposed buildings in unique and site-specific ways. The courtyard model allows us to combine a typological study with preservation constraints. We propose that each courtyard is to be rented and occupied by a different relevant entity. As such, the ward becomes a site for a number of collaborative, satellite campuses for education, research, and technology development.

The ward is centered on the existing shipyard area which is turned into a shared common zone for all of the campuses, comprised of a commercial building, an art zone, a sculpture park, and a recreational facility. Additionally, the southeast courtyard becomes a shared facility which serves as a combined workshop and convention center, which takes advantage of the currently existing warehouse's scale. The four East campuses of the ward are defined programmatically as: educational, performance, research, and the aforementioned shared workshop and convention center. {▲1–3}

"How much information do you need to discover or simulate, in order to make a scheme that is engaged in some culture of the place?" **Alan Plattus**

▲ **PDB:** I'm reminded of Wesleyan, where Kevin Roche did all these infill buildings that shared a common architectural and material language and they were inserted into a series of radically different buildings. Your interventions are so particular and even Eric Owen Moss-like, where you slam through a building; I think your technique should stay more subtle, and not indulge in these bourgeois play games of blowing away existing buildings and creating enormous difficulty and demolition and reconstruction. Just do the project at hand which is about managing down to a certain scale of courtyard, space and make a whole series of small campuses that share the streets and things. ▲ **IB:** I'm looking for the urban infrastructure. I was a little surprised when you showed what was new and what was existing. From an urban perspective, that's one of the major flaws, this lack of an overarching logic. ▲ **EM:** My only hesitation would be making L-buildings because I think that gets a bit too cutesy—you just make a bunch of these generic buildings. And when you do that, all the things in the context produce difference, including the water. I wonder, if you tested this on the rest of the site, if you'd find the same thing—that if by being fairly generic, everything becomes different because every piece of the site is different. It's the great lesson in urban design: you just organize the site in such a way that it just picks up difference. ▲ **GM:** There's something here that we've seen handled differently, in other words, thinking about what happens to this over time. This seems to come out fully programmed to me, which is curious. What makes universities interesting is not necessarily the buildings or organizations, but what they do with them over time and how they begin to add on meanings and other things. I'm sitting here thinking you're almost making this too generic. ▲ **AP:** I wish Dean Stern were here, because the conversation Jonathan, Mahdi, and I had in the course of the semester was: imagine, if you will, that Stern, in doing the two new residential colleges, had been forced to keep all of the buildings that were on the site. Just like these buildings, they were not deterministic. They had each their strong character and position on the site. They referred to diverse formal patterns of habitation—one was a big house, one was an armory building where the sculpture department was. There's an interesting methodological question here that's been running through the studio, and these guys engage it specifically, which is: how much information do you need to discover or simulate, in order to make a scheme that is engaged in some culture of the place? I think some of these comments give you an additional layer of information that you could have added to the buildings themselves. I'm still interested in what the theoretical limits of this are.

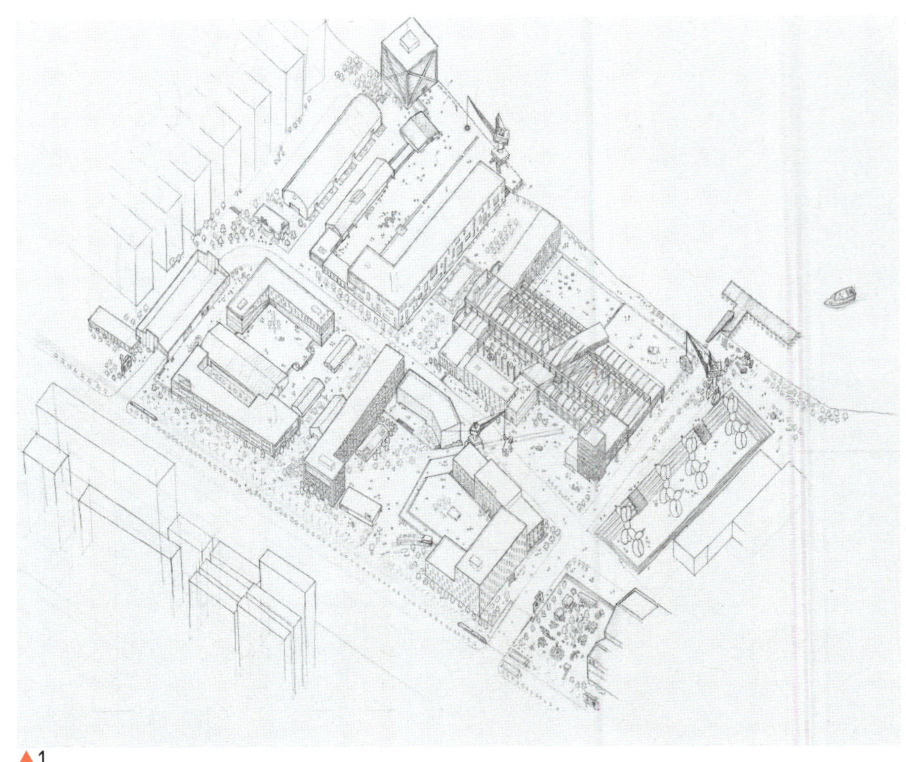

▲1

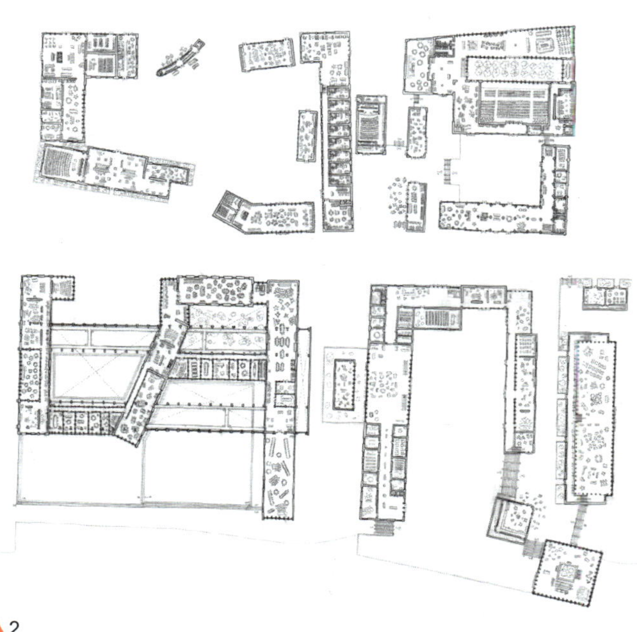

▲2

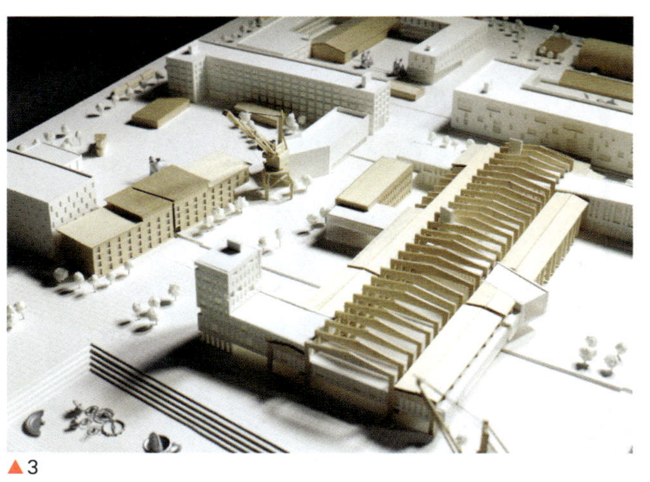

▲3

MATTHEW WHITE
& CARL CORNILSEN

Chinese cities are developing at rates unseen in modern history. Known around northern China for years as "Beijing's Little Brother," Tianjin is no exception. The city has recently surpassed both Beijing and Shanghai in achieving the highest growth in economic production per resident of any Chinese metropolitan area. This explosive growth means Tianjin faces a new challenge of being "one city with two faces." As the modern services sector takes hold, the city is in danger of losing the industrial base that has fueled its rise. Tianjin is developed industrially, yet disconnected from its status as a creative mecca. The planned relocation of the old Tianjin XinHe shipyard is an opportunity to bring these opposing forces together. URBN BRWRY seeks to harness Tianjin's economic engine to sponsor a civic realm wherein creativity is linked to industrial production. Assuming that production capacity is fundamental to creative output, URBN BRWRY presents an adaptive reuse of an agro-industrial tank farm. The brewery creates a platform for a community of microbrewers to collaborate and innovate, while creating an opportunity to produce at an industrial scale. The URBN BRWRY will be a hub for the creative economy of Tianjin. The city could incubate the type of entrepreneurial innovation that can power long-term, sustainable growth. [▲ 4–7]

"Rem Koolhaas proposed putting an island in the middle of the Charles River, and you know why? He wanted to connect the business school to everything else." **Ben Wood**

▲ **FB**: I have a problem with the island. To me the interesting part of this is the orange and the purple fabric that really does start to address programing issues, and it's a successful urbanscape. Why do an island, if not to shorten the distance to the other side when there's nothing on the other side? If you would have put a giant beer world over there, then I would understand, because there's more of a reason to cross over. ▲ **BW**: Rem Koolhaas proposed putting an island in the middle of the Charles River, and you know why? He wanted to connect the business school to everything else. ▲ **IB**: One of the issues, not to harp on the island, is that you could have done what you're doing through the development of the actual riverfront, and I would have done it with smaller moves that have a bigger impact rather than the opposite. Meaning, once you're on that island, despite the fact that we're looking at it in a particular scale, it feels like just another piece of land. If that was the desire you could look at how you deal with the edges of the water, possibly through porosity, extension, even an archipelago happening at a smaller scale that might have had a greater impact than the kind of mass island. That said, I think repurposing the existing infrastructure on the site is fantastic. ▲ **CH**: It's an interesting thing, isn't it? If the land value increases as you get closer to the water, you just increase the amount of land that is close to the water—it sort of makes sense. I think the idea of bringing water to every bit of it is great, but I agree with the point that you just end up with more middle land mass to deal with that you didn't need. ▲ **BW**: About the comments about the island being too much—those of you who haven't lived in China for sixteen years can say that, but China is with it. We all grew up and went to schools like MIT and Harvard and Yale, but many in China grew up in an agrarian society. They build and tear down islands every day if it serves their purpose and we should recognize that. They also make cities that are famous for beer like Tsingtao. So, it's not pie in the sky, what these guys are doing. ▲ **AP**: There's a slightly more radical and maybe vaguely unrealistic idea that I've been interested in for some time. I think many of us that grew up when American cities were industrial saw local breweries, stockyards, industrial areas that you actually could walk through, they were not walled compounds. The sense of industry as something that exists behind an electric fence, which of course permeates China and other places; finding those aspects of it that can be opened up again and not just become art galleries, is perhaps a little quixotic but also a really provocative idea.

▲ 4

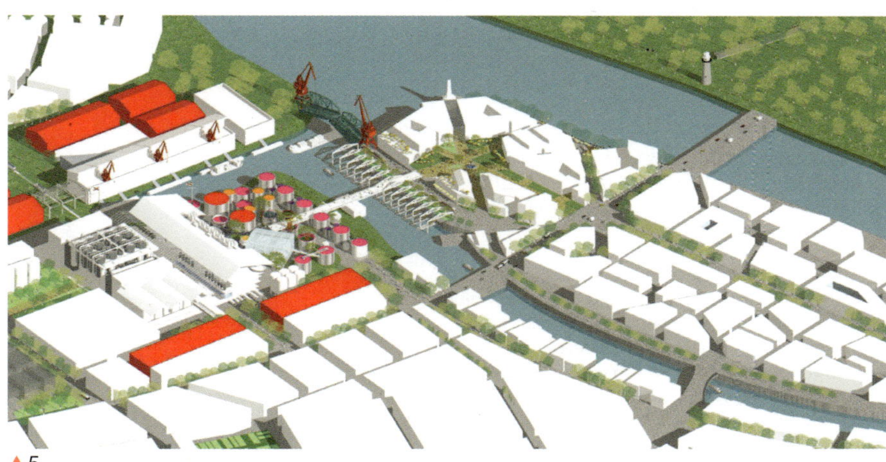

▲ 5

▲ 6

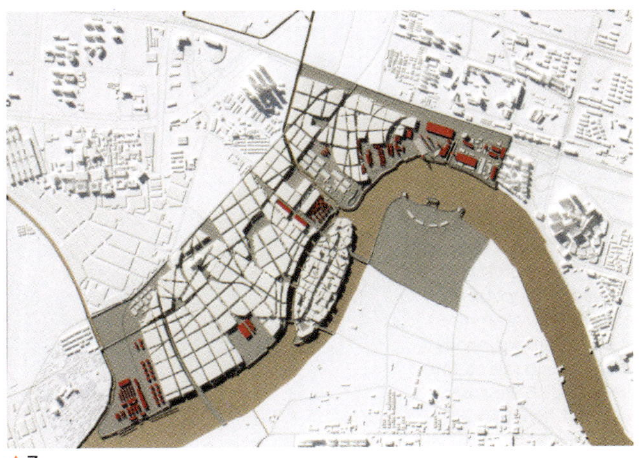

▲ 7

JULIE KIM & DANIEL NGUYEN

Tianjin Industrial Waterfront Redevelopment envisions a mixed-use waterfront district that connects to a greater network of urban development along the river's northern edge while retaining the grid of the site's industrial past to maintain a diverse urban fabric. Through the relocation of the Tanggu Railway station, the site becomes a vital link to Beijing, Tianjin's city center, and the new Central Business District via the planned high speed rail extension. A variegated urban street network and pedestrian promenade constantly draw residents and visitors to the water's edge with a main pedestrian axis that becomes a promenade toward the river. The end of the promenade is met with a waterfront theater with sub-axes that lead back inland toward the old shipyard factory building and crane yard, now used as a convention center and sculpture park. Restaurant and shopping amenities are embedded in a corridor of hotels that include ground level retail linking the train station to the convention center. The proposed master plan investigates the duality of the city and the water's edge as building envelopes respond to the varying conditions set up by the two edges. {▲ 8–11}

> "You designed this piece, but if you came to it another day you could just design another one, and what's missing in this is a larger rule." Ila Berman

▲ IB: I'm looking for more strategies that are specific to the way in which the urban morphology develops. I'm asking myself: when are the green fingers defined enough and what programs them, and what happens when built form intersects with them? I feel like you designed this piece, but if you came to it another day you could just design another one, and what's missing in this is a larger rule set for how a kind of mass customization or even the diversity of urban form develops at this scale. ▲ AP: One's expectation might be that the river, because of your interest in it, would be the dramatic edge, but you've chosen to fold the edge into the depth of the site in order to realize your scheme. I think it's clear that they wanted to make a miniature city from the very beginning, and in the mix of uses it simulates, for better or for worse, the things you'd come to expect to find in a bigger city or region. So I think the numbers are important here—how many people live and work here—and if there is going to be enough for a degree of autonomy which justifies its own train station. ▲ DP: One thing that's fascinating about this project is that there seems to be an ambition to explore alternatives to the monotony of one architect doing sixty towers. So, to me what's interesting about this model and the implication of your plan is that you can have a city based on some urban design principles around public space, around streets, around a network of pedestrian routes and connections, and set it up in a way that makes some big decisions around massing and density. For me, if you accept the idea of a train station here—which I do, because this is a huge opportunity—you've got a lot of density around the station, which I think is more important than putting it by the waterfront. ▲ GM: I'm trying to think about it at the pedestrian scale, where it really does feel like if you live in the residential buildings, you'll never want to fight your way over to the plaza, and if you do you'll be fighting through many lanes of traffic. It's fascinating that it's very strong visually and responds to the demands and scale and site, but putting myself there it seems so impervious. ▲ EM: When you have a building that's twenty-five stories tall, is pretty formidable, and then you have streets that are always cutting across them, which I think you haven't accounted for. The secondary street hits a building at a corner that becomes prominent in your plan and doesn't react three dimensionally yet. Those kind of things would give you the coding that would tell you how to respond to these sorts of things locally. You could get rid of fifty percent of those that cut through the fingers while still allowing for the green space to be something other than sculpture parks with giant pandas in them.

▲ 8

▲ 9

▲ 10

▲ 11

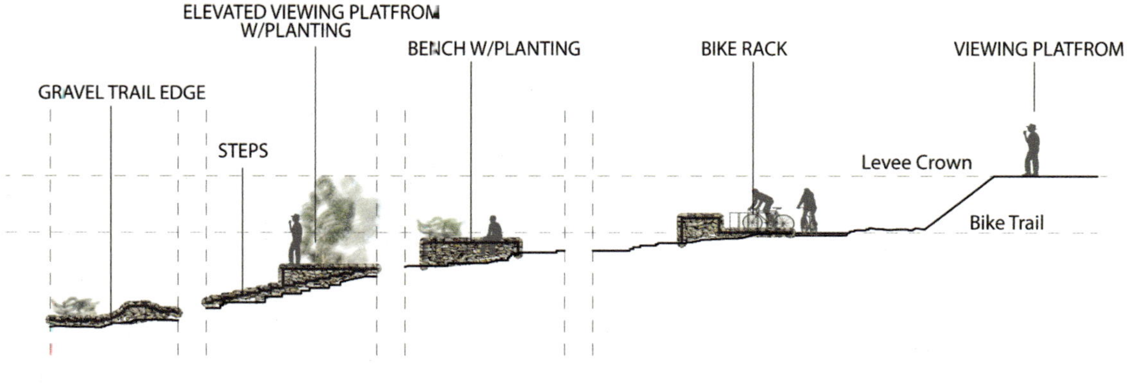

■1

■2

■3

4226a
Ecological Urban Design
Alexander Felson

This course lays the groundwork for students from the School of Architecture and the School of Forestry & Environmental Studies to collaboratively explore and define ecologically driven urban design. The goal was to work as an interdisciplinary group to cultivate a perspective on the emerging field of urban ecology and to develop approaches to implementing urban ecological design. The transformation of urban ecology from studying a system to shaping urban ecosystems was a primary focus for the course. The course concentrated on the following questions: How do we define urban ecosystems? How do we combine science, design, and planning to shape and manage urban ecosystems? How do we implement effective and adaptable experimental and monitoring methods specific to urban sites and human subjects in order to conduct viable urban ecological research? The course used the Earth Stewardship Initiative, a large land-planning project developed for the Ecological Society of America in Sacramento, CA, to create a real-world project where interdisciplinary teams worked to combine ecological applications and design with the goal of shaping urban systems to improve the ecological, social, and infrastructural function of city components.

DAPHNE BINDER, STANLEY CHO, SARAH SUGAR, AMY WEINFURTER

Our design focuses on improvements to Reach One of the American River Parkway, a stretch of greenbelt along the American River, just north of Sacramento, California. Despite its close proximity to downtown, this reach is less widely used than upstream sections and suffers some of the most severe ecological threats. Its restoration could result in enormous potential benefits, both for the flora and fauna that rely on the river, and the park users who frequent the parkway. To physically and interpretively reconnect the river to its floodplain and the floodplain to the city, our project establishes points of explicit visual continuity across the river system, making use of the elevation differential between the levees and the parkway. The design also formalizes physical links between the river and the parkway, enhanced with functional infrastructure that serves to conceptually blur the hard line between the river channel and its floodplain. {■1}

GABRIELA BAEZA-CASTANEDA, JASON KURZWEIL, ALEXIS WEINTRAUB

Our project focuses on Resilient Park Ecosystems. We think of a resilient park ecosystem as one that continually adapts to change and disturbance. In the context of an urban environment, we consider an ecosystem to include all of the human and nonhuman members of the community that pass through the parkway. As an urban "park," we consider it essential that the park serve the residents and visitors of Sacramento, both as a functioning ecosystem and as a place to enjoy spending time outdoors. We see the parkway as a raw space with vast potential. Our vision is to impose a system of nodes and networks that draws people into underutilized areas of the ARP and highlights underappreciated features. In order to make visible the historical, cultural, ecological and recreational opportunities within the park, we identify, categorize, and map points of interest throughout the parkway. We then develop a system of nodes and connecting pathways intended to bring people to these locations and create spaces that encourage them to stay and enjoy them. We use three design elements to accomplish this vision: ① Establishing points of interest and networks of historical, cultural, ecological, and recreational features. ② Establishing nodes with repeating architectural elements and interactive display stations. ③ Creating regional identities. {■2}

ALICIA POZNIAK, JOHN SHIVELY, PAMELA SOTO

While searching for an opportunity to improve the American River Parkway through designed experiments, we focused on addressing three major issues: soil and habitat restoration and disturbance, programmatic use, and species diversity. The resulting designed experiment proposal seeks to enhance public recreation while also supporting ecological restoration efforts. The project creates a series of habitat "patches" located within the "open" and "closed" ARP landscapes of grassland/savannah and riparian forest/scrub. The patches contain planting plots encircled by colored fence poles to identify the experiment in the existing vegetation. Accessible plots acting as native gardens are located along the existing parkway bike path allowing for public interaction and educational opportunities. Exclosure plots are located off the bike path but within view for comparative analysis. The plots are to be planted and enclosed with deer fencing at staggered intervals to reveal successive stages of growth. The experiment tests the impacts of herbivores and human recreation on the landscape's capacity for ecological regeneration. {■3}

Interface: Guggenheim Helsinki
Joel Sanders

<u>Critic</u>
Joel Sanders ⟨**JS**⟩

<u>Instructor</u>
Josh Dannenberg ⟨**JD**⟩

<u>Jurors</u>
Stella Betts ⟨**SB**⟩, Tatiana Bilbao ⟨**TB**⟩, Cara Cragan ⟨**CC**⟩, Jean Pierre Crousse ⟨**JPC**⟩, Peter Mackeith ⟨**PM**⟩, Eeva-Liisa Pelkonen ⟨**ELP**⟩, Joseph Rasa ⟨**JR**⟩, Marc Tsurumaki ⟨**MT**⟩, Billie Tsien ⟨**BT**⟩, Ari Wiseman ⟨**AW**⟩, Tod Williams ⟨**TW**⟩, Mabel Wilson ⟨**MW**⟩

In June 2014, The Solomon R. Guggenheim Foundation and the municipal government of Helsinki announced an open, international competition to design a Guggenheim affiliate in Helsinki, Finland. A new Guggenheim Museum will expand the Guggenheim museum network. The Museum will showcase internationally significant modern and contemporary art from the 20th and 21st centuries while also specializing in local Nordic art and architecture. The museum building will be in close proximity to the center of the city, in the Eteläsatama, or South Harbor area, a major passenger port welcoming cruises from Stockholm, Sweden and Tallinn, Estonia. The site is 18,520 square meters and the floor area designated for the museum building is 12,100 square meters, of which 4,000 will be devoted to exhibition space. Under the agreement, the Guggenheim Foundation's role is to provide its brand value, overall direction, oversight of programs and access to its collections while the City of Helsinki will be responsible for development and construction costs ⟨estimated at €140 million⟩ and the annual operating fund. A $30 million licensing fee will be raised by private donations.

Supporters and critics are divided over this development. Those who oppose the museum argue against the large costs to taxpayers and believe that a Guggenheim franchise will threaten Finnish culture and identity and cite setbacks that other Guggenheim affiliates have faced around the world, including the Vilnius Guggenheim Hermitage and the Guggenheim Abu Dhabi. Spearheaded by Helsinki's mayor Jussi Pajunen, supporters are inspired by the success of the Guggenheim Bilbao, which transformed the Basque region into a thriving tourist destination. Advocates also claim that a new museum will bring economic and cultural capital to Helsinki, heighten global visibility of Finnish art and culture, and serve as a community center for residents and tourists.

Ari Wiseman, Deputy Director at the museum and Cara Cragan, Director of Architectural Projects and a 1999 graduate of the YUAG, agreed to participate in our advanced studio with the hope that our research and out-of-the-box design thinking would shed new light on their unfolding initiative. Students' challenge this term was to address the issues and concerns raised by both constituents, even if that meant modifying or reinterpreting the official competition brief. If the Guggenheim Bilbao inaugurated the era of the photogenic icon designed by a star-architect, Guggenheim Helsinki required students to invent an alternative vision for an inclusive community oriented art museum that caters to regional as well as global interests. In addition to providing an opportunity to develop a site-specific proposal for a high profile building that is garnering international attention, the Guggenheim Helsinki provided a vehicle for us to engage broad issues that are reshaping the future of the contemporary art museum and the discipline of architecture.

JULCSI FUTO ✳

Responding to the Finnish artist community's cri-tique of the Guggenheim as an elitist institution, this project extends the program of the museum to include education to both make it relevant to the local community and bridge the gap between art and the everyday. Instead of using the Guggenheim brand to create monumentality and iconicity that is disconnected from the Finnish cultural heritage and risks reducing Helsinki to a one-liner, this project ties into the low, courtyard-filled urban fabric of the city. The pavilions and courtyards respond both to the islands and plazas that define Helsinki's urbanism and the graceful subtlety of the city.

The striated landscape connects the market and the ferry terminal and responds to the two different sides of the site. It is crenulated at the water, continuing the language of the bays at the shoreline, while its linear edge faces the park and defines the boundary of the site. The undulating landscape creates elevated viewing platforms, sunken gardens, and pools presenting a transition between the waterfront and the park.

The nested volumes of the five pavilions allow for a seamless insertion of new program. An education hub, multi-media projection rooms, artist residency, and library at the core of each pavilion are flanked by an ancillary ring of exhibition spaces which transition into the unticketed exhibition spaces. This interstitial space—the "container"—links the pavilions and encloses courtyards in the interior of the building. The fifth pavilion, the ferry terminal, is linked to the building with a canopy. The strategy of nesting is also used in the section; each nested volume within the pavilions is lowered in section, prompting a gradual descent into the central, and most intimate core. The contrast between the programmed pavilions and the open "container" linking them prompts free meandering and fosters an active, self-curated engagement with art. (▲1–4)

> "<u>And</u> <u>sometimes</u> <u>being</u> <u>an</u> <u>artist</u> <u>means</u> <u>you</u> <u>don't</u> <u>want</u> <u>to</u> <u>see</u> <u>the</u> <u>public.</u> <u>I just</u> <u>need</u> <u>to</u> <u>do</u> <u>my</u> <u>work</u> <u>and</u> <u>have</u> <u>an</u> <u>institu-</u> <u>tion</u> <u>support</u> <u>me.</u>" **Mabel Wilson**

▲ **TB:** I like this project because it's bringing the archipelago into the city at a different scale. It works even if the museum interrupts the path of people. You can still see continuity through the buildings. ▲ **MW:** I really appreciate the nested quality of the project, and I think it's very interesting when you look to the top of the map and see all those courtyards. It's a new public space inside there. We think we live in a world where we can see everything, but we don't. Not everything is transparent. I think this strategy gives you an opportunity to embed and create varying degrees of publicity or privacy within the building. I especially appreciate that because, when you said artist or residency, I thought "Oh my god, they'll be exposed!" and sometimes being an artist means you don't want to see the public. I just need to do my work and have an institution support me. That's what a residency is supposed to do, and I think your strategy allows that. Then when artists want to be public, they have zones in which they can make themselves public. I appreciate the way this lets them do that in various ways. ▲ **MT:** Yes, I really appreciate which this s one of the projects that has really emphasized the idea of seasonality. Mapping through this labyrinthine landscape, although it has no walls, allows and disallows certain passage because of the way you're working with the landscape's section. It seems to have this capacity to develop a dense and complex network of pathways that are under your control. This is the project that makes us think there must be some tidal variation. You should induce some water movement. ▲ **JR:** You might think about something that can become a convertible space and how it becomes part of the community. It's a space where program isn't defined, but it can be defined by a program that is inserted into it. It lets the community come into the building and have ownership conceptually. It would have a presence within this very nice, organized, systematic, yet free-flowing space. ▲ **JS:** It's almost like a non-program. ▲ **JR:** Exactly. Maybe it becomes the nesting space that's open to the possibility of inserting something into a fixed program. ▲ **JS:** I think you've grappled with the programmatic specificity in a good way.

▲1

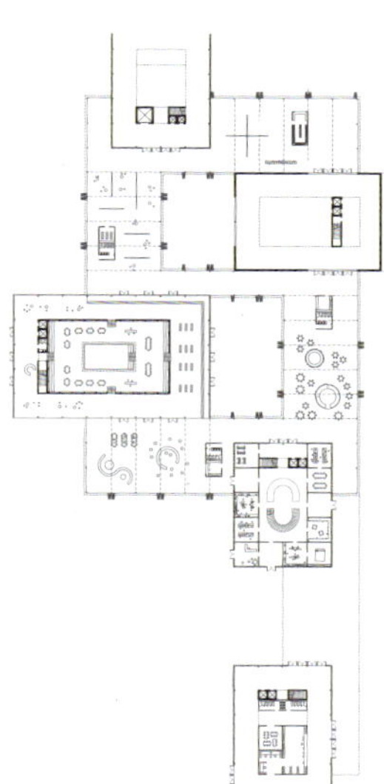

▲2

▲3

▲4

MICHAEL COHEN & TYLER PERTMAN

Our project attempts to not only infuse Helsinki's South Harbor with life and energy, but also address some of the key urban issues of the city and speak to the current trajectory of the international art market. In the contemporary art world, the production and consumption of art is polarized. The act of artistic creation is alienated from large-scale global art events where art objects are perceived as commodities. This project aims to reverse this division by integrating space for art-making with a large-scale exhibition hall. Additionally, this multi-purpose facility creates a public amenity on an urban scale while fostering new opportunities for public-private partnership.

The exhibition hall, a generic field of columns, is located at the center of the project. The flexible nature of this space allows it to absorb a diverse range of events including international exhibitions, private art fairs, and commercial conventions. While the interior of the hall is a mechanism for private enterprise, the hall's expansive roof is co-opted as public domain. Rising out of the ground on the northern part of the site, the roof is a topographic pedestrian infrastructure that connects to the adjacent park and ferry terminal. Additionally, the roof surface can be used for outdoor recreational activities and events. Floating above the exhibition hall on the southern end of the site is a rectangular bar of stacked artist's studios and exhibition spaces. The studios present the opportunity for an artist-in-residence program and are interspersed with shared facilities such as a media lab, library and maker-space which both artists and the public could access. An extended harbor walk connects the hall to the residential bar and provides views out into the harbor and back towards the Cathedral. {▲5–8}

"Everybody gets their own real estate. It seems like that's a decent solution."
Eeva-Liisa Pelkonen

▲ **MW**: I don't know Helsinki. I've never been there. I've only ever seen the maps. It seems like this is a site that should accommodate multiple strategies. It sits on the water. It can be read against the larger city, and usually you see these huge buildings. Somehow the scale isn't working. You could work more on the integration of the elements. We start to see it somewhat in the section, but when I look at the model, there is something slightly off at this scale. Look at the artist cell in relation to the rest of the building. Maybe there should be more medium-scaled spaces that they could operate as they move closer to the water. It scales the building. ▲ **MT**: The scale of the building seems so inaccessible at the scale of this grand staircase gesture. It feels right in the beginning. I feel a little bit less this way about the plinth. I don't object to the scale of the plinth, per se, but I think it's a question of how you take advantage of that relatively enormous surface area that you're producing both horizontally and vertically to create this sense. Then, with the plinth itself, I think you start to operate in really interesting ways in perspective by slipping below the plane, beginning to make interesting visual interactions between above and below. I wonder if that could happen even more. I wonder if it is a place where you are not just being outside on top of the plinth or inside and underneath it, but I start to imagine a series of interstitial spaces that somehow occupy the between in different ways. It's just an occupied roof, but it's something that has a density to it. ▲ **ELP**: I like the fact that you had started to make this interstitial space. It's not just the plinth, but there is this interstitial space you start to carve out between the programs and so forth. Could the housing go there? You could stick it in as kind of a terrace. Everybody gets their own real estate. It seems like that's a decent solution.

▲5

▲6

▲7

▲8

ROSS McCLELLAN

Using the international Guggenheim Helsinki competition as a point of departure, this scheme overlays the critical programs of the museum onto existing paths of movement and systems of infrastructure in and around the harbor. This creates new public spaces by improving connectivity between the primary city promenade to the north and the distant infrastructure to the south. Submerging the new museum programs into existing infrastructure generates a hybrid program that benefits both parties. Public space and art displays generate traffic from the ferry terminal, and increased activity from a wide range of visitors enhances the museum. This new hybrid typology generates an iconic museum for Helsinki and offers an opportunity for the Guggenheim institution to reinvent its reputation. Rather than creating iconicity through the placement of a foreign architectural object, the scheme creates an iconic museum experience integrated with the city's infrastructure. {▲ 9–12}

"One thing that I wonder about is whether or not the strands you're operating with in your very elegant and beautifully resolved proposal suffer from a certain degree of sameness." **Marc Tsurumaki**

▲ **AW:** One of the challenges of the current situation is a degree of frustration from the Helsinki populous regarding previous competitions that have been held in the same harbor front. There was a museum, which was never built, and then most recently a south harbor competition, which you may have seen. The increase of access to the waterfront has been a primary objective for decades here. Whether it breaks the rules and therefore made itself obvious to you, or it's an idea that came in the middle of the night, I think it's a very valuable way of beginning. ▲ **SB:** I'd like to start by saying I think it's a really strong proposal in the way that you've started to look at this urbanistically by connecting all of these different modes of transportation and different paths. I'm also really interested in hearing about the diagram you had that was a gallery and the terminal. I think that's the big idea aside from this urban move. To what degree did the gallery have to change, and to what degree did the terminal change in order to allow those two to be married? I have no doubt you went through a more in-depth program interrogation to get to this point. I'm curious because it's a fascinating hybrid, but no doubt there is ultimately compromise to some degree. ▲ **MW:** It makes sense to think about these as lines of movement. I think you have handled it very well by dealing with it in terms of a series of ribbons and strands that can move through in very particular ways. I find the plans very elegant, and the site plan is beautiful. ▲ **MT:** One thing that I wonder about is whether or not the strands you're operating with in your very elegant and beautifully resolved proposal suffer from a certain degree of sameness. Think about a bicycle path versus a pedestrian path. Maybe they're both asphalt, but they are different dimensionally, and have different requirements in terms of speeds of movement, etc. As much as I like the intentions of the proposal to blend these things together to a point where they're almost indistinguishable, I wonder if there's another way that ends up resulting in the current proposal, which benefits from a higher degree of differentiation among the parts. Maybe the gallery strand would be a little bit different from the terminal strand. Maybe the things coming in from the park would be different material from the things coming in from the terminal market. I think the tendency for everything to get rendered in the same way {both literally rendered in terms of images, but also architecturally rendered} should be revisited.

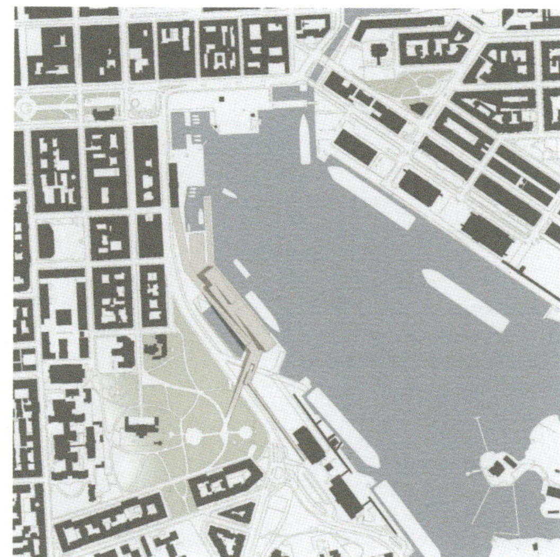

▲ 9

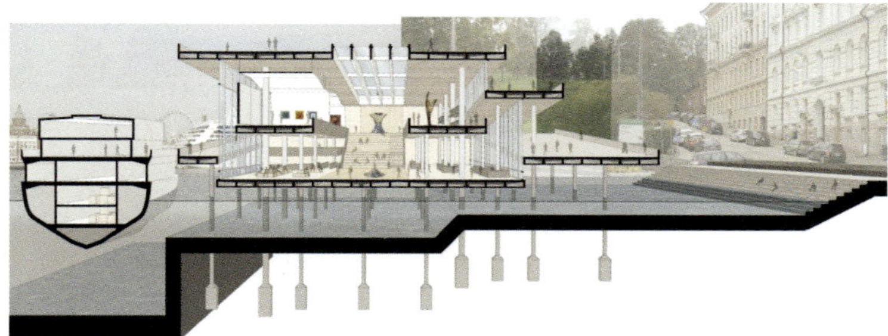

▲ 10

▲ 11

▲ 12

Post-Professional Design Studio
M. Arch II

Critics
Edward Mitchell {EM}, Aniket Shahane {AS}

Jurors
Ila Berman {IB}, Anya Bokov {AB}, Lorna
Congdon {LC}, Eva Franch i Gilabert {EFG},
Brian Healy {BH}, Susie Kim {SK}, Fred Koetter {FK},
Michael Kubo {MK}, Gregg Pasquarelli {GP},
Alan Plattus {AP}

The purpose of the studio was to introduce the incoming class of post-professional degree students to a number of urban and architectural issues germane to the current discipline, as well as to foster a dialogue between the faculty and students about the status of the discipline and to help students develop their own design project.

Over the past several years, the post-professional studio has looked at the historic development of central New England. Earlier work studied the cities of southern Massachusetts and their potential revival. These sites are a network of connected yet independent towns with their own histories and future potential. A book *A Train of Cities* was published by the school on that work. More recently the focus has shifted to the hub of that network, the city of Boston.

In recent years Boston has undergone a renaissance. After decades of limited growth and flight from the city center, Boston has revived, in part, due to the increased investment in research and development fostered by its major educational institutions, but also due to a growing desire for the dynamic life offered by urban living. The past two studios looked at sites along Fort Point Channel and in Cambridge, part of the regional transportation network and slated for new residential and/or lab development. These sites exemplify the changes to the city and anticipate new patterns of urban development. These changes are projected to bring Boston up to the standards of other international centers of business and research and change its reputation as a provincial city of small neighborhoods. The studio project calls for a new Boston City Hall. The studio looked at the issue of renovating the existing building, but did not entertain the idea of a physical renovation which only serves to reveal an atrophied engagement with the architectural issues that the building initially addressed. We were not interested in turning the clock back so as to preserve the urban fabric of times past and promote a simplistic return to historic origins.

Instead, the studio was concerned with revisiting the disciplinary moment in which the competition was launched, namely, the end of High Modernism. We wanted to use the studio investigation as an opportunity to engage the subsequent debate about the role of a public building in the city.

The program for the project and the site was taken directly from the 1961 brief with some modifications so as to acknowledge existing buildings since constructed. For purposes of the studio, the site proper remains the same as it was in 1961, but the context incorporates the physical and conceptual problems of the contemporary city.

Design Risk:
Design Reward

Gregg Pasquarelli,
SHoP Architects

Tonight's lecture will be about the rules that our brilliant professors, mentors, and leaders taught us, and how we broke them all.
① *Don't have more than two partners who actually put their names in the firm.* By acting upon the ferocity of our convictions, we seek to recast the role of architects as those who reveal coherence in chaos.
② *Don't build in your own city.* I think we were able to break this one by heavily involving ourselves in the politics around space.
③ *Don't work with developers too much.* The more you go toward the political side of things, the more freedom you get to go in the exact opposite direction and push ideas.
④ *Don't be nice.* How you treat your people matters. We have never had an unpaid intern in the history of our office, we will not work for dictators, and we will not work in countries with indentured servitude.
⑤ *Don't talk about beauty.* Humans need beauty as much as we need air, water, and song, particularly when it is the fingerprint of human action in the anonymous vastness of our times.
⑥ *Don't get involved in means and methods.* If you take risks and push the envelope, you better damn well know how that building goes together.
⑦ *Don't try to do it all.* Technologies are making complexity transparent and allowing us to challenge the status quo at every turn. I am proud to be an architect. I believe we can make a huge difference. We need to take risks. We need to break the rules, and I think we can have an incredible time with our lives doing it.

Work Play

John Patkau
{Norman R. Foster Visiting Professor}

The act of imagination can take many forms. It is most commonly an expression of cultural purpose, of environmental response, and of construction and technology. The more inclusive the imagination is to the diversity of circumstances which surround a project, the more complete the work of architecture. And then there is the issue of craft. For us, craft is intellectual in the first instance; it is the construction of ideas. It is a rigorous set of relationships which form an armature for the ongoing development and elaboration of the project. Craft is also aesthetic—a product of the sensibility of mind and eye. Finally, craft is physical—the material product of mind and hand and the hand's extension through technology. Like the act of imagination from which the architectural project is formed, I believe the more inclusive the craft, the more complete the work of architecture.

CHARLOTTE ALGIE ✳

A city hall is the smallest form of government representation where architecture will inevitably define a community's sense of the political machine. Boston City Hall Redux starts with a pinched scale, sensitivity to interior spaces, and human-scaled urban thresholds. Mayoral duties are increasingly nomadic—adrift in the city, within school gymnasiums, or at local businesses. Meeting rooms thus become a crucial programmatic hinge. For the reprised Boston City Hall, they become specific and unique pavilions, defined as both interiors and within the landscape. Since the mayor deploys his work to the more private rooms of constituents' businesses and homes, the city hall should reflect and focus on the scale of the room. The ground level of linear, semi-public spaces serves to unite disparate City Hall departments as a network between the municipal and administrative teams, as well as the interface for visitors. The project imagines groups of visitors walking the line bridges and linkages and stopping at small public squares. Visitors are given the opportunity to survey both through and into the offices of their representatives. Space is pushed to the limits of smallness and evokes Boston's Georgian laneways. The scale makes the encounter between the government and its constituents more informal. City Hall becomes a permeable urban threshold. (▲1–4)

> "The whole scale of it is so miniaturized that it looks like a mini-city for city-kitty. You need some sort of major event there like a horse race." **Susie Kim**

▲ **IB:** Why is every room or element figured independently of all the others? I want to know why things are figured the way they are and what the relationship is to the other pieces. There might be seven different meeting rooms here, but each is a different shape, and I don't understand why. ▲ **BH:** I do. I think what she is trying to say is there's a collection of individuals, and the collection is indicative of the commonality among disparate citizens. ▲ **IB:** But where is the collective? What I see is a bunch of individuals strung together, but what is missing—and what City Hall represents—is the collective. ▲ **AP:** It's too small. That's a big part of her idea. In a sense, all of these things have gotten too big, and local government can no longer be differentiated from national government because they all occupy the same gigantic, monolithic structures. What is overlaying all of this—and I'm having a sidebar conversation with Ila about it—is John Hejduk's masks. More than an Enlightenment project or Archigram or Metabolist, there is an individualized, poetic sensibility. You've had a private intuition about what each of these spaces should be and then it's been rendered public. I'm not sure it should be drawn like a practical project. The illusion that you've worked it all out on another functional level is not doing it justice. The sections are what I'm intrigued by, and the plans are just a key. ▲ **RAMS:** In 1961, as government was getting bigger, city governments were beginning to set up satellite agencies in various neighborhoods, and that was the way to get at community engagement. Your building does reflect that. They have broken down some of the functions and installed them in the neighborhoods. You've really produced an extremely bureaucratic scheme. ▲ **SK:** I don't know if this is what you want, but it does bring to mind not only Archigram but also walking buildings, which are fabulous. The whole scale of it is so miniaturized that it looks like a mini-city for city-kitty. You need some sort of major event there like a horse race. ▲ **IB:** I'm glad Bob brought up the outpost within the city—the field condition—because that's exactly what you are reflecting. What happens when you bring the collection back to the site, and what developed the language of all the symbols you used? You created a language of a series of figures and shapes that I don't buy as just being different. One logic is that you pull these spaces from the urban environment, and there are some qualities that come with them. When you bring them together, you have to negotiate the differences. I feel the thing you set up becomes too arbitrary as a language, and there is a relationship of signification and symbolism that you have to take on.

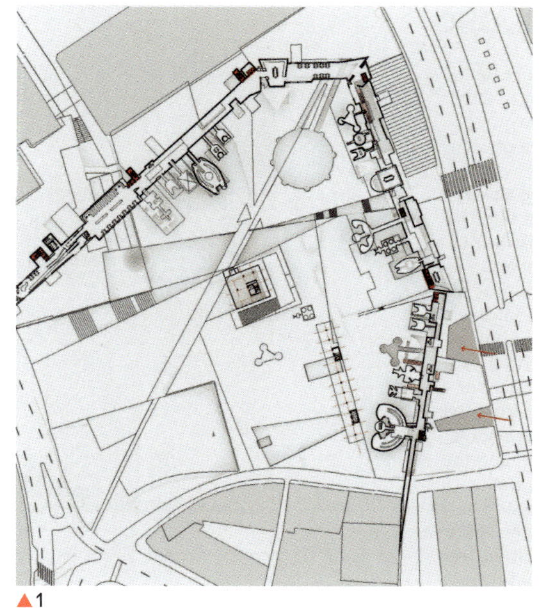

▲1

▲2

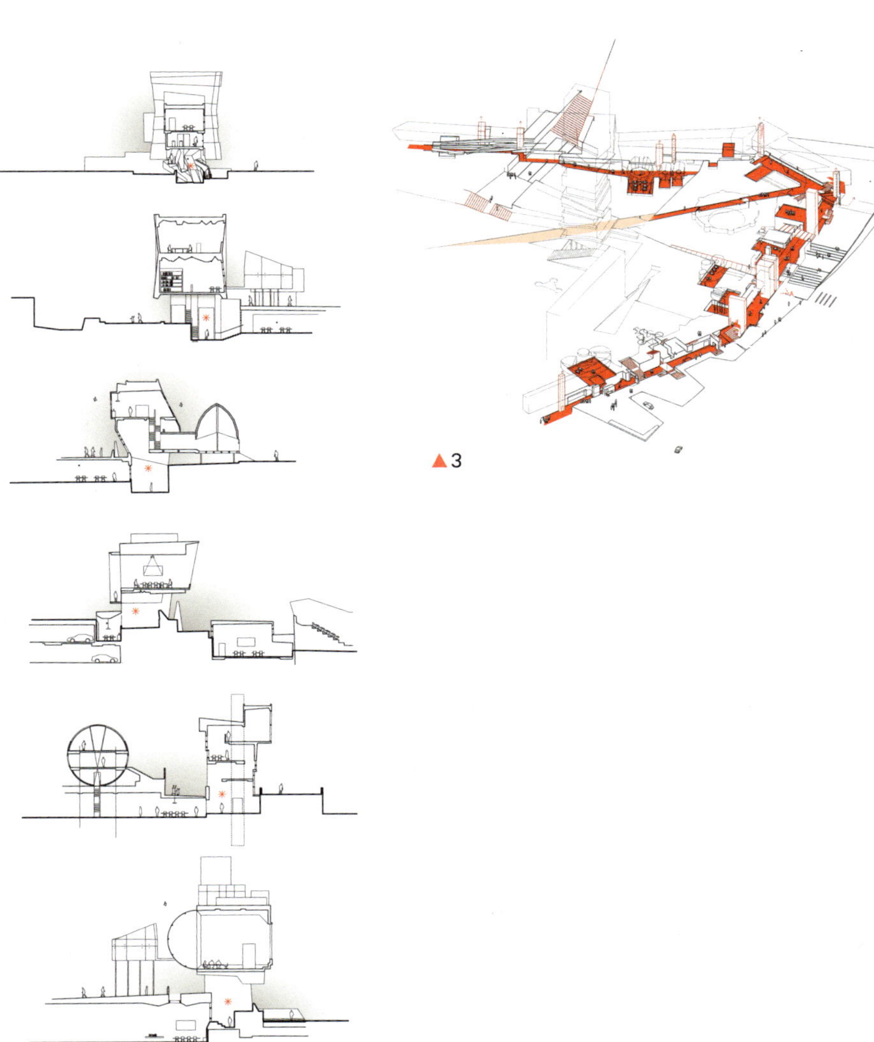

▲3

▲4

ROBERTO JENKINS & EUNIL CHO

We propose a mixing chamber that encourages interaction through shared public programs. Our project is a gathering hub for urban life—a microcosm of the city that brings in a multitude of public amenities.

The project engages with the existing site by creating a "ground" that organizes access into the site. It links the three nearby subway stations into a dynamic urban plaza with a centralized location in the city, and a connection to existing infrastructure leading to the airport and other major landmarks. It follows the pedestrian flow from the neighboring Faneuil Marketplace and creates a central courtyard adjacent to four lobbies. The aggregation of program stems from a couple of issues in the existing scheme. The existing building and plaza don't encourage movement throughout the site, and the single, municipal program manifests as a singular mass with a centralized entry and a limited number of visitors. By adding a hotel, commercial offices, a subway hub, and a series of urban amenities, the project aims to create more interaction between urban life and the traditional functions of City Hall. {▲ 5–8}

> "What you're celebrating is the neo-liberal privatization of government interests through this formal continuity of the hotel and the retail as the dominant thing."
> **Michael Kubo**

▲ **AP:** There is a linguistic level to this project, which we haven't talked about much today. I read your scheme as a rhetoric of continuity: surfaces flow into each other, and there is a continuity of floor plates expressed on the facade. The building has an intention to express that kind of openness and continuity, but the way the building works is actually quite discontinuous. If I'm a mayor and I'm going to an important city council meeting, what are my options in terms of getting there? There are actual pathways, then there is what your building is telling me: the expression of the actual place. I have a feeling, and it's not entirely negative feeling, that this is a perfect foil to the 1961 City Hall. Just as it was of its time, right at the heart of the Brutalist movement, quoting all of the right sources by some incredibly sophisticated, precocious of architects, this is the perfect 2014 update. ▲ **BH:** In a cynical way? ▲ **AP:** No! Not in a cynical way, in an observational way. ▲ **BH:** I thought Alan was going here: If there is a desire in program to break up different functions, why do they all look the same? Why do they all have the same language? ▲ **MK:** The linguistic question is what you're celebrating implicitly, versus what they were celebrating in 1961. What is the difference in the political climate? The project was emblematic of a specific realm of emblematic expression in architecture. What you're celebrating is the neo-liberal privatization of government interests through this formal continuity of the hotel and the retail as the dominant thing. I agree that you're being totally earnest about it. It's now a cynical observation. ▲ **IB:** I very much appreciate the massing and morphology of the building in relation to the larger urban environment and what it is as an entity unto itself. I almost feel like these are two different projects: the plans versus what I'm reading as a three-dimensional thing. Morphologically, I very much appreciate its mediation of the urban environment in terms of scale across the site, and dealing with the types of difficulties within that space. It acts like a knot and makes sense of it, while at the same time producing something that stands alone. The difficulty is the promise of this continuity. I might believe in it entirely as a three-dimensional object, but the plans are driving me crazy. There is this default condition: a double loaded corridor. There is a belief that the continuity will translate through all aspects of the project, but it doesn't. It should be about how you move through the entire building. And you didn't take advantage of the roof—it should tie together the logic that you're operating with. It's all about figuration and not about what it does.

▲ 5

▲ 6

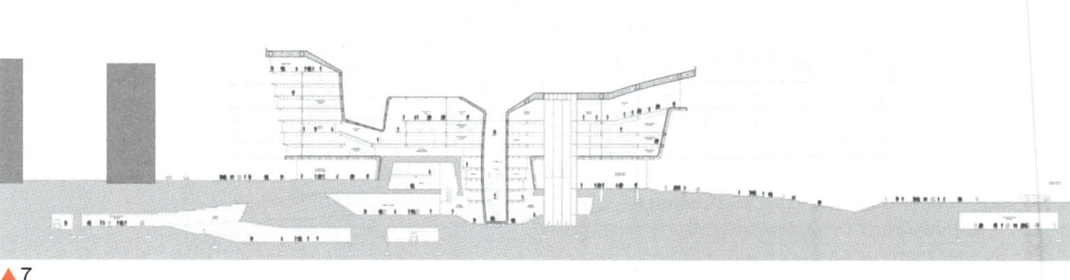

▲ 7

▲ 8

KARL KARAM, ADIL MANSURE, ABDULGADER NASEER

Contemporary social interactions, business, and politics are evermore crossing traditional hierarchical boundaries. We believe City Hall should reflect this change and that its symbolic, vertical and singular unit model is no longer valid. Instead, while retaining some of its key bureaucratic functions, City Hall should provide a seamless, continuous platform between itself and the city.

A platform punctuated by a series of dynamic spaces would suppress the symbolic role of the complex, establish a horizontal plane, and celebrate both traditional and progressive urban performances. City Hall campus would spread across the site in a series of spaces clustered around an oversized working space: the hall. The assembly chamber morphs into the adjacent building and provides access through Pemberton Square. Such a move allows the public to access city council meetings. The mayor's office strategically faces Faneuil Hall to create a plaza that allows the mayor to both interact with Bostonians and watch over them. It also establishes a physical link to the assembly chambers by crossing over the existing road through the campus, the subway station, and into the chambers. That link establishes an axis along the plaza and exposes elected officials to the constituents. The hall is a large, sunken space marked by two types of columns that navigate through three different types of furniture—areas which furniture accommodate for different functions between city and city hall seamlessly. The light walls above, flooding the space with natural light, allow for various vantage points into the hall. The project, in its totality, proposes a new model for the state in the urban realm. (▲ 9–11)

> "You're like a box of cereal in a Walmart."
> Robert A. M. Stern

▲ **RAMS**: When I looked at your model, you know what I thought it was a scheme for? A train station. It has all the tracks below and the concourse above. What are you thinking? What is a city hall? ▲ **AP**: This is not so strange. If you start to explore the contemporary architecture of government, what's driving the relationships are considerations of security, enclosure, and confidentiality as well as modern ideas of efficiency and organizing work. There is a discourse here that forces us to reconsider the way in which government buildings are positioning themselves. ▲ **RAMS**: Well, you are talking about two different things here. You will always have to deal with security and the disabled, but it does not change the fact that, when an important decision comes out of the Supreme Court, there are always people standing on the steps. When you are designing anew, you should be able to embody the symbolic ideals of government and meet the needs of modern people. ▲ **SK**: I don't think you believe there should be a city hall and it needs to disappear, but what would go on top of this? Are you just saying this is all garbage? ▲ **RAMS**: You have no idea of scale. There is a huge space, and you have little droppings. City hall is something that people can gather around. That's what architecture does. Your job is not to control society, but to enable society. You can design a church for a religion that isn't your religion. You can understand their beliefs and create an environment. You can't just say: I'm not that religion. It shouldn't exist. They have no right to exist, or whatever. ▲ **MK**: So you are against the polemical competition proposal that one does to move the discipline forward? ▲ **RAMS**: If you think it's going to move things forward, then you take the risk. But you're likely not to move things forward and you're not going to get the job. I actually believe that architects go to architecture school to learn how to master the discipline and ultimately succeed as architects; not to be critics of society. ▲ **MK**: Are those separate? ▲ **RAMS**: Yes, they are. There is a difference. I think this is a very juvenile critique: it doesn't answer the question about what it's like to be under that plaza with hundreds of people sitting and little streaks of light coming from above—very horrible. You're like a box of cereal in a Walmart. ▲ **MK**: You haven't given yourself the representational tools to mount the argument as a critique.

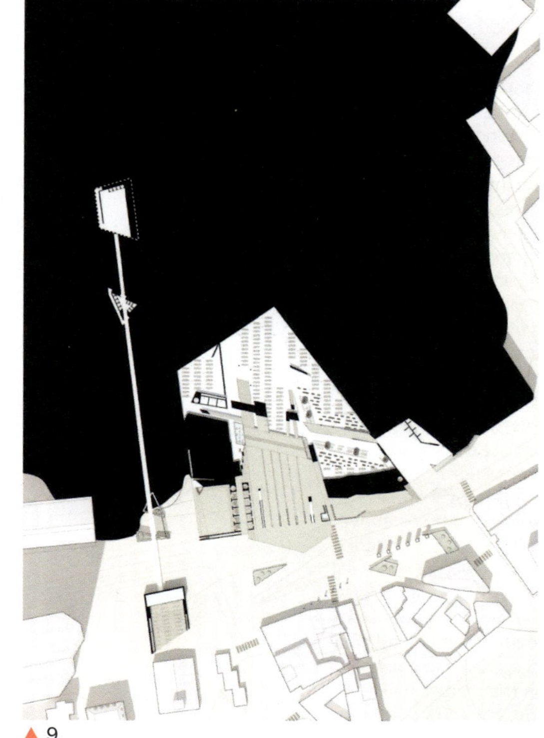

▲ 9.

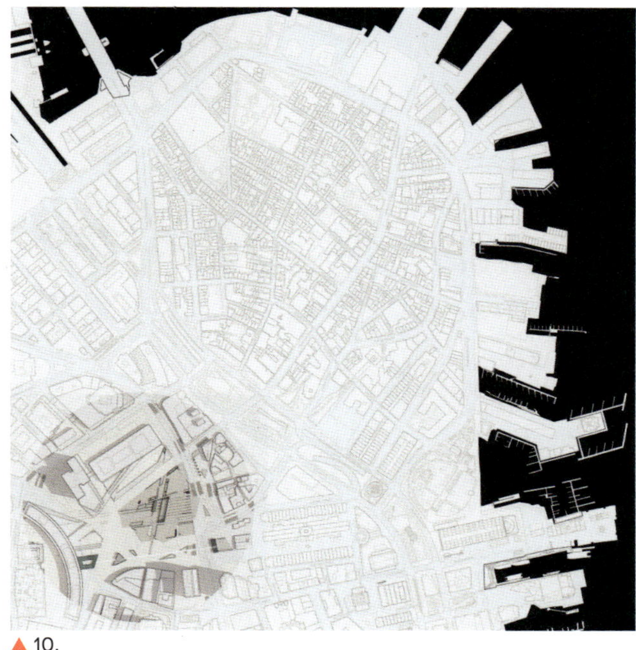

▲ 10.

▲ 11.

DAPHNE BINDER & JARED ABRAHAM

In our proposal for a new Boston City Hall, we considered this civic institution a space for individual and communal public demonstration, from paying your parking tickets to protesting the mayor. We believe city hall must incite interaction between citizens and their representatives while still providing a place for the private deliberations of government officials. A series of overlapping urban rooms connect diagonally Cambridge and Hanover streets, constituting a central hall for visitors to migrate through or occupy. The mass of city hall is at once voided by the central hall and at the same time frames its chambers. It is broken up so as to allow site connections on an East-West axis between Cambridge and Congress Streets through a series of ramps. All city hall departments can be accessed along the central hall's ground floor or by large public cores that take you to the upper-level offices. While separated on the ground floor, offices above bridge over the main space and enable interdepartmental circulation and spaces for collaboration.

Programs that are essential to city hall's identity—the city council chamber, the reference library, and the mayor's office—are located within and adjacent to the central hall's main space. The council chamber, positioned within the central hall, is enclosed by rotating partitions that allow for the public to inhabit the space when the council is not in session. The undefined central hall lends itself to multiple uses and public functions. (▲12–15)

"We elevate experience by confronting the world with architecture and representing the things we already know in order to experience something else."
Ila Berman

▲**RAMS:** You need a symbolic front door. City Hall is still something that school children are brought to and introduced to government with. It's not just about paying your parking ticket. It has discourse about contentious neighbors, angry about some development or school bus—and it's not an office building. Where do I go to get married? Every building needs a front door. ▲**IB:** I fear the discussion devolving when we make certain assumptions. That there should be a front door—I don't buy that. On the one hand, whether there is one door or five doors, how you deal with entry should be part of the project. That is a position in relation to the project, because the assumption that there is a default is the same thing as saying that a door is not an opening, but it's actually a thing that hinges and opens, etc. ▲**RAMS:** You're telling students not to have doors and hinges? ▲**IB:** Modernism spent so long trying to deal with this condition of opening and entry—to get rid of classic default icons, saying, "a door looks like this, a window looks like this." ▲**RAMS:** Give us a break! That is so cliché of an opinion and so disastrous to architecture. ▲**IB:** I'm sorry, but that's my position. We elevate experience by confronting the world with architecture and representing the things we already know in order to experience something else. This is, and should be, a part of what you're doing. The question is, then, what are you proposing? It's more about the clarity of that. I don't want us to default to what the public was saying in the first place: "Yes there should have been a single entrance." I don't think half of city halls actually do that, and they present what they present as an architecture. That's what you should be putting forward and discussing, how entry happens. ▲**RAMS:** You starved architecture to death. If the Canadian way is to stake out everything that gives texture and detail to architecture, it's a sad, sad sight North of the fortieth parallel. When I looked at that drawing on the bottom, at least I saw a spritz of spirit in that drawing. But I don't see that anywhere else, including the translation from the bottom drawing to the rendering. Why don't you have drawings instead of renderings? ▲**AP:** Instead of facilitating two-thirds of the school's budget to nothing but renderings, take all that equipment away. ▲**RAMS:** No, students learn for themselves what they need to do and not do. You don't take away the horsepower from the car, you tell people they shouldn't drive at ninety miles per hour down a little, quiet, residential street.

▲12

▲13

▲14

▲15

UNDERGRADUATE STUDIES

Yale School of Architecture offers an undergraduate major in architecture to students enrolled in Yale College. The purpose of the undergraduate major is to include the study of architecture within a comprehensive liberal arts education, drawing from the broader academic and professional environment of the Yale School of Architecture. The curriculum includes work in design, history, theory, and criticism of architecture as well as urban studies. As a liberal arts major in Yale College, it leads to a Bachelor of Arts degree with a major in Architecture.

Director of Undergraduate Studies
Bimal Mendis

250 Methods and Form in Architecture I
Bimal Mendis and Trattie Davies
{◎1–3}

450 Senior Design Studio
Turner Brooks and Adam Hopfner
{◎4–6}

251 Methods and Form in Architecture II
Joyce Hsiang and Jennifer Leung
{◎7–9}

249 Analytic Model
Elijah Huge
{◎10–12}

494 Senior Project Design Studio
Steven Harris and Marta Caldeira
{◎13–15}

490 Senior Research Colloquium
Karla Britton

◎1. Katherine Colford

◎2. Harper Keehn

◎4. Andrew Kim

◎3. Edward Wang

◎5. Katrina Yin

◎6. Marisa Kaugars

◎ 7. Katherine Colford

◎ 10. Jose Gomez-Acebo

◎ 12. Thaddeus Lee

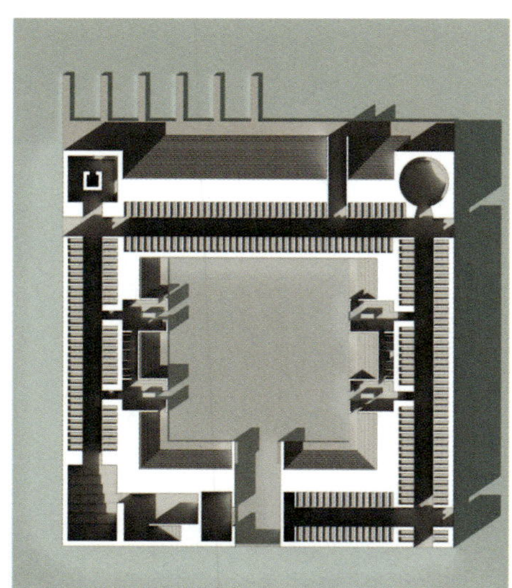

◎ 14. Edward Oo

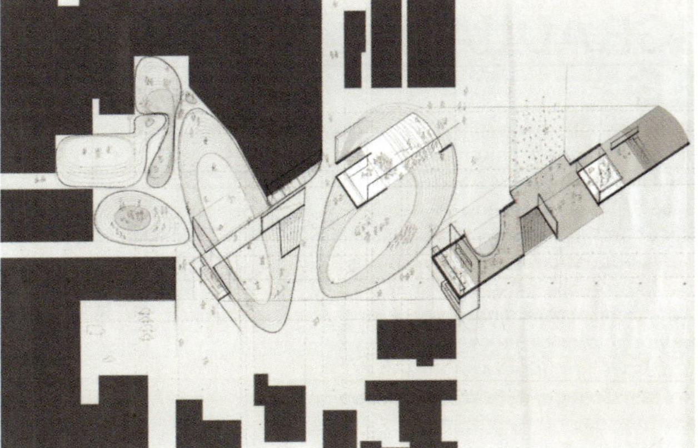

◎ 8. Edward Wang

◎ 9. Sijia Yang

◎ 11. Nadya Stryuk

◎ 13. Elif Erez

◎ 15. Katrina Yin

Retrospecta 38

Senior Research Colloquium

CONSTANTIN GEANAKOPOLOS

When the first Puritan settlers laid eyes on New Haven in 1638, they noted its position at the confluence of three significant geographic features: a harbor, a series of rivers, and the picturesque formation of East Rock silhouetted against the horizon. Today, the Mill River District remains perhaps the last area in the city where the relationship between harbor, river, and rock still can be perceived with strong, visual connection.

New Haven's waterways once anchored industries that brought the city great wealth. In the 19th and early 20th centuries, the Mill River District's network of infrastructure made it the most strategic area in all of Connecticut to operate a coal-powered manufacturing plant. By mid-century, however, the automobile, alternating current electricity, and containerization technology had made all of those former advantages obsolete. Abandonment, outdoor storage, construction laydowns, garbage dumps, and seas of parking now are much more common to the area than manufacturing.

MAGGIE INHOFE

When I began my research on Stourhead, I admired the many perspectives I read on the landscape, but I ultimately found that they failed to account for the entire 2700 acres of the Stourhead landscape. Instead, they focused on a small portion of the landscape, the famous picturesque garden centered around the main lake. Kenneth Woodbridge, the premier scholar on Stourhead, proposes that this garden is an allegory for *The Aeneid*. Another lesser-known reading of the site comes from Michael Charlesworth, who sees the landscape as a Herculean allegory. Though Henry Hoare II, owner and designer of Stourhead's garden, certainly employed iconography from both of these sources, I think it is wrong to deem the garden an allegory and prioritize one interpretation over the other. Each only discusses portions of the circuit walk around the lake and ignores the estate as a whole.

The landscape, and Hoare's work on it, extends far beyond the garden and the lake. In order to best understand the purpose of Mr. Hoare's creation, all aspects of the estate must be considered, especially those that are not part of the formal garden. The portions of the landscape that surround the periphery of the lake and extend far to the north and west of the house itself are designed, but not manicured. They stand in stark contrast to the dammed lake, cleared pathways, and classical architecture of the circuit area. They cannot be ignored as Woodbridge, Charlesworth, and others have done. I would like to focus on the regions of the landscape beyond the lake and, in discussing the work that Hoare did outside of his formal templescape, show that the two different parts can come together to redefine the reading of Stourhead as a whole.

JOSHUA ISACKSON

In the decades following China's reforms in 1978, small-scale water towns in China's Yangtze River Delta have changed significantly in appearance and function, reflecting the shift from the planned economy to the individual pursuit of wealth. The aesthetic value of the water town has grown in significance while the commercial function of agriculture and trading has diminished—as has the traditional way of life. A vestige of pre-Communist China, the water town has been embraced as a place of beauty and unique history and serves as a nationalist rallying point as well as an emblem of China's rich culture. Once a place to live, farm, and engage in regional trade, the water town has increasingly become a place dedicated to attracting tourism and spurring investment throughout the Jiangnan region. As a result, the canals have become not just aestheticized, but increasingly ornamental. Restoration, replication, and abstraction: these three strategies of manipulating the water town are the confluence of attempts at cultural preservation, economic growth, and tourism as well as reconciliation with globalization and development of a contemporary Chinese architecture. The replication, restoration, and abstraction of the Chinese water town reveal, to an increasingly large degree, the transformation of Chinese water town architecture and urbanism from lived reality to ornamental and aesthetic function—the purpose of which is modernization, nation-building, economic growth, and Westernization. This senior essay develops a narrative of the water town's fate by examining the intentions of each method, the process of historic preservation undertaken at each site, and the results.

MASTER OF ENVIRONMENTAL DESIGN

<u>Program</u> <u>Director</u>
Eeva-Liisa Pelkonen {**ELP**}

<u>Critics</u>
Michelle Addington {**MA**}, Karla Britton {**KB**},
Peggy Deamer {**PD**}, Keller Easterling {**KE**},
Karsten Harries {**KH**}, Dolores Hayden {**DH**},
Alan Plattus {**AP**}

<u>Visiting</u> <u>Critics</u>
Ed Eigen {**EE**}, Rania Ghosn {**RG**},
Anthony Vidler {**AV**}

The Master of Environmental Design {M.E.D}
program is a two-year research-based program of
advanced architectural studies culminating in a written thesis or independent project. The program is
intended for students, including postgraduate and
mid-career professionals, who seek an academic
setting to improve scholarship and research skills,
to explore a professional or academic specialization,
and to sharpen critical and literary expertise. The
program provides foundation for a career in writing, teaching, curatorial work, or critically informed
professional practice, and may, in some cases, provide a basis for future Ph.D. studies in architecture
and related fields. Environmental Design is broadly
defined as the study and research of the aggregate of objects, conditions, and influences that
constitute the constructed surroundings. Those
studying in the M.E.D. program are encouraged to
understand the larger cultural and intellectual factors—social, political, economic, technical, and aesthetic—that shape the environment.

<u>Roundtable</u> <u>Discussion</u>

◙**RG**: A common theme here was addressing
the issue of scale. I think it's interesting to think
about what kinds of methodologies are set up
by the students to understand the different
relationships between things. The students
adjusted the particularities as well as their large
conceptual ideas. ◙**AV**: This is not just self-
contextualizing: Architecture and Architecture and
Architecture. That is the old way of going about it.
We're going straight to the heart of architecture's
formative influences: the economy, society,
politics, the programs—that which produces an
architecture of one form or another—whether
that's Architecture or a trailer. When you look
at economics and politics and social conditions
for answers to questions like where, how, and
why you would practice, that's incredible. ◙**ELP**:
Never have we had such a politically charged class.
They came here as advocates. The forces that
shape the built environment: this was a founding
principle of the program in the late 1960s. It was
exactly this, not architectural history, but the built
environment. This body of work is very close to
those original principles. ◙**EE**: Interdisciplinarity
is important. What can you learn about American
history or the welfare state or shopping? What can
architectural history teach that other history can't
learn by other means? Interdisciplinarity, if it's not
reciprocal, doesn't mean anything. We're just in a
subordinate position. The audience for your work
should not just be people within architecture or its
history, but these people whose books and articles
you read to help you with your work. They should
read what you have to say, because you could teach
them something as well. You are contextualizing
architecture for other disciplines. ◙**KE**: There
is an idea that there is a dilution of disciplinary
knowledge, but it's the complete opposite. Other
disciplines need operable and durable spatial
variables as evidence or test beds. So many are
looking for that kind of evidence. You can see
that this work today begins to bring those spatial
variables to the center of focus. ◙**AV**: And it takes
these virtual variables and spatializes them. It's like
an economic chart: suddenly, you can see things in
a way that you didn't see them before. These ideas
take root.

First Years

SHIVANI SHEDDE

**Anomalous Space: Subterranean
Infrastructures in Colonial India**
This research focuses on the production of space
in colonial India that resulted in the creation of differences in the Indian landscape. Beginning with
the survey documentation under the Department of
Survey of India, this thesis will investigate how the
Indian landscape was mapped, archived and eventually transformed through land-based extractive
industries—the mine.

The thesis highlights the colonial survey project as a process of simultaneously making visible
and rendering invisible. That is, while mining prof-
its had global ramifications, the mines themselves
were hidden, subterranean constructions, that
would never be encountered except by those working them. Similarly, while the survey projects were
an exercise of gathering information about the colony, they were relegated to archives to be accessed
by an elite few. The mines were therefore an ultimate expression of territoriality that instituted new
social orders.

By giving an account of the historical change
instituted by colonial extractive practices, this thesis will shed light on the new spatial configurations
that arose to enable efficient administration, discipline of the population and swift extraction from
the colony. My analysis seeks to render palpable the
protean nature of the relationship between state
and space and body in colonial India as constituted
through its various representations and institutional
frameworks. Ultimately I will look at the contradictions in the way nature was seen, ordered, remade
and rendered invisible in the creation of these subterranean infrastructures.

PREETI TALWAI

My M.E.D. thesis will investigate the interface
between people and screen technologies in digital
retail innovations. Particularly, I am interested in the
implications of these immersive retail experiences
for the embodied experience of shopping, and the
relationships engendered between the consumer-
subject, the screen, and the objects of consumption themselves. By bridging theoretical frameworks from multiple disciplines, the thesis will use a
series of case studies in the United States that highlight the complex relationship between self, space,
and screen in a rapidly technologizing and globaliz-
ing context. These case studies include "connected
stores," shoppable windows, virtual fitting room
technologies and interactive wayfinding.

In recent years, much has been written about
embodiment and technology, but architectural
interpretations of interactive screen technology,
particularly with respect to questions of consumer-
ism, ownership, and identity, are rare. On the other
hand, the vast body of scholarship on spaces and
cultures of consumption rarely accounts for the
role of the body, or the convergence of commercial
space and interactive screen technology. In an era
where personal technology is ubiquitous, and opportunities for consumption abound, it is important to
bridge this gap in scholarship to more humanisti-
cally and synthetically theorize the physical-virtual
interface. The thesis contends that screens, of various forms, have always been integral parts of the
retail environment. With this foundation, the thesis
will explore how changing relationships between the
subject, screen, and object throughout retail history
are involved reciprocally with retailers' manipulation
of desire and consumers' creation of identity.

GENEVA MORRIS

**Life in One Room: Austerity and
Small-Space Living**
Renters are seeing shrinking unit sizes nationwide.
As developers seek higher density and higher revenue per square foot to offset rising land value and
construction costs, more and more small-scale
units are being developed. Like any building-type,
small space units embody both the financial constraints of their time and the dominant societal,
political, and architectural views. The story of small-
space living types underscore an understanding of
the social dynamics of the built environment: how
public policy has both encouraged and impeded
certain types, how the single-room unit has been
revived in the form of the micro-unit, how such a
development can exclude the most vulnerable communities, and how rhetoric of "substandard" and
"slum" fueled the destruction of hundreds of thousands of units.

The minimal dwelling unit offers a rich prism
through which to parse shifting representations and
ideologies of place and family life in American cities and the urban crisis of an ongoing housing shortage because its materiality is always bound up with
an intricate assemblage of meanings. Studies of
the architectural and spatial artifacts, discourse
surrounding those debates, and the economic
and social conditions that gave rise to these housing formats ground this work. Tentatively, these
case studies include: single room occupancy units,
cage hotels, kitchenette apartments, and micro-
apartments. This thesis will analyze how changing notions of domesticity, privacy, gender, race,
and class have contributed to different manifestations of small space living arrangements in the built
environment.

Second Years

ERIC WYCOFF ROGERS

Progressive Cities: Planning, Reproduction, and Power in the American Metropolis

In the Progressive Era, new technologies of power were distilled and deployed in the development of political and economic reproductive apparatuses that sought to shape the city in ways consistent with the requirements of power. In looking back on the era, one must remember that most of the mechanisms by which today's economists or politicians manage the economy did not exist. The thesis focuses on four groupings of upperclass reformers whose legacy has been treated as progressive, yet whose reforms ultimately preserved capitalist power relations: the National Municipal League, the early city planners, the *Better Homes in America* campaign, and the Federal Housing Administration. The reformers were not conscious about the economic processes that they were manipulating, yet they were nevertheless conscious of power and influence. The factional "disorganization" that was leading to a decline of ruling class power in the late 1800s was visualized by the National Municipal League in the unplanned urban conglomeration of late-nineteenth century cities, and they addressed this issue, ultimately, through a consolidation of administrative control—largely over infrastructures, utilities and other physical features of the city—in municipal government. The League was eventually successful in placing "expert knowledge" in command by "creating an educated and intelligent public in the matter of municipal government"[1] that would demand municipal control by expert administrators, out of the reach of democratic interference. The city planners, observing the physical city, which operated as a proxy for "the economy" in a time when this term did not yet exist, sought to combat the ways in which economic inefficiencies and social ills were hindering commerce, and they addressed the urban manifestations of these problems as a means of resolving the economic contradictions of commerce. "Congestion" of streets was rectified in a way that shored up capital, and got it flowing again. The *Better Homes in America* reformers sought to use the intimate setting of the home to manipulate the subjectivity of its occupants —especially children. Girls were expected to participate in the informal economic sphere of the home, whereas boys were trained to deal with the formal economics of the house—its construction, procurement and sale. The goals of "reducing household drudgery" and educating children on the pragmatic chores of daily domestic life were stand-ins for dealing with systemic economic issues of the informal sphere in a direct and rigorous way. The Federal Housing Administration, some years later, devised a strategy for "conducting the conduct" of the homebuying public, maintaining both a targeted interest in homebuyers themselves, and particularly with publications after 1934, to influence society's influencers themselves to spread the FHA's message. The issue of employment was understood in relation to the slowdown in construction and manufacturing, and was correspondingly addressed through housing and infrastructure. By creating a specific financial climate, the FHA was able to encourage other entities to produce the kind of built environment that would lead to maximized consumption, both in the present and down the road. In all of these cases, groups formed consciousness of their interests through the problematization of urban conditions and extended various defenses of these interests. Ultimately, this projects shows the way that urban development, arising out of a discursive problematization of issues within the built environment, were related to, but not necessarily directly determined by, economic processes of capital. Since discourse was ultimately the origin of actions that intervened in the built environment, the history of interventionism, packaged into the Progressive Era, was really a series of distinct, contingent moments in which immanent sets of interpretations of urban problems were organized into marginally coherent programs of power and control.

[1] Woodruff, Clinton Rogers, "The National Municipal League", in Proceedings of the American Political Science Association, Vol. 5, Fifth Annual Meeting (1908), pg. 131.

BRENT STURLAUGSON

Housing Power on Pine Ridge Reservation

On April 17, 2013, a group of housing activists arrived at Union Square in Washington, D.C. after traveling over 1,500 miles from Pine Ridge Reservation in South Dakota. The purpose of their journey, announced by Paul Iron Cloud, the chief executive officer of Oglala Sioux Lakota Housing, was to "to show Congress the need for Indian housing." To demonstrate this need, Iron Cloud and his fellow activists brought evidence supporting their claim. There, parked on 3rd Street NW in front of the United States Capitol, was a gooseneck flatbed trailer carrying fragments of a two-bedroom, one-bath house. The week before, Iron Cloud had testified before the Senate Indian Affairs Committee a few blocks away, where, in his words, "everybody reads from a piece of paper, saying big words and all this stuff. But you know, I spoke from my heart." This time, however, Iron Cloud brought more than a testimony representing a problem; he brought the problem itself.

"The Trail of Hope for Indian Housing," as the demonstration was called, sought not only to expose the need for improved housing, but also to express related concerns. To this end, a printed vinyl banner affixed to the side of the demonstration house read, "IT'S ABOUT JUSTICE. Lack of reasonable housing on Indian Reservations causes many problems. Education, Health Care, and the Economy on the reservation all suffer." For these activists, the demonstration house served as a medium for communicating their political concerns. Once used as a tool for delivering values consistent with federal interests, the same house, through dislocation and disarticulation, subverted these interests in favor of tribal concerns. Power, in this instance, traveled through material networks to link distant groups across time and space, a process that relied on an vessel capable of carrying a range of interests. Far from the natural outcome of a neutral process, evidence from Pine Ridge Reservation renders the house as a politicized object capable of housing power.

This thesis examines housing on Pine Ridge Reservation in South Dakota. By foregrounding housing, I emphasize the enduring effects of space in reservation politics. In this framework, politics becomes legible through the space it creates, and as such, I argue that housing registers political activity between the Oglala Sioux Tribe and the United States government. Guiding my investigation are three core questions. Why is reservation space different from nonreservation space? What are these differences? How did they develop?

Archives, interviews, and government documents comprise the evidence for my research. In the interpretation of this evidence, I draw on theories of settler colonialism from Patrick Wolfe and Lorenzo Veracini; power from Michel Foucault, Bruno Latour, and James C. Scott; space from Keller Easterling and Eyal Weizman; and historical agency from Ned Blackhawk and Andrew Needham. The organization of this thesis reflects the material properties and spatial composition of housing on Pine Ridge. The three core chapters describe developments in log, frame, and trailer housing. With this organizational strategy, I highlight the differential effects of housing according to its spatial configuration and material composition. These properties map loosely onto the chronology of reservation development, which enables a historical narrative that privileges space, rather than time, as its central protagonist. By exploring the interaction of land and housing, this thesis seeks to describe the imbrication of space and politics. In analyzing this imbrication, I argue that political struggles occur in and through reservation housing. In particular, I contend that the specific materiality of housing enables a prescribed range of activity while disabling an alternative range. As such, I contend that housing power registers the shifting interests of political encounters on Pine Ridge.

BENYAMEEN GHAREEB

Housing Crisis in Kuwait: Toward a Viable Alternative

Despite having one of the highest Gross Domestic Product per person in the world due to high returns from the export of oil, most Kuwaitis cannot afford to buy housing and, accordingly, are completely dependent on the government to fill that need. This leaves about half the population on an ever-expanding housing applicant list. Moreover, about ninety percent of the citizens work for the government. These two crises are compounded with depleting oil reserves and an unstable global market. In the past few months, the price of oil has plummeted a staggering fifty percent, which has rightly highlighted the gravity of the current predicament.

Among other secondary causes, the current setting was mainly engendered by the government's policies six decades ago. In the 1950s, Kuwait was set on a radical transformation path from a primitive mercantile trading port town into a modern socialist welfare state made possible by newfound oil wealth. The existing urban fabric was almost completely razed and a new central business and civic district was erected in its place. It was done sporadically and left many abandoned plots behind. Residents of demolished dwellings were relocated into automobile-oriented housing suburbs outside the new downtown and served by an array of welfare services. Urban development for the most part did not take place except through the government, and by the government in the case of housing its citizens, which was produced at a very slow rate. To put things in perspective, the current backlog of housing applicants has reached 111,000, whereas the country has built about 140,000 housing plots since the 1950s. This means that a "second Kuwait" will be needed in the near future.

Within a public policy context, this project will be divided into two main parts: study of the crisis (background and analysis) and four policy options to reduce the applicant backlog. The four options will explore: first, the status quo; second, involving the private sector with regulation and oversight by the government while keeping current development policies (automobile-dependent suburbs); third, involving the private sector—again, with regulation and oversight—but with radical changes in the current urban form to make the built environment more integrative of various uses and become less dependent on the consumption of oil; and finally, using a policy of leased housing welfare, as opposed to ownership. The final chapter will vie for the third option since it will make the market more affordable while providing the framework for diversifying the economy by encouraging an emerging class of entrepreneurs coupled and also reducing dependence on oil consumption.

ERIC PETERSON

Planning for Capital: The Urban Development Corporation and Urban Crisis in New York

This thesis examines the history of the New York State Urban Development Corporation (UDC), a public authority founded in 1968. The UDC was one of the most important experiments to reform postwar urban renewal amidst the 1960s "urban crisis" and built over 30,000 units of subsidized housing throughout the state in just eight years. While led by urban renewal veterans like Ed Logue, the UDC departed from past modernist housing efforts by eschewing large-scale clearance in favor of experimentation with new design types created by vanguard architects and and by working directly with community groups. The UDC experimented with the creation of mixed-race and mixed-income 'new towns' and made generous use of new federal programs intended to bridge the vast inequalities created by suburbanization and urban disinvestment. The corporation's planners undertook a highly ambitious housing agenda even as they were stymied by escalating unrest in some of the most impoverished neighborhoods in New York City and State.

For New York Governor Nelson Rockefeller, one of the principal champions of the UDC, the organization was a key part of his efforts to create a more socially conscious capitalism and sought to balance capitalist growth and inequality through the "politics of building." The thesis explores how, as an attempt to resolve the contradictions of a brand of liberalism that by the late 60s was wearing its limits, Rockefeller turned to private financial markets, experimenting with new financial mechanisms. These experiments, coupled with the decline of federal housing subsidies, ultimately subjected the UDC's ambitious housing agenda to the volatilities of private credit markets. In 1975 the UDC nearly declared bankruptcy and contributed to New York City's own bankruptcy. Both grew reliant on heavy private borrowing from many of the same banks and financial underwriters. After defaulting on its debt obligations, the UDC was retooled to become a powerful economic development agency working to help the private sector in the creation of commercial real estate.

Study of the UDC pushes back against drastic claims of the emergence of neoliberalism in New York during 1970s. Transformation of Keynesian institutions of urban planning must take broader account of the contradictions of those institutions, especially as they privileged the use of financial capital and the interests of the city's banks over those of the low-income communities policymakers often declared themselves to be working in the name of. I argue that the turn to revenue-dependent financial mechanisms such as mortgages and municipal bond markets played a crucial if unexamined role in subverting ongoing attempts throughout the postwar era to undertake comprehensive planning in creation of an integrated metropolis. The UDC transformed from a "catalytic" agency working towards social integration of New York State's communities to a single entity restricted to minimizing public expenditure in the service of economic development. This shift illustrates many of the institutional factors that have helped to create the metropolitan landscapes marked by infrastructural and social inequalities that we live in today.

ANDREW RUFF

Architecture of the Unknown

The unknown is a spatial construct. The cartographic term *terra incognita*, "unknown territory" or "unknown land," describes spaces which lie beyond the extents of the known world. These spaces are both physical and imagined; though they are represented in cartography and literature, they are ultimately speculative fabrications at the edges of the known world. In this thesis, I explore *terra incognita* as a philosophical construct intimately bound to the production of space.

Unexplored, uninhabited, and undocumented, the unknown persists at the periphery of the map. In medieval and Renaissance cartography, mapmakers often grafted symbols and mythical creatures into the peripheral spaces of the map, in those regions just beyond the reaches of sovereign control. This practice created a paradox between the objective geographic survey and the interpretation of space through symbolic imagery; a paradox which was most articulated within *terra incognita*, the dynamic, uninhabited lands dwelling on the tenuous horizon of the known universe. Here, the symbol served as a projection of man's desire to occupy the unknown, operating as a mediator between the impossibility of the infinite and the tactility of the immediate.

Yet the unknown is not simply geographical space awaiting exploration. The unknown exists at the scale of the microcosm and the macrocosm, it pervades our being and inflects our perception of the world. All human enterprise whether in art, science, religion, philosophy, or architecture, thrives because of the desire to know, understand, and give shape to this infinite expanse. As a consequence, human history can be understood as a trajectory marked by a ceaseless expansion of the known world into *terra incognita*. To encounter the unknown requires specific strategies, tactics, and armatures: spatial practices of discovery, speculation, projection, and creation. These discrete spatial operations ultimately operate as structural mediations between the known and the unknown and create, what I consider, the architecture of the unknown.

By framing the exploration of the unknown within the practice of architecture, I hope to inscribe a certain scale and tactility to the spatial instruments which mediate between the divergent scales and manifestations of *terra incognita*. The unknown takes many forms: the frontier, the wilderness, the imaginary, and the infinite, each of which has a parallel binary in the interior, the city, the real, and the finite. These latter, more grounded corollaries constitute the familiar terrain of architectural practice. In the construction of buildings, landscapes, and cities, architects operate in a constant negotiation between the substantive and the speculative, between the tactile and the imaginary. Sets of possible binaries begin to frame the fundamental project of architecture: to create something from which there was nothing through the accumulation of form, image, and space. Not unlike cartographers who illustrate maps of unseen lands, architects manipulate the realities of space and materials in a never ceasing project of constructing the world: however, as an architect, the endless cycle of producing space without critical introspection not only devalues the practice of architecture, but neglects to consider the relationship between architecture and broader environmental conditions. Architectural practice disengaged with the possibilities of the world produces spaces which lack significance and dynamism. Spaces which only engage the known are stagnant, insular, and sterile, incapable of impacting the territories and landscapes just beyond its delineated borders. In this thesis, I hope to uncover moments of friction between the known and the unknown which generate new implications and possibilities for spatial practice.

Contemporary Architectural Discourse Colloquium
Minor Architecture: Destabilizing Major Narratives

Program Director
Eeva-Liisa Pelkonen {ELP}

M.E.D Student Organizers
Benyameen Ghareeb, Eric Peterson, Eric Wycoff Rogers, Andrew Ruff, Brent Sturlaugson

Organized by second-year M.E.D. students in collaboration with the director of the M.E.D. program, this colloquium explored the concept of minor architecture and sought to destabilize major narratives. While many discourses and practices strive to assert the autonomy of architecture in its image or form-making powers, a minor architecture embraces the manifold conditions—ranging from political and economic factors to cultural imaginaries—that constitute the contemporary built environment. Through lectures and conversations with theorists, historians, and architects, we searched among the detritus of everyday urban space often neglected by contemporary architectural curricula seeking paths and opportunities ripe for speculation or intervention. This year's colloquium explored a range of invisible, even subversive, conditions that affect the role of architecture in the built environment. We hope that these explorations will inform emergent methods for alternative, disruptive practices—or minor architectures. Contributors to the conversation included David Gouverneur, Bill Rankin, Craig Buckley, Andrew Herscher, Felicity Scott, Quilian Riano, Laura Barraclough, Meredith TenHoor, Cindi Katz, and Todd Reisz.

VITTORIO LOVATO & EUGENE TAN
Guide to Minor Economies
In his *Unreal Estate Guide to Detroit*, Andrew Herscher posed the question: What can we learn from Detroit? The city is clearly home to a complex and visible urban situation. With over 200,000 vacant or abandoned properties scattered throughout the city, Detroit remains in a situation wedged between future dissolution and past economic solvency. Detroit's problems of valuation seem insurmountable given the vastness of its economic decay and its dependency on extreme economic change for its future salvation. Labor is exchanged for a new form of capital; it is a capital not based on monetary gain or profiteering but ethical responsibility, cooperation and community. They contribute to the capitalist structures but exist adjacent to its major economy. Events and collective engagement establish spatial meaning through occupation of urban territories. Detroit is one of the only cities where the small practices and the large practices have taken on exaggerated and highly visible forms. Detroit provides a fertile ground for the study of the minor and the major as they unfold, negotiate each other, and attempt to shape the city into their own image. Social-cultural anthropologist Arjun Appadurai speculates that economic value emerges from an exchange not of objects or commodities, but of sacrifices. Giving up one object for another during the process of economic exchange gives the exchange value onto itself. In many cases in Detroit, these alternative practices sacrifice their labor to meet basic needs. What makes them distinct from typical economic forms is that these sacrifices are not for private gains or unproductive activities, but the transition toward a spatial commons for the benefit of the collective community. This disassociation of material gains suggests that these practices trade on the development of knowledge and the immaterial formation of the social. The writings of Julie Graham and Katherine Gibson speculate on these immaterial labor practices. Their goal is to highlight these minor practices by devoting academic attention as objects of study and investigation. In this sense, making them visible, political objects uses knowledge in a performative capacity to generate economic change. Therefore, Detroit is uniquely positioned to make these hidden events and alternative economies visible by virtue of their quantity and capacity to attract attention within the community and leverage the urban landscape. The question becomes, is this level of unprecedented visibility tantamount to building new spatial values within the urban landscape—an urban landscape in which the conflict between the major ambitions of the capital elite and the neighborhood initiative are capable of working together? Perhaps time will tell.

SOFIA SINGLER
A Subversive Syllabus
Architecture aims to serve everyone, yet its pedagogy is restricted to a select audience. Education that incorpates minor architecture disrupts this constraint. In order for architecture to reach its full potential as a vigorous discipline that strives to create places and spaces that frame human life in all its complexity, the field's educational framework must be exposed to a wider audience. An education in minor architecture expands and extends formal architectural education from a strictly tertiary target group to a much younger audience. "Minor" in both a literal and metaphysical sense, it dismantles the hierarchical and exclusive character of contemporary architectural education and strives to strengthen the discipline's role in society by making it more accessible and understandable to all. The recognition of architecture created by non-architects is increasingly salient, and crediting individuals and teams with no formal architectural education for the authorship of works of architecture is no longer unheard of. Understanding and appreciating minor architecture created by people who lack the formal qualifications of an architect, specified by professional organizations or licensing bodies, contributes to a more holistic and diverse conception of architectural design and practice. A wealth of informal architectural education exists; many that complement, enriche, expand, challenge, question, and even deny the canon of architectural education as we know it. A particularly powerful strand of such informal training is minor in the most literal sense: architectural education for children and youth.

DOCTORAL STUDIES

Director of Doctoral Studies
Alan Plattus {**AP**}

The five-year doctoral program prepares candidates for careers in university teaching, cultural advocacy and administration, museum curatorship, and publishing. It aims chiefly, however, to educate teachers capable of effectively instructing future architects in the history of their own field and its manifold connections with the culture at large.

The program forges a unique combination of professional knowledge with a historical and analytical grasp of key phases in the history of architecture, especially those that have a demonstrable share in the field's current state and the critical issues it faces. The program secures sound training in historical study and historiography, imparting technical knowledge and awareness of intellectual trends that inform the reception and role of architecture around the world. The history of science and technology {as well as its reception in popular culture and the arts}, the history of media, and an understanding of architectural practice are as important as the fine arts and literature.

Entering students with sound professional preparation engage in a concerted course of study that leads directly to dissertation research and a doctoral degree. The student's field of interest is defined by the end of the second year, at which time the director of doctoral studies assigns the student an adviser, who may or may not be from the School of Architecture. At the end of the second year and after the student has taken the three oral examinations, the director of doctoral studies, in consultation with the student's adviser, appoints a dissertation committee for the student. The dissertation committee guides and monitors the student's progress in writing the dissertation and evaluates the dissertation upon completion.

By the end of their second year, doctoral students normally complete all course and language requirements. Oral examinations are taken on topics relevant to the student's doctoral research. Examiners question the candidate in the presence of the director of doctoral studies and the thesis adviser.

During the third year, candidates present and defend a preliminary proposal for a dissertation topic, consisting of a topic statement, detailed program of research, and an annotated bibliography. By the end of the third year, students begin dissertation research and writing, submitting drafts of the dissertation chapters as they are completed.

◊ 2. Mario Bettini, acoustical diagram of an elliptical theater {1642}. The Baroque strategy of focusing sonic "rays" was an important precursor to the modern theory of reverberation.

Working Titles

❶ Surry Schlabs, 4th Year Ph.D. Candidate
Slouching Towards Architecture: John Dewey and the Limits of Modern Art

❷ Anna Bokov, 4th Year Ph.D. Candidate
Teaching Architecture to the Masses: VKhUTEMAS in the 1920s

❸ Tim Altenhof, 4th Year Ph.D. Candidate
Inside/Out: Blurred Boundaries and the Constant Breath of Modern Architecture

❹ Ioanna Angelidou, 4th Year Ph.D. Candidate
Savage Machines and Urban Condensers: Type, History, and Anti-technology in the Design Theories of Kazuo Shinohara and Oswald Mathias Ungers {1955–1985}

KYLE DUGDALE
Dissertation Director: Karsten Harries

Architecture After the Death of God: Urie Birnbaum's "Der Kaiser Und Der Architekt"

Early in 1924 a small Viennese publishing house began printing copies of a lavishly illustrated fable, Uriel Birnbaum's *Der Kaiser und der Architekt*. Set in Peter Behrens's severe Antiqua typeface and accompanied by plates rendered in an ink wash technique of astonishing lucidity, it is ostensibly the story of an emperor who is haunted by the dream of a wonderful but evanescent heavenly city, and who turns in perplexity to his architect. The architect's prodigious city-building efforts culminate in the construction of a tower, a thing of immensity and beauty, an enduring monument to the architectural project. It is the fate of this tower that shapes the story's conclusion.

It is clear that Birnbaum's text can be read on a number of levels—historical, political, philosophical and theological. But it is articulated, first of all, in a vocabulary that is explicitly architectural. Conceived in the years immediately after World War I, Birnbaum's cities bear close comparison to the fabrications of Expressionism, which provide a primary point of reference. But his argument also exposes architecture to broader intellectual claims, suggesting that the architect must grapple with problems far beyond the limits of the building site. And if architectural introspection has often been precipitated by provocations external to the discipline, Birnbaum's narrative is not alone in adopting the central motif of the Tower of Babel, understood as an archetype of the architectural project.

The book fell into oblivion almost immediately, and has left little trace in architectural consciousness. Speculations as to the reasons for this forgetfulness yield several suggestions: the book's publication—costly, delayed and incomplete—contributed to the failure, that same year, of its publishing house; its appearance coincided with the fading of an already moribund Expressionism, to which it seemed inextricably tied; its author found himself increasingly out of step with contemporary enthusiasms, despite having tasted, not long before, of the fruits of critical acclaim; and his opportunities for exposure soon suffered the effects of growing anti-Semitism before being extinguished altogether under the rise of Nazi power. The few assessments that do exist have tended to consider Birnbaum's work either in retrospective relationship to the Expressionist tendencies of which it offers such a clear critique, or as the predictable product of a conservative mind, a retrogressive artefact that is therefore readily swept away by the currents of modernity. Both approaches place Birnbaum's text at a dead end that leaves little room for further exploration.

This dissertation studies it instead as an articulation of preoccupations that, ninety years later, have not yet been dismissed from among contemporary anxieties. Approaching Babel as a recurring paradigm in the architectural narratives of modernity, and devoting particular attention to its extraordinary resurgence during the early decades of the twentieth century, it tests the hypothesis that the Tower can stand as a marker of the predicament of the architect who must build in a self-consciously modern, godless world. {01}

Awarded Yale University's Theron Rockwell Field Prize, 2015

JOSEPH CLARKE
Dissertation Director: Kurt W. Forster

The Architectural Discourse of Reverberation, 1750–1900

The auditory environment occupies a curious status in architectural discourse. Designers have professed concern for acoustics since antiquity. Sound is uniquely able to transform the emotional character of an environment, and its spatial management can have profound political consequences, determining whose voices are heard and by whom. Sometimes, sound has been invoked as an ideal model for architecture itself, a figure for the immersiveness and dynamism to which the discipline can only aspire. Yet sound has also proven remarkably resistant to critical conceptualization. Fleeting, intangible, and unseen, acoustical effects have rarely been understood as more than secondary or supplementary factors in a building's design.

My dissertation reconstructs an architectural discourse of sound, marking off a field of key concepts, historical references, and political distinctions within which contemporary acoustical design choices can become meaningful. It follows a specific genealogy of 18th- and 19th-century European architects who sought to redesign the auditory environment of modern theaters. At the center of their investigations was a familiar yet elusive effect of sound in space. Just before a sound dies away, it can seem to hang in the air briefly as a kind of diffuse liveness. This phenomenon of reverberation occurs when energy waves reflect rapidly off the surrounding surfaces and reach the ear at intervals too short for them to be recognized as discrete echoes. Reverberation seems to be a uniquely modern concern, not recognized as a distinct architectural effect before the late 18th century.

During the Enlightenment, in response to the auditory demands of an ascendant bourgeois public, two architects in particular worked to understand the enigmatic phenomenon of "resounding" in large buildings: Pierre Patte, who sought to rationalize sound in orthographic drawings, and Claude-Nicolas Ledoux, who contended that it was fundamentally other to visible phenomena. It was the German architect Carl Ferdinand Langhans who finally proposed a model of reverberation as a distinct architectural effect, produced through the reflection and diffusion of sound. His model of reverberation influenced Richard Wagner's music-dramas and the highly reverberant *Festspielhaus* built for their presentation at Bayreuth in 1876. Wagner's artistic enterprise necessitated a new level of technical sophistication in performance hall sound, fueling demands for an applied science of acoustical engineering, even as his influential aesthetic ideas provoked aesthetic theorists to posit "reverberant" conceptions of architectural space. This divergence of technical and cultural ideas of reverberation led eventually to its dropping out of architectural discourse, to be taken up instead by scientifically-trained engineers.

By tracing the 150 year arc of reverberation, the dissertation shows it to have been a hotly contested issue whose elaboration cut across the grain of architectural modernity itself, putting pressure on disciplinary techniques of orthographic representation, principles of empirical scientific investigation, models of subjective experience, and assumptions about architecture's social purpose. This account sheds light on the structure of 18th- and 19th-century knowledge about the physical environment within and beyond the conventional limits of architectural thought, revealing the unrecognized contributions of acoustics to the spatial ideas and auratic pretensions of modern architecture. {02}

◊ 1. The front cover of Uriel Birnbaum, *Der Kaiser und der Architekt: Ein Märchen in Fünfzig Bildern* {Leipzig and Vienna: Thyrsos Verlag, 1924}

Independent Study
Fall & Spring

DIONYSUS CHO, ANNE MA
Advisor: Mark Foster Gage

Artifice
Taking advantage of the control afforded by the gaming engine in manipulating the user or environment, ARTIFICE proposes a multi-directional gravity space; the response is one that must treat all surfaces as habitable, defined only by the gamer's intentions. Whether in the design of a room or a puzzle, the challenge provided by the constant shifting of the concept of up creates a new experience in the interaction with the environment. This is greatly enhanced by the VR capabilities of the Oculus Rift, which tosses the user in a tumultuous world rather than viewing events cinematically. ARTIFICE is an experimental immersive experience developed as an "eccentric" game utilizing the Oculus Rift and powered by Unreal Engine/Blueprints. {01–2}

AMIR KARIMPOUR
Advisor: Kevin Rotheroe

Ornamental Tectonics
Mass customization and production have compromised two key components in contemporary design: craft and innovation. Contemporary tools allow us to make design decisions so quickly that little time is left for critical decision making. Parallel to this, as tools become increasingly advanced, designers become more reluctant to exploit them.

Islamic ornament was used as a starting point in a semester-long investigation, specifically because Islamic ornamentation incorporates both strict geometrical patterns and free-form arabesque calligraphy. The project hinged on the development of an analog-to-digital process: detail images were created, then manipulated digitally to become digital models which were subsequently fabricated. This process was repeated multiple times with various materials and methods and in a variety of sequences. This iterative process produced a taxonomy that showed a range of glitches in the fabrication process and variety of hiccups in the computational software used to generate images and forms. Instead of rectifying these idiosyncrasies, they were used as moments of inquiry that allowed for new iterations. The design of the both process and objects were a feedback loop that allowing for greater control over craft. {03–4}

MEGHAN LEWIS
Advisor: Dolores Hayden

The Architecture of Selective Memory
Ruins play a crucial role in the development of cultural identity and narrative. When ruins are preserved, they act as architectural historical records. When ruins are destroyed, the cultural diversity and historical narratives they record are destroyed alongside them. While the aesthetic appreciation of American ruins is visible in the profusion of websites, publications, and exhibitions dedicated to photographing Detroit and other cities, the social and spatial implications of the destruction or preservation of these ruins requires further exploration.

Though the history of settlement in contemporary America extends as far back as that of other nations, there has been relatively little study of the ruins resulting from the decline of its ancient settlements. The ruins of early indigenous populations of the United States, such as those found at Mesa Verde or Cahokia, are few in number when compared to the vast number of ruins found in other countries. Through case studies in Turkey, Greece, Italy, Cambodia, and America, my independent study aims to put American ruins in a larger global context with a longer history of appreciation and preservation. {05}

STANLEY CHO
Advisor: Dolores Hayden

The Wicked Glazier [1]
On February 15th 1929, Walter Benjamin wrote a letter to Sigfried Giedion expressing deep admiration and excitement for Giedion's book *Bauen in Frankreich*. In this letter, Benjamin writes that after a few passages he decided not to continue with the reading until he could get more in touch with his own related investigations—presumably on the subject of new architecture. However, when Benjamin was ready to return to Giedion's book, he began reading it backwards.[2] It is not that Benjamin literally read *Bauen in Frankreich* from back to front like a Japanese novel; but what is implied is that he read it for his "own transformative extensions and rewritings."[3] Benjamin's own investigations through Giedion hoped to reify modernity via architecture. However, there is a discrepancy between the writings by Benjamin about the exhilarating potential of the 19th century poet and the architectures of iron, glass, and concrete—of new technologies. Though both investigations are equally brilliant, one can simply observe the present age and comprehend that architecture has not led us into a modern world as Benjamin imagined, and has perhaps instead contributed to an unprecedented era of Bourgeois living. This essay seeks to re-trace the contexts of the 19th century, where Marcel Proust writes about Charles Baudelaire, to revisit them in the company of Benjamin, who writes about both Proust and Baudelaire, and to depart with him at the modernist turn of the century. It is in the context of these texts and the interiors circumscribed by Honoré de Balzac that texts about Surrealism, Expressionism, Dadaism, Functionalism, and Cubism, texts which followed long after, will be looked at with a kind of telescopic lens—as a kind of retroactive discourse—from a room of the old world, where despair and optimism were fiercely latent in the mundane.

[1] The title of this essay comes from the title of a poem, "Le Mauvais Vitrier," from a collection of prose poems by Charles Baudelaire entitled Le Spleen de Paris {1969}.

[2] Detlef Mertins, "Modernity Unbound," 88.

[3] Ibid., 97.

TYLER PERTMAN
Advisor: Mark Foster Gage

Qualities over Quantities, Mind over Matters
Aesthetics has existed as a key part of architectural discourse since Roman times. It has been the subject of an enormous amount of consideration and debate. The idea of beauty in the theory of architecture arrives as early as Vitruvius' *Ten Books on Architecture*. Vitruvius believed in *venustas*—beauty or delight—along with *firmitas*—strength or firmness —and *utilitas*—functionality or commodity. Since that time, beauty and, to a greater degree, aesthetics have always been a central part of architectural theory, yet somehow as a product of modernization, scientific reason, and criticality, contemporary architectural theory has failed to embrace aesthetics in the same way as Vitruvius all in favor of *utilitas*. In abandoning *venustas*, current architectural thought has been increasingly plagued with quantitative measures of success, rather than qualitative metrics. Architecture too often serves a third party ideal—whether it is capital efficiencies, environmental efficiencies, or social efficiencies. Not that these goals are irrelevant or useless, but they have become superfluous to Architecture. When prioritized above Architecture itself, these agendas are damaging to the discipline and its discourse. Object-oriented ontology {OOO}, a nascent branch of Speculative Realism, is an ontology that places objects and their qualities at its center. Its methods offer an opportunity to reframe the current quantitative approach to architecture in favor of a qualitative approach. The time has come for the discussion in architecture to return to something relevant to the discipline itself—something the discipline can have a command over. The matter at hand is that of qualities. The further architecture spirals towards its loss of agency, the worse its prospects become, not only for the profession itself, but for all the possible good that architects can offer. Our inability or hesitation to discuss the aesthetic realm, to talk about delight and beauty, and to use language that describes the deeper qualities of objects could be the proverbial nail in the coffin. Object-oriented ontology is bracing. It is intellectual, and it has a spirit of curiosity and language that opens architecture to a new way of talking and thinking. It liberates the imagination from burdens of quantitative measurements and the detriments of undermining and overmining. Object-oriented ontology prioritizes the mind over less relevant matters. Through theories posited by OOO, Architecture will regain its integrity and perhaps reclaim its status as the mother art.

JONATHAN SUN
Advisor: Alan Plattus

What Are We Preserving When We Preserve Urban Public Space?
Urban public spaces are an important part of the urban environment and support the physical, social and mental health of an entire region. Surely while the primary goal of preservation is to preserve sites of historical significance, the greatest urban benefit of preserving spaces is that it also maintains the presence of these spaces in cities. Without preservation, public space is at risk. The study examines systems of preservation at municipal, national and international levels; these are the New York City Landmarks Preservation Committee, the US National Historic Landmarks Program, and the UNESCO World Heritage Center, respectively. In order to understand how to preserve urban public spaces, one must first understand the organizations of preservation and the implicit and explicit systems they use to evaluate significance. Without understanding how and why these spaces are valued by preservation organizations, we risk losing these ever-important players in our cities. {06}

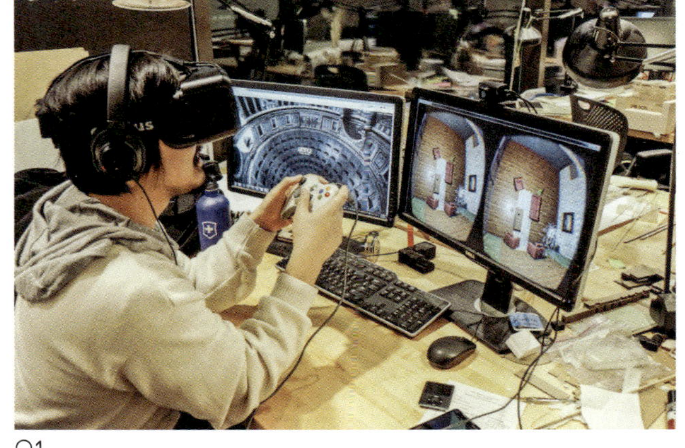

01

02

03

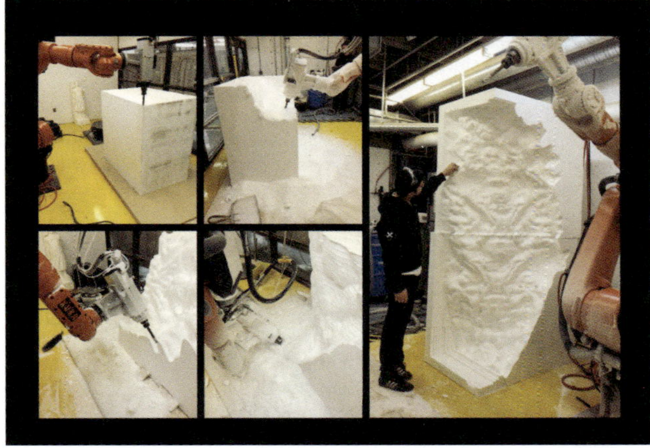

04

05

06

Yale Urban Design Workshop 2014-2015

Director
Alan J. Plattus

Project Manager
Andrei Harwell

Faculty Associates
Alex Felson, Edward Mitchell, Douglas Rae

Fellows 2014–2015
Matthew Rauch, Jack Wolf

Founded in 1992, by Alan Plattus, then Associate Dean and Professor at the Yale School of Architecture, the Yale Urban Design Workshop {YUDW} is a community design center based at the School of Architecture. Since its founding, the YUDW has worked with communities across the state of Connecticut, providing planning and design assistance on projects ranging from comprehensive plans, economic development strategies and community visions to the design of public spaces, streetscapes and individual community facilities. Clients include small towns, city neighborhoods, planning departments, Chambers of Commerce, community development corporations, citizen groups, and private developers. After nearly a decade in a storefront on Chapel Street, the YUDW relocated in the summer of 2014 to a second floor office on the corner of Chapel and Howe Street, in New Haven's Dwight neighborhood, two blocks from the School of Architecture.

In all its work, the YUDW is committed to an inclusive, community-based process, grounded in broad citizen participation and a vision of the design process as a tool for community organizing, empowerment, and capacity-building. A typical YUDW project may include design charrettes, focus groups, and town meetings, as well as more conventional means of program and project development. These projects are staffed mainly by current graduate professional students at the Yale School of Architecture supervised by faculty of the School, but often also include Yale College undergraduates, recent graduates of the School as full-time staff, faculty and students from Yale's other professional schools {including the Law School, the School of Forestry and Environmental Science, the School of Management, the School of Public Health and the School of Art}, as well as outside consultants and other local professionals.

Recent and current projects include downtown and neighborhood plans for the Connecticut towns of West Haven, Woodbridge and Bridgeport, and a redevelopment plan for the former site of the town hall in North Branford, CT. In 2014, the YUDW completed a comprehensive master-plan for Fishers Island, New York, which addresses the stabilization of the year-round population of the Island. A new plan to establish a Thames River Heritage Park between Groton and New London, Connecticut was completed in spring 2015, including plans for a water taxi system and the design of a comprehensive identity and signage package. Following on the success of a pilot water taxi project in the region last September, the project is now moving towards implementation. In the summer of 2015, the YUDW will begin work on a major coastal resiliency plan for Bridgeport, CT, funded by the U.S. Department of Housing and Urban Development through the State of Connecticut. {□1–4}

□1

□2

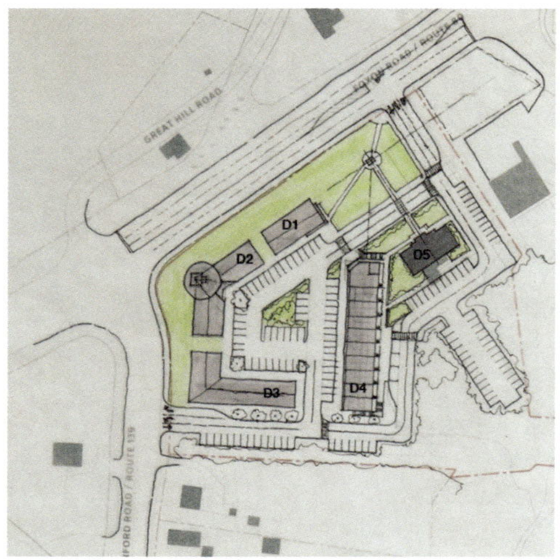

□3

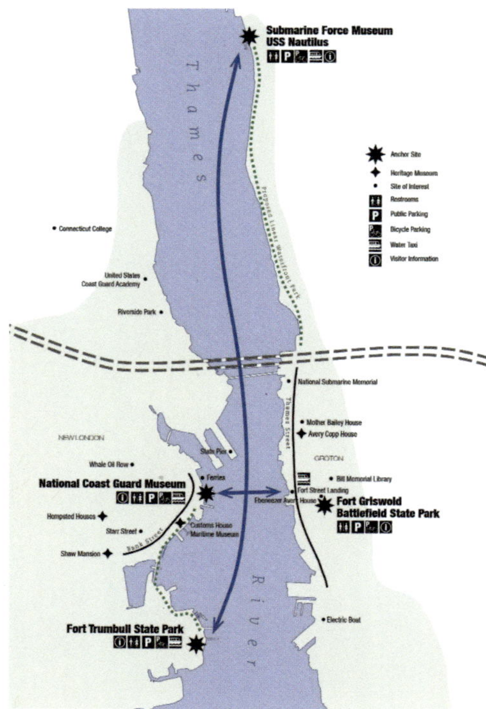

□4

Archaeology of the Digital Ⅱ:
Media and Machines

Curated by Greg Lynn, "Media and Machines" marks the second phase of the Canadian Centre for Architecture's research project initiated with the exhibition "Archaeology of the Digital", which was displayed in our gallery during Spring of 2014. Featuring work by Asymptote, Karl Chu, Bernard Cache, dECOi Architects, ONL, and NOX, the new exhibition concentrates on architecture's engagement with digital technologies from the 1990s to the early 2000s. The six projects presented a range: from the design of buildings to the design of interactive media, interactive robotic mechanisms, and generative algorithms. The installation at Yale is sponsored in part by Elise Jaffe + Jeffrey Brown.

Curator: Greg Lynn
Graphic Design: Johnathan Hares

Yale School of Architecture
Publications 2014-2015

Cultural Cues
Joe Day, Tom Wiscombe, Adib Cure
& Carie Penabad

Cutural Cues is the sixth book featuring the work
of the Louis I. Kahn Visiting Assistant Professor-
ship, which brings young innovators in architectural
design to the Yale School of Architecture. This book
includes the studio research and projects of Joe
Day of Deegan Day Design in "NOWplex" a cinema
in L.A.; Tom Wiscombe of Tom Wiscombe Architecture in "The Broad Redux," for a new interpretation
of the Broad Museum in L.A.; and Adib Cure & Carie
Penabad of Cure Penabade in the studio "Havana:
Housing in the Historic Center." The studios explore
contemporary interpretations of the implications of
cinema, the museum, and housing, taking cues from
their complex cultural and urban contexts. Along
with student work, interviews with the architects
about the work of their professional offices and
essays framing the themes of the work are combined with insight into the pedagogical approach
of these practitioner-educators. Edited by Nina
Rappaport and Jeffrey M. Pollack ('14) the book is
designed by MGMT.Design.

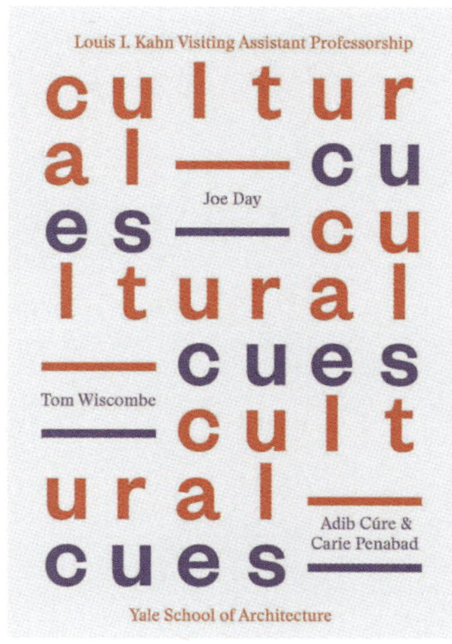

Social Infrastructure: New York
Douglas Durst and Bjarke Ingels

Social Infrastructure: New York is one of a series
that documents the Edward P. Bass Distinguished
Fellowship at the Yale School of Architecture. This
book includes the studio led by Douglas Durst of the
Durst Organization, a leading New York firm known
for spearheading sustainable high-rise developments, architects Bjarke Ingels and Thomas Christ-
offersen of BIG, and Yale faculty member Andrew
Benner. The studio explored potential synergies
between public and private programs in the design
of inhabited bridges crossing major waterways in
New York City. The featured projects here demonstrate a diverse range of approaches for combining
residential, cultural, and commercial activities on
complex and dense infrastructural sites in imaginative and productive ways. The book includes interviews with the professors, an essay by Bjarke Ingels,
and the studio projects. Edited by James Andrachuk
('13), Nina Rappaport, and Andrew Benner ('06) the
book is designed by MGMT. Design.

Exhibiting Architecture: A Paradox?

Exhibiting Architecture: A Paradox? brings
together a collection of essays that are an out-
growth of the eponymous symposium at the school
in Fall 2013. The forum was convened by associate professor Eeva-Liisa Pelkonen (M.E.D. '94),
David Andrew Tasman (M.Arch '13) and curator
Carson Chan. The ambition of exhibiting architecture entails paradoxes: how to exhibit something as
large and complex as a building or a city, and how to
communicate something as elusive as an architectural experience that unfolds in space and time. To
be sure, architecture poses a challenge to exhibition
as a medium. What is it we exhibit when we exhibit
architecture: should we be satisfied with photographs of buildings and sites or should we aim to
display whole buildings or fragments and models of
them? These were among the questions the organizers posed to the group of architectural and art
historians, practicing architects, and curators who
were invited to participate and contribute essays to
the book. Their discussions address the exhibition
as a medium and challenge the preconceived idea of
what architecture is by examining a range of possibilities as to how architecture is made, experienced,
and discussed. The book was designed by Amy Kessler to guidelines by MGMT. Design.

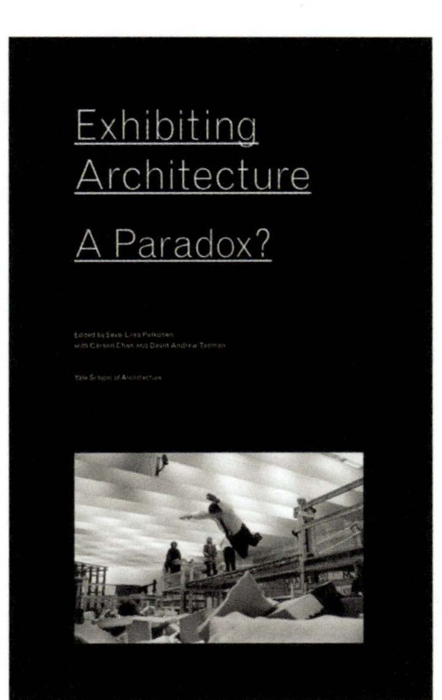

Spring

Factory Shop
Greg Lynn

<u>Critic</u>
Greg Lynn {**GL**}
William B. and Charlotte Shepherd Davenport
Visiting Professor

<u>Instructor</u>
Nathan Hume {**NH**}

<u>Jurors</u>
Michelle Addington {**MA**}, Brennan Buck {**BB**},
Hernan Diaz-Alonso {**HAD**}, Mark Foster Gage
{**MFG**}, Florencia Pita {**FP**}, Richard Schulman {**RS**}

In an effort to eliminate inventory, reduce the time
and expense of transportation, duty and tariffs, and
to get into closer contact with consumers a new
model of manufacturing and retailing has been
developing: the merger of the factory and the retail
brand shop. Until today, the architectural response
has been to adapt the museum type to this phenomenon; examples include Coop Himmelblau's
BMW Welt, UN Studio's Mercedes-Benz Museum,
the Stuttgart Porsche Museum and Audi Mobile
Museum Ingolstadt. These buildings tell the story
of the companies and their products through spatial promenades ending in shops, inventory and test
tracks adjacent to corporate headquarters. This
studio will begin with the type of the factory and
instead of exhibitions of corporate legacy it will
bring the dynamism of final assembly, testing, training and tuning to be experienced by visitors.

The studio had a chance to interact with the
senior leadership of the Piaggio Group and to visit
the Vespa Factory in Pontedera and Moto Guzzi
factory in Mandello for background and inspiration.
Students observed the integration of a test track
and vertical manufacturing at the Lingotto Fiat Factory in Turino as well as contemporary small production factories in the "Motor Valley" of Modena.

The studio spent some time becoming familiar
with contemporary fabrication and assembly processes. Industrial scale processes familiar to Yale
Architecture students at that of an architectural
model were examined at the scale of transportation
manufacturing, namely for their ability to transform
the assembly process and introduce it into showroom and retail environments. In the same way that
the gantry crane was introduced into the building
structure of the 19th and 20th century factory, so too
can the universal robotic arm, 3D printing head and
CNC mill be introduced into the factory store. The
integration of these machines into the structure of
the building and its experience by visitors was the
primary focus of the studio.

EMAU VEGA ✳

The "Small Urban Factory" rethinks the prevalent factory type in favor of a full-service station in the urban context. Customers, enthusiasts and the general public become part of the spectacle of the factory. The concept sees the factory not only as a place for the assembly of new motorbikes, but also as a place to sell, service, repair, customize, train, and entertain. The architecture becomes an important negotiation of these multiple programs. It is developed as a system that allows the interweaving of the two major programmatic functions: the factory and workers, as well as the service center and visitors.

The scheme takes the typically flat, continuous factory floor and thickens a few areas to create figural volumes of space within it. This inhabitable poché allows the service center and visitors to coexist with the factory and its employees. The visitor is allowed to experience the factory in an orchestrated manner without interfering with its daily operations. The factory floor also extends above the volumes, thereby relegating certain assembly line processes to a space between the faceted volumes. The result is a distinct spatial experience of compression and expansion. The project seeks not to reveal the entire assembly process to the visitor, but rather reframes the experience of catching glimpses of the process while moving in and out of the embedded volumes—a spectacle unto itself. As the visitors move from the outside in, the path is conceived as an extension of the road folding into the building and onto itself. The circulation path winds through the main hall and within the thickened volumes. {▲1–4}

"You know what the type is: it's a zoo—you go in though and see a certain thing, but there is this vast infrastructure behind the elephants that you'll never see." **Mark Foster Gage**

▲**FP:** Your project is about span. You don't have columns. I imagine the span to be the length of your building, and I am assuming for that span you'd need a certain width of the slab. That slab width is the concept of your project: it opens up to make these pockets. But the way these pockets are happening in your project now is a stylistic or mannerist one. ▲**MFG:** Columns wouldn't necessarily destroy the skin. The visitors are already getting a highly curated view. You can have them view where there are not columns. I appreciate that you have this big and open warehouse thing. We know that works as a historical reference to what a factory is. In that vastness, you manage to get an experience of intimacy and coziness with the visitor. ▲**HDA:** I kind of like that he's keeping all the feeling to the interior—it's not in the center, but I am thinking: "attack the entrance." All the energy is pulling to that moment, that space. It is certainly the clarity of the project: I walk in, I am in the showroom, surrounded by all those unique spaces; every time I go in, I am reminded. It's very clear idea. ▲**MFG:** You know what the type is: it's a zoo—you go in though and see a certain thing, but there is this vast infrastructure behind the elephants that you'll never see. ▲**HDA:** This project embraces the factory aspect of it. Of course there's a sense of spectacle, but not everything has become a theme park. Because one of the cool things when you go to a factory is it's like walking into a secret society they allow you see things that most of people can't. The moment it becomes a pure spectacle, I start to be suspicious—this is not a real thing. So the idea that you can still keep that sense and quality of being in a factory—O.K., it's still curated, has some spectacle too, but it doesn't go overboard. Even though it looks like a little bit a museum, it doesn't feel like it has a museum strategy. ▲**MFG:** It maintains the sense of vastness. Most of the schemes have the viewer stationary, and the products moving. The visitor is coincident with the product. And you can even exaggerate it more, so you start out with parts, and when you're done with the experience, you'll be standing next to the same product made of those parts. There is a coming together and breaking away; the speed of the manufacturing and of the spectacle.

▲1

▲2

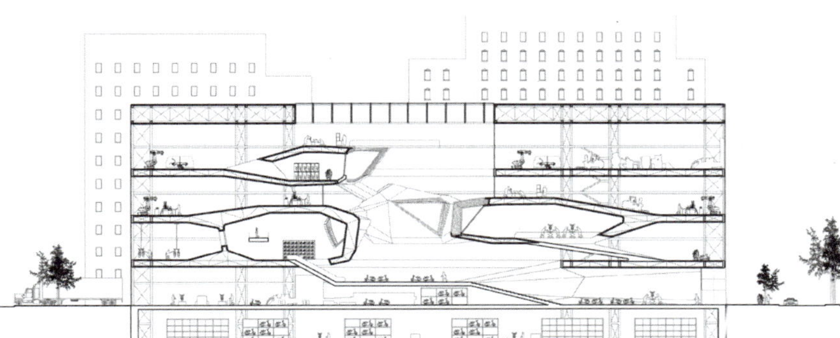

▲3

▲4

PERRY WEXELBERG

There is something inherently compelling about seeing parts become a whole during the manufacturing process. The culture of conspicuous consumption was created by the very process of observing and being in the shopping arcade or mall. The proposed project for a motor vehicle factory works under the notion that the new culture of conspicuous consumption arises from objectifying and demystifying the production process.

Motorcycles and scooters are social objects that inspire people to connect around a common passion. Motorbike enthusiasts have long congregated in informal spaces at a variety of scales, from public parking lots to the family garage. This new urban factory proposes to organize manufacturing functions, retail spaces, and maintenance facilities around a large central space so motorcycle and scooter fans can experience the manufacturing process while also providing a new type of informal space. The large central void in the factory acts as a contemporary arcade and makes a spectacle of the retail and production space. The canyon-like space is defined by sculpted walls and apertures that create a series of views. In addition to enlivening the main void, the views are arranged to allow a series of framed and layered peeks into the process. Motorcyclists visiting the building experience the factory by riding parallel to parts moving along the factory floor. The ground plane articulates where bikers, pedestrians and automated factory carts are meant to move as well as congregate. ▲ 5–8

"You're starting from assumptions about how people get together and maybe it would just be interesting to see how people park their bikes and where they put their barbeques" **Mark Foster Gage**

▲ **MFG**: It kind of feels like partying on a traffic island. I think the idea is so super compelling. It's a space that's volumetrically very generous, but in terms of plan not very generous. I wouldn't want to barbeque on the island. You barbeque on the traffic island because there is no nicer place to be. ▲ **MA**: Maybe this is a case where being very pragmatic would actually help you be more inventive. You can't possibly have visitors, autonomous vehicles, and people motoring around in the same space. So the question becomes: can you have the circulation simultaneous and contiguous without actually crossing paths and without being in jeopardy of touching? ▲ **FP**: You can advance the arcade. The arcade is flat. Sometimes you have landscaping, sometimes you have benches. So you brought the big idea of the arcade, but you didn't advance it to involve vehicular items. So how do you advance the arcade with that? For example on a lake, there is this huge project in Russia by Michael Maltzan. And it's a kind of low budget, it's like a quarter mile housing tower. It has a shopping arcade. And since there are so many dogs downtown and they don't want them walking on grass, every piece of grass is elevated. So you have the trees on top of those things. It has the environment, but not accessible green. All grass is elevated, and pedestrians walk around them. But it's really strange when you see six foot tall grass. So that is their solution to an urban problem and a social problem. There's so many ways urban furniture doesn't work, so how do you also address that? They make shopping malls look like living rooms. It's an issue of how you engage the privacy of the house, and give privacy to the public space. So as a problem it opens a whole area of research for you, but your project takes the first step. ▲ **MFG**: Did you look at Sturgis, the Harley convention? It's like 500,000 people or something, and the whole center strip of Sturgis becomes this continuous party gathering. You're starting from assumptions about how people get together and maybe it would just be interesting to see how people park their bikes and where they put their barbeques. In terms of some programmatic way to start designing that space. Because the space is generous, it just doesn't feel like it's programmed appropriately, or could accommodate the program that you're asking it to. ▲ **Perry Wexelberg**: I think partly why it manifested as a street is because a lot of those events like Sturgis are on a street. ▲ **MFG**: Right, but that's not where all the action happens. It goes all the way back to the bars and parking lots. I don't know, maybe that's your next studio. Sturgis studio. ▲ **GL**: The jury will be median-aged 75.

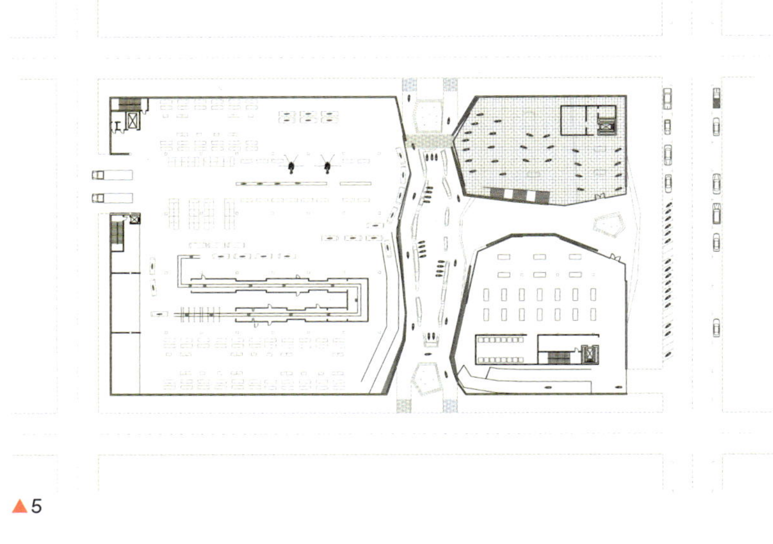

▲ 5

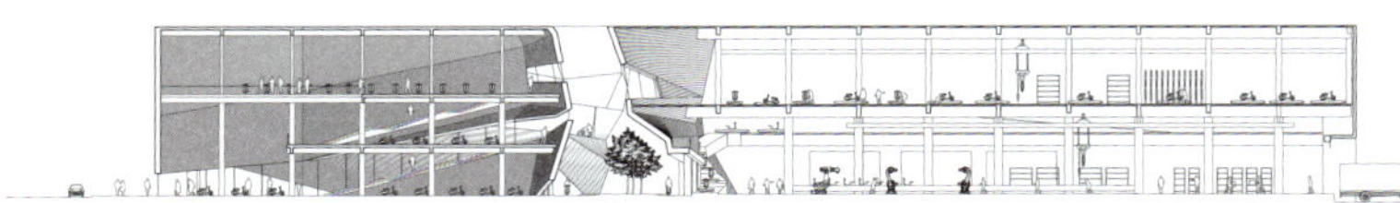

▲ 6

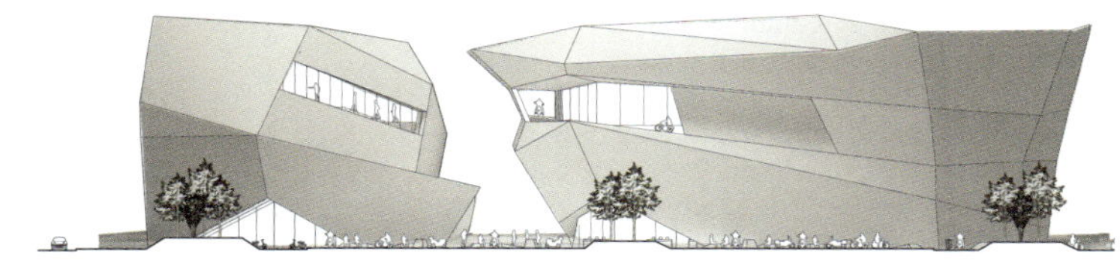

▲ 7

▲ 8

HUI ZHEN NG

Factory tours have often been criticized and associated with zoo visits, wherein companies capitalize on the spectacle of factory workers. This proposal is a response to the zoo-like dynamic of the factory tour; all workers and robots are hidden, save for occasional glimpses of products in motion as they travel along the assembly line. By focusing on the transitory moments of the assembly line, the project frames the factory experience as one of mystery and surprise. By offering only glimpses of inventory travelling to and from various work stations, the visitor anticipates the next moving object along the line—whether it be a small object like a wheel or fabricated system like a chassis. The inventory enters the visitor's view by gliding along the roof, travelling down to the wall and back into the ground. The visitor is engaged in a precarious moment and suspended in a figural space. Instead of a linear assembly line, the project reorganizes the production line at various angles, allowing the visitor's path to weave into the production line. The resulting spatial knot creates a moment of dynamism and intensity which contrasts with the orthogonal factory box. The moiré effect of the façade is activated by the moving inventory. This same flickering is perceived on the exterior through the building's perforated double-skin, a feature that additionally produces a subdued sense of movement along the street. The overall experience of the factory is further activated by the assembly line from the urban context while the element of surprise is enhanced as the visitor goes further into the building. The visitor walks into the building from the street and traverses the building in a loop, all the while experiencing a constant change in section. [▲9–12]

> "What you're engaged in is way more interesting than the damn little Vespa itself." **Michelle Addington**

▲**GL:** The idea is that you are on the ground, find yourself on a bridge and all these crazy things and cars are flying all around you. ▲**FP:** You see it only from between all of the knots, not from all the knots. You enter a knot and then you exit a knot. ▲**Hui Zhen Ng:** Yes, so it's about a very specific moment. You will never have an overall spectacle of the factory. ▲**RS:** Just the objects inside move. Your idea for this visual is what? Where did it come from? How did you decide to make it look like that? ▲**MFG:** Just say you're a genius. ▲**RS:** No, but it came from somewhere. You didn't just say— ▲**MFG:** God! Baby Jesus! ▲**RS:** No, but it's a legitimate question. ▲**GL:** What do you think? Is it photogenic? ▲**RS:** Extremely. It's beautiful. I was shot down for asking a very banal question. ▲**GL:** They were ruled surfaces, meaning they were all made out of lines. And you played around with different ways of articulating them. It's the sticks with the gaps that make the moiré patterns. ▲**RS:** I appreciate it, so I wanted to find out how your mind worked to come to that. I want to know your secrets. It's genius to be able to, if it's real, to photograph something like this. So many great possibilities, visual concepts of light, shape, shadow, and volume of space that would be a treat for a photographer. ▲**MFG:** One thing I always talk about on Hernan's reviews is *Alien*. The first *Alien* movie where you never see the alien makes it kind of creepier and more interesting. One aspect that unites these comparisons is that it doesn't just flat out show you people putting handle bars together. I think it's that glimpsing quality that you're using as a decorative moiré pattern, which is pretty interesting, but I do think that there is something about the withholding of some of the aspects of it that makes it not a didactic thing but an aesthetic thing that I really appreciate. I think it's a beautiful, pleasurable project. ▲**HDA:** It's much more curated and focused. In a way, I would argue some of the other projects, even with the animations, are much more cinematic quasi-documentaries, vignettes. This one for me is much more theatrical, much more of a stage. ▲**MFG:** For me it's just electrifying. ▲**MA:** The artifact itself, the thing supposedly you are there to see, is the one thing that you're not going to see. But you're not even curious to see that because what's there and what you're engaged in is way more interesting than the damn little Vespa itself.

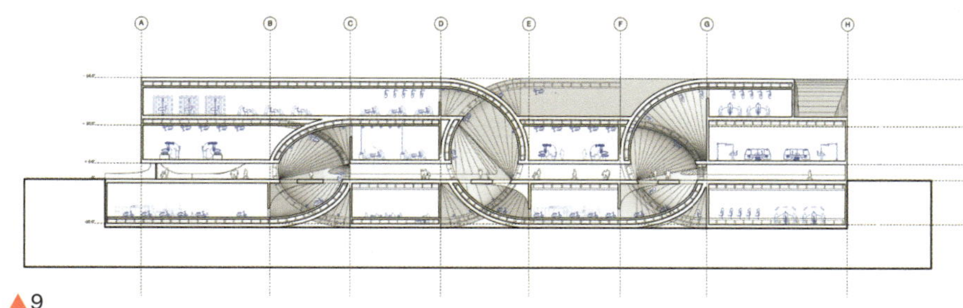

▲9

▲10

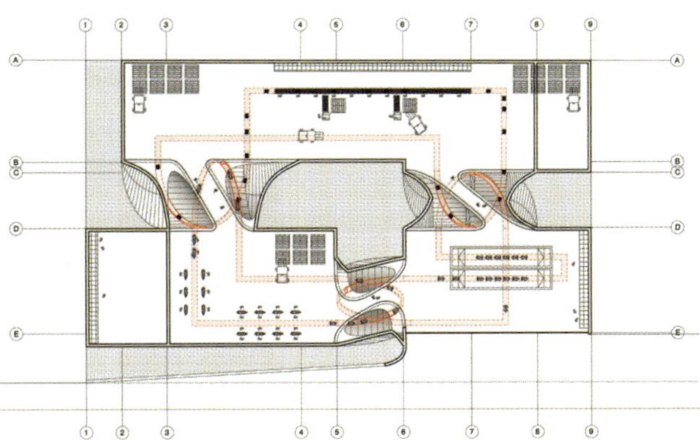

▲11

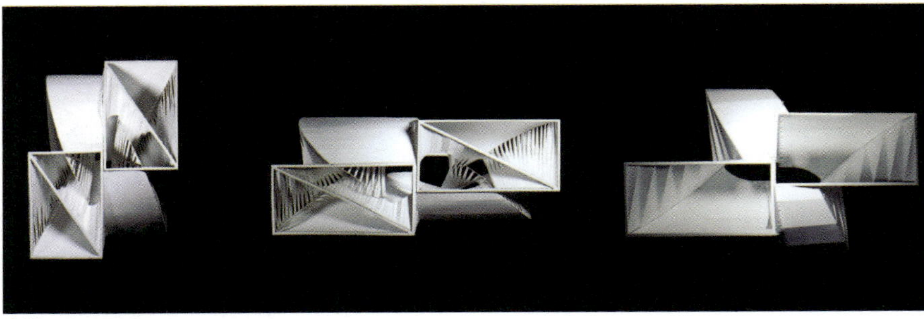

▲12

Chicago Studio
Thomas Beeby

Critics
Thomas Beeby {TB}
Bishop Visiting Professor

Jurors
Deborah Berke {DB}, Judy Di Maio {JD}, Kyle
Dugdale {KD}, Peter Gluck {PG}, Benet Haller
{BH}, Stephen Kieran {SK}, George Knight {GK},
Leon Krier {LK}, Aric Lasher {AL}, Jonathan Levi
{JL}, Barbara Littenberg {BL}, Robert A. M. Stern
{RAMS}

The studio explores the possibilities of single family infill housing in a major American city. Chicago has a long tradition of small wood-framed houses from the time of the founding of the city in the mid-19th century until the great fire of 1871. Rather than providing institutionalized collective housing, the city's response to the fire disaster was pre-cut minimal wooden shelters to house the thousands of homeless citizens. To this day, the single family house remains the ideal of the vast majority of Chicago's population that is currently housed in its historic neighborhoods. These neighborhoods were built by immigrants and remain diverse today, although many have transformed their origins and racial characteristics over time with each new wave of immigrant workers from afar. However, the heart of each neighborhood remains its cultural and religious institutions with the historic neighborhood schools, churches, and synagogues focusing the communities' shared interests.

The methodology of this studio focused on programmatic synthesis as a continuous process. The participants of the studio designed every aspect of their small dwelling in complete resolution, with all the assemblies, systems, and finishes—including colors, furniture, and landscape. The studio demanded attention to both discipline and imagination, characteristics required in order to be an architect. This was an opportunity to design a dwelling that is fully rational and buildable. The students visited Chicago and experienced its architectural legacy, which ranges from Richardson, Sullivan, and Burnham, to Wright and Mies as well as the work of current architects.

BENJAMIN SMITH ✳

On the south side of Chicago there is a need for more than just new housing stock; the communities located there are in need of jobs. With the relocation of the historic stock yards many residents lost their primary source of income. Joblessness forced many to move to other parts of the city. Today, vacant lots abound. This design is intended to be a prototype which reincorporates a place of production into the home. This place of production acts as both a shop and a classroom. The design maintains a domestic facade on the street while the shop and classroom are accessed from the back alley. One first builds this house then teaches two neighbors how to build similar houses. Those neighbors in turn teach two more neighbors how to build. Thus, the house becomes not only a place to dwell, but also a didactic tool and a place of production. The house uses simple materials and construction techniques; a balloon framing system rests on top of a concrete plinth. The main floor of the house has spacious but simple living and kitchen spaces which have access to an open-air terrace between the house and the back entrance to the shop. The second floor of the house has two bedroom suites. The shop is accessed through the back alley by a stair and lift. It has clerestory windows all around which allow for ample light and give the house above the appearance of floating. There is also a light well which draws light through the middle of the house providing both light for the house and shop and views between the domestic space and the productive space. This project not only proposes a design for infill housing on Chicago's south side; it proposes another, perhaps, not-so-new way to build and to live in our cities. {▲1–4}

"You can spend your whole life figuring out how to be simple." Steven Kieran

▲ BH: What are planners but failed architects after all? I have to say the historic investigation of what you've presented is fascinating and really is more in the area of urban design. The social component makes it much more of an urban planning approach. And what you're doing is going back to the 1880s and 1890s characteristics of Chicago, which resists the segregation of uses. This is before zoning, and so the city grew for a long time only constrained by the pattern of streets. ▲ DB: I actually love this project, and I think your biggest mistake was the polycarbonate because I think it's this red herring. It's about how this is going to be a cool building when what's really cool is the urban idea. You could clad it in panels borrowed from off-site but it's not about what it's clad in. It's the idea of how you use unused land, of how you bring people together, of how you teach new skills, of how you build something that essentially anyone can build and how you take the back yard and make it four-season space. I think it's completely fantastic, and I think you should forget the seduction of one cool material that performs terribly, and just make it a building. ▲ AL: It's truly a piece of vernacular Chicago wood architecture and it doesn't pretend not to be. It could adopt any number of expressions as many Chicago buildings do, but it has a really useful generic aspect to it. It's not an individual work of art, but really a prototypic solution. ▲ DB: I'm telling you, if you had set the assignment for yourself that every single element in the house a person could buy at Home Depot, this would have been extraordinary. That could have been a row of the cheapest, work-with-your-framing, two foot skylights that brought light down to a double height basement that allows the kid on the second floor doing homework to lean over and shout "Mom! Help!"—that is so much more meaningful and exciting. It's the Home Depot house that has a really interesting city idea. If I were in Chicago I'd say "Stick it to ya! This is what we need." Forget if it meets the code, this is what we need to do. ▲ SK: The most potent ideas here are the absolute simplest and it's so freaking hard to be simple as an architect. You can spend your whole life figuring out how to be simple. It's a system. It's got social premises. It's got economic premises. It's a comprehensive idea.

▲1

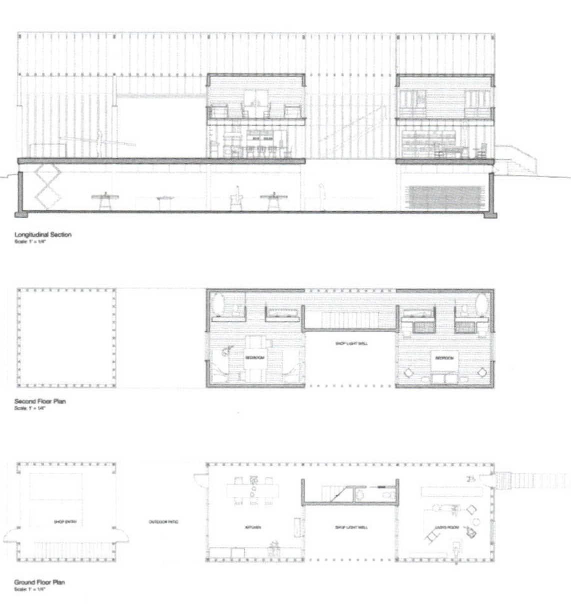

▲2

▲3

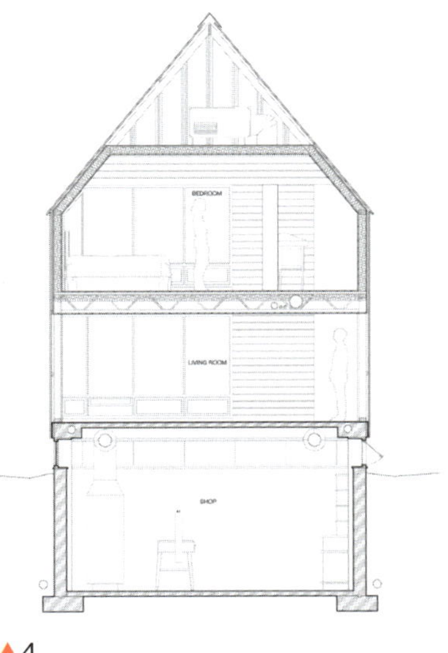

▲4

OLEN MILHOLLAND

This single family home is two distinctly different houses in one, both sharing the same suite of bedrooms at the center. Housing must necessarily include a place to sleep and that very space tends to be the room most sheltered from the climate. In this project, the bedrooms are grouped together into one conditioned bar that then shapes the rest of the house. The bar shades the spaces below from the sun, and lifts the spaces above it towards the sky and the views. The spaces above and below are the more public and social spaces of the home and mirror each other in plan. Everything that exists above the bedrooms exists below, only inverted and offering a different way to experience the current weather. This house adapts to the climate by offering different ways of experiencing it. While most houses offer inside or outside, sheltered or exposed—a binary limited by the time of year—the home is adaptable to the seasons. Throughout the year, it is both warm and cool, shaded and sun-lit, formal and casual and at once a space of activity and relaxation. The aim of the design is to resist limiting the way you can experience nature, but also offer new, inventive ways to inhabit a home. {▲5–8}

"If I lived next to it, I'd immediately go down to city hall and protest." **Robert A. M. Stern**

▲ **RAMS:** It's a very interesting formal exercise, of course, but it's not a very good house. I mean, if you had children, where do they play? I think you don't understand how children play. But I'm more concerned—and I've been concerned about this other times when Tom's had a studio, is how these houses fit into the neighborhood. So I'll make my little speech and then I'll leave. I think this is the most aggressive, un-friendly, un-urban thing. I mean, if I lived next to it, I'd immediately go down to city hall and protest. Absolutely! ▲ **BH:** It reminds me of the Robie House which has this basement that goes way out into the front yard and the neighbors to the north complained. ▲ **SK:** I rarely agree with Bob about anything, but I will agree that there's some aggression in the streetscape. You let the porches on the houses read forward as the objects on the street and pulled this back to have just as powerful an idea. But what I do really enjoy here is your production. It is spectacular. You work really hard, diligently and carefully, systematically and comprehensively. It is completely depicted. ▲ **JL:** It also has a strong premise. I think the idea of making the three levels of a house completely distinct worlds is quite strong. I think what's not as strong is the distinction of the layers in the other direction. I think the little notation of different kinds of curves is very flaccid as a way of describing the differences between those layers depicted so beautifully in the rendering. That's a very compelling kind of a house to occupy where you have views from one layer to the next to the next. It's a very complex environment with the scales of foreground, middle ground, and distant views. It's really about the opening, the aperture, breaking apart the room and the vista activating the rooms by the depth of experience. ▲ **RAMS:** I promise to go but I want to offer one more dissenting view. ▲ **JD:** We know that's why you came. ▲ **RAMS:** No I came to praise Caesar, not to bury him. But, all these windows on the side—there are other peoples' houses here. So the privacy issue is intense the way you've made it. Typically in row houses, by Frank Lloyd Wright or Joe Blow, whether Chicago or anywhere else, there are almost no windows on the sides, and you bring light in from the center and from the back end where you can control it. This seems so perverse. So these people sitting here, there curtains will be closed all the time or they'll be on display. ▲ **Laurence Lumley:** But isn't the project about being perverse? I mean the whole thing is perverse. You're on display. You're swimming in this pool and your naked body appears in the public living room. You're also putting this gold heaven into this poor neighborhood suggesting a hedonistic and material world. ▲ **RAMS:** Don't you think that this design, conceptually, is not that of a row house? It's of an object building in a landscape. It's a pavilion.

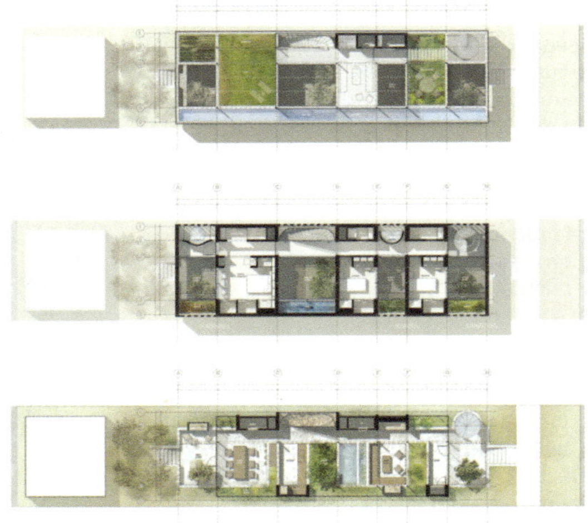

▲5

▲6

▲7

▲8

LEAH ABRAMS

This house for Chicago tackles the problem of infill housing by proposing a simple but robust concrete construction system. Chosen for its affordability and durability, precast concrete panels create a strong skeleton that is softened by more refined interior finishes. The massing is designed to take advantage of southern exposure with a series of terraced floorplates. The stepped section allows significant light and productive garden space to be integrated into all three bedrooms. In contrast, the shallow northern front facade is designed simply as a friendly and contextual face on the street. The spaces of the house are conceived as a series of experiences connected by a meandering circulation path. On the ground floor, the front entry hall serves as a formal and informal social space—a place to entertain guests or simply cross paths with other members of the household. The kitchen is enlivened with a large light well over the sink that connects to a rooftop greenhouse. It also looks down over a sunken dining room that is level with the backyard to create a seamless flow between indoor and outdoor spaces. On the second floor, two small bedrooms each have a private solarium as well as access to a garden. The third floor contains the master bedroom suite, complete with an outdoor terrace and access to the rooftop greenhouse. [▲9–12]

"I was told once by Colin Rowe that coffee tables are forbidden." Judy Di Maio

▲AL: The way that you draw it and you built the model is so—there's so much love in creating a place for humans. Architecture can be so abstract and that's a very important part of it, but I think retaining some relationship to the central idea of what it means to live in a house is really important, and it's demonstrated in the way you've designed your building. ▲SK: The issue of meandering in a relatively small house is you wind up with lots of space lost to movement. ▲LA: I don't really see it as space lost, though. You have a sequence of rooms and you just move through the rooms, so essentially there is no circulation space. You just have to experience the rooms as you move through them. ▲DB: I love how populated your model and your drawings are. All that is absolutely fantastic, but I want to talk about making rooms in a house, because rooms need walls and axes—organizational axes. This is going to sound so petty, but you have a three bay window here which has a very strong center. Do you see the relation of that center to the center of your fireplace? I don't care that it's not on center of the façade, but this room is impossible to furnish. ▲PG: I think the episodic method of looking at the house is its strength. That's what everyone has responded to positively, but it's also its weakness. There is a sectional structure that's very clear but when I see the big section, it's drawn so lightly you don't really understand how you get down that cascading piece. ▲JL: It's a very provocative project. I've spent my career creating buildings that are integrated objects; integrated inside and out. What's provocative about this is—I think it's rather clumsy on that level—that it's lived through your imagination. The reason that you did all the furniture—you put a lot of effort into the furniture, maybe as much as the building in some ways—is because that's the way people live in a home. People interact with the furnishings and the furnishings become projections of their way of living. It's a house of the future because I think houses will become less and less understood as objects, and more and more understood as sets of experiences. ▲JD: I have to say this first, I just can't resist. I have people come into my house who say "Judy, couldn't you buy just a big sofa so everyone could just lie around?" and I'm just like "Why? I like all my chairs!" These chairs I have, they're not very comfortable and I don't have a coffee table—I never did, I was told once by Colin Rowe that coffee tables are forbidden. Not that I always listen to him, but it was very interesting. He seriously thinks they don't work. But it's something worth thinking about—the notion of living and living around.

▲9

▲10

▲11

▲12

XS: "Micro" in Japanese Architecture and Urbanism
Sunil Bald

This seminar focused on trends in Japanese architecture and design culture over the past twenty years— both the culture that developed since the bursting of the bubble economy and the architectural excess it enabled. The course looked at architectural, urban, and aesthetic concepts that embrace the diminutive. Topics included the contemporary Japanese house, micro-urbanism, return to nature movements, and concepts of both the cute and monstrous. These were explored through a series of lenses that engage tradition, pragmatism, sustainability, gender, and nationalism.

PHILLIP NAKAMURA

This paper investigates the role of extra-small in *Chashitsu* architecture. The *Chashitsu*, or teahouse, suggests a space that is not large enough to be a house but exceeds the expectations of a room. Attributed to architect Kazuo Shinohara as the "discovery of the design of an interior object," the drawing analysis uses the traditional representation and design method, the okoshi-ezu, or folded drawing, to examine the spatial composition of three examples: Sen no Rikyu's Tai-an {1582}, Koji Fujii's Chochikukyo tearoom {1926}, and Hiroshi Sugimoto's Mondrian {2014}. The drawings are then reconstructed into orthographic projections to further explore the Chashitsu as complex interior volume. However, the *Chashitsu's* significance extends beyond an autonomous volume; through its juxtaposition of scale, it negotiates the individual's relationship between room, house, and city. {■1–2}

BELINDA LEE & HAELEE JUNG

This paper explores Japanese animation as a laboratory where new ideas about architecture and urbanism are both generated and tested. These animations represent the in-betweenness of Japanese culture, residing neither solely in the imaginary world nor the real world, reflecting the desire of the society but expanding it further with artistic imagination. The animations combine the irrational and familiar in a way that is visually compelling, relating to the way we see the world now—a synthesis and appropriation of different time periods, architectural styles, and scales to create a world that is both fantastic and whole. Scale in anime is perceived in relation to human body and can distort viewers' sense of scale. At one point, the viewer would be fully immersed in the built environment, but at other points the viewer would escape from it, reducing everything to a single image. With the added dimension of speed, anime turns the solidity of architecture into a fleeting image. {■3}

CYNTHIA HSU

The built environment of the Japanese city has the unique potential of becoming a collection of houses as temporal microcosms—at times devoid of urban context, isolating itself from the outside world—yet possessing a sense of dynamism and vitality that excites the viewer. These microcosms appear as art objects, often tailored to such a level of specificity to the occupant that it is nearly impossible to negotiate the possibility of another using the space. A combination of an urban and economic framework with a culture of impermanence residing in the Japanese subconscious sets up the conditions for these unique projects precisely because of their temporal nature. These microcosms produce an obvious tension between the fantastical and the banal as these art object buildings that occupy typical lots declare their individuality ignoring their immediate context. While radically different in form, they appear to have a shared cultural and ideological context in place of its lack of context with its immediate surroundings. Western criticism has always dismissed Japanese cities as chaotic and disorganized. Rather, it is of interest to analyze the existence of these microcosms as another building type unique to Japan.

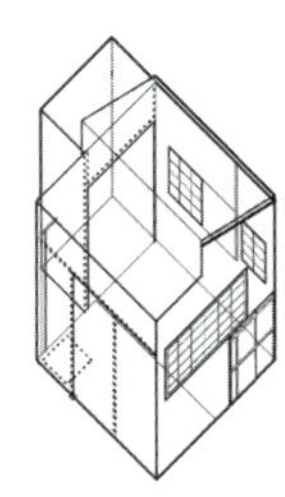
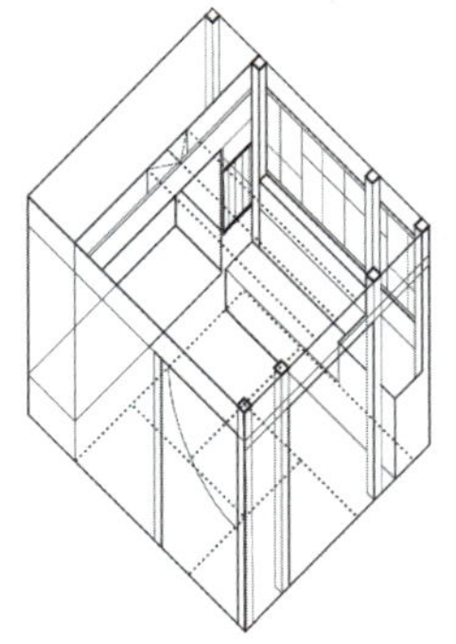
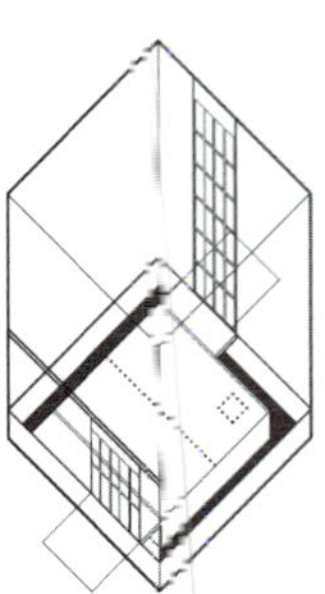

■1

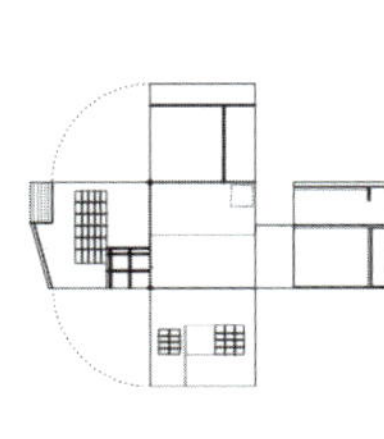
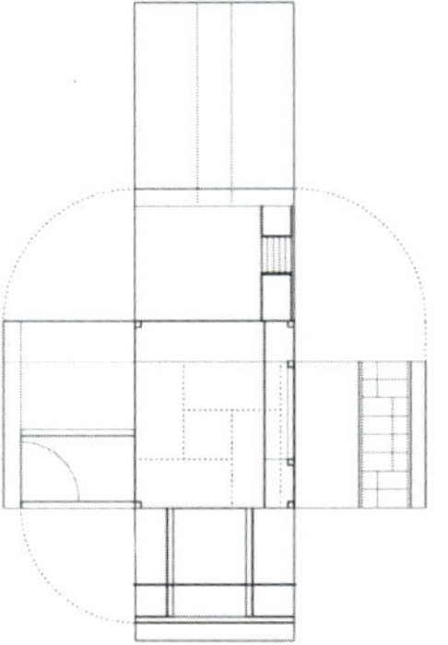
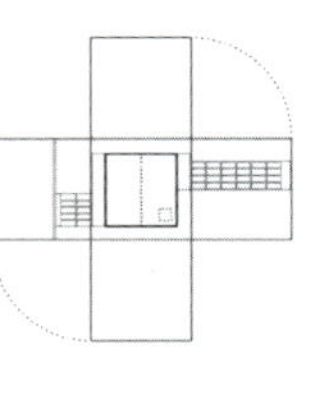

■2

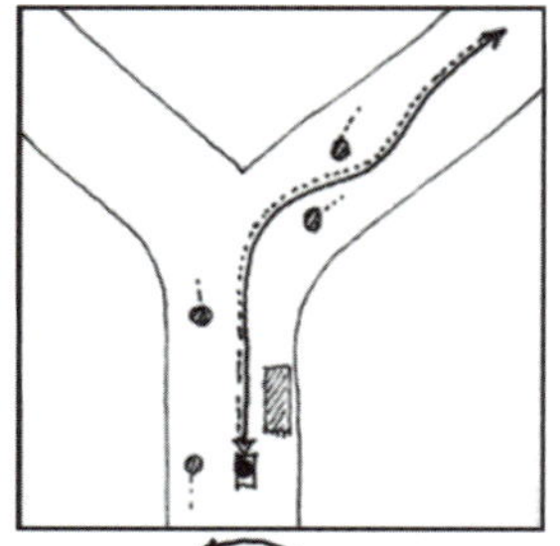

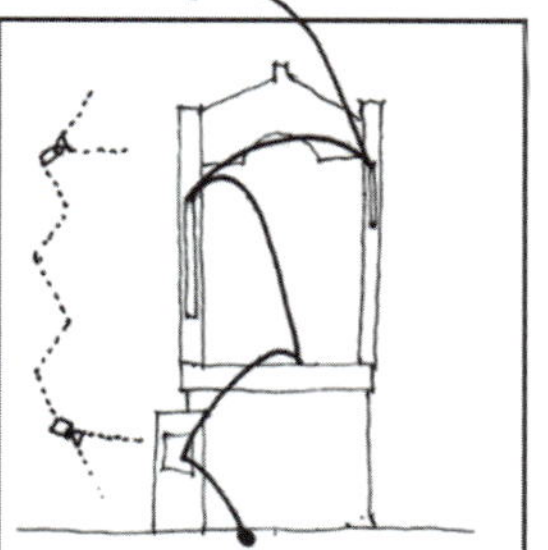

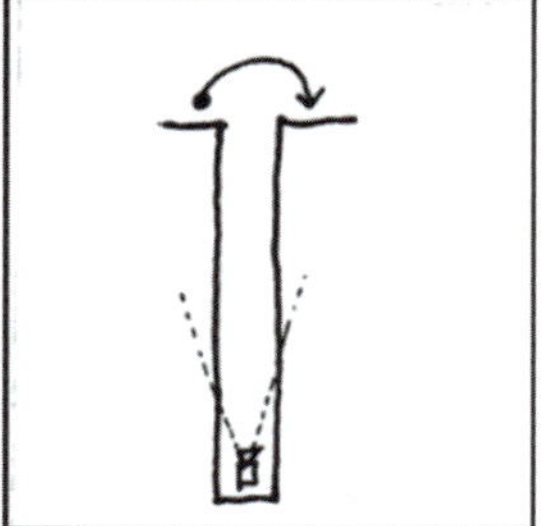

■3

History of British Landscape Architecture
Bryan Fuermann

This seminar examines the history of landscape architecture and of the idea of nature in Britain from 1600 to 1900. Topics of discussion include Italian and French influences on the 17th-century British garden, the Palladian country house and British agricultural landscape, Capability Brown's landscape parks as national landscape style, garden theories of the picturesque and of the sublime; Romanticism and the psychology of nature; the creation of the public park system, Arts and Crafts landscape design, and the beginnings of landscape modernism. Comparisons of historical material with contemporary landscape design are emphasized throughout the term. The collection of the Yale Center for British Art is used for primary visual material, and a trip to England over spring break, partially funded by the school, allowed students to visit firsthand the landscape parks studied in this seminar.

MELODY SONG & HAELEE JUNG

The project is a fictive Red Book for Tom Stoppard's play *Arcadia*, which is set in an English country estate in 1809. In the play, the transition of British landscape design—from the Brownian landscape to the Picturesque—appears as a backdrop. Mr Richard Noakes, the landscape gardener, is charged with bringing Lady Croom's garden up to trend. Inspired by Humphrey Repton's Red Books, Mr. Noakes has a watercolor book that illustrates the existing state of the gardens, and on a flap mounted on the same page, his improvements. We have created what might have been Mr. Noakes' Red Book. The landscape improvements are derived from the text, and the formatting of the book replicates Humphrey Repton's original. The description the improvements are inventively pieced together from Repton's writings on Blaise Castle, the pavilion at Brighton, and William Gilpin's "Observations on the River Wye, and several parts of South Wales, relative chiefly to Picturesque Beauty." [1]

BENJAMIN SMITH

Within the British landscape one can find many different structures. Some of these are follies whose singular purpose is to either act as an eye catcher on a distant hilltop or compose a picturesque scene; however, some of the structures that one might encounter in these estates are connected to the agrarian needs of a working landscape. These small buildings may look like follies, but they are in fact architecture for animals. Many of the large estates in England have extensive deer parks which served as a recreational pastime for the residents and guests. This Gothic pavilion which almost looks like a castle with its spires and pointed arches is actually a shelter for deer. [2]

KIN TAK YU

As England began to transform into an overseas Empire it became interested in exotic cultures, architecture, and landscape gardening—an intrest which introduced a wide variety of styles to English gardens. Most of these imported architecture and landscapes were interpreted through Western tradition. Rococo and Gothic were combined with Oriental designs, ultimately creating styles such as Anglo-Chinois, Turquerie and Moresque, each unique to England. Three significant examples of follies were selected and reconstructed digitally using existing drawings. The resultant models of the Chinese Pagoda at Kew Gardens, the Turkish Tent at Stourhead, and the Royal Pavilion at Brighton represent the *Chinoiserie*—Islamic and Indian styles from 18th-19th century British landscape architecture. [3]

BELINDA LEE & STEPHANIE JAZMINES

This set piece for the play *Arcadia* was made in the style of Inigo Jones, referencing the British gardens of Stowe, Stourhead, and Castle Howard. [4]

■ 1

■ 2

■ 3

■ 4

Is Less Enough?
100,000 Houses
for San Francisco
Pier Vittorio Aureli

<u>Critic</u>
Pier Vittorio Aureli {**PVA**}
Louis I. Kahn Visiting Professor

<u>Instructor</u>
Emily Abruzzo {**EA**}

<u>Jurors</u>
Tim Altenhof {**TA**}, Sunil Bald {**SB**}, Neeraj Bhatia
{**NB**}, Peggy Deamer {**PD**}, Peter Eisenman {**PE**},
Maria Guidici {**MG**}, Surry Schlabs {**SS**}, Alan
Plattus {**AP**}

The studio asks students to take a position towards
one of the most urgent problems in architecture:
the project of housing. More specifically, the studio
will be asked to design 100,000 affordable houses
for a city that is, at the moment, suffering one of the
most dramatic housing crises in the US: San Francisco. There are two main questions implied within
this project: What is the social and political meaning of housing in an age that has made of "scarcity,"
"crisis," "resilience," a fundamental *modus operandi*
of economy? Can a project that operates at the
scale of the city still be an "architectural project"?
  This is an opportunity to radically rethink the
architecture of domestic space. Since the beginning of its history, housing has been the exclusive
embodiment of one type of human association: the
nuclear family. In this way, housing has prevented
other forms of association based on values such solidarity and sharing. The studio agenda is not against
the nuclear family, but sees the latter as only one
possible form of association among others. For this
reason, an important goal of the studio is to rethink
domestic space beyond the typical form of a family
home. Rather than beginning with the design of the
family home, the studio will propose to start from
the most basic form of living space, the room. We
propose to take the room at face value, stripping
it of the expectations and preconceptions created
by the last three centuries of typological discourse.
Today, as practicing architects, we work with a pre-
set toolbox of purpose-intended rooms, which can
just be shifted around and given a different position
or different form while in fact still fitting the same
diagram—the nuclear family apartment. But should
a room have functions at all? Should an apartment be divided in rooms? Are the standard sizes
requested by law a way to protect the citizen, or a
straitjacket to enforce a certain behavior? Addressing the room, and starting a project from the room,
does not only mean to question the functional subdivisions we normally take for granted. It also means
to challenge the idea of what is public and what is
private within the house itself. With the best possible intentions, architects have tried to propose new
horizons for the family apartment, playing with double levels, different distribution patterns, new models of furniture. However, we have hardly criticized
the basic articulation of living spaces into a preor-
dered set of rooms. Taking the room as the first element of a project for living space might allow us to
see the question of housing on completely different
terms from the ones we normally work with.
  The studio is organized as a research studio,
which encourages literacy with historical precedents not as a matter of erudition, but as a way to
engage with the very meaning of our discipline and
its historical significance in the face of fundamental
human problems such as the need for housing. The
studio sees the production of drawings and images
not as mere illustration, but as a specific argumen-
tative language through which to propose ideas for
architecture and the city.

MICHAEL COHEN ✳

This project is a medium-scale building that offers affordable housing for middle-income freelancers in San Francisco. Suitable to the existing density of the city, the intermediate scale of the project, which sits between the townhouse and the tower, enables independent inhabitants to form residential cooperatives. Limiting the size of the community supports the effective sharing of space and domestic tasks, engendering a collective consciousness that is essential for the precarious worker of the disenfranchised middle-class. While the project is contextual in scale, the autonomy of the building is made evident by its cubic form and isotropic façade. The regularity of the exterior clearly marks a limit to the city and conceals the project's unique spatial and social interior. The nine-square grid defines the plan of the project. The walls between the square rooms are thickened, to create a poché space that accommodates the biological functions of living. Within this compact territory, private living cells border the façade whereas shared kitchens, storage and dining areas are centrally located. Circular rooms act as inhabitable vestibules that mediate the transition between the private cells and the centralized shared facilities. In contrast to the highly prescriptive poché space, the eight squares on the border of the plan are empty and double height. This type of generic space is particularly valuable to freelance workers who lack the structure of a conventional work environment. Devoid of the demands of household management, the unprogrammed, but formally specific, outer squares permit sovereign interaction between individuals, thereby engendering entrepreneurial collaboration, solidarity, and political action. The center square, which is indisputably unique, contains a monumental circular staircase that establishes a collective center for the community and affirms the wholeness of the architectural object. The distinct formal difference between the generic squares and the compressed realm of biological maintenance communicates the social and political structure of the project. (▲1–4)

"Why representationally or organizationally does the status of perfection announce itself again and again and again?" **Peggy Deamer**

▲ **MG**: To be honest, you could start to pick on these things like what does the scale of the community mean, but I have to say one thing before anything else: it is so mind-blowing from the architectural point of view. That is one of the most amazing plans that I've ever seen, not only in a student project, but recently. The fact that you use the poché but you use it in a modern way, and it makes sense typologically, or anti-typologically, is absolutely incredible. ▲ **SS**: I really love the kind of appropriation or assimilation of the Palladian poché of the project. The transition from the curvilinear geometry to a more rectilinear one speaks to a transition from an interior disorientation to a kind of exterior reorientation. In some way— metaphorical, mystical, numerological, or other— it relates strongly to your discussion of political or social interaction. And though there's a certain elegance, there's also a slippery re-insertion of hierarchy. There's a privileging of the units, which are on the level with the double height space. It is a positive privileging. There's always going to be a hierarchy of some sort in a multi-story building in the context of any collective. I think the possibility of hierarchy within a pure collective arrangement is quite interesting. ▲ **SB**: The one thing that I don't like is the disguising of the plan with the elevation. There are some weird carving acts that you're doing in the plan, but then they end up disguised in the elevation. You create this system then you replicate it in the plan and the section, and then that consistency creates an anomaly. And then that anomaly actually creates something that adds value to the relentlessness of the plan and section. ▲ **PD**: Related to the question about the masking of the interior difference on the outside—the perfect cube. We can see that everyone today's interested in stripping down difference, and idealizing. We could call it consistency, but it's idealizing perfection, in some way. I'd be curious from your point of view about what the status of that is. Why representationally or organizationally does the status of perfection announce itself again and again and again? ▲ **PVA**: It's a fundamental issue.

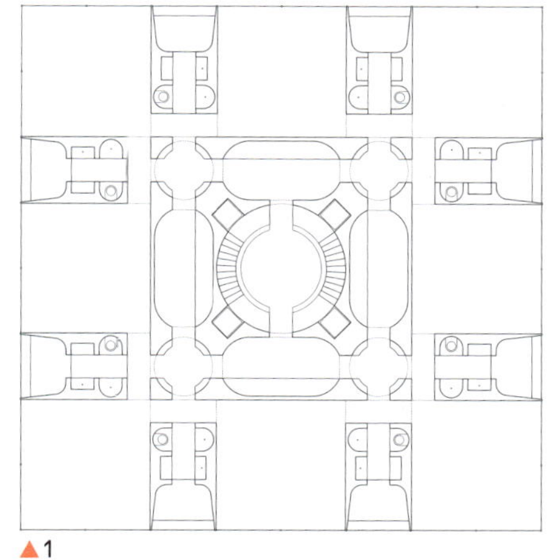

▲1

▲2

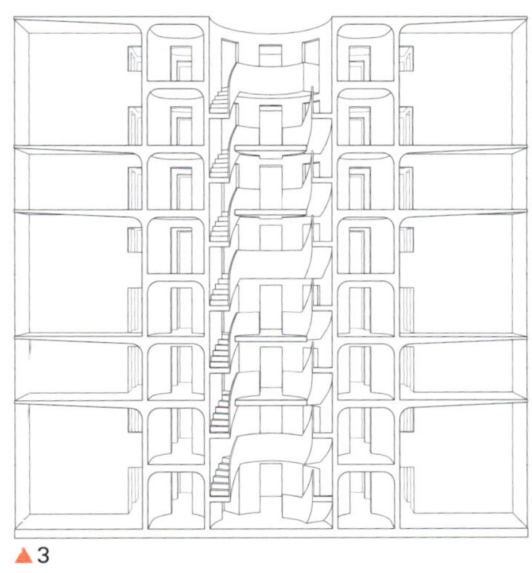

▲3

▲4

SOPHIA SINGLER

This project subverts lot division logic and reclaims the center of the city block as shared space—the courtyard. The scheme comprises groups of open-air courtyards, around which the housing units are organized. The court is a space that can be claimed by no one and thus belongs to everyone—the land becomes a gift yet again. For monks, the cloistered courtyard provided separation from the distractions of laymen and the life of the city outside. In similar fashion, the shared outdoor space of the court expresses and defines the rituals of the residents living around it, endowing the complex with a sense of organization as a city within a city. In Nordic *Kollektivhus* models of communal living, a housing block was seen as a built manifestation of a particular life form that the building's residents shared—the ground floor was dedicated to activities defined by residents themselves, and living units were set on higher floors. In this manner, the ground floor spaces that enclose the court reflect different residential groups' forms-of-life: young families in one court transform them into a day care center and playground, artists in another convert them into studio and gallery spaces, tech workers and students in a third mold them into co-working hubs. Domesticism becomes an opportunity to construct a form-of-life where the boundaries between everyday life and shared rituals are eradicated. In San Francisco, zoning laws dictate that ground floor functions in the Mission District and 16th Street area must house commercial activity. Thus the shared ground floor not only becomes the common ritual space of the court's residents but also links the project to the city via entrepreneurialism. By employing the courtyard type as a device to construct a city within a city, the court rejoins the political with the domestic, intertwining individuals' personal lives with the rituals of the community and fostering a sense of sociopolitical and economic organization among residents, while referencing to San Francisco's history as a locus of neighborhood activism. [▲ 5–8]

"What is the scale of the collective? At this point, collective becomes so unfamiliar, we could call it totalitarian."
Peggy Deamer

▲ **SS:** I really love how diverse the spatial arrangements can be. I remember the kind of bedtable-desk apparatus from midterm, but I think you've much more successfully integrated that old Mission approach to flexible living through furniture to a project about a collective. ▲ **SB:** I have a problem with the corridors, and part of it is because of practical reasons, but the other part is that you said you didn't want to privilege one side or the other. But I think this notion of the communal and the city, or the enclosed communal and the city does privilege one side of the other. When you say that you want to have the same condition on each side then it immediately draws you to the center. Here it's the toilet that occupies the center of your building—the services. So you get into a situation where you have the most private thing in the center and move to the outside. ▲ **PD:** It's interesting because I was looking at the two corridors and the absoluteness with which you said, "No, you don't own a window!" Here you're always reminded that the community exists first and that the building is owned by the community, and you just can't get away from that. As a political position I just have to admire the stridency of that. Once I buy, I don't own a window, and I'm always reminded of the collective. Then I get interested in that collective. What is the scale of the collective? I get nervous about the size. At this point, collective becomes so unfamiliar we could call it totalitarian. ▲ **RAMS:** Have you studied or made a determination of how many people form a communal group of a reasonable number? I think monasteries have a structure that is beyond social—they have a ritual and it's totally controlled. At Yale in the residential colleges they think a suite with more than six people is a recipe for disaster. Eight is the absolute most because beyond that it becomes uncontrolled, and nobody is responsible for keeping the kitchen clean. Thirty people is a very big group. For example, in your year you're fifty people, but we break you up into ten or twelve people, and even then it's hard to get people to agree on dinner. What you have is not communal. It's the opposite. It's cellular.

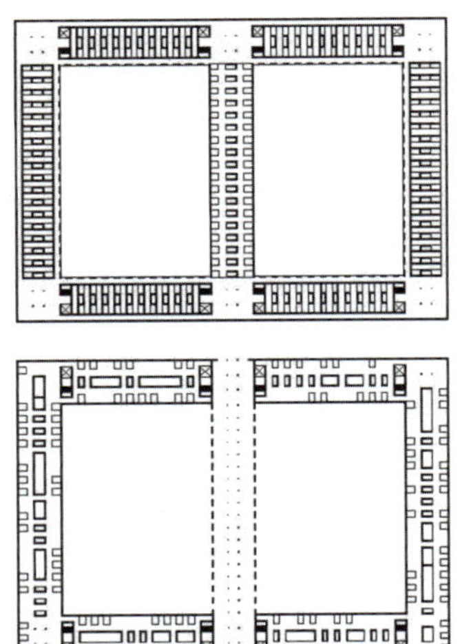

▲ 6

▲ 5

▲ 7

▲ 8

Walking from Site to City

Rafael Birmann
ƐEdward P. Bass Distinguished Visiting
Fellow in ArchitectureƷ

I was eager to learn the trade. One of my many issues was with architects. In Brazil, most architecture schools would never do something like the Bass fellowship—bringing business people to interact with students. First of all, they despise real estate. Only public buildings with a social agenda were considered worthwhile. Young architects are taught that clients are obstacles in the way of great projects. Back in 1980, I was starting to develop my first office building and wanted to work with one of the most acknowledged architects in São Paulo: Gian Carlo Gasperini. I started explaining the project and he said, "Come back in two weeks, I will have the conceptual design." I said, "But I have some ideas, and I want to discuss them." Again, "Don't worry, I understand the needs. Come back in two weeks." I walked out of his celebrated office and never went back.

Architecture is the sole art that cannot fulfill itself without a third party. The architect needs clients, and not only because she is the one who foots the bill, but she also sets the parameters, the market reality, budgets, and all sorts of limitations. That's real creativity   to design within constraints. That's the real deal.

Kairos, *Chronos*, Time, and Space: Designing for Humans in a Digital World ƐDavid W. Roth and Robert H. Symonds Memorial LectureƷ

Douglas Rushkoff

The highfalutin Greek ideals of *Chronos* and *Kairos* occurred to me while I was watching "The Real Housewives of Orange County" with my wife.

It was amazing to me how much trouble these women had communicating with each other. They can't connect, and I realize that these women are falling victim to the technological problem that I think we as a society are falling victim to as well. They are using technology to try to lock down time, rather than to enter the present moment. These women have used Botox to try and lock chronological time at age twenty-nine, and, in doing so, they have made themselves unavailable to the actual moment in which they are in a room with another person.

Time on the clock is *Chronos*. Human time that we can only understand through interpretation or feeling is *Kairos*. When I first encountered the internet, I saw it as something that was going to make more time. I graduated college in 1983 at the height of the Slacker Era. For those of you who missed it, the whole idea of slack was not to be lazy; it was to have more time to do the things you want.

TAMRAT GEBREMICHAEL
& NICHOLAS MURAGLIA

The project reinvigorates the residential hotel model for a new generation of precarious workers by reclaiming an object of housing infrastructure lost in the evolution of domestic space: the core. All domestic activities such as sleeping, cooking, eating, and cleaning are consolidated within the core, liberating the periphery space of prescribed functions. The project proposes a system of cores with degrees of sharing and privacy embedded in its organization; a single core is always shared between multiple residents and operates as a partition that mediates the private and collective spaces. The core is not only reclaimed in terms of its functionality, but more importantly becomes the critical element of collective living that restructures and provides clarity to domestic space and ritual. The core system is not predicated on any specific form or type. As such, the project may be deployed in three different forms specific to three different urban conditions in San Francisco: the high rise tower in the Financial District, the bar building in the mid-scale blocks along the city's transit corridors, and the one-story building in the former industrial areas. While the scale and form of the project adapt to these different site conditions, the grammar of the core system remains the same, providing a legible urban form to the precarious subject. As opposed to the existing urban structures which conceal the presence of a residential hotel's inhabitant to preserve an illusion of stability, the project represents this new form of inhabitation. The project aims to reconfigure domestic space as one defined by mobility and collective living, providing both an interior space and a legible urban form through which these subjects can recognize themselves as a new political body in the city. (▲ 9–12)

> "Sleep is the last vestige of community because it's the time when we rely on each other not to murder one another."
> **Surry Schlabs**

▲ **SS:** I really love the kind of glyphic quality to the cores as they sort of march along. We've been talking about legibility and readability, and I really love the fact that each one of these little cores become a kind of glyph unto itself and when strung along refers to a certain building type. ▲ **SB:** You think of core as having to do with vertical mechanical systems and so forth but there also seems to be a conflation of things you can dimension that occupy cores, or behavior that you might be able to predict that you can dimension. Everything that you can't predict or maybe the sort of open space seems to be a stand in for something else. That the bed is part of the core is interesting. You are thinking of sleeping as an act of efficiency. ▲ **SS:** The question of sleep is an interesting one in the context of this studio. I think the projects that we've looked at have tended to frame it as a very private action or time. In Jonathan Crary's recent book *24/7*, he described sleep as the last vestige of community because it's the time when we rely on each other not to murder each other and take all our stuff. So, I don't know what that says for this project, but the notion of sleep as simultaneously the most private act we commit and the most public in terms of framing our relationship to a community or a collective is an important one. ▲ **NB:** What I like about this plan is that there's an interdependency between the cores and their adjacency. If you thought about not stacking the same module on top of each other, it could be an interesting sectional play. ▲ **MG:** You are pushing back a series of things that are not really in the core in architecture anymore, but they used to be in the past. I have the impression that one of the most violent typological things to happen to the modern house is the moment that the kitchen, which used to be the source of heat and cooking, was not used exclusively for heat. That could be really interesting, as this is not possible anymore in the buildings we have today because we actually blur the meaning of the cores as you show them. But you are pushing back everything again, so in fact that technical space there is anything but secondary. It could almost become a poetic element.

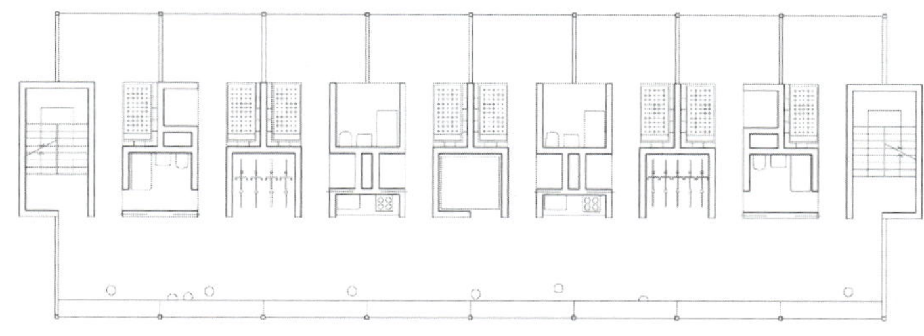

▲ 9

▲ 10

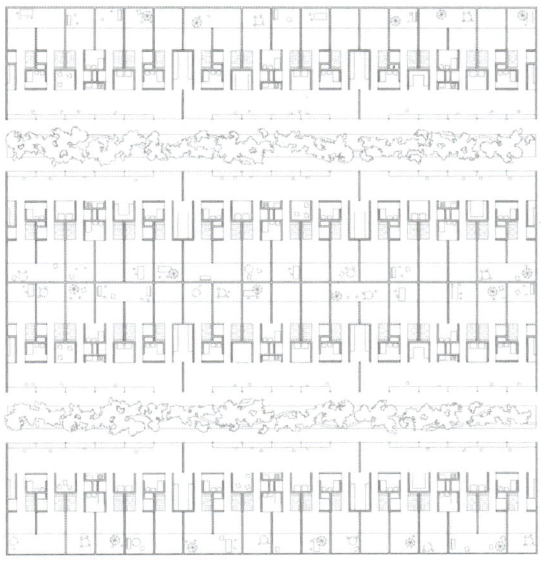

▲ 11

▲ 12

3266b
Building China Modern 1919-1958
Amy Lelyveld

MICHAEL KOLTON, CLARISSA LUWIA, EDWARD WANG, BOYUAN ZHANG

The search for an architecture that is both Chinese and modern has been underway for more than a hundred years. At the beginning of the last century, many were looking for just such a new language of building—one that could be both culturally specific and international. China started this grappling early, and it continues to this day. This architectural quest has run parallel to radically changing ideas of what China and Chinese ought to represent. This seminar examines experiments in Chinese building during three important periods: around the May Fourth Movement {1919}, during Nationalist China {1927–48}, and in the inaugural years of the People's Republic. Each period had its own mindset, but in all of them the reimagining of Chinese architecture was considered of paramount importance. While this course reviews the "tradition" of Chinese architecture, its focus is on the "experiments" in changing it. Students' research concentrated on case studies using primary resources located in Yale University's deep research collections {e.g., Sterling Memorial Library's periodical holdings and Manuscripts and Archives collections, along with the Divinity School's records on China-based missions}. This class generated a comprehensive timeline which here includes the investigations of Edward Wang: *Seeing Red— Investigating Communist Theater and Film from Liberation to the Great Leap Forward* {green}, Boyuan Zhang: *Henry Murphy's Compasses— Reading the Drawings of Yenching University* {red}, Michael Kolton: *Rebalancing Light and Dark—The Skies in Building China Modern* {blue}, and Clarissa Luwia: *The Stage of Cultural Construction—The Case of Tiananmen* {orange}. {■ 1}

1230b
Patternism
Brennan Buck

The proliferation of algorithmic software over the past five years has completed a transformation in digital design culture from the smooth to the patterned. Undulating virtual surfaces have been supplanted as a default design mode by hyperarticulated assemblies of parts—facade panels, structural members, and fabricated components. Yet the same topological logic lies beneath both the digital surface and these more recent computationally composed assemblies: smooth repetition and variation and a lack of hierarchy and difference. This course seeks an understanding of algorithmic logic at a technical and conceptual level and speculates on its potential beyond tectonic assemblies and topology-based sensibilities.

JESSICA ANGEL

The volume represented in the series of drawings is generated by an interpretation of the Villa Farnesina's floor plan. The relationship between the external pentagonal massing and the fragmented interior rooms was the focus of interest to generate the form in Grasshopper. The formal concept is reinforced graphically by colors and hatching influenced by Italian Futurist paintings. {■ 2}

NICHOLAS MURAGLIA

The project originated with an interest in gestalt perception, specifically in the work of Josef Albers, who uses color and line to create oscillating hierarchies that play with the language of graphics and make us aware of the conventions we rely on to "read" a drawing. I wanted to produce drawings which were more explicitly suggestive of layered depth and scale, but still retained the same unstable hierarchy which draws attention to the act of reading, first, by using color to establish relationships of depth which conflict with the reading of

layered space. Then I wanted to emphasize this tension between graphic and three-dimensional space by using a self-reflexive "alphabet" in which the line work defining the volumes is a hatch pattern generated from the master diagram, which organizes these volumes in space; the reading of the graphic "letter" begins to compete in hierarchy with the volume "word" which it defines. {■ 3}

HUI ZHEN NG

The project uses the concept of erosion to generate difference and complexity, where the central octagon is eroded by two neighboring spheres. Using only one additive and one subtractive module, the booleaned octagon is extruded and repeated on the X,Y, and Z axes to form a figural module. However, each form progressively erodes more as the size of the spheres increase. One drawing element, the contour line, is used to define points, edge, texture, and form—to erode a seemingly precise, patterned space into an ambiguous one. {■ 4}

1222b
Diagrammatic Analysis
Peter Eisenman

While the subject of formal analysis has often been studied, rarely has the distinction between form and content, and more importantly, between geometric form and topological form been articulated. The study of the diptych in both painting and architecture, which is essentially a relational {i.e. topological} and thus non-static, may do that. When making abstract schemata of architecture, the numbers three and nine are traditionally used whether as a tripartite façade or a nine-square plan. Very rarely is a four-square plan or a two-part façade proposed, and when it is, it is as a two part opposition—solid/void, orthogonal/gridded, or round/smooth. Such a binary opposition, which has underpinned thought in most disciplines, seems today to be insufficient or inadequate to deal with the complexities of the built environment in the post-mechanical age. In other disciplines in the humanities, foremost among them linguistics and philosophy, binary oppositions and paired relationships have come under an intense critique. The object of the class was to produce a new matrix of solutions that deal with the possibility of partial as opposed to fragmentary figures, and simultaneously deny the political power of symmetrical frontal imagery inherent in triadic relationships.

EUGENE HAN

In Narcissus and Echo, as found in the House of the Ephebus {Pompeii, AD 62-79}, the functional roles of Lacan's mirror stage are masterfully portrayed in laconic efficacy. The two subjects are pensively fixed towards the reflection, while the ominous gaze of the reflection opens the threshold between the subject's *innenwelt* and *umwelt*. This separation of Narcisuss' head with his *imago* masterfully alludes to the Lacanian fragmentation of the subject's own identity. The painting decapitates the head of Narcissus to produce the subject's own gestalt of "self." The dialectic circumvents the visual "reality principle", and achieves "a voyeuristic-sadistic idealization of the sexual relation; a personality that realizes itself only in suicide" {Lacan, 1949}. During this exchange between the subject and his image, Echo remains a bystander, transfixed on her own inability to separate Narcissus from himself. {■ 5}

DORIAN BOOTH

When read as a diptych, Francis Bacon's *Study for a Portrait, 1980* reveals complex spatial relationships present in neither his true diptychs nor triptychs. The figure sitting for the portrait is split by a mirrored zone {the hinge of the diptych}, which acts as not only a means of division, but also of connection. The hinge here creates both a separated and coupled figure, concepts that Gilles Deleuze discusses in relation to Bacon's work. Although Deleuze assigns the separated figure to Bacon's triptychs and the coupled figure to single paintings, here

both are present and indebted to a diptychal reading. The left-hand side of the painting is thus read as a space of legible structure and stasis, whereas an altogether different figure and space emerge on the right; this right-hand, mirrored space is one of flatness, constantly in flux as both figure and space become altogether structure-less. {■ 6}

2216b
Materials and Meaning
Deborah Berke

This seminar urges students to probe material usage, in terms of detailing, context, embedded meaning, and historical precedent. The course examines how variations in joinery affect a built work, what opportunities materials afford architects in design and construction, how architects make material selections and decisions, and what meanings material selections bring to a work of architecture.

JINGWEN LI

This project tries to create a joint detail between three dissimilar materials: timber, plastic, and metal. By using threaded metal rods as a bracing system, the different material panels could be suspended and rotated flexibly. Those pieces of panels are overlaid with each other to conceal the joint behind and achieve an abundant quality of shades. {■ 7}

ZACHARY VEACH

This image reconceives Frank Lloyd Wright's 1890 Winslow House as an imaginary timber structure. The original home in Chicago's Oak Park neighborhood is a Roman brick structure on a cast stone coping. Below the low, wide roof is a terra cotta band obscuring the second story. This dark band works in conjunction with the shadow of the overhanging eave. Taking a cue from the ornamental banding, horizontal materiality, and prominent roof structures found in vernacular Polish timber architecture, the reimagined house is made of log cabin-like joinery. Ornament is reconceived according to principals of wood craftsmanship. The roof, made of small, pointed wood shingles and contrasting wood species, enhances the ornamental banding. {■ 8}

AMANDA BRIDGES

In design, chemical properties of materials sometimes become secondary to their historical, aesthetic, and formal functions. Rather than substituting one material for another in construction, perhaps there are opportunities to join the dissimilar materials to create an integrated approach. My project is an experiment in material interaction founded in the fundamental traits of two materials: aluminum and wood. As molten aluminum was poured into a sand and foam cast holding the section of lumber, the aluminum seeped into the wood's exposed pores and crevasses. Moments of interaction are visible in the result by burn marks in the wood, which, as the metal cooled, sealed the two materials together in a tight bond. The result of this violent process is a delicate, yet dynamic fusion of two materials. {■ 9}

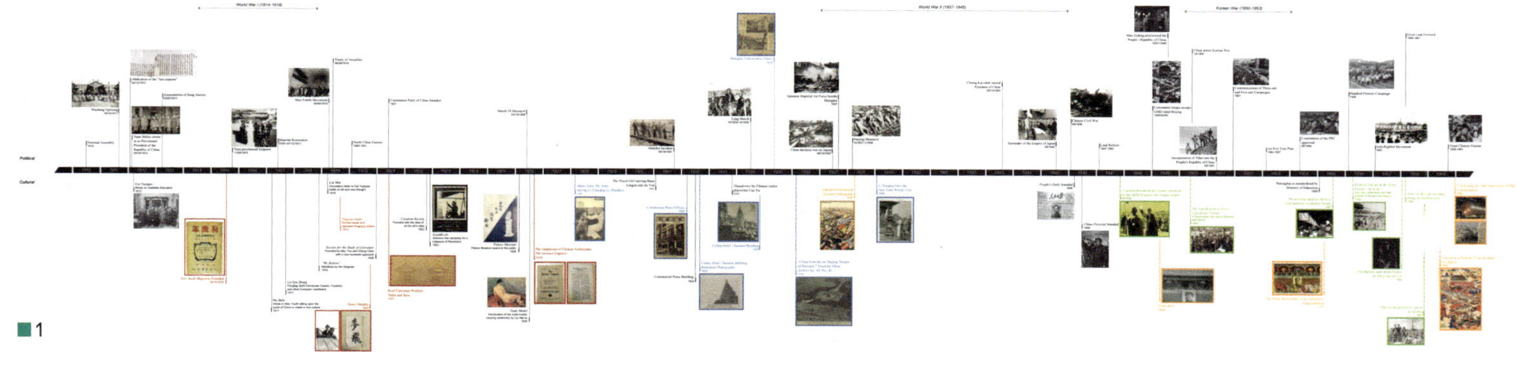

1

2

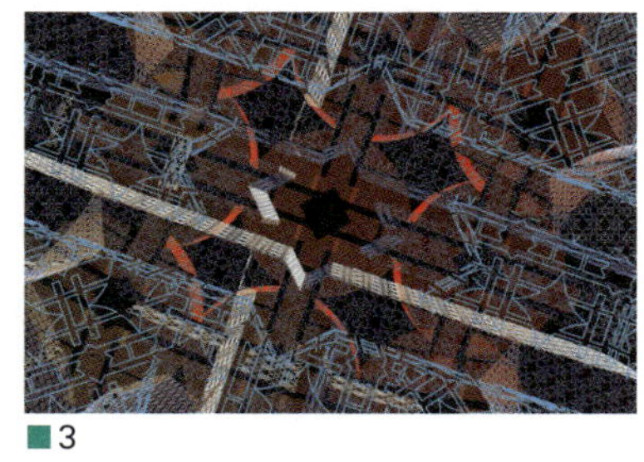

3

4

5

6

7

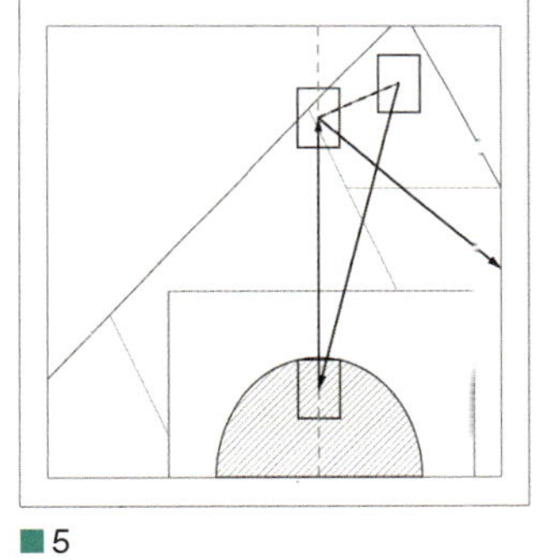

8

9

Masses to Flesh.
Surfaces to Flowers.
Hernan Diaz-Alonso

<u>Critics</u>
Hernan Diaz-Alonso {**HDA**}
Eero Saarinen Visiting Professor

<u>Instructor</u>
Austin Samson {**AS**}

<u>Jurors</u>
Jackie Bloom {**JB**}, Miroslava Brooks {**MB**}, Peter Eisenman {**PE**}, John Enright {**JE**}, Mark Foster Gage {**MFG**}, Ferda Kolatan {**FK**}, Greg Lynn {**GL**}, Fabian Marcaccio {**FM**}, Florencia Pita {**FP**}, Ali Rahim {**AR**}, Marcelo Spina {**MS**}, Peter Trummer {**PT**}, Robert A. M. Stern {**RAMS**}

The central aim of the studio is to design a new Secession Exhibition Hall Building in Vienna. The studio focused on architectural speculation as cultural advancement. Proposals strove to answer the larger question: what is the formal project today in relation to the tissue of the city? The studio explored possible solutions by creating a dialogue between conventional exhibition space and formal idiosyncrasies—all by way of ethereal masses and self-camouflaging malware. Very precise digital techniques were used to stitch together architectural pieces. Considering the incredible shift in architecture in the wake of the digital revolution, the proposed projects reexamined the possibilities of form generation in terms of aesthetics, building, fabrication, and overall design principles. The digital shift also forced architects to rethink the philosophical and ethical underpinnings of their practice. Idealistic or even utopian goals were replaced by a revived curiosity for an unapologetic interest in progress, often pursued for its own sake. In the context of these conditions, the studio focused on the production and manipulation of "formless" or edgeless masses. Distorted reflections, animations, renderings, and biosynthetic replacements served as an aesthetic catalogue for the production of architecture. An understanding of butchery, carving and reassembly often guided the massing and formal decisions of the work. Specifically butchery combines techniques of mutilation and organization that will serve to inform the studio. A commitment to the "useless"—to a body of work and to projects in which cultural advancement and technological refinement are central—was an emergent theme as the studio progressed; understanding all the while that architecture is often incapable of true newness and perhaps can only innovate at best. In many ways, the projects argue that the main contribution of computational architecture is the possibility of "New Coherencies," that is, the same type of ornamental architecture prevalent in late 19th century Vienna, albeit with meat masses rather than floral surfaces. The "redone" Vienna Secession buildings proposed are the same square footage, program, and collection as the existing building. This is a not a cloning operation; this is mutant evolution.

**LAUREN RAAB
& MICHAEL MILLER** ✳

This project proposes a hanging garden park to replace the Secession Museum in Vienna, Austria. The scheme is composed of a continuous path of platforms and stairways, which connect a series of small internal and external galleries. In the tradition of the *Raumplan*, the garden becomes a dynamic three-dimensional space. The original ornamental dome from the Secession Building is reinterpreted as interior space, while the exterior architectural components call into question conventional notions of structure, form and ornament. The main entrance to the structure is located at street level and leads into the largest of the four golden spheres. Each of the spheres is completely enclosed and can be used as gallery space to showcase visiting artists' work and permanent exhibitions. Starting at the entry, two paths of circulation weave through the structure, moving visitors between the enclosed galleries and large exterior garden platforms for sculpture. The project was represented and explained exclusively through animation. This method of representation allows opportunities to convey the complexity of the three-dimensional hanging garden. Multiple series of M.R.I.-type section cuts that move through the scheme vertically and horizontally in the animation explain the sectional and plan qualities of the building and convey how the individual pieces fit together and pierce into the ground. The final animation drifts between gentle trips of insanty, rendered in *Alice in Wonderland* colors mixed with a Viennese psychosis. (▲1–4)

"I think it's dangerous to validate an architectural project based on its relationship to history." **Mark Foster Gage**

▲ **PE:** Every discipline has precedents. There aren't any great filmmakers, writers, sculptors, etc. that don't take from their discipline themselves. There's no such thing. Derrida wrote a great essay on the original and the copy. What Derrida argued was that when Heidegger studies Hegel or Derrida studies Heidegger, it's not that Heidegger is the precedent. What Derrida does in the copy is transform the copy into an original. And so the whole idea is to take precedent and copy from it into an original. ▲**MFG:** But another reading of that is Harold Bloom's *Anxiety of Influence*, when you're reacting against something that already exists which seems more like what they're doing. I think it's dangerous to validate an architectural project based on its relationship to history. Otherwise Leon's studio would be the most successful ever. ▲**PE:** That's not the kind of history I'm talking about at all. ▲**MFG:** What makes your history better than his history? ▲**PE:** What I'm saying is that he takes history as classical. That's not the history. ▲**MFG:** But so are the histories you choose. ▲**FK:** So the critique is a lack of ideology? ▲**PE:** My critique is that it is difficult to understand the work. I asked a student in my class, "Why do you think you're at Yale?" And the person said, "To learn to be original." And I said, "In the land of originality, idiots are king." Because there always has got to be some animating thing other than just dropping from the sky. ▲**MFG:** Why is it more important to judge this against other work as opposed to just discuss it relative to its effects on the viewer? You're discussing it conceptually based on relationships rather than effectually based on its impact. What effect does it produce? Do we have to validate the projects based on their relationship to anything else other than what effect it produces? ▲**HDA:** But, for example, if you take certain cliché from certain cinema. You take the general superhero, right, so Superman for a long time was happy and married and blah, blah, blah. Then the second life as the Man of Steel makes Superman into something else. So there's a kind of aesthetic and cinematic effect, but it has some correlation and a way to place it in a contemporary context using basically the same elements, just changing certain, specific effects. ▲**PE:** Many years ago, when I was teaching with Michael Graves, I used to tell the students, you have to do Michael Graves and not believe in it, but learn what it is. So, I think this is a terrific studio; the students are learning Hernan Diaz-Alonso. I just need to know more about what that is. See, I was very clear on what Michael Graves was.

▲1

▲2

▲3

▲4

HANK MEZZA

This proposal works extensively with cutting. The exterior is an aggregation of pieces which bear the markings of slicing and recombination. While all different, one could insinuate that these pieces were once part of the same original whole, violently separated and then quickly reassembled. Thus, continuity is broken by protrusions, rough overlapping, and deep scars. Within the voids created by these masses is a gold membrane which houses exhibition spaces. Without naturally flat surfaces, guests are given access through a scaffolding of platforms and stairs. Inverting the use of gold in the original secession building, this interior entity peeks out of the bottom of the building, as though it is standing on legs. This appearance suggests that the building's relationship to the site is tenuous at best and creates a tension with the ground that confronts the classical stability of the surrounding context. Despite the alien nature of the geometry, the building retains strong suggestions of symmetry. The front façade is composed of four relatively equal components, the plan consists of a central hall with three side spaces, and the overall mass rests on three nearly symmetrical legs. Combined with a radically new formal language, this symmetry puts the project directly in dialogue with the building's secessionist counterpart. ﹝▲5–8﹞

"I was looking at the relief of this building, and I was thinking about popcorn and chewing bones." **Fabian Marcaccio**

▲MS: There is something relentless in it, almost the brutality of the masses which maybe in the context of studio is actually quite interesting. The fact that you make these masses that are hovering over—they meet the ground in a very strange way. And one thing for me is the impact of the medium—the animation as the way you make this thing, and also the animation as the way we are actually seeing this versus the more disciplined medium of plans and section. A section through a building like this would have done a very different thing to the legs meeting the ground. ▲FM: The situation of the mapping, actually, in your case of this band map that travels and distorts and creates a relief like places is a good example of a humble use of gesture. And the way they circulate is a really simple and works even when the envelope breaks with the geometry. I actually enjoy that a lot. I was looking at the relief of this building, and I was thinking about popcorn and chewing bones. ▲HDA: I'll tell you right now, my next studio is popcorn. It's popcorn architecture. I'm saying it in public. Not here, in Sci-Arc. In Sci-Arc I can do whatever I want. ▲PE: It seems you can do whatever you want here. ▲FP: It seems the texture mapping is a rationalization of the under-symmetry of this form, and you don't need that. What is nice about popcorn is that you can have architectural elements, which is the ground relationship, but then you can have a texture that has nothing to do with that. It would have been fantastic if you built up. Here you have a grain, you're dialing the concrete, and then maybe you're not mapping it correctly so sometimes it has a glitch. Those things should be done on purpose. Fabian said the popcorn on the form, and I saw the way you did the animation where they pop up like that, then they kind of bundle together, and of course it's a surface. It has no mass, but if you see the grain of the grid, it's really strange how it tries to be architecture. ▲FM: The metaphors of explosion and destruction, even if they are controlled, are a taboo subject in architecture. That's why architects have a fascination with Matta Clark, because it's not controlled. ▲PE: Matta Clark? ▲FM: Yeah. Everybody talks about that because he can make a hole in a building. No architects can do it because it's a wall, and you cannot get away with it. But it's an interesting thing that we could really study more. Especially the controlled demolition, the popcorn. ▲MFG: Back to deconstruction. ▲FM: Pop! And you have something else. ▲MFG: Neo-deconstruction.

▲5

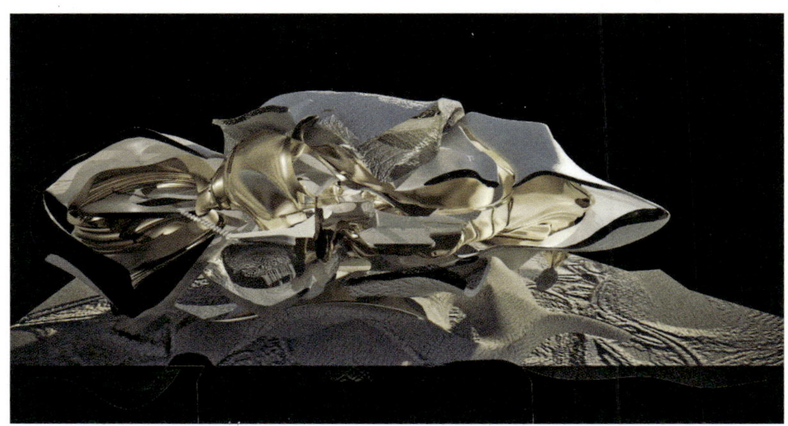

▲6

▲7

▲8

HAELEE JUNG & JACK WOLFE

We begin with the creation of coral structures
through continuous surfaces that folded back on
themselves. These become monolithic figural forms
that are then carved along straight lines. The cut
frames the building within the site. Like a window
frame, the building captures a single moment in a
landscape or a cut object form. Rather than a dis-
creetly bound form, the cut suggests an infinite continuation of the object. The interior is carved with
boxes to create occupiable space as well as to provide a regular geometry to read against expressive
form. Our surface treatment for the coral structures
is inspired by Otto Wagner's floral motifs and his
treatment of ornament as continuous surface patterns, uninterrupted by architectural elements. As
opposed to the classical model of ornament, which
embellishes structural elements, Wagner treats
walls as textiles. We introduce Wagner's vertical
landscape to our reinterpretation of the Secessionist Building as the ornamental system. Our final system is a membrane structure that lives within the
body of the cut mass. These flexible gallery spaces
expand and contract to accommodate changing
exhibits. Conceived as a singular entity that procre-
ates through cell division, these spaces suggest a literal corporality—the inhabitation of the body itself
as opposed to the classical notion of scale and proportion in relation to the body. [▲ 9–12]

> "Right now, you have a 100 billion dollar
> budget. If you had a 100 million dollar
> budget, I want to see what you would
> have to remove." **Mark Foster Gage**

▲**MFG:** It is interesting that you have an
argument for the cute part at one scale, and, what
do you call it, evil? ▲**Jack Wolfe:** Gross. ▲**MFG:** And
the gross part at another scale. The stair and floor
scale is totally and aesthetically inert. It seems very
separated. Cute here at this scale, gross here at this
scale, and generic at this scale. Is that just an after
effect? ▲**PT:** It looks like you are using architectural
cuts for floors, for facades, and for grounds. But
then I think you are using a butcher cut, basically,
under the window, and that makes up these poche
things. ▲**FP:** I noticed another thing that you have
done that I think is quite smart. Peter was asking
about how you address the site. You guys address
the site with these perpendicular cuts, so you have
an invisible envelope. You don't recognize it as a
cut, but as a façade. The cow stuff I'm not sure I
understand. The gross stuff is actually not gross at
all. ▲**HDA:** This studio is not about the pursuit of
affect. ▲**MS:** I think the definition of the surface and
the texture is quite important. Imagine, just as an
example—your project has many different degrees
of curvature. Imagine if, when it was flat, it was
Murakami-esque, and when it was curved it became
fleshier. What if the whole meat or flesh thing
had appeared on the underside of the Murakami
surfaces? ▲**JE:** It seems that we're all talking about
this dichotomy. I think Mark was saying, "Would
it be more strange and uncanny to be looking at
something that was cute?" As I look at it, all of
a sudden I realize it is part of something gross.
▲**MFG:** When you cut off a project like that,
it implies that it could just go on forever. Like
it's not a composition, it's a system, and you've
just taken out a chunk of this system. ▲**PE:** I
think it's great. ▲**MFG:** Crazy. ▲**PE:** Why not?
▲**MFG:** You can't have a world-encompassing
system that you're taking chunks of, and then
have an argument that they don't have enough
contextual relationship. ▲**PE:** They don't, in this one
they didn't. ▲**MFG:** I don't think that really qualifies
as a design. ▲**GL:** I know they're all together. But
it just raises questions about editing. ▲**MFG:** I
wonder why there's so many moves in the form.
Right now, you have a 100 billion dollar budget. If
you had a 100 million dollar budget, I want to see
what you would have to remove. ▲**FP:** But these are
also compositional issues, I think everything here
could be in a movie. Like how do you work with the
frames? Where do you stop the camera? ▲**MFG:**
Peter likes the chopping. If you scaled it up four
times, and then chopped it against the sides, I'll bet
it would be a much more interesting project. **PE:**
Chopping in all directions. ▲**FM:** You win the prize
for idiosyncrasy.

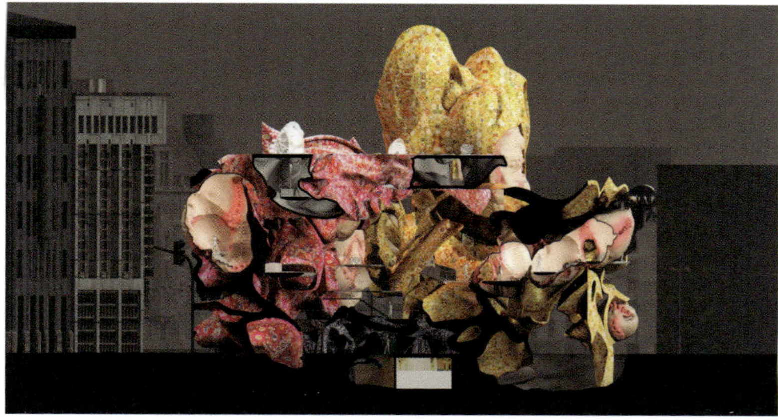

▲ 9

▲ 10

▲ 11

▲ 12

Exploring New Value in Design Practice
Phillip Bernstein & Brian Kenet

How do we make design a more profitable practice? Design practice has traditionally positioned building as a commodity in the delivery supply chain, valued by clients like other products and services purchased at lowest first cost. Despite the fact that the building sector in its entirety operates in large capital pools where significant value is created, intense market competition, sole focus on differentiation by design quality, and lack of innovation in project delivery and business models have resulted in a profession that is grossly underpaid and marginally profitable. The profession must explore new techniques for correlating the real value of an architect's services to clients and thereby break the downward pressure on design compensation. This seminar redesigns the value proposition of architecture practice, explores strategies used by better-compensated adjacent professions and markets, and investigates methods by which architects can deliver—and be paid for—the value they bring to the building industry.

JOHN KLEINSCHMIDT & ADAM WAGONER
Prefabulous
Prefabrication at the scale of an entire building demands an acceptance of change and the shouldering of additional risk from myriad entities in an industry that is already fragmented, uncoordinated, and litigious. Rather than bite off more than we can chew, what if we focus prefabrication on one discrete element of a building? Targeting one specialized piece allows for rapid prototyping and a more focused feedback loop, which might enable us to refine the product in order to maximize its benefits to the design and construction industries without fundamentally changing the entire structure of how those industries operate. Large-scale disruption is a long-term goal; in the meantime, targeted disruption is the name of the game. With this in mind, we have created a design-build firm that aims to harness the "circular economy" to rethink residential kitchens as a service that we lease rather than a product that we sell. Our flat-pack kitchens are modular and made of high-quality, durable materials that can be easily recycled and reused. By leasing kitchens, we enable easy remodeling and reduce initial hard costs of new buildings by spreading the cost of the kitchen over time.

Reinforcing Urban Tissue: Strategies to Reactivate Public Space and Integrate Community
Tatiana Bilbao

Bernard Rudofsky predicted the death of urban public space in American cities because they were being dehumanized by planning that favored automobiles. This model was reproduced throughout the world, especially in underdeveloped countries trying to develop along American lines. Planning for automobiles led to broken communities with social tensions, crime, and lack of social cohesion. Public space, which can be an important activator of a community's cohesion and success for the quality of life, lost its significance in the city and in society. While many efforts to regain public space have been successful in having a positive impact on the development of a community, there is not a clear strategy that can be applied to all cities. This seminar analyzed successful and unsuccessful cases of public place-making in underdeveloped countries in an effort to create a series of reproducible strategies to reactivate public space and to serve as a way to critique and propose new urban planning ideas today.

APOORVA KHANOLKAR
Modernizing Mumbai: A Vertical Facelift for the Slumdog City
This paper takes the form of a speculative study, examining one of the most controversial large-scale urban interventions in South Asia in recent years—The Bhendi Bazaar Redevelopment Proposal in Mumbai, India. This planned comprehensive overhaul of a high-density mixed-use precinct in the heart of the colonial city is the first of its kind in scope and impact and promises to change the face of the metropolis and the lives of millions. After a long and complicated approval process mired in legal, social, and planning roadblocks, it is finally slated to begin construction this year. The paper charts the agency and urgency of the project in transforming the area from squalid marketplace to swanky 'global' district vis-à-vis Mumbai's past and current urban ambitions, gauging its position and impact on the region's larger social, political, economic and communal landscapes. The scope of investigation primarily hinges around the question of whether the scheme's decontextualized, fragmented western aspirations are so fundamentally flawed in their origins that it is but a recipe for disaster from the get-go, or whether this much-maligned yet rather courageous proposal can become the city's own Cinderella Story and pave the way for the kind of urbanity that Mumbai desperately needs.

EUGENE TAN
The Social in Singapore's Smart Nation
Singapore thrives on being a test bed for new urban ideas. From Corbusian public housing to Metabolist-inspired megastructures, the city must be continually rebuilt in order to remain globally attractive and regionally competitive. Singapore's latest reinvention is the architecture-negating Smart Nation initiative. Officially launched in 2014, its seeds were planted eight years before with the founding of the National Research Foundation. It funded strategic alliances with renowned institutions such as MIT, ETH Zurich, and TU Delft on the grounds that research would align with and enable Singapore's national agenda. Fulfillment, community, and free expression are promised in the Smart Nation. However, using the work of Max Weber, Georg Simmel, and Jean-Jacques Rousseau as lenses for viewing these research driven interventions, quite the opposite is observed. These negative social scenarios have nothing to do with space, but revolve around technology. This obsolescence may give architects a chance to take stock. While Singapore or other smart cities may have detached themselves from architectural invention or criticality, there is enough evidence to suggest that spaces of resistance can emerge within these cities of hyper-connectedness. They may also catalyze unprecedented degrees of technological embrace, aiming to empower inhabitants beyond current smart city proposals.

Writing on Architecture
Carter Wiseman

The goal of this course is to train students in the principles and techniques of nonfiction writing as it applies to architecture. The course includes readings from the work of prominent architects, critics, and literary figures, as well as reviews of books and exhibitions, opinion pieces, and formal presentations of buildings and projects. Class writing includes the development of an architectural firm's mission statement, drafting proposals for design commissions, web texts, and other forms of professional communication. The main focus is an extended paper on a building selected from a variety of types and historical periods, such as skyscrapers, private houses, industrial plants, gated communities, malls, institutional buildings, and athletic facilities.

ISAAC SOUTHARD
Ghost House
Its presence looms large over the gridded city yet tourists ask time and time again, "Where is it?" Hidden from view it begs to be discovered, but its silhouette deceives. Landlocked in the fabric of an old neighborhood, it is both artifact and abstraction. "Ghost House" is an architecture of art and history; a landmark that continues the reading of the past. Ghost House is a memorial to Benjamin Franklin and the house he built for himself in 1760 on the same site in Philadelphia. The memorial was designed in 1970 by Venturi Scott Brown & Associates and consists of an abstracted steel frame that follows the outline of Benjamin Franklin's original house. The plan of the house is represented in the paving materials of the court. White marble suggests the interior walls and gray slate the space between. Raised planters and steps provide places for the public to congregate, rest, and contemplate. Smooth faced concrete viewing portals are superimposed over the court marking locations of previous archaeological sites below. As a memorial, Ghost House is loaded with historical significance. It suggests the architecture of the Revolutionary Period, the influence of Benjamin Franklin, and the complex history of the United States. As a work of architecture, however, its significance is much subtler but nonetheless profound. Ghost House revolutionized how we perceive history and marked a turning point in the design of representative structures. Rather than reconstructing from inadequate historical documents, its constructed silhouette allows the viewer to read his or her own interpretation of what once was, as if to admit the unstable soil on which the foundations of historical reconstruction rest. The design is a quintessential work of the post-modern era in its dialogue with both historicist and modernist principles.

Venice: Urban and Architectural Histories of a Maritime Republic
Daniel Sherer

This seminar explores Venice, a place where multiple histories of politics, commerce, religion, art, and science intersect, all of which presuppose a unique reciprocity of architecture and urban form. This course traces the genesis the city from late antiquity to the present; investigates how political myth and urban reality are implicated in the Piazza S. Marco, the Rialto, and the Grand Canal; and studies how singular forms of continuity and collective memory shape the interaction of type and morphology. The seminar also examines the various formal, functional, and structural strategies that architects have deployed when coming to grips with the singularity of Venice. The second half of the seminar analyzes the challenges faced by contemporary practices when negotiating with the historical image of a city. The course ends by repositioning the Venice Biennale in terms of the dialogue it has fostered between the contemporary culture of the spectacle and the diverse imperatives of historical understanding.

ALISSA CHASTAIN
Over the centuries, Venice has positioned itself as the heir of Rome and the Byzantine Empire; and physically accumulated layers of spolia from all over the world because of its position as the center of trade routes. This intentional mythology is demonstrated through the careful repurposing of spolia. Venice synthesizes the aesthetic traditions of multiple cultures to create something distinctly its own. Venice has a difficult history with modern architectural projects. Part of this is due to a distrust of outsiders. There were only two modern architects to have significant work built in Venice: Ignazio Gardella and Carlo Scarpa. Casa alle Zattere is Gardella's only project in Venice, but it is one of the city's only completely new projects. When seen from afar the building looks as though it could have

been there forever. The quiet architecture allowed for its construction in the first place, and Gardella leverages the subtle exterior to exercise more design freedom on the interior and at a smaller scale. Carlo Scarpa was born in Venice in 1900 and grew up in Vicenza and Venice before attending the Academy of Fine Arts. He has three major projects in Venice, all of which are interior and renovation projects. With the exterior architecture already in place, Scarpa had the freedom to experiment with his own aesthetic. The most unifying trait that emerges from his work is the fragmentation of the surface at material joints. Scarpa's knowledge of his motherland gave him unique insight into the city's architecture, which profoundly changed the nature of his designs. Because Venice is an island, everything has to be built. It is a place of accumulation, and Scarpa's architecture is one of careful expression. This modulation of the ground plane and construction of overlapping elements is taken to its furthest extent in Scarpa's work at the Fondazione Querini Stampalia in 1963. The water enters the main level through the screens on the canal and moves into the gallery space. The water level changes based on the tides and season. The interior floor acts as a bridge or container that floats above the water. The visitor is physically aware of the loss of the ground plane.

HUGO FENAUX

The Masieri Memorial: Frank Lloyd Wright and Venice

The urban condition in Venice has always been tenuous. Even more eloquent than the fact that Venice rises like reeds from the lagoon, the practice of new construction within the city has been an area of rather strong contention. On one side, the conservationists parade Venice as the frozen remnant of an idyllic, bygone era, and on the other, the modernists seek to claim for Venice a foothold within modernity, vying for a resurgence of the old Venetian power—Rome in the lagoon. Many architects have tried to build on the tumultuous islands of Venice, and all too often, regardless of the proposals worth, those lacking in native blood were rebuked: Louis Kahn, Frank Lloyd Wright, Le Corbusier, and Peter Eisenman among them. While their sites and strategies may all differ, the unifying categorical description as foreigners was the first of many issues that plagued Venetian architectural climate. The story of Wright's unbuilt project in Venice is one that treads, with heavy steps, the fragile precipice of change: on the one, side Venice's historical identity, and on the other, its place within the future. While such a smalland modest project spurred such an intense debate, the true legacy of the Masieri Memorial was bringing to light these concerns of conservation and larger issues related to identity, and the assumption of identity, within a project of architecture. The discourse that followed set the stage for large-scale urban protection strategies that changed the course of architecture in Venice in the later half of the 20th century.

ALICIA POZNIAK

Venice: Part and Whole, The Development of Piazza San Marco and the Doge's Palace

By the fall of the Venetian Republic in the late 18th century, Piazza San Marco had become its principal urban space. The city's most civic institutions defined its perimeter, the arrangement of which has remained largely unchanged to today. Symbiotically, the Doge's Palace or Palazzo Ducale located at the Piazza's head, had developed as the Republic's house of governmental power. Both these urban components share complex and blurred histories and their developments are intertwined. However, the genesis of the Piazza spatially and formally emerged as a macrocosm of the Doge's Palace complex. This is not to say the development of one has been entirely influenced by the other, but that the courtyard type of the Palace is reproduced in the urban form of the city's largest and most important *campo*—Piazza San Marco. There are three main developmental periods of the Piazza and Palazzo. The first began in the 9th century with the establishment of the Palace as a fortified *castrum*, said to be influenced by Diocletian's Palace in Spalato (Split, Croatia). The second period during the 12th century saw the major reformation of the Piazza and consolidation of the Palace reflecting Venice's rising power. In the final period during the Gothic and Renaissance years, the Palace was formally completed and the Piazza widened at its hinge point around St Mark's campanile. Interestingly, the final urban composition had influence elsewhere beyond Venice which describes a circle of time. Between 1860 and 1928, in Split, Croatia, a new Republic Square was built after Venice's just west of the ruins of Diocletian's Palace. The symbolism of transplanting the Venetian Piazza back to its origins in Spalato is prodigious. It reinforces the immortalisation of Venice spatially and ideologically and ultimately demonstrates the inherent part to whole relationships of the city's generative urban components: Piazza San Marco and the Doge's Palace.

3239b

Launch: Architecture and Entrepreneurialism
Keller Easterling

This seminar studies the designer as entrepreneur. Contemporary entrepreneurs usually understand not only how to capitalize a business but also how to play market networks with the viral dissemination of both objects and aesthetic regimes. While the architecture profession has absorbed many of the technologies that markets use in their population thinking, practice is nevertheless structured to support architecture conceived as singular creations. This seminar considers both historical and contemporary moments in architectural and urban design when architects conceived of buildings, building components, or formats as repeatable products—products that, in the aggregate, may have the power to create an alteration to a local or global environment. The final project is a business/design-plan wherein students serve as each other's publicists.

ANDREW STERNAD & ANNE HOUSEHOLDER

Welcome to the Bloomburbs

Historically, home ownership has been an essential part of the American Dream: kids playing sports in the front yard and the street, families grilling out in their back yards, and neighbors chatting porch to porch. However, the characteristic spaces we imagine are often highly underused. Privacy is valued over productivity in both social and environmental terms. Bloomburbs, Inc., is a for-profit agricultural enterprise that identifies this space and puts it to use in collaboration with local communities. Not only are the environmental, spatial, and cultural implications great, but in time the transition from Boomburb to Bloomburb could catalyze a complete redevelopment of the suburban streetscape. As part of their planning, Bloomburbs require a pre-engineered community center from which agricultural operations are based. This facility can be rented for multiple uses, such as a micro distribution hub for national delivery services during peak holiday seasons. Auxiliary spaces at the distribution center may also be rented for events such as small concerts and meetings. As the community naturally turns over, 2% of each home purchase will be allocated to the sustenance of the landscape in a fund specifically setup for each respective subdivision. As this fund grows over time, each Bloomburb will shift to become a semi-independent co-op with its own management structure. Our organization will stay involved as a land management company for a percentage of the annual harvest revenue. Bloomburbs, Inc., aims to demonstrate the value of rethinking suburban landscapes. Over time, we aspire to grow beyond left over spaces and use the entire zone encompassing streets, driveways, and lawns as a new public common space. In the future, a broad swath of public greenspace, a new suburban common, will bind homes and subdivisions together. By reconceptualizing the notion of public and private amenities, Bloomburbs, Inc., offers a comprehensive, long-term lifestyle retrofit for suburbia.

SUSAN SHUO WANG & KAROLINA CZECZEK

Chameleon Properties

Housing, immigration policy, and urban transformation are controversial and contemporary issues. As architects and urban planners, we see opportunities in creating more thoughtful connections between real estate, immigration, and planning to benefit the city and its inhabitants. Current investment channels often seek returns in the easiest ways. This flood of capital attenuates increasing class divisions and the globalized nature of capital and human migration specifically in steel and glass towers that are affecting the financial structure of real estate and reorganizing our urban landscapes with new symbols of economic inequality. Chameleon Properties seeks to engage with five land-use and financing phenomena: 1. a transformation of the American urban skyline producing spaces that are secretive and often vacant, 2. the emergence of taller, skinnier, richer skyscrapers in New York City, 3. the influx of foreign capital into US real estate, 4. an existing immigration investment program, and 5. an urgent housing shortage. By combining mutual interests and subverting the logic of existing models, our proposal aims for results that are bigger than the sum of their parts. Our company employs an investment strategy in which foreign investors capitalize on US real estate for return and permanent residency status. Chameleon Properties uses these funds to subdivide existing vacant apartments into Single Room Occupancy dwellings that fulfill the demand for housing. A portion of the investment is then channeled to establish businesses that provide amenities and jobs to the community—grocery stores, swimming pools, childcare and co-working spaces—negotiating different urban densities and development models to create a win-win situation for investors, the public, and our company. By inverting the secrecy of investments, we divert typical flows of investment into the city and encourage creative uses of capital to support local communities.

SAMANTHA JAFF, PEARL HO, MADELYNN RINGO

Memory Parks

The cultural stigma surrounding contemporary funerary architecture and burial practices stems from 18th—and 20th—century traditions and a concern with sanitation, population growth, as well as a social, political, and religious relationship with human mortality. The cemetery has evolved into an island of the dead—completely removed from the quotidian space of society. The problem of current cemeteries lie not in a shortage of burial space, but rather in our cultural conception of appropriate burial space as well as how that space can function on the urban scale. By freeing the burial site of its land-locked position on the outskirts of the city, the cemetery can be broken up and mapped onto vacant urban lots, thereby creating a network of smaller "Memory Parks." These places rethink the site of the burial ground and its adaptation to an urban context. The cemetery is paired with other programs to become a public amenity and a way to generate money for the city; programming these sites provides incentive for buyers and investors to acquire and develop vacant lots. Rather than having one large cemetery, the project proposes to shrink them in size and increase them in number. This fragmentation inspires a more local and individualized idea of the final resting place for the urban environment. Our cultural relationship with mortality is changing from one that suppresses and ostracizes those at the end of their lives, to one that accepts time, nature, and human limitations. The space of funerary practices and their relationship to the city must be reconsidered in light of this more meaningful and productive engagement with death. Memory Parks are a first step in that direction.

Unreal City
Niall McLaughlin

Critics
Niall McLaughlin {NM}
Norman R. Foster Visiting Professor

Instructor
Andrew Benner {AB}

Jurors
Pier Vittorio Aureli {PVA}, Julian Bonder {JB},
Frida Escobedo {FE}, David Kohn {DK}, Jennifer
Leung {JL}, Petia Morozov {PM}, Alan Organschi
{AO}, Surry Schlabs {SS}, Mike Tonkin {MT},
Billie Tsien {BT}

Recently, London's mayor suggested that the city should seek greater devolved powers from the United Kingdom. This sprawling urban area generates a significant proportion of the nation's wealth. It does so by selling knowledge and services to the world. If it became separate, it would take its place among very few autonomous cities that operate without any natural hinterland, thriving off the abstract movement of international trade. It already has formed an international community through its inveterate appetite for immigration. Almost no one in London is from London. To be really at home there you need to be from abroad. How would you make public architecture in a city so divorced from the key determinants of place: people, landscape, ways of making things from what lies nearby? Architects in the 20th century produced an abstract language for buildings to signify this duality—everywhere/elsewhere. It gradually replaced classicism as the representative system of choice to embody the more abstract institutional values associated with modernity. We wonder whether it is possible to reconsider the representative capacity of architecture. At heart, public architecture has always laid claim to be a representation of the world. This studio looks at the possibility of designing buildings in London that can create public meanings in the context of an autonomous world city. We are interested in how cities emerge over time through a repeating process of doing and undoing. There is no final form, only the next iteration. In this, we observe an analogy with the design process itself. Perhaps design could be a process of doing and undoing; one in which ideas emerge through making, and making is stimulated by emerging ideas. Doing again and again is about testing, rehearsing, or shifting your point of view. As a process of trial and error, doing and undoing suggests the production of difference, the gaps that exist between intention and outcome, between the previous and the next. Doing can also be seen as a ritual act analogous to everyday habitation, the rhythms, cyclical repetitions, and irregularities that determine the social life of buildings and cities.

We are particularly interested in addressing the question of architecture's representative capacity through the relationship between ideas and material practice. We see instances in architecture where meanings have evolved out of material or constructional necessity. Conversely, we often see new kinds of material practice being brought into being to answer the challenges of novel ways of conceptualizing the world. We are interested both in the truth and fiction of materials: their ability to reveal and to deceive. To "fabricate" means to make by skill and labor, or by assembling parts or sections, but also to devise a legend or a lie, to fake or forge a document. We find the idea of material metamorphosis and the ambivalent potential of fabrication inspiring for architecture today. We question the extent to which materials can continue to reflect the geography and socioeconomic position of a specific site and we look for material innovations that can transcend the limits of place.

ALISSA CHASTAIN ✸

The basis for "Unreal City" is London reimagined with devolved powers. Receiving devolved powers gives London greater autonomy and governmental control which would precipitate the need for more regional government centers. The proposed assembly buildings are representative of the different boroughs of London. This new devolved government examines the nature of government, especially small-scale government, and the type of spaces that it requires. An important part of this studio was the process of making and unmaking. A series of artifacts were made that reflect how government could be visualized as a procedure or new kind of space. These artifacts then began to be incorporated into the architectural ideas of the building. The project began by rethinking of an older studio project. The goal was to invert a more traditional theater type—a single space within poché—so that everything lives within the wall. The result was an L-shaped wall with a series of punctures and setbacks. This wall was then aggregated to enclose a central square space with expanding layers. The functional and inhabited space of the new wall creates a labyrinth and makes a space for procession and a series of small spaces that could become a model for a new type of government. Rather than having a singular large area for gathering, the building favors circulation through a series of small spaces. {▲1–4}

"You capitalize on the banality of the service space." **Pier Vittorio Aureli**

▲PVA: It's an extremely well resolved composition. In a plan like this, you have both the most institutional spaces, which are also the most interesting spaces, and then you have service spaces. You capitalize on the banality of the service space by creating solid walls, which then become the main element to define your own space. Actually, it's very similar to what happened in this building. Rudolph really hated closets. So in fact, the building is full of storage hidden between walls, which keeps the walls very thick and also very clean from objects. ▲SS: This notion of privileging the interstices—the in between spaces in the building which revolve around a democratic seated government—is really powerful if you consider an interpersonal dialogue the germ of democracy. Dialogue is something that happens between people. Here you have a project where one is constantly passing between things, and there is ample opportunity for random unexpected and potentially productive encounter. With that said, there's also the danger of this becoming something like Kafka's *The Trial*, where one passes through the interstices and suddenly finds him or herself captured by the bureaucratic apparatus of the state. I prefer the kind of first reading. ▲BT: I like the relationship that you have with the water and with the canal. And I feel like it makes the water have a very beautiful relationship with the buildings. I too have a slight worry that one could be wandering the halls. So I think the idea of a labyrinth is good, but I think that it might be worthwhile to make more clear the primary way through, so that if you needed to find something fairly quickly you understand that you can go and become lost, but you also understand that there is another level of clarity that helps you get there. ▲NM: We asked each student to show us a piece of work from their previous portfolios that they wanted to take forward, then on the basis of Lars von Trier's *The Five Obstructions*, we asked them to recreate that piece of work five times under different exacting conditions to see how we could get them to interrogate what was habitual to them. What you're seeing mostly in the background of these projects today is people breaking lots of eggs and hoping to make an omelet. What's interesting about you as a student is you never broke an egg once. And I'm not saying that's a good thing or a bad thing, but it's certainly unlike everybody else in the studio. ▲PVA: The way you say it seems almost like a negative comment. ▲NM: I'm not sure that you didn't struggle enough. It's not about the amount of effort or struggle. It's that there is an architectural idea contained in this and it gets reiterated again and again, and it gets elaborated. I find the singular nature of your development process not a good or a bad thing, but as something that is worthy of comment.

▲1

▲2

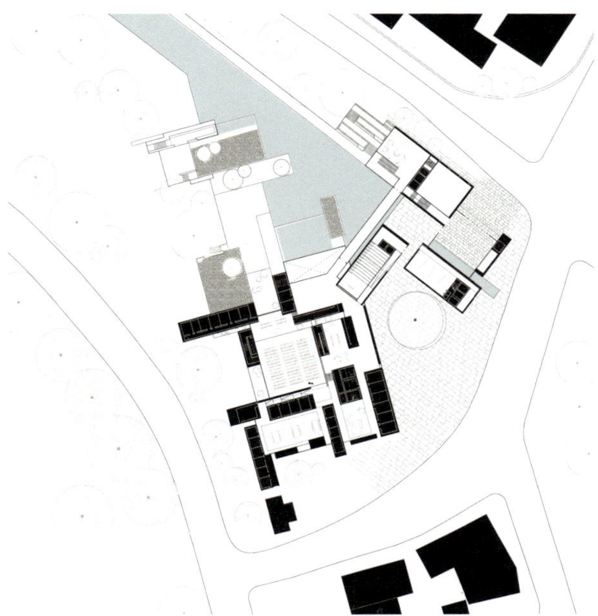

▲3

▲4

MAYA ALEXANDER

East London, and more specifically Whitechapel, is a neighborhood that has always been a destination for the newest citizens of London. Defined at the turn of the 20th century by its bustling docks and robust working class population, it has now become a cultural center for Bangladeshi people in London. However with growth and mobility, the Bangladeshis are slowly moving out and yet another new constituency, primarily eastern Europeans, have begun to move in. The transient nature of this neighborhood was a departure point for imagining a civic space that could accommodate the current population, but also acknowledge the adaptive nature of the community. Using the existing row houses located on the site as an anchor, this project seeks to express the codependence between history and governance and a diverse and changing populace. The row house type, which dominated the urban fabric of this neighborhood a hundred years ago, is now limited to vestigial moments. In most cases, these human scale buildings have been replaced with larger structures that have restricted public access and minimal open space. The "Meeting Wall" is a scaffolding structure that traces the footprint of the historic row houses on the site. On the eastern end, the scaffolding is mirrored and supports itself to create a meeting hall for public assembly. The western side is supported by tension cables which connect back to the row houses and create a shaded plaza that people can gather in for more informal assembly. ❴▲5–8❵

"There are possible figures for the architect that are between the absolute abnegation of authorship and the master of the universe." **Niall McLaughlin**

▲**PVA:** You idealize East London, which to me represents the main problem of how London is turning itself into a city that is not made for people but for cash. East London is right now being heavily gentrified and, actually, one of the Trojan horses of this process is exactly public space. We have to realize that right now public space is becoming extremely problematic, because often it's used as a kind of stooge to open up processes of transformation of renewal which sometimes turn very aggressive to other populations in spite of the good intentions of the architects. There is a trend of participation. We are very seduced by this idea, but the reality is very different, we are much more apathetic to the construction of the city. Certainly we don't have involvement of people in the 12th or 14th century people had in the construction for their own city. ▲**SS:** I think there is a symbolic richness to it as a sort of scaffold, not just a physical scaffold, with an explicit reference to the gothic, but as a social scaffold too. Maybe it's overly romanticized, but this apparatus can support a range of different social functions in the public square. The reference to the gothic is apt. It's important to remember that the gothic revival wasn't just a stylistic movement run by architects, it was about making small things and about enriching the lives of everyday people through the creation of beautiful objects. ▲**DK:** Maybe the funny thing about your project is it's almost too beautifully made. It's a really beautiful model and the model has a kind of completeness that is slightly at odds with the incompleteness you're looking for. What does it mean that it's beautiful, but you're trying to make it a social project? ▲**JL:** I keep thinking of some examples from art practice and art history. I'm thinking Thomas Hirschhorn. The cultural artifact is a sense of shared patrimony. It's part of the language of incompleteness but also rigor. I'm curious, how demountable is this? ▲**NM:** I'm moved by the formal aspect of the scaffold. But I'm slightly concerned that there's a political conversation that says there are only two poles: an architect that is the great controller of all things, or the entirely participatory project in which there's no authorship at all. There are possible figures for the architect that are between the absolute abnegation of authorship and the master of the universe. I do feel that this is a project where you know what kind of architect you're going to be. I have a feeling it does set a program for you as an architect.

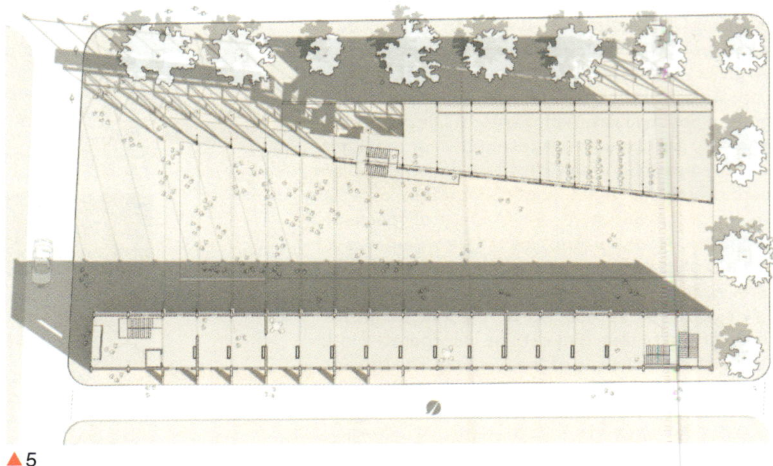

▲5

▲6

▲7

▲8

JULIE KIM

Whitechapel Community Center is an immigration center servicing an evolving immigrant population in the borough of Tower Hamlets and Greater London. It addresses the issue of democracy as an opportunity for the underrepresented to be represented. Built conceptually and spatially off the scale and idea of one voting booth, the first threshold into the building is composed of a series of permanent voting frames. Each consecutive space doubles in size and program and accommodates offices niches, classrooms, meeting spaces, and a long assembly hall. The hall sits above the initial voting booth signifying the collective voice. The building's poche follows a similar pattern of growth as the voting frames thicken to allow bookshelves, small closets for chairs, circulation, and restrooms. The construction sequence aligns with the logic of the building's concept as it is composed solely of wooden panels and slats. The building investigates the idea of democracy as a true collective voice of the people as visitors and users are combed through the fin-like building from the booth into the long assembly hall. As the façade of the building becomes a machine for democracy to occur on a regular basis, the procession of casting a vote, walking through the booth, into or past the line of sequentially growing spaces, and emptying into the large assembly hall reveals how the individual voice transforms into a part of the collective identity. [▲ 9–12]

"You industrialized political participation, which I find a very apt commentary or the way democratic participation has been reduced today." **Pier Vittorio Aureli**

▲MT: It has a feeling sort of like an agricultural building, like you're leveling democracy to some sort of bureaucratic medium, but then the poetry of going through them and arriving in this big space is fantastic. When you go through the House of Lords and House of Commons, the spaces get bigger and bigger until you get to the House of Lords and it is seven stories tall and you're sitting in this chamber. The scale is ridiculous. You have scale in the plan working, but I wonder if there's a way to make the section work as well. Because it's a wonderful piece of work. ▲SS: The term 'combing' didn't bring up agricultural associations but rather hair as a sort of ultimate metaphor as a relationship between the individual and the collective. I'm ambivalent about everything being comprised of individual hairs as it were, but I really enjoy the procession from small scale to the collective. And the notion that you could use these as voting booths during elections is a really nice thought for me. Here we often use schools for voting, but then ironically they close the schools for security reasons, and then you have to keep your kids home which is a pain in the ass. Whereas on the west coast in San Francisco you have polling places in the back of laundromats, and pizza places, which I think is really wonderful. I can imagine that you pass through the voting block on your way to some other collective function ▲PVA: I like this breaking down of the unity without losing the legibility. Introducing more bittersweet notes might make the project more interesting because it's also controversial that you reduce the whole issue of democratic participation to the voting booths. From my point of view—sticking to an ancient definition—there is an anti-democratic idea of voting booths, which were introduced as a shortcut to avoid discussion, which is the very essence of democratic practice. For me the voting booth is an industrial machine to create consensus and to rule by majority, which is actually in ancient democracy considered a very anti-democratic attitude. So, there is something very ironic in your voting machine. You industrialized political participation, which I find an apt commentary on the way democratic participation has been reduced today. For me, this one of the most fundamental symptoms of our post-democratic ethos. What redeems this programmatic aspect is the issue of legibility. One of the profound democratic deficits in our cities is the lack of legibility of architecture and urban form, and the way it defines collective and individual domains.

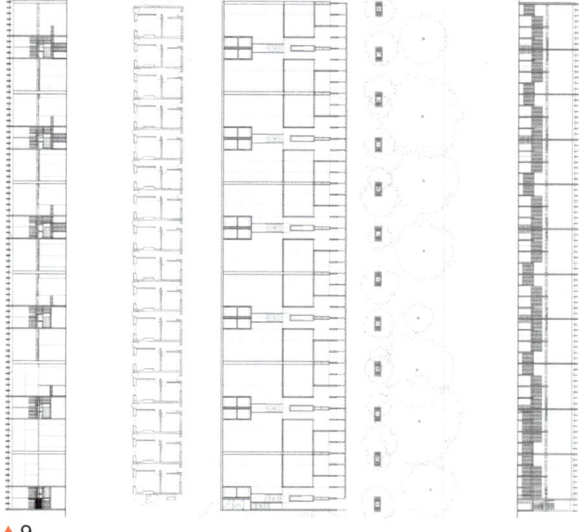

▲ 9

▲ 10

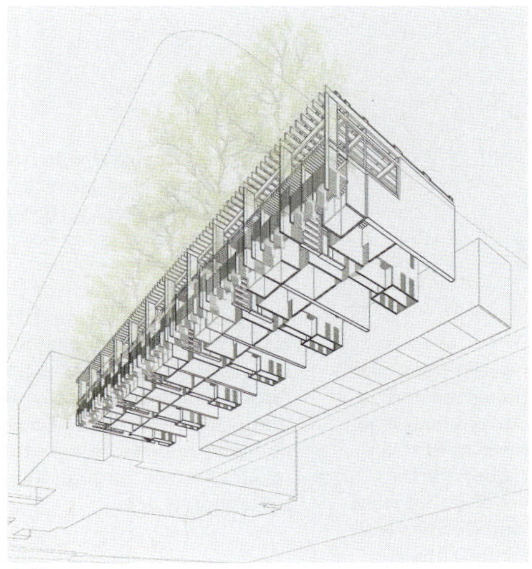

▲ 11

▲ 12

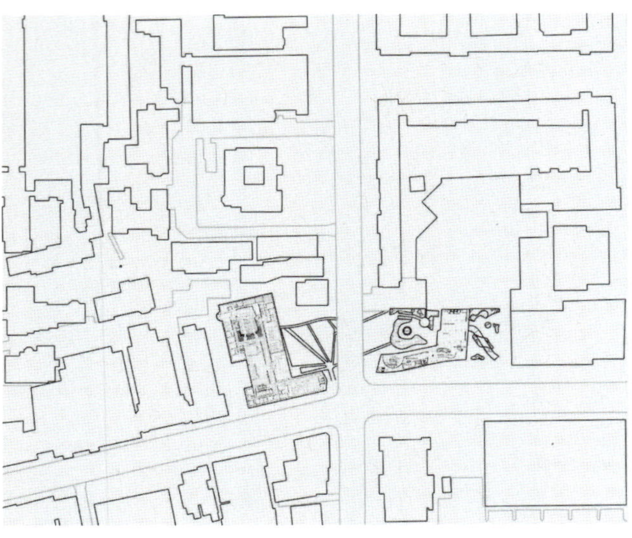

■1

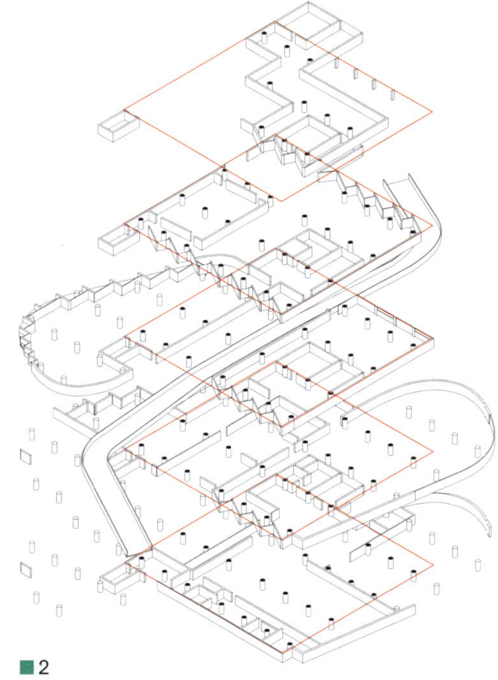

■2

■3

3214b
Construction of Exactitude
Karla Britton

This seminar critically considers modern classicism, not only as a compositional design method and as an evocation of precedents, but also as a language of clarity, reduction, and economy resistant to an unquestioned avant-gardist predilection for the "new." Beginning with the fixed principles that were the legacy of 19th-century French and German Neoclassicism (unity, symmetry, proportion), the seminar continues up through the Rationalism and Formalism that followed the Second World War. Issues explored include the concepts of the ruin and monumentality the Modern Movement's analogies to the classical and the representation of interwar national and political ideologies. Works studied include those by architects, literary/artistic figures, and theorists such as Richardson, Garnier, Perret, Le Corbusier, Rossi, Asplund, Lutyens, Terragni, Speer, Mies, SOM, Kahn, Valéry, Gide, de Chirico, Calvino, Rowe, Krier, Eisenman, Stern, Porphyrios, and Colquhoun.

LAURENCE LUMLEY & ADIL MANSURE

Our study began with a simple idea as a key to Hejduk's strange and elusive world: central to his work is the body. Animating and personifying inorganic bodies with qualities of human or animal bodies is a theme visible through many of his later works. His project can be seen, then, at least in part, as a continual investigation of the analogy of the building as a body. This metaphor is an old one, particularly in the western tradition of classical architecture, and it continues to manifest itself in contemporary practice. In Hejduk's case this manifestation takes the form specifically of a "renovation of the body", as Alberto Perez Gomez has argued. His mysterious architecture operates as an attempt to hold the body together in the face of its modern torture and invest it with meaning as perhaps the last refuge or 'sanctuary' of the soul. This essay explores how, exactly, Hejduk goes about this renovation. It analyzes his work in terms of four classic instances of the body/building metaphor, and shows how he transforms the traditional analogy. If the façade is considered a face, then for Hejduk it is rather a mask, if cladding is skin, it becomes armour, so too structure as upright posture becomes collapsed posture and finally, and perhaps most enigmatically, the inhabitant becomes the soul. In so doing we hope to demonstrate the following: Hejduk reveals himself through this lens—architecture and metaphor as one.

RAPHAEL DE LA FONTAINE & DANIEL LEDFORD

In 1960 the Yale Art and Architecture Building was completed across York Street from Louis I. Kahn's Yale Art Gallery. This analysis aims to answer a central question: how would Paul Rudolph's A&A Building respond to a different architect's Art Gallery design? We present the hypothetical situation in which Lucio Costa and Oscar Niemeyer's Brazilian Pavilion for the 1930 New York World's Fair replaces Kahn's Art Gallery. In this hypothetical, we reconfigure Rudolph's design for the A&A Building, following closely to his own principles of environment explicated in his 1950 publication "The Six Determinants of Architectural Form." Through the analysis of the existing building's reciprocities with its neighbors, and site, paralleled with Rudolph's design philosophies, the project illustrates iterative steps projecting alternative form, massing, and orientation to the hypothetical scenario. The proposed alternative plan shows the A&A relating to Niemeyer's building through a shared continuation of courtyard space that directs and orients the walker in the city scheme. The two buildings form a gateway to campus at the crossing of Chapel and York Streets. (■1)

LUKE ANDERSON & MICHAEL COHEN

Le Corbusier's 1910 Dom-ino model is a vital joint in the construction of architectural continuity from antiquity to the present. Located at the nexus of theory, construction, tradition and modernity, Domino is iconic as both an image and a design methodology. Simultaneously interpreted as abstract and exact, Dom-ino can be read as a highly specific construction system and a conceptual diagram. For the art historian Colin Rowe, "The famous perspective drawing is...the initial didactic statement of the spatial concepts of the modern movement...In the concentrated energy of a few simple gestures are contained implications which for the next 20 years are to condition the development of modern architecture". This project aims to unpack the complex heritage and legacy of Dom-ino. (■2)

3223b
Parallel Moderns
Robert A.M. Stern

This seminar puts forward the argument that what many have accepted as the mutually exclusive discourses of tradition and innovation in the modern architecture of the first half of the 20th century—respectively identified as the "New Tradition" and the "New Pioneers" by Henry Russell Hitchcock in his *Modern Architecture: Romanticism and Reintegration* (1929)—in fact share common genealogy and are integral to its history. The seminar explores in-depth key architects working in the "New Tradition" and goes on to explore its impact for postmodernism in the 1970s and 1980s. The possible emergence of a new synthesis of seeming opposites in the present is also considered. (■3)

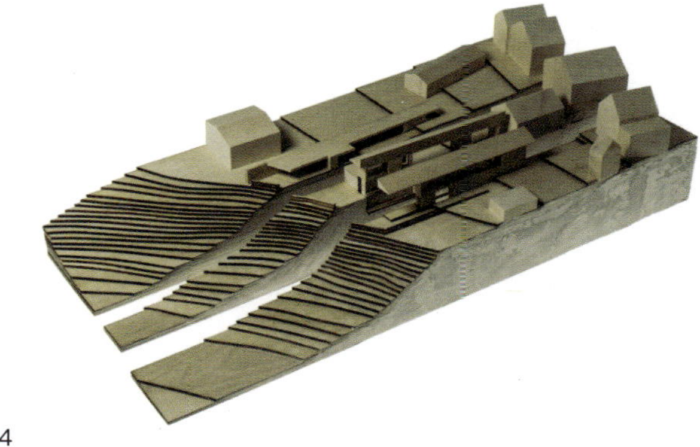

■ 4

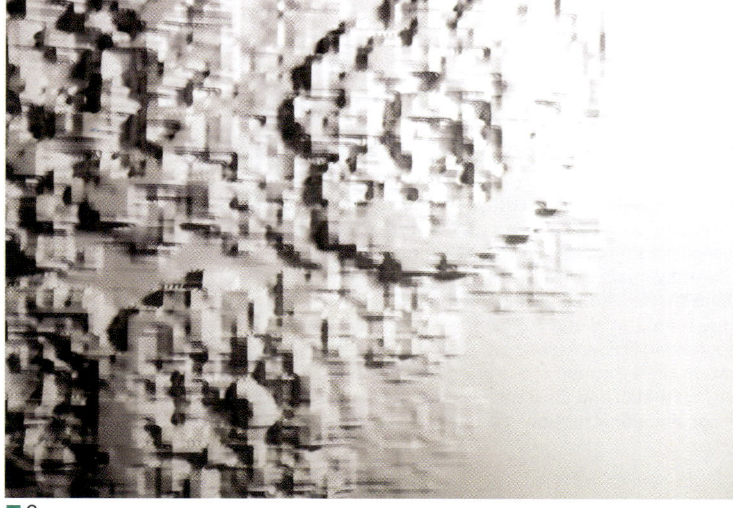

■ 6

■ 5

■ 7

1226b
Sites and Building
Steven Harris

This seminar investigates buildings and their sites. Conceived as a vehicle for understanding the relationship between site and building through critical analysis, the course examines ancient, historic, and contemporary works of architecture and landscape architecture. Material includes works by Hadrian, Diocletian, Michelangelo, Raphael, Palladio, Durand, Schinkel, Lutyens, Asplund, Aalto, Wright, Mies, Kahn, Neutra, Saarinen, Scarpa, Bawa, Krier, Eisenman, Ando, and Gehry. The seminar focuses on site organization strategies and philosophies of site manipulation in terms of topography; urban, suburban, and rural context; ecology; typology; spectacle; and other form-giving imperatives. Methods of site plan representation are also scrutinized.

JASON KURZWEIL

Through concrete, Zumthor's home in Haldenstein, Switzerland echoes the morphology of the region's vernacular architecture, even though it is inward-looking and sets itself apart from its neighbors. A castle in ruins looms on a bluff that overlooks the home; the two are not so different. No doubt this is his own fortress, a manifestation of the famed reclusiveness of the architect. Within, touches of wood and curtains warm the otherwise Spartan concrete dwelling and suggest an extension of the garden. Its program, largely disposed about the central courtyard, turns its back on the street. Approaching the home and studio, one finds few clues of entry. A blank concrete wall with a nondescript door provides passage to the studio. It is a one-sided opacity and supports Zumthor's penchant for working with his back to a wall, while views remain open before him. The home and studio opens to the courtyard and to the inaccessible precipice of mountains beyond. ⎰■ 4⎱

2219b
Craft, Materials, and Digital Artistry
Kevin Rotheroe

This course reviews materials and manufacturing processes especially suited for digitally crafting aesthetically unique architectural components and surfaces. Cross-fertilization of digital and conventional modes of making is emphasized, as this approach often enables economically viable opportunities for creative expression. This is a hands-on, project-based seminar addressing fundamental theoretical issues in the transformation of ideas into material reality via representations, hand-operated tools, and CNC-automated forming devices.

CASEY FURMAN

This work explored the properties of geometric decomposition via a feedback loop of digital and manual means. The purpose of these experiments is to introduce the human hand and error into a digital process. I began my tests with a hand-drawn geometric pattern and translated it into the digital realm and decomposed the pattern in a multitude of ways, both digitally and physically. In later studies, through digital tools, I was able to superimpose dense textures and patterns which created an architecturally replicable form which was then fabricated with foam. The use of a soft material such as foam made it possible to manually edit the resultant form, while still leaving intact the evidence of CNC and digital fabrication. ⎰■ 5⎱

RACHEL GAMBLE

This work examined the translation of a one-dimensional photograph into a three-dimensional architectural surface. Two separate but concurrent lines of research were carried out to achieve the same end result—one, the digital manipulation of the photographic data; and two, learning and cultivating different material and fabrication techniques. By modifying the layers of information in the original image, opportunities to explore texture, depth, and the interplay of shadow and light presented themselves when translating to three dimensions. The final iteration of the photographic data was used to digitally fabricate a surface that combined this research into one single physical artifact sculpted from Corian via subtractive milling techniques. ⎰■ 6⎱

MINU LEE

This project focused on the production of a scale model of an external facade through the process of analog to digital representation. This culminated in an aluminum cast panel that could be mass-produced through a sand-cast molding technique. With an attempt to re-envision the Brutalist motif of Rudolph Hall, its ribbed and uneven characteristics throughout the building interior were traced on paper. The qualities of such traces, which could also vary through the intensity in which they were hand-traced, were then digitally translated into 3D extrusions. The level of these extrusions would change according to the gradient of the traced textures that resulted in a smooth but dynamically fluctuating wall. This model was then 3D milled with high density foam that would become a mold for the aluminum cast panel. The result was a take on addressing the ribbed and bush-hammered concrete through the integration of the unexpected nature of manual labor and the digitally-enhanced output. ⎰■ 7⎱

The Chair
Timothy Newton

The chair has been a crucible for architectural ideas and their design throughout the trajectory of modern architecture. The chair is both a model for understanding architecture and a laboratory for the concise expression of idea, material, fabrication, and form. As individual as its authors, the chair provides a medium that is a controllable minimum structure, ripe for material and conceptual experiments. In this seminar, students develop their design and fabrication skills through exploration of the conceptual, aesthetic, and structural issues involved in the design and construction of a full-scale prototype chair.

■ 1. Amir Karimpour

■ 2. Stanley Cho

■ 3. Isaac Southard

■ 4. Emily Bell

■ 5. Sheena Zhang

■ 7. Dionysus Cho

■ 9. Anthony Gagliarci

■ 6. Emau Vega

■ 8. Jeannette Penniman

■ 10. Olen Milholland

■ 11. Meghan McAllister

■ 12. Jared Abraham

The Brutalist Epoch: Histories, Theories, and Criticisms {George Morris Woodruff, Class of 1857 Memorial Lecture}

Anthony Vidler
{Vincent Scully Visiting Professor in Achitectural History}

Once coined, New Brutalism had, and still has, an after-life. Despite all the arguments for "ethics" rather than aesthetics, by the late 1960s, Brutalism was attacked by the public and from within, by both the supporters of a Gropius style Modernism and the initiators of what, already in 1960, was termed "post-modernism" by Nikolaus Pevsner. Pevsner always hated Brutalism. "Sculptural" and "personal" like Le Corbusier's Ronchamp, Brutalism represented for him "self-expression of the artist-architect," "a fervent avoidance of lightness, of anything that could be called elegant, and also of anything that could be accounted for purely rationally" and, "forms of overpowering—what shall I say? Yes: brutality."

Le Corbusier, as usual, had the last word. He who had been credited with inventing the Brutalist surface was rightly annoyed when the Harvard administration called the Carpenter Center "Brutalist," writing to Sert in May of 1962, he retorted, "*Béton brut* was born at the Unité d'Habitation, where there were eighty contractors and such a massacre of concrete that there was no way of imagining how to construct useful relationships through rendering. I had decided: leave everything *brut*. I called it *béton brut*."

Origins and Translations

Niall McLaughlin
{Norman R. Foster Visiting Professor}

The second place drawing had been designed by a fellow named Shane de Blockham. He had worked at Louis Kahn's office, and come back from that office with an extraordinary sense of what architecture was. We had him as first years and fourth year; the impact that he had on us as first years was an idea of what architecture was about. It was profound. He felt that architecture became architecture when it could not be spoken about, and much of our teaching was conducted in silence. He believed strongly in the power of institutions, with the room as the bedrock of architecture. These drawings show the Kahnian spirit that he brought to the school, and that discipline was central to my education: his notion of the power and mystique of the architect was something he brought to Louis Kahn.

Disheveled Geometries
Mark Foster Gage

Kitbashing originally emerged from the hobby of plastic model building and involved using pieces from multiple model kits, glued together in unexpected arrangements, in order to produce objects that seemed strange and otherworldly. This technique was adopted heavily by designers of 1970's science fiction films such as *Alien, Star Wars, Blade Runner,* and numerous other films that predated the emergence of digital special effects. For this seminar, we aimed to build on research conducted in previous years of this course, but move it in more nuanced formal and theoretical directions involving slippages of perception between forms and figures, and figures and content. [■1–2]

3237b

Human/Nature
Joel Sanders

Our global environmental crisis poses the challenge of devising a new model of ecologically responsible, interdisciplinary practice that brings together two disciplines—architecture and landscape architecture—that have been professionally segregated since the 19th century. We look at this issue from a cultural and historical perspective, tracing the ideological origins of the architecture/landscape divide to another Western polarity—the false opposition between nature and culture, human and non-human—dualisms that are deeply rooted in Western literature, philosophy, popular culture, and even notions of gender and sexuality. [■3–4]

OLEN MILHOLLAND

During the 1960's and 1970's, environmentalism and conservationism shifted from fringe issues to a central theme in the American cultural consciousness and political discourse. With the rise of environmentalism came the vilification of certain industries that became emblematic of the harm being inflicted upon the earth. One specific sector that garnered special attention was the mining industry. The abandoned sites of mines and quarries were singled out in the public media as they occupied large expanses of visible landscape and were viewed as eyesores. With his newfound reclamation projects starting in 1970, Smithson saw himself as a possible go-between for the worlds of art, ecology, and mining. Aiming to reshape the public's view of the corporations, Smithson tried to work with the mining industry in these publicized sites to create new land works that would recast the dilapidated sites in a different light. Just as mountains were seen as ugly protuberances in the 17th century and are now viewed as beautiful through a shift in artistic conscious, Smithson sought to do the same for mines. In opposition to the ecological beliefs of the day, Smithson didn't hold the abandoned sites up as proof of wrongdoing, rather he saw them as visually appealing unto themselves and ideal places to set his art. While some see Smithson's work with the mining industry as aligning him with evil, he viewed the mines as just as inevitable as the Earth's own processes that created the minerals being mined and therefore outside the realms of right and wrong. It is this detached view of the world as an entropic inevitability that allows Smithson the ability to mine it for all of its aesthetic potentials untainted by morality, thereby improving it.

■ 1. Robert Hon

■ 2. Kiana Hosseini

■ 3. Charles Kane

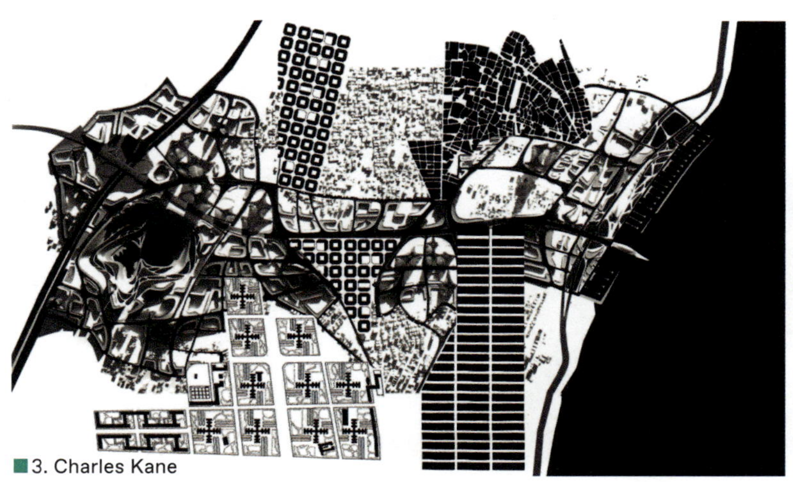

■ 4. Andrew Dadds

A New New Haven Shorefront
Leon Krier

<u>Critic</u>
Leon Krier {**LK**}
Robert A.M. Stern Visiting Professor

<u>Instructor</u>
George Knight {**GK**}

<u>Jurors</u>
Ioanna Angelidou {**IA**}, Thomas Beeby {**TB**}, Kip Bergstrom {**KB**}, Michael Crosbie {**MC**}, Barbara Littenberg {**BL**}, Benjamin Northrup {**BN**}, Liam O'Connor {**LO**}, Robert A.M. Stern {**RAMS**}, Anthony Vidler {**AV**}

The recent construction of an I-90 highway bridge over New Haven Harbor is a late demonstration of the dumb urban and traffic planning which has fated New Haven since the urban renewal horrors of the 1950's. The Planning Department was then appropriately nicknamed "The Kremlin" in the *vox populi*. It is time that the "End of Urbanism," so poignantly documented by Professor Doug Rae's study of New Haven, is ended. This studio's project was undertaken as an operative critique culminating with a New Urbanist proposal for the Quadri-Centenial Anniversary of New Haven's foundation in 2038. The location of the city on one of the most spectacular Oceanside estuaries is now sadly only experienced when driving on the I-90 or looking down from an airplane. To remedy this catastrophic debility, the studio masterplan foresees the future highway bridge to cross the harbor between City Point and East Shore Park at once opening 400 acres of prime urban land for development notably for four new urban quarters and a new civic center facing the Harbor Bay. The students' projects are located in a set masterplan. Each student planned a typical mixed use urban block and a public building as well as the landscaping of the surrounding public spaces, in order to exercise the extraordinary range of typological and stylistic possibilities of vernacular building and classical architecture, of housing private and public activities. The studio visited exemplary shoreside towns and villages in Europe like Luzern, Riva del Garda, and Portofino.

Conceived for the year 2038, Leon Krier's master-plan for New Haven not only places emphasis on the city as the "cultural capital of Connecticut," but also maximizes on its potential as a key location in the Northeast region. The New Haven Capitol addresses both neighborhood and national scales. Based on previous statehouse plans, the parti of the building is simple in its conception: a central hall and two flanking rooms. Facing New Haven, the building is a monument with a neighborhood scale. To achieve this, the block is broken down into smaller-scale elements while the center remains open as public space. The other governmental programs occupy separate adjacent buildings to form a campus. On the side facing the harbor, iconicity becomes a key factor. This is addressed by the height of the building—a tower to be seen from great distances. The plan remains compact, heeding to the essentials, and larger monumental gestures acknowledge the public. The park within the center of the block contains an open pavilion. The lantern provides views of the city from above, and the colonnade walk on the southern side capitalizes on views of the harbor. The building itself makes multiple references to the emblems of Connecticut. The capital features the egg and dart motif symbolizing the robin; the neck of the column features a mountain laurel motif; and the corners of the tower feature the founders of Hartford and New Haven. Moving the state capitol to New Haven gives greater meaning to the state's motto: "Qui Transtilut Sustinet" or "He who is transplanted sustains." [▲1–4]

"I forgot to bring my United States flag to this review." **Robert A. M. Stern**

▲**RAMS:** A lot of designers of U.S. capitols are actually looking outside of the U.S. ▲**GK:** But we have so many great precedents here in the United States, architect Stern. ▲**RAMS:** Yes, I forgot to bring my United States flag to this review. When I look at what you've done, there is something a bit William and Mary about it. ▲**AP:** Well that might be good, because when the capitol is no longer needed, you can recycle it as a residential college. ▲**BL:** I have a question about the asymmetry, only because I think it comes down to the political system, which is a two party system right now, more or less. How does that manifest itself in the architecture? That might be an angle that you look from: the history of Connecticut and the politics. I wonder if that's a better perspective, because it's more broken down, and I think there's a way to explore some of those issues in form. ▲**AP:** When the Capitol started out, they just had a house for the senate. There was no colonnade leading to it. The centerpiece was built later, and the dome was built during the civil war. There are these wonderful early views of the bicameral operation with a void in the middle. I wonder if, given the waterfront and that shaft of space without a central feature, but rather with things on either side, that might not be an interesting idea to play around with. It might not be workable, but this is a fantasy. ▲**TB:** This looks great to me. I think it's an extraordinary building. ▲**LK:** This was a long struggle which ended with a triumph. ▲**RAMS:** It's a wonderful concept. This shows you why, in the Beaux-Arts days, they didn't have open juries. ▲**LO:** I think the way you chose to present your main elevations was very brave. You should do some graphic analysis, though. Compute it. Get the shadows right. It would look so much better and so much more convincing. ▲**LK:** But I think now computers are considered traditional representation. Digital plans and sections are the convention. She studied a lot of precedents, but none of them showed up in her hand drawings. Now finally, it's a very good composition. I think it would be worth the digitization. It's time to make it concrete.

▲1

▲2

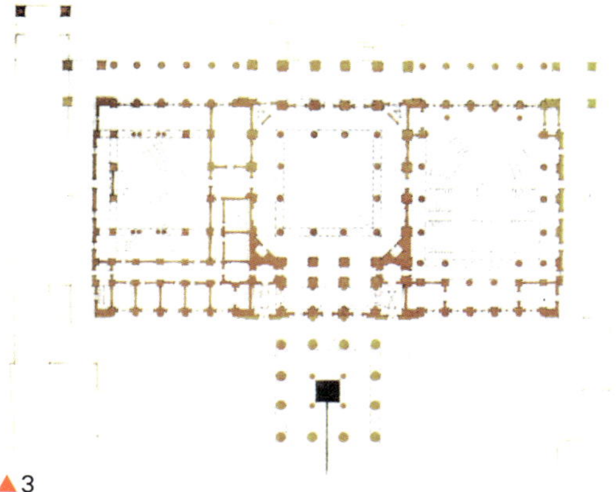

▲3

▲4

MENGSHI SUN

This project rests on the southernmost corner of the overall master plan adjacent to the ferry terminal and waterfront promenade. The central plaza becomes a core that connects to the neighborhood market, the church, and the memorial hall. Restaurants, stores, dental clinics, and other local commercial spaces are also distributed along the plaza. The roads between each neighborhood are shared by both vehicles and pedestrians similar to the roads of Nafplio, Greece. Each neighborhood consists of six residential buildings that share one central garden. Automobiles are not allowed to access the central garden. Commercial function happens along the waterfront promenade and the plaza with arcades defining spaces of public uses. This language helps to create a pedestrian-friendly environment. The other sides are occupied by residential housing embracing a private courtyard. The first story is lifted four feet above ground to block the view of passersby. The proportion of each component is carefully designed to blend in with the vernacular context. Along the promenade, a variety of activities take place. Vegetation and paving help to break down the scale and offer pleasurable public space. Due to the severe weather of New Haven, it is impossible to sustain sandy beaches along the coast. Instead, stairs occur occasionally to provide access to the water. As one of the public buildings on site, the market develops a mixed language of classical colonnade and vernacular building style. The two bays on each side are given over to independent shops, while the sky-lit open-air central space is designed for temporary vendors. The building plays with pairs—white columns and brick walls, colonnades and arches, wood trusses and steel skylights—which all come together to create a space that will become a new center for the city. [▲5–8]

"How many identical villas can you add before you have too much of the same? Is there no limit? This is a great community, but do you think you run the risk of monotony?" Michael Crosbie

▲BL: I think the issue of whether your housing is in a neighborhood or a block is important. Essentially this is a block—or at least I would call it that—it's like they do in La Cariola in Rome. I wonder, if you think of it as a block, do you really want people to come inside the streets at the interior? Should that be private or controlled access space with people living in those units? ▲Mengshi Sun: The pathways are all open to the public, but the cars don't enter them. They only go along the side of this one large block. Only pedestrians have access to the large gardens. ▲BL: Aren't you concerned with having residential privacy? They'd have to keep their shades down all the time. ▲Mengshi Sun: Yes, that's why I lifted the base of the first story one and a half meters. People can't have a direct view into those spaces, which also gives more height to the retail space on the ground. ▲MC: So you've got this base that goes around the sides that do not have the loggia. ▲BL: Very clever. ▲TB: What happens in that leftover half? ▲Mengshi Sun: That is mechanical. ▲LK: There is a separate section for residential or commercial. You can also conceptually lift the circulation. ▲BL: It could be very nice for the housing, to have a lifted backyard. Just the people on the block have access. You'd still have the visual openness and trees, but it would be less public. It's a direct amenity with views for the residents, indirect for others. By having natural light flood in here, with the punched openings, you would illuminate the parking garage. ▲KL: In Rome, the property line is in the middle of the alleyway. ▲TB: How much can you build? How many identical villas can you add before you have too much of the same? Is there no limit? This is a great community, but do you think you run the risk of monotony? Do you build six of these or sixty? ▲Mengshi Sun: I think this type with the central courtyard at this scale can expand. I find the site plan quite weird, because there is no sense of scale consistency anyway. If we had larger developments for the public, this housing could expand to the entire area.

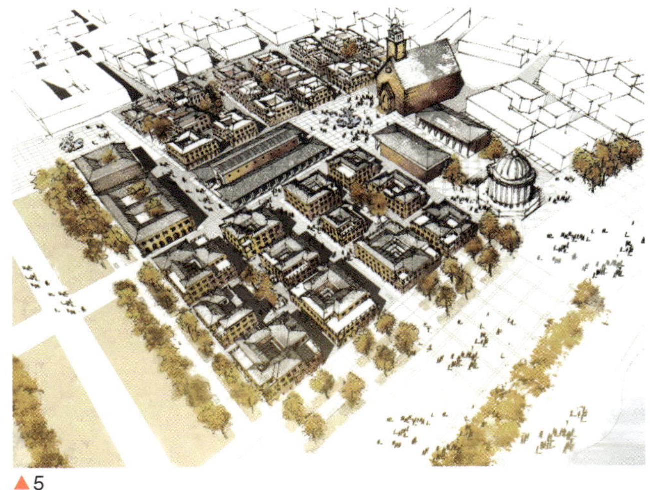

▲5

▲6

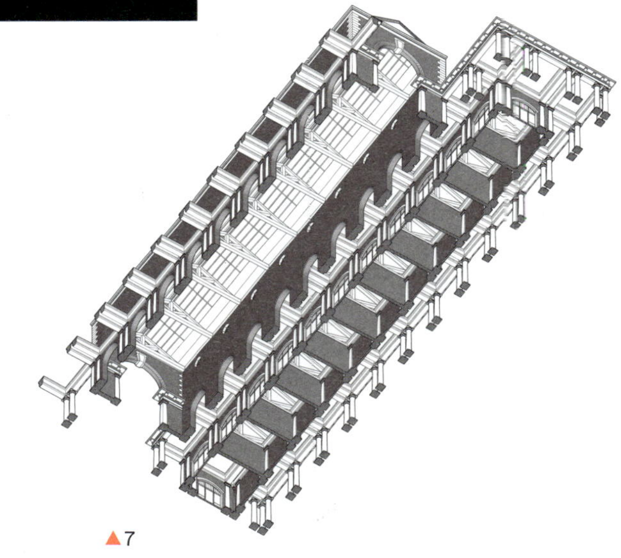

▲7

▲8

IAN SPENCER

The City of New Haven has undergone a number of unfortunate purges of its traditional fabric with the goal of urban expansion and infrastructural improvement. The net result has been has thwarted these goals. Key transit locations have become entirely isolated from the city center by a wholly unintelligible, non-pedestrian urban system. Working from a master plan developed by Leon Krier, this project proposes a new, traditional waterfront quarter and the re-routing of I-90 around the city. Cass Gilbert and Frederick Law Olmsted's "Plan for New Haven," demonstrates the need for a radical re-working of the land between The Hill and Downtown. Merging the Gilbert-Olmsted plan with the traditional fabric proposed in the Krier plan forms a new urban fabric with major axes along Church Street and Highway 1 that provide direct access to The Green, Yale-New Haven Hospital, and the Old Campus of Yale. The Knights of Columbus building now serves as a strong urban marker to direct pedestrian travel, and Union Station not only accommodates a larger number of travelers, but celebrates train travel. In this new scheme, passengers ascend within the building into two carriage buildings and out onto a raised plaza which leads down to the platforms. From the city, a new clock tower marks the station's location from afar, while a new pavilion directs traffic. Based on Gilbert's original, the new portico protrudes slightly to provide shelter and give relief to an otherwise flat elevation. With these changes, Union Station and the surrounding district of New Haven can become the new symbols of the city and a paradigm for future development. [▲9–12]

> "It's a kind of architectural Freudian slip."
> Anthony Vidler

▲AV: I'm very interested in the fact that you're moving this building to the street edge. I'm appreciative of the fact that you're moving this towards the Green or, in fact, bringing the Green closer to this building. ▲BN: You mentioned Cass Gilbert's excellent plan, which was executed well. I love what you've done with the neighborhood and these complex blocks. You've created lots of wonderful spaces. It seems like there's a missed opportunity to create that type of connection to the front of the train station though. Living in New Haven, it can be hard to find the station. The plan that you've come up with is this dense neighborhood with these wide boulevards. ▲TB: I like the space—it's very nice. But it's a type of old European train station where trains are actually sitting in the space. Whereas, in this one, they're down one level—you don't see them. The station is activated by the people moving through to the trains instead of by the trains themselves. ▲RAMS: That's how Penn Station was. You could travel above the trains because they were electrified, so there would be no smoke. It's actually a 20th century type, not a 19th century one. ▲TB: But this looks like an old European train station in that it's a station where there are more users. I just don't understand what's going to happen up there. It's so big. Are there enough commuters? ▲AV: If this truly is a square, as someone said, then the station serves as a separator between the old town and the new. You haven't really made the diagram expressing the old town and your plan for the new to convince us. ▲BL: It's a kind of architectural Freudian slip. What he's suggesting is that this piece should have been more centered in this drawing and that your area of study should encompass both sides. Perhaps your judgment suggested that we're centered there on what exists, and we don't permeate the new stuff, whatever that might be. The station is so frontal now. And one thinks of that façade as difficult to balance—I suppose you could put a crazy modernist façade on the back. The time spent on the building leads us to think it's less about the town planning that's going on around it and more about the building as a bridge. ▲LK: Trains used to be something dirty. They smoked and made noise. But this celebrates the tracks. It's fronted by linear boulevards that create paths through the town. Trains are a nice thing now—they are a stamp on the city.

▲ 9

▲ 10

▲ 11

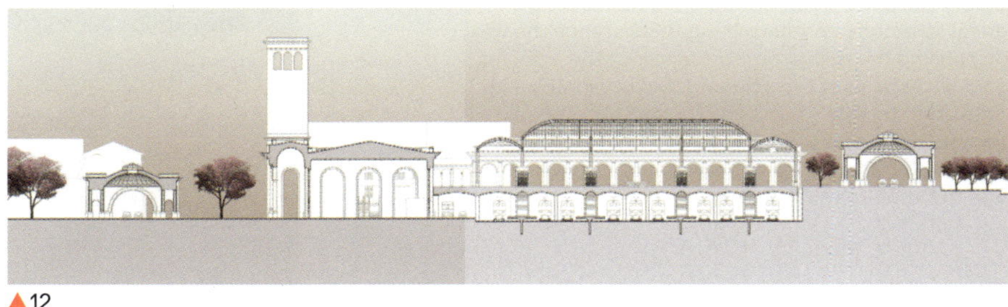

▲ 12

Design
Computation
Michael Szivos

Computational machines, tools once only considered more efficient versions of paper-based media, have a demonstrated potential beyond mere imitation. This potential is revealed through design computation; the creative application of the processes and reasoning underlying all digital technology—from e-mail to artificial intelligence. Just as geometry is fundamental to drawing, computation affords a fundamental understanding of how data works, which is essential to advance the development of BIM, performative design, and other emerging methodologies. This seminar introduces design computation as a means to enable architects to operate exempt from limitations of generalized commercial software; to devise problem-specific tools, techniques, and workflows; to control the growing complexities of contemporary architectural design; and to explore forms generated only by computation itself. Topics include data manipulation and translation, algorithms, information visualization, computational geometry, human-computer interaction, custom tooling, generative form-finding, emergent behavior, simulation, and system modeling.

HUGO FENAUX

As posited by theorists in the sixties, the architectural machine speculated on the potential for a new relationship between designer and machine—one that would not only facilitate design, but also advance it. This iteration of the architectural machine represents a desire to understand the fundamental meaning of medium. While an artist's hand has the potential to portray meaning and desire through simple and tangible media, the traditional output for the computer is conversely sterile. The drawing machine attempts to bridge the gap between the hand and the computer, giving the computer a means of representation that encourages error, autonomy, and personality. ⟨■1⟩

BORIS MORIN-DEFOY

Working in tandem with a Montreal-based music composer, I created a five-minute piece that reacted intrinsically through its code to the music and the grid of the architecture of Beinecke Library. The work was projected on the façade of the iconic library as part of Yale University's Lux Festival. Following a positive response from the audience, I created a series of stills from that piece. The code generating those stills was then redrawn in an experiment with the CNC cutter, switching the blade attachment for watercolor brushes. ⟨■2⟩

JACK WOLFE

This project translates a graphic representation of sound into a physical form through a machine. The processing script translates the audio amplitude into distorted rings that aggregate vertically at a controlled rate creating cylindrical structures. The machine uses the same logic as the script, but the printed form is affected by external forces of gravity, thermodynamics, and centripetal force. The interactive experience results in a wax mold for investment casting, and the form is determined by live audio input. The audio input controls the radius of cylindrical structure by determining the distance the wax dispensing nozzle is from the center of the spinning disc. The speed of the spinning disc is variable and regulates the rate of aggregation and splatter distance. This machine is conceived of as a prototype, allowing for alterations of components from one wax iteration to the next. ⟨■3⟩

■1

■2

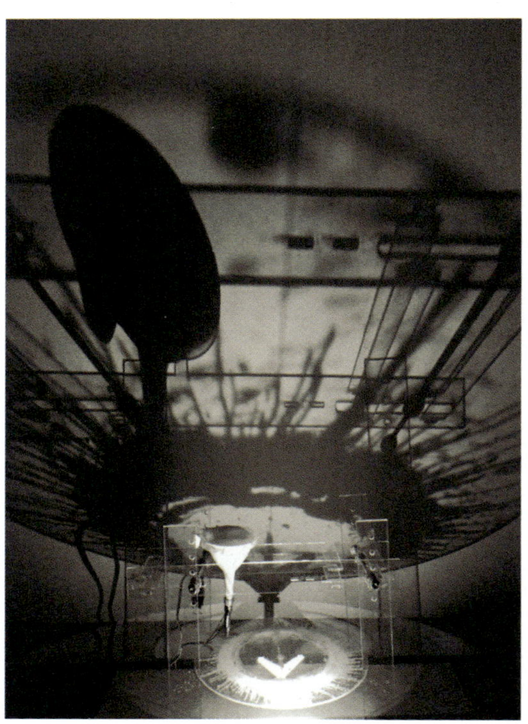

■3

Drawing Projects
Turner Brooks

Each student admitted to the course came pre-pared with a particular subject that was investigated through the media of drawing for the entire term. There were weekly evening pin-ups of the work in progress, in which much of the discussion focused on the act of "seeing" and finding the "mark" on the paper which conveys the varied meanings of the subject matter. (■1–6)

■ 1. Charles Kane

■ 2. Charles Kane

■ 3. Dima Srouji

■ 4. Dima Srouji

■ 5. John Kleinschmidt

■ 6. John Kleinschmidt

Diversification: How to Regenerate Social Housing in Mexico
Tatiana Bilbao

<u>Critic</u>
Tatiana Bilbao {TB}
Louis I. Kahn Visiting Assistant Professor

<u>Instructor</u>
Andrei Harwell {AH}

<u>Jurors</u>
Karla Britton {KB}, José Castillo {JC}, Frida Escobedo {FE}, Terence Gower {TG}, Galia Solomonoff {GS}, David Kohn {DK}, Ed Mitchell {EM}, Niall McLaughlin {NM}, Robert A. M. Stern {RAMS}, Mike Tonkin {MT}, Sara Topelson {ST}, Sarah Whiting {SW}, Carlos Zedillo {CZ}, Anthony Vidler {AV}

A very ambitious social housing policy was created in Mexico during the mid-seventies to provide an affordable solution to the housing deficit at the time. The solution gave many Mexicans access to resources to find real homes, but its implementation grew without control, creating suburban ghettoes in every city in the country that might have been lacking connection to the urban centers, infrastructure of any type, services or nearby jobs. These housing complexes, some of which exceeded 20,000 units, are being abandoned little by little, with some already reporting at least 50% vacancy. The government has launched several policies that are stopping the sprawl of this type of developments, but is not giving many solutions to the existing problem besides repainting the houses to resell them. This studio focused on understanding the conditions of these complexes, finding architectonic solutions to reintegrate these housing developments, and transforming them into a space that could be reverted from abandonment and could also be the detonator for its surroundings. INFONAVIT {National Institute for Social Housing} was a major sponsor for the studio and covered the travel expenses of the students.

JULCSI FUTO & KAROLINA CZECZEK ✳

The objective of this project is to turn Real de Palmas, a low-income workers housing settlement of 60,000 inhabitants near Monterrey, from an agglomeration of houses into a self-sufficient city. Different scales of interventions respond to problems ranging from underused backyards, lack of public amenities and civic programs, nonexistent employment opportunities, and need for more housing. The urban strategy takes advantage of the existing structure while allowing for organic growth. Rezoning the central spine of Real de Palmas lends program and function to the road system. Enlarging sidewalks and introducing bike lanes prioritizes pedestrians on the currently underused road. Building extensions to houses and introducing commercial activity along the spine yield new work space for the inhabitants. The "carpets" work on the scale of the neighborhoods and connect existing green areas to offer a place for community activities. Comprised of unified paving material, urban furniture or planting, and covered recreational areas, the carpets are designed to provide a sense of identity for each neighborhood. The "backyards" recall the *Vecindad* housing type and convert underused backyards into shared spaces. This intervention is a more efficient use of space and creates new relations between the neighbors. Pockets, anchored around existing civic buildings, break the relentless grid of houses and introduce recreational, cultural, and civic programs. (▲1–3)

> "I like the European city discussion because the craft of city making has to do with time." **José Castillo**

▲SW: The fact that you proposed different scales of intervention that require the state level and a very localized one, as well as just the adding of a room, to me is exactly taking on Tatiana's mandate to the studio of something that's a very big vision but operates at different scales and has a utopianism to it. In the end the urbanism that you proposed has a kind of normative scale to it—it manages to make the big pockets operate not as neighborhood centers but as part of this larger necklace of amenities. ▲RAMS: There's nothing utopian about it. Utopias are a wonderful world that we'll never have and this is a very real world that we hope some people will have. But I think it's kind of relentless. It's still very like sprawling suburbia—there's all of these very small and fundamentally identical houses. ▲EM: Would you compare the public spaces and the existing thing to the Siedlung, the Hilberseimer settlement plans, the Costa schemes, or anything else just to get a sense of how much of this stuff you would need? Or would be appropriate or would measure the politics of the existing paradigms. Not cities but the settlement plan. ▲NM: The thing I enjoyed a lot in your description is when your individual houses began to pair up with each other and share spaces in between. Maybe it's that European part of me that wants you to form a circle, create a space that feels as though it's been carved out of something. ▲RAMS: One small thing that was typically done in the early part of 20th century urban conditions in America and England—the ends of the blocks have special units that turn the corner and close the vista from the street down the back yard so you make much more of a room of the backyard—and if you could have a few more of those, if you look at the plan of sunny side gardens, it's next to a railroad yard in a very banal part of Queens in New York, where workers housing has worked for three quarters of a century, it does those kinds of things, and creates also walkways as opposed to streets. JC: I like the European city discussion because the craft of city making has to do with time. What I find incredibly appealing is that you've taken up the task of answering the question that's become the elephant in the room, which is if architecture has a way to address the problems of housing in the city today. Can architecture, as Bob has argued, do something to retrofit and make out of these relentless sometime horrible environments something more meaningful and attractive?

▲ 1

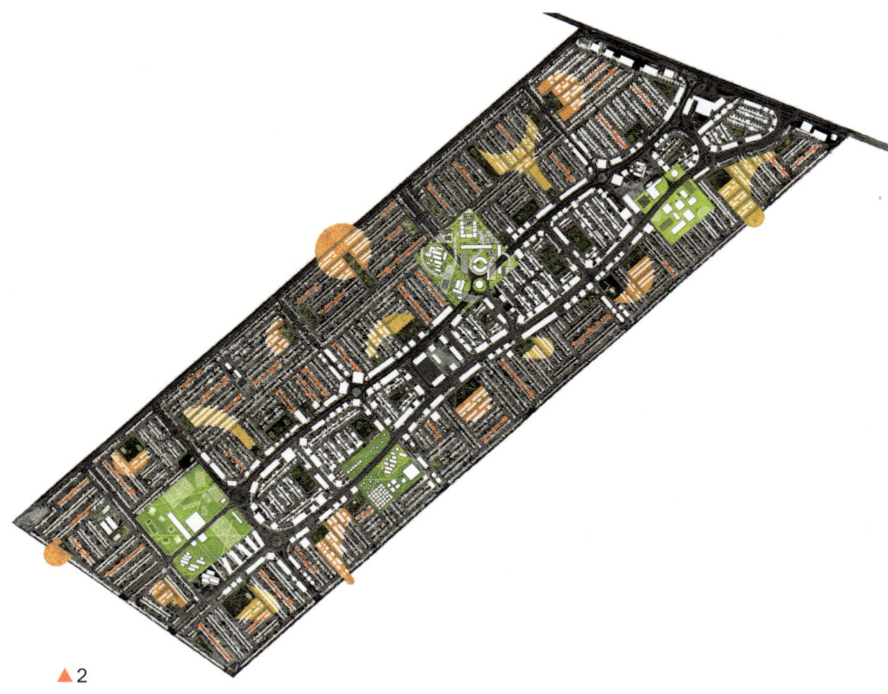

▲ 2

▲ 3

KARA BICZYKOWSKI & AMANDA BRIDGES

Despite Chulavista's close proximity to Guadalajara, this development is marred by a high percentage of abandonment and lack of nearby employment opportunities. The scarcity of basic services and disconnection to the city center make living conditions fall far below satisfactory standards. After studying the continuing nearby trends in uncontrolled growth, we employed design solutions to formally and programmatically curb urban sprawl. Our project is comprised of a series of architectural, urban, and environmental interventions along the southern boundary of the site that will stimulate positive growth and reconnect the large housing development to Tlajomulco, the municipality's center of government, and Guadalajara's rich cultural and economic resources. This proposal uses the new Bus Rapid Transit system to connect Tlajomulco and Guadalajara. This relocates residents in the most abandoned and crime-ridden areas along the development's edge, as well as the young population, and lowers the rate of car ownership. With these factors in mind, our project provides identity and connectivity to Chulavista by creating a dense urban edge that physically reinforces the Conavi federal housing boundary. This new edge to the city provides services to support the development, mixes live-work housing strategies to accommodate local business and economy, provides recreational amenities, promotes the regional agricultural practices through community farms, urban gardens, and, most importantly, creates exterior spaces for residents to congregate during social events. Here, the linear edge city becomes the framework for Chulavista's unique identity. [▲4–7]

> "Soviet linear city schemes were mentioned earlier, but there are even earlier American utopian schemes that look similar. I think what this project leans toward is a new idea of collective living."
> **Ed Mitchell**

▲JC: Is this about aggregation or disaggregation and fragmentation? I'm actually fascinated with the way that you frame some of your initial assumptions about the site, and maybe the right question to ask is how you deal with edges. Is the solution to retrofit this neighborhood based on the work that people do inside of it, or work that is done on a surface level—this intersection between agriculture, landscapes, and built form? From Soria y Mata in Madrid to the Soviet linear cities, to even a more watered down transit-oriented development approach, there's a long tradition of this. You could even approach in this in a historical sense. ▲MT: Maybe you want to dissolve the edge. One thing this is like is the Pasolini film, *The Gospel According to Saint Matthew*, where the city of Matera is almost hollow entirely underneath. These underground caves were used for storing wine and wood, which makes me think of what you're doing here. It also makes me think of a Greek hill town. What you've done is filled in the side of the hill, and that's broken the link with the landscape beyond. What you always want to do is the opposite. You want to open it up as much as possible. It's beautiful what you've done, but it would be more beautiful if we felt it could work like a Greek hill town. It could have these little paths that wind their way up, opening into squares and public spaces. So it's really beautiful, but what you probably should have done is tested the architectural language against the ambition. ▲EM: Soviet linear city schemes were mentioned earlier, but there are even earlier American utopian schemes that look similar. I think what this project leans toward is a new idea of collective living. The fact that I can detach those houses from underneath shows me you don't know what that stuff is. There are American utopian schemes similar to this that were based on mobility—the new thing after the second half of the 19th century. The new thing was a kind of collective housing, so that everyone could get everywhere, and the model of the community was already embedded in the architecture.

▲4

▲5

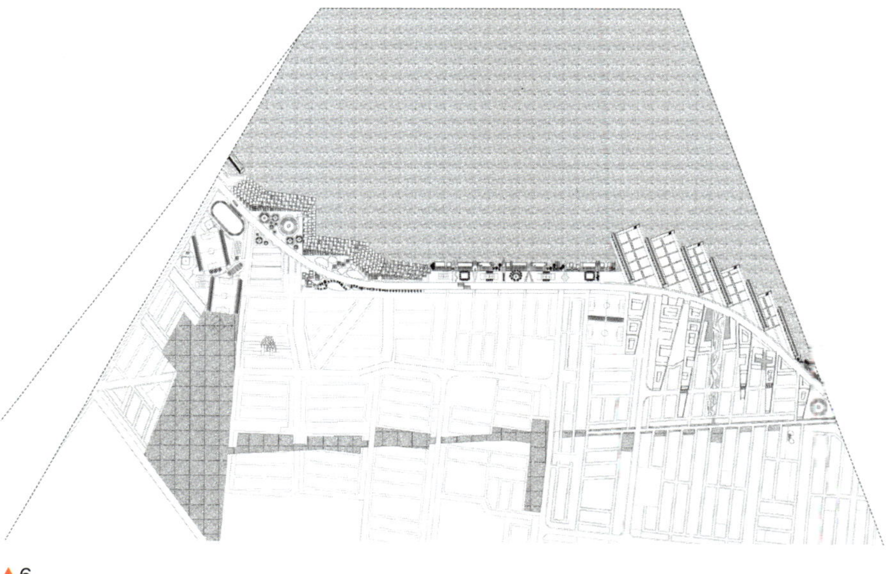

▲6

▲7

MEGHAN MCALLISTER
& MEGHAN LEWIS

The Mexican community of Villas Otoch has a high rate of abandonment due to the transitory nature of many migrant workers seeking wage labor in the tourism industry of Cancun. Many of the migrants are from indigenous communities, and their traditional community practices are hindered by the monotonous housing stock with poor ventilation and little communal outdoor space. We are proposing an indigenous university that will provide more localized employment opportunities while also empowering residents with a means to pass on and sustain traditional knowledge in an urban setting. This new university type would enable education practices to blend with home life and be distributed throughout the neighborhood at the scale of a room. The university includes prototypes for housing that renovate the existing structures to double the amount of shaded outdoor space while still maintaining approximately the same density. Both the housing and university prototypes will encourage residents to build on the second floor, opening up additional communal, shaded living spaces on the ground level. The university components and associated housing will be built first, and then the existing fabric is expected to incrementally morph over time. [▲ 8–11]

"The elephant in the room is whether architecture can resolve the problems that architecture created." **José Castillo**

▲**SW:** Why a university? Why not a series of training facilities or forms of vocational assistance to this community. It's hard for us to get our heads around what it means to put a university in here. It seems like it might be an aspiration to education. I can't tell if just vocational help or training facilities would be too close to a Band-Aid for Tatiana, and you wanted to go more extreme. ▲**AV:** If you place a large non-indigenous population within an indigenous population, you're going to get a complete transformation of the economics of the commercial strip and so on and so forth. What we're really looking for is not the idea of something dropped in, but something emerging. So do you have any sense of the process by which something can build up, be assimilated, be transformed? ▲**NM:** In your analysis of the issue, two things that you pointed to are the almost immediate failure of a new building stock and the vacant sites that have been set aside for public institutions, which are then never developed. Your answer seems to be more building stock and institutions, but it seems to me that the failure of the existing buildings and institutions is a symptom of an underlying problem that can't be addressed by more buildings and institutions. I was really interested that you, as an architect, said that the people around here are actually very good at building things for themselves, and yet your solution to it, in the way that architects do, imposes architecture as another kind of building culture on top of it. ▲**EM:** What you're assuming about universities is that universities are an imposed condition on a community. If you think about how universities grew through the classical model, like Yale, it was for the clergy and it built up over time. The technical universities were usually in support of the industry at the time, so, for example, RISD was built in support of the textile industry. When superimposing a university you have to already have a program to support that university—it has to support some other institution in order to make it viable. So to me, if you're going to do something with education, it has to be education for what? ▲**JC:** I celebrate the effort to address this challenge, because the elephant in the room is whether architecture can resolve the problems that architecture created. I don't think any of the students or the jury members truly believe it's only about architecture. Does architecture have to say or do something regarding this problem? And that's why I think symbolic architecture plays a big role. I'm thinking of Siza's Quinta de Malagueira and the choice of the raised aqueduct and its piping. It becomes the equivalent of a Roman aqueduct to produce a sense of civicness, connecting it to the infrastructure. That choice is fundamental, and it seems to me that your choice of the disaggregated university complex in Latin America is problematic.

▲ 8

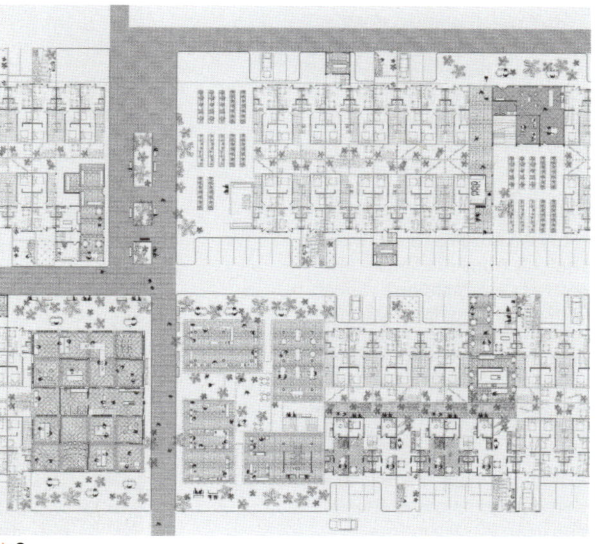

▲ 9

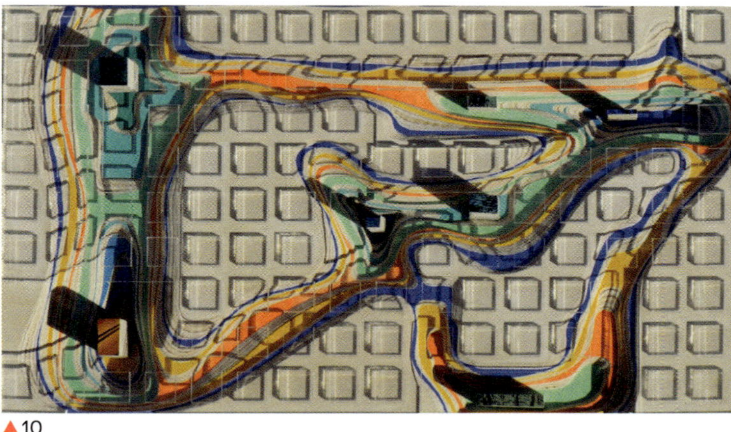

▲ 10

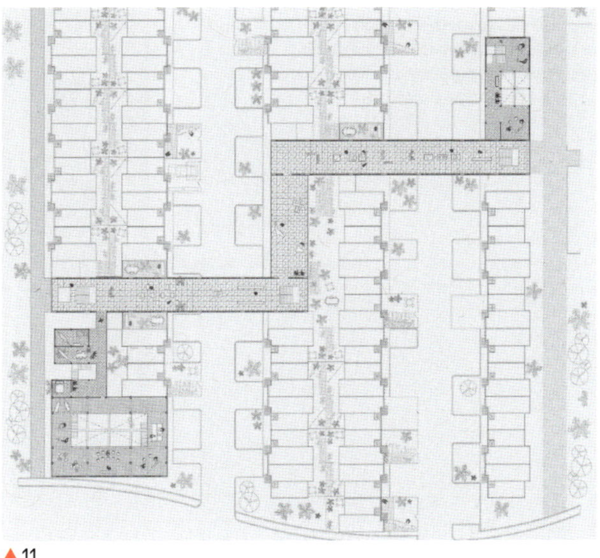

▲ 11

Paranoazinho
Rafael Birmann
& Sunil Bald

<u>Critics</u>
Rafael Birmann ⁅**RAB**⁆ and Sunil Bald ⁅**SB**⁆

<u>Instructor</u>
Andrei Harwell ⁅**AH**⁆

<u>Jurors</u>
Louis Becker ⁅**LB**⁆, Barry Bergdoll ⁅**BB**⁆, Tatiana Bilbao ⁅**TB**⁆, Ricardo Birmann ⁅**RIB**⁆, Keller Easterling, ⁅**KE**⁆, Martin Finio ⁅**MF**⁆, Masami Kobayashi ⁅**MK**⁆, Jennifer Leung ⁅**JL**⁆, Ed Mitchell ⁅**EM**⁆, Alan Plattus ⁅**AP**⁆, Robert A.M. Stern ⁅**RAMS**⁆, Sara Topelson ⁅**ST**⁆, Anthony Vidler ⁅**AV**⁆, Sarah Whiting ⁅**SW**⁆

A vision of a city born of that initial gesture which anyone would make when pointing to a given place, or taking possession of it: the drawing of two axes crossing each other at right angles, in the sign of the Cross. ⁅Lucio Costa, "Plano Piloto," Modulo, 18, Rio de Janeiro, June 1960⁆. Thus began Lucio Costa's poetic, though nebulous, competition entry for the city of Brasilia. The Cross, with its spiritual weight, was quickly translated into a bus station and tangled roadway interchange between the Monumental Axis of governmental buildings and the artery of commercial, hotel, and residential superblocks. Brasilia was born with the car central to its conception, and the result is a City of the Future that is decidedly anti-urban. Twenty kilometers from the north edge of Brasilia lies Sobradinho. Also planned by Costa, but as a settlement rather than a city, Sobradiho had a primary *raison d'être*— to house the workers who built the city. Between Brasilia and Sobradinho lies a 16 million square meter estate known as "Fazenda Paranoazinho", where 30,000 middle class homesteaders—and commercial strips serving that population—have made their homes on top of irregular settlements lacking legal tenure. There are also expanses of open land filled with mango trees, two meandering rivers, and a dynamic topography. UPSA, a company founded by Rafael Birmann, is developing this site into a city for 150,000 inhabitants. However, Paranoazinho is not being conceived as an isolated entity, but as a new regional urban center—a heterogeneous residential, commercial, and cultural hub between the homogenous urbanities of Brasilia and Sobradinho. In addition, Paranoazinho's development will be transit-oriented, prioritizing pedestrian, bicycle, and public transit over the automobile. Finally, the new city will be anchored by a diversity of public spaces, the largest being a linear park that takes advantage of the river and the rich ecology it supports. Two of Paranoazinho's public centers, a neighborhood park and an urban plaza, will bookend a gently curving 800 meter artery that will be the city's commercial and cultural hub. As planned by UPSA with Gehl Architects, this Destination Street will be humanly-scaled, pedestrian-oriented, and programatically diverse. In short, everything Brasilia's monumental axis is not. It will also be the first part of Paranoazinho to be developed—a place to precede the city. The Destination Street will be both an anchor for the city's future population and an attraction for the region's current population.

APOORVA KHANOLKAR ✳

This project's primary point of investigation is the agency of the architect in the planning process, particularly within the framework of the blank-slate urbanism of Lucio Costa's Brasilia. The 90 by 120 meter block takes the form of a bar-and-mat scheme, where the bars house a variety of residential units and the mat. The aim is to create a developer-friendly model of mixed-use urbanism where the role of the planner is to maintain an overarching vision, but also relinquish part of that control to market dynamics, social forces, and the community itself. This idea of possibility and flexibility is implemented in two ways. One, by means of a systemic organizational module that generates both the public and private program, i.e. the mat and the bars. The second is a strategic deployment of service armature that allows the site to be developed intuitively. These possibilities carry over into the residences, where a module-based organization makes it possible to combine units to become a variety of dwellings—from studios to penthouses. Each apartment is a cross-ventilated, single-loaded unit fronting an open veranda. The option to purchase an open well allows residents to convert the space into a bedroom, study, terrace, or patio. While one of the bar's facades is a louvered acknowledgement of Brasilia's modernist legacy, the other is a pixelation of the community's own expression. The block is designed to fit within the existing master plan, can also take on a prototypical role where different permutations of its many parameters come into play at different instances. It is looked at as a top-down exercise in providing an armature within which the bottom-up organic forces of urban growth are allowed to proliferate. (▲1–4)

"It's not a question to be shoved under the table of architecture." **Robert A. M. Stern**

▲**JL:** The façade is the proof of concept in the project. And I'm also curious about this flat division between the world above and below. I wonder if that might actually be the threshold of tension. What kind of negotiation happens there? I was thinking that additional program, not institutional necessarily, but essentially you also have this strange diagram of dwelling and selling, and I guess one of the things that's so interesting about the favelas, is the upstart forms of collaboration. That's an opportunity that is somehow inherent in your project, because of the sensitivity that it's showing to a neighborhood idea. There's a kind of middle scale between the infrastructure and the very flexible unit. ▲**AP:** The inside is perhaps more interesting than the perimeter, which I guess is not such a bad thing. That's where I want to be, I think it's generally a good thing. My desire is that those bars not be seen as kind of ghostly presences floating on top of the active world of entrepreneurship, but touch down on the street. ▲**RAMS:** Well Alan, you said, and Tatiana agreed, that it's not more important to have an interesting interior than to have the exterior expression. And I think that goes to the heart of the problem—the difference between housing and architecture of multiple dwellings that people live in, which doesn't have a very nice word. Housing automatically takes you into this realm of diagrammatic perfection, of the orchestration of everything, without much attention paid to the image—the collective image buildings can convey—to lift or depress the spirit of the people who are going to live there. Collective residence is very, very important. Being a resident there starts on the street. I'm not saying it's something you haven't addressed. It's more about the discourse of the critics than your scheme. But it is true, looking at your drawings, which are very beautiful, they fall a little short of what this would be like sitting on the street in Brasilia. Or you could say there's something that could happen in Brazil that's different than what's happening in Mumbai. Indeed in Mumbai, things are changing. Things are taking on more of an expressive role. How much expression is appropriate is another question. But I think it's not a question to be shoved under the table of architecture. That's what architects do—they give expression to bodies and people and objectives of developers, whether they're public or private or whatever.

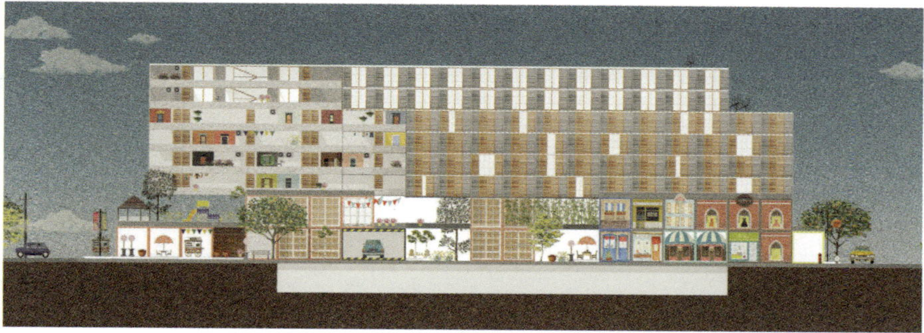

▲1

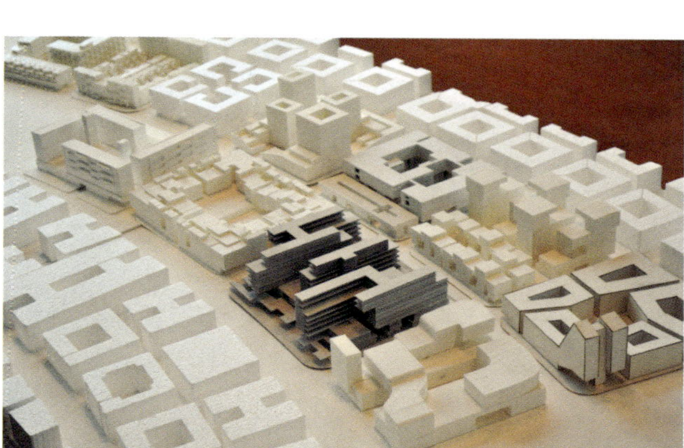

▲2

▲3

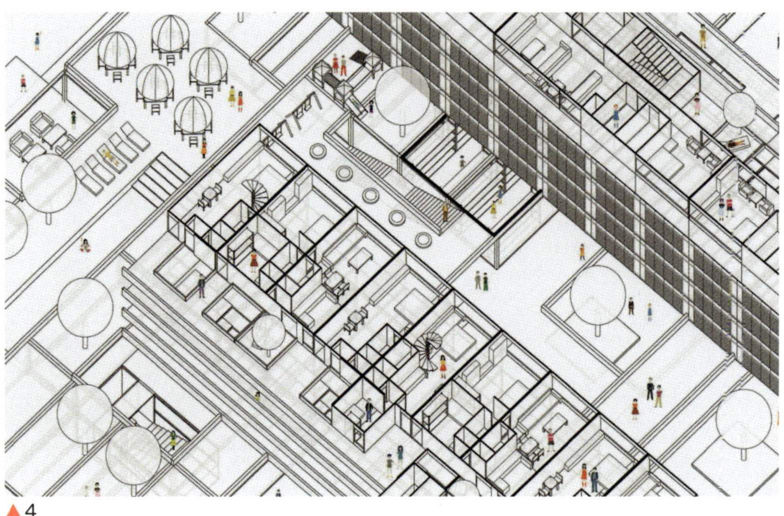

▲4

KIN TAK YU

This is a proposal for a micro-urbanistic environment that integrates low density and high density housing within a 100 by 100 meter city block outside of Brasilia. A formal strategy that combines multiple scales of massing accentuates the drastic height changes characteristic of urban environment. The block is subdivided into two smaller parcels—the parcel adjacent to the destination street is mixed use with ground floor retail space and housing above. Duplexes and townhouses are mixed with smaller scale frontage for retail. A central retail courtyard space is introduced to encourage the pedestrians from the main street to circulate and shop within the block. The housing types placed along the "destination street" are duplexes and townhouses and address the need for smaller scale frontage for retail programs. A central retail courtyard space encourages the pedestrians from the main street to circulate and shop within the block. The courtyard's perimeter of duplexes and townhouses maintains a small sense of scale. Large cascading towers feel less imposing behind the smaller housing blocks while managing to incorporate high density condos. Although the change in scale between the housing types is radical, this project also attempts to design a sense of community by establishing various types of shared and private outdoor spaces throughout the city block. The duplexes and townhouses have series of shared small garden terraces and a private roof garden. The cascading condo towers have large communal terraces that can be connected at higher levels. {▲5–8}

"It's a tricky thing to actually have collective space within a privatized living arrangement." **Martin Finio**

▲**SW:** You've created a density across the site so that the courtyard is a sign of the number of people there, but since the courtyards are for more than one unit, you're creating a different scale of the collective. It emphasizes the individual apartments and others have emphasized the whole square. You're introducing this middle scale. What I'm not quite getting is how many units congregate around these open spaces or use them. ▲**MF:** I think it's also proved to be a troubling composition just in terms of the way humans tend to be territorial about those kinds of spaces. I don't know, it's a tricky thing to actually have collective space within a privatized living arrangement. ▲**RIB:** There is an important issue there about having kind of a semi-private space. This is more toward the private than it is toward the public. This is a space just for four apartments and if you don't get along with one of them, it's going to be hell. If you have those places on the courtyard or on the rooftop and you need a barbecue place and you just go somewhere and sign up for it that day, it's a different kind of logic. But I don't know, I like it. I think it could be sorted out somehow. ▲**MF:** As the president of one of these co-ops, I can tell you it is hell! Like if there was fixed furniture in part of this, you don't become responsible for it. It's interesting territory, how to it figure out. ▲**AV:** There are small co-ops in New York where there are three or four floors of brownstones and the roof. And the roof is shared and the quarrels are intense. ▲**AP:** I'm wondering, actually, because I think the level of porosity is probably not quite believable on the ground floor. You've gone through the trouble of making these do-si-do massing situations in the back; I wonder if you ever considered putting them back together again? In other words, having gotten it to that point, just consolidating it into those two or one solid block. The potential efficiency of the circulation of that court would be fabulous and certainly better than what you have. We've been talking about blocks and buildings and the relationship to streets and blocks and how many buildings you get on a block and how those buildings are expressed. And I think this is an extreme of what Keller called micro-urbanism.

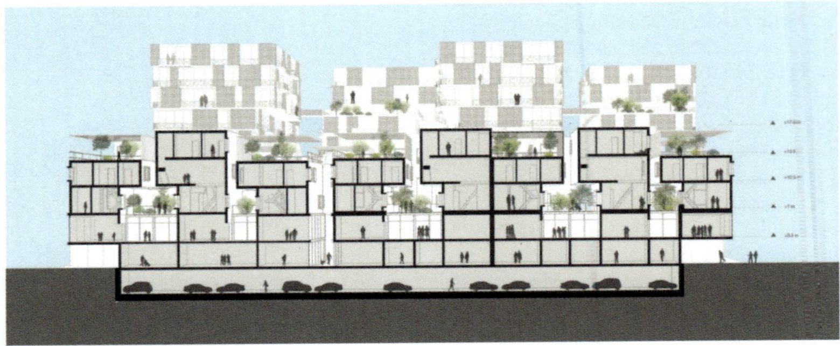

▲5

▲6

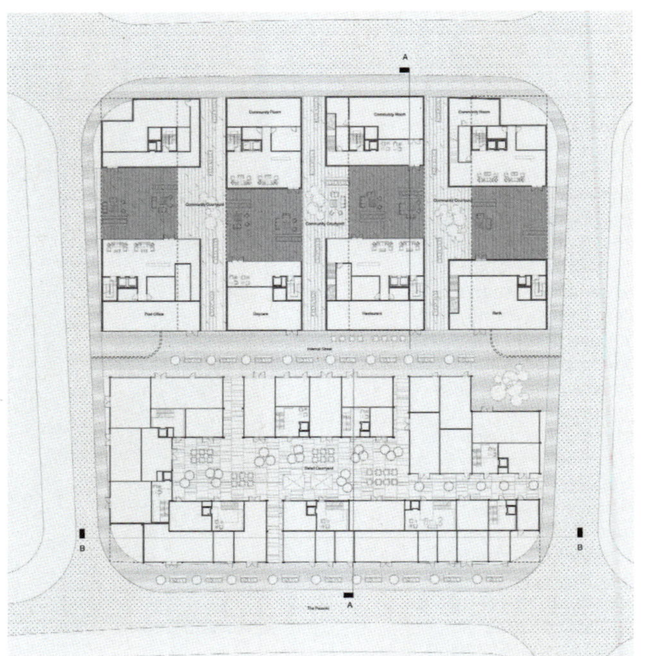

▲7

▲8

Today is the Greatest Time in History to be an Engineer {Gordon H. Smith Lecture}

Steve Burrows

This epoch is the first time in the history of this planet that mankind has learned how to adapt Earth to ourselves instead of the other way around. We now have control of Mother Nature. The future of this planet is now in our hands for the rest of the time we occupy it. This change is irreversible, and sustainability is no longer a choice for any of us. Time is also an influencer of design direction. We discover daily that nature has evolved solutions over millions of years, and we can replicate that in our buildings. Examples like natural ventilation replicating termite mounds or using trees in bloom as seasonal solar shades are allowing us more freedom to design lower life-cycle cost buildings. When technology connects the two sides of the brain completely, I envisage a more gender-balanced construction industry in which buildings are built twice as fast and for half the cost of today by people who understand the occupants more fully. A future where buildings are part of a city ecosystem and where examining thousands of options in a heartbeat to find the optimum solution allows more creativity and time to deliver the designs we dream about.

Shaken Not Stirred

Hernan Diaz-Alonso
{Eero Saarinen Visiting Professor}

The title of this lecture has to do with the digital turn and its changing notion in theory and discourse. As you can see, the modern James Bond is too busy doing stuff—killing people, having sex with women. These are all the wonderful things Bond does to waste time. I was always much more interested in the production of a discourse that is embedded in the doing, as in film or fashion. That's my thing with "shaken or stirred"—to hell with it, give me the drink.

The greatest contribution that digital tools bring is the possibility of new coherences. In the beginning of the 19th century of German Rationalism and Romanticism, the idea that those could coexist was impossible. Computers allow us to be super-rational beings who are open to the idea that we can be contaminated and produce new coherences.

I could argue that we are in kind of a secessional digital period. The secessional moment was when we were trying to reclaim the sense of individuality in the midst of the industrial revolution. Now, I would argue that the digital mechanisms many of us are trying to figure out deal with how to reclaim the sense of the problem we are trying to solve. So the notion of reciprocity is not for everybody, but it is something that fascinates me. I am obsessed with that.

ELVIRA HOXHA

The outskirts of Brasilia present a unique problem. Designed by Lucio Costa only fifty years ago the city center has become a living monument that hampers development by refusing growth. The studio focused on learning from Brasilia's missed urban opportunities and proposed to design a new urban spine. This project explores how one of the blocks of this refashioned city would function both locally and within the larger proposed master plan. Influenced by Brasilia's modernist architecture as well as vernacular building types, this project explores a more connected way of urban living. The architecture seeks to create a city center teeming with life and energy. The plan is divided by a commercial strip that supports the residential component. In the center of the residential housing is a semi-private courtyard with facilities to accommodate the needs of the residents. The undulating façade and landscape creates pockets of privacy to allow for intimate social interactions that foster the culture present in the city. The building is clad in combinations of rich, dark woods contrasting with the stark white of the smooth stucco finish. This treatment reflects local building practices and plays off the large Brazilian pines that are characteristic of the area. The residential block is composed of a series of buildings which function individually but are also linked through a continuous passageway. Each building is composed of townhouses in the lower level and topped by apartments. The block is a unified mass, composed of smaller piece, which act independently while being linked together. [▲9–12]

"<u>Marketing</u> <u>guys</u> <u>would</u> <u>say</u> <u>we</u> <u>are</u> <u>crazy</u> <u>to</u> <u>do</u> <u>this</u>." **Rafael Birman**

▲SW: What is your take on what it means to live in this kind of organization? I can't tell if you're solving a problem with a certain degree of density and elegance, or if it's an argument about what it means to live here. I think it's trying to create an enormous amount of differentiation. But I also think you've created a coherence through the language. So even though it's super busy and kind of crazily dense, I actually think it works very well in creating both difference and a clear agenda for the housing here. ▲MF: You can't underemphasize the power of having pulled that street through as a pedestrian way. It's incredibly powerful, not only because of the continuation it creates at the pedestrian level, but also because of the asymmetry it gives you to the block views and the potential it creates for solving for the problems it sets up. I could imagine there's a kind of middle-scale of architecture that's being used to secure this area and close this off by some kind of gate so that it still feels very connected to everything but gives some privacy to the residents. ▲EM: You could make it a garden like you get in Brooklyn Heights on the promenade, where people's backyards are actually facing into there. They're not as high as you are there, but they're gardens. ▲RAB: Townhouses are not a common type in Brazil, so lately we don't really see anyone developing them. The issue of security is a strong thing, and it's not that you can't make it safe, it's just that the idea of putting your door up front in the street becomes a perception of insecurity. ▲RIB: The perception of insecurity is a very strong feeling. What most developers are doing is what we call condominium clubs, which are buildings that are surrounded by a fence and a gate. Everybody wants that. Here, we're swimming against the tide because we aren't doing a condominium club, and you'll have to face some opposition from the consumers. But we think of the condominium club as destructive to the urban tissue, so we won't do it. ▲RAB: Marketing guys would say we are crazy to do this. They would hear the briefing of the project and say it's not going to sell. But I think what's interesting here is that we have the scale to do it, because if you do it inside one block in Sao Paulo, it would be a disaster, but if you do this at a scale where you have this whole neighborhood, where things happen along the street, I think we can push this.

▲9

▲10

▲11

▲12

Books and Architecture
Luke Bulman

For architects, the book has been an essential tool for clarifying, extending, and promoting their ideas and projects. This seminar examines the phenomenon of the book in architecture as both an array of organizational techniques {what it is} and as a mediator {what it does} Arguably, outside of building itself, the book has been the preferred mode of discourse that architects have chosen to express their intellectual project. Because a lasting impression relies partially upon durability of message, the book remains the *objet par excellence* among media. In addition, the book finds itself in a privileged position as an instrument of discourse. Through case studies, the first portion of this seminar examined the relationship of book production to a selection of contemporary and historical practices, including each project's physical and conceptual composition as well as how each project acts as an agent of the architect within a larger world of communication. The second part of the seminar asked students to apply ideas in a series of three book projects.

MAYA ALEXANDER

"Now if ever, in this place and in this mood, the traveler can abandon himself to the rich pastime of window gazing." This excerpt from Walker Evans 1950 *Fortune* article "Along the Right-of-Way" was the genesis of this book, which is meant to be both a temporal and precious documentation of travel. The mere act of printing a photo has become a complicated endeavor and we all too often scroll through endless photo streams on our screens. This book asks you to feel the weight of the printed photo. The actual prints are juxtaposed with images on newsprint. The translucenct quality of the newsprint and the weight of the printed photographs interact with each other and create unexpected moments as you read the book—not unlike travel itself. {1}

KAROLINA CZECZEK

This book project explores Google imagery of cities, infrastructures and landscapes as a source of information about current spatial planning and its implications. Concurrently, the project emphasizes more abstract and pattern-like qualities of such structures. The first set of books uses real imagery and is accompanied by the text *Zone: The Spatial Softwares of Extrastatecraft* by Keller Easterling. The second set of books, with the same images, manipulated by CMYK color level, focuses on the aesthetics of such photographs and is accompanied by text *Color as Field* published by the American Federation of Arts. The proportion of images to text in the book is 2/3 to 1/3. {2}

ZACHARY HUELSING

250 Images That Matter to Architecture is a visual exploration composed of 250 images that present the polished ideal of architecture in relationship to the fluid, lived experience of the built environment. The book uses images collected from domestic interior design product catalogs, exhibition catalogs, and personal photographs. {3}

1

2

3

4235b

Credentials: The Professions of Urbanizing
Todd Reisz

As the close of the 1960s found cities in Europe and North America designed into obsolescence, urbanization unfurled with conviction in other parts of the world. The following decade could have been an era of true global expansion for the architectural and planning professions; however, there are many examples of where they were dismissed in favor of other enterprises, namely large-scale engineering companies and so-called technical and management service providers. The products of these urbanizing professions set in motion the global rules for and expectations of modern notions of the city. This seminar identifies and pursues case studies of expansive infrastructural projects in such places as Turkey, Pakistan, Iran, Iraq, Saudi Arabia, and the United Arab Emirates. Through these case studies, students seek out the credentials and historical tracks of performers who have delivered urbanization.

MAYA ALEXANDER & JOHN-THADDEUS KEELEY

When Optimism Gets in The Way: Sudanese Agricultural Development in the 1970s
In the 1970s, Sudan was a very different kind of nation. Indeed, as late as 1982, even as the country lurched toward a reinitiation of a devastating civil war, Sudanese officials might have said their country was on the brink of becoming the next Saudi Arabia—a nation overwhelmed by wealth from its resources. Ten years earlier, the Addis Ababa Agreement had brought an end to the first Sudanese Civil War, and the nation seemed primed to finally capitalize on their economic potential as the largest country in both Africa and the Middle East. It was in this context that the Rahad Irrigation Project, an enormous agricultural infrastructure scheme, was developed. While waiting for its windfall from oil, the Sudanese government saw massive potential in their other great resources, land and water. With financial backing from western countries, the World Bank, and their newly prosperous neighbors, Kuwait and Saudi Arabia, Sudan undertook the construction of its first state-run and state-planned national farm. Despite the optimism, Rahad was not the economic success the Sudanese government had hoped for and, just as the project was nearing completion in the mid-1980s a series of economic and political disasters befell the country. Still, the physical presence of the scheme remained as a symbol of Sudan's potential as a global agricultural powerhouse. Today, a new kind of optimism is being imported from China. Investors see Rahad as a prime testing ground for GMO cotton, which can be exported to meet the extraordinary demand from the east. The plans alone are a potent reminder of how much hope Sudan had for Rahad four decades ago, and how quickly optimism can falter in the face of reality.

MEGHAN MCALLISTER & JASON KURZWEIL

Make No Little Plans: The Forgotten Ambitions of Saudi Arabia's Cities
Planned in the late 1970s, Jubail and Yanbu Industrial Cities aimed to become the backbone for a newly diversified oil industry in the Kingdom of Saudi Arabia. Strategically placed on opposite coasts with a pipeline connecting them, the myth of two cities rising from the desert became a popular provocation for the late 20th century imagination. With the seemingly impressive claim of being the world's largest civil engineering project, Yanbu and Jubail are a statistical accomplishment, but most residents see these cities as places to work, but not as places for living long-term. Architects and urban designers from Skidmore, Owings & Merrill who designed the original master plans revealed some of the buried ambitions for these two cities to be more than the prototypical company town. Ten times the area of Manhattan, these were among the first cities planned and built "from scratch" at this scale. While these American architects saw the cities as an exciting opportunity for place-making and

a testing ground for building ideal cities that fused western-planning principles with Islamic prototypes, the Kingdom of Saudi Arabia saw these cities as lynchpins for building a secure and prosperous nation. The concept of city-building as nation-building perhaps proved fruitful economically, but the notion of designing from a *tabula rasa* may have been flawed from the start. Can cities built purely as economic infrastructure ever become cohesive, permanent communities? Should the Saudis just admit that it is inherently impossible for cities to engineer their way out of feeling like an engineering project? Are Jubail and Yanbu cities at all or overblown industry centers?

MAHDI SABBAGH & DIMA SROUJI

A Legacy of Aspiration: The Iraq Development Board
British command in Iraq was terminated in 1932, yet under the Iraq-British Treaty, Iraq was not fully independent. The treaty assured British control and was backed by the recently established Iraqi monarchy and the rural *shaykhs* in the region. When it was clear that Iraq would soon receive significantly increased oil revenues in 1949, the British Embassy encouraged Iraq to set up a development board. This would for the first time enable the state to invest 70% of its oil revenue into large-scale development. To chronicle the infrastructural development in 1950s Iraq, this piece highlights and visualizes the relationship between the Iraq Development Board {IDB} and the foreign consultants that were involved with Iraqi development at the time. Specifically, water control and irrigation infrastructure were presented as tools of stability and prerequisites to modernity. What both documents from the Iraq Development Board and foreign consultants have in common is a downplaying of the political reality of Iraq at the time for the benefit of a political narrative of progress and modernization. Ultimately, the IDB's built legacy has carved itself onto Iraq's environment and remains relevant today. The Tharthar Dam near Samarra made the headlines in April 2010 when news reports responded to a YouTube video titled "ISIL militants take Tharthar Dam in Iraq." The Iraqi army was quick to deny ISIS had taken control of the Tharthar Dam. The message was still clear. Water infrastructure in Iraq today, as in the 1950s, signifies and symbolizes agency and power over land and people. Whoever controls the dams controls Iraq.

3268b

Reinterpreting the Enlightenment
Anthony Vidler

This seminar studies the works of architects and artists from Nicolas Poussin and Claude Perrault to Jacques-Louis David and Claude-Nicolas Ledoux through the lenses of successive reinterpretations of the Enlightenment in the modern period. Conventional ascriptions of the "Age of Reason" {Ernst Cassirer, Emil Kaufmann} were thrown into question by post-World War II philosophers {Theodor Adorno, Max Horkheimer} and later by poststructuralist critics {Michel Foucault, Jacques Derrida}; these critiques were countered by a new interest in typological form {Aldo Rossi, Bruno Fortier} that founded Neo-Rationalism on a reading of Enlightenment visions of city structure. The engaged historical interest in the reinterpretation of the French Revolution and its cultural effects {Maurice Agulhon, Mona Ozouf, Robert Darnton} together with a revived utopianism of the later 1960s opened the texts of Enlightenment architects, hitherto seen as "dei∞cult," to scrutiny with respect to the literary accomplishments of the late 18th century. More recently, the return to a study of the idea of "nature" in the work of Bruno Latour and Félix Guattari has stimulated a sense of the "modernity" of the Enlightenment's views of the environment, for better or for worse.

ANTHONY GAGLIARDI

The Mathematization of Architectural Theory
Antoine Picon, in *French Architects and Engineers in the Age of the Enlightenment*, coins the end of the 18th century as the primordial schism between art and science as well as architecture and engineering. This is supported by the *Encyclopédie* in the mid- to late-1700s, edited by Denis Diderot and Jean le Rond d'Alembert, which classifies architecture under the faculty of imagination rather than with the sciences under the faculty of reason. Yet, at the turn of the century when arts and sciences are being compiled together into one archive of human perception, the theoretical advancements made within each discipline are strikingly parallel. A rigorous decomposition, categorization, and reconfiguration of elements can be seen in both fields; there are inflections of empiricism within the arts. The ambition of this research is to rouse correlations between dominant pedagogies of architecture and science at the end of the 18th century. This essay begins with Antoine Picon's argument for the isolation between the architect and the engineer and follows the tutelage and work of Gaspard Monge, Jean-Nicolas-Louis Durand, and Claude Nicolas Ledoux. The hope is to identify specific similarities between the theory of mathematics and the theory of architecture at the end of the 18th century.

STANLEY CHO

An Architecture of Ephemerality
Although we typically think of Ledoux and his monumental forms having a kind of permanence and massiveness about them, I propose in my essay "An Architecture of Ephemerality" that Ledoux had a perspective that was as light as the ephemeral. The ephemeral signifies what is necessary and temporary, those normal and accessible things that should endue the opposite of *amoure-propre*, a concept of Jean-Jacques Rousseau where esteem is contingent on the society of others. The opposite of *amoure-propre* is a self-esteem that does not depend on *La Règle du jeu*. Like with Emil Kaufmann, the essay traces a narrative of architecture history *von* Ledoux *bis*…Modernism. But, instead of finding similarities in volumetric form and geometries, it emphasizes the ephemeral, the unpredictability of the quotidian; that which is always eluding form and, if anything, can only be catalogued in an encyclopedic fashion. The paper attempts to make this argument beginning with Ledoux's project on the Ornamental Barn, continuing through d'Alembert's *Encyclopédie*, then paintings of Ozenfant & Le Corbusier, and landing on the architectural projects and manifesto of Hannes Meyer.

STEPHANIE JAZMINES

Square, Triangle, Circle. Then The Windows: The Poetry of San Cataldo Cemetery
The mid-20th century experienced an unearthing of the Enlightenment. Through Kauffman's publications, revolutionary ideas of an architecture aimed at expressing character, creating atmosphere, and composing through form became accessible and permeated the architecture scene. In 1967, after publishing *L'architettura della Città*, Aldo Rossi translated and introduced Boullée's *Essai*. According to Rossi, the compositional theories set forth by Boullée encompass two major characteristics of absolute validity and modernity: the construction of a logical process of formal investigation and, within that, the primacy of the conceptual, emotional, and operational. In translating and investigating Rossi's "Introduction" and his notes in *I Quaderni Azzurri*, it is apparent that the design for San Cataldo cemetery in Modena draws heavily from Boullée. Rossi expands on Boullée's "architecture of shadows," not only as a physical entity, but also as an understanding of light relative to nature, man, and the essence of time. In the passage of light and the manipulation of shadows, Rossi produces an environment that speaks directly to man's own mortality. The dialogue between the design in Modena and Boullée's writing presents architecture not as "the art of building" {Vitruvius}, but rather, as poetry.

3225b
Religion and Modern Architecture
Karla Britton

The design of religious architecture challenges the creative capacities of prominent architects, yet this domain has largely gone unnoticed within the field. In an interreligious and interdisciplinary context, this seminar offers a fresh examination of the history of modern architecture through a close analysis of a single building type—the religious building. This course opens a discourse between the disciplinary perspectives of philosophy, theology, liturgical studies, and architectural history and theory. These perspectives also enhance an understanding of the influence religion has come to exert in contemporary civic life and the concretization of that role in the construction of prominent religious buildings. Questions addressed include: How can the concept of the "sacred" be understood in the 21st century, if at all? In a pluralist society, in which the spiritual is often experienced individually, how can architecture express communal identity or tradition? How are concepts of the ineffable realized in material form?

SOFIA SINGLER

In-Between: On the Theology of Alvar Aalto's Unrealized Funerary Chapels
The theologically nebulous, or even inconsistent, character of Alvar Aalto's unrealized funerary works may be seen as evidence of consciously crafted ambivalence rather than mere passivity or refusal to take part in the theological discourse of the 20th century. Significant developments in recent scholarship have called attention to the self-reflexivity of the Modern project and have questioned the "the assumed hegemony of total secularization as a social and political project."[1] Aalto's funerary projects provide further evidence for a more nuanced narrative of the relationship between modernism and religion, where religion is neither accepted or denied. The theological ambivalence of Modernity is at play at various scales in Aalto's funerary projects. The massing and composition of the three complexes can be justified by functional demands but also invoke powerful theological connotations; their composition refers to Lutheran doctrine whilst questioning liturgical tradition; the ornamentation simultaneously reinforces and challenges traditional Christian symbolism. Indeed, true modernity entails entertaining "simultaneously conflicting conceptions of the world."[2] From the scale of the surrounding landscape to the scale of the interior detail, Aalto's funerary architecture is, at once, both humanist and religious; Christian and pantheist; rational and irrational; perfect and decaying; geometrically rigid and organic—it is truly Modern. This consciously constructed ambivalence demonstrates that a dismissal of Aalto's funerary projects as unrelated to religion is fallacious. His funerary chapels sit in the interstice between religion and reason, constructing an in-between space that frames but does not dictate the religious experience of the individual.

[1] Renata Hejduk & Jim Williamson, "Introduction: The Apocryphal Project of Modern and Contemporary Architecture," in The Religious Imagination in Modern and Contemporary Architecture: A Reader, ed. Renata Hejduk & Jim Williamson (New York: Routledge, 2011)

[2] Gustavo Benavides, "Modernity," in Critical Terms for Religious Studies, ed. Mark Taylor (Chicago: University of Chicago Press, 1998), 190.

MINU LEE

The Meaning of Sacred in 21st Century Catholic Church
Pursuing the concept of the sacred is one of the most difficult problems facing religious architecture today. As globalization eases the dispersion of foreign cultures the transfer of values and inter-religious dialogues become increasingly common. That outbreaks of fundamentalism sometimes annihilate existing religious identities are a problem that reaches the field of architecture, since the discipline has, over time, acted as a system that materializes the sacred. Architecture thereby constructs a self-referential system for its followers. It is important

to define the extent to which the formal experimentation of contemporary architecture has room for a dialogue between the sacred and the profane. Peter Eisenman's Fall 2014 studio "The Unreason of the Modern: The Transformation of the Sacred" produced five separate Catholic church projects that actively argued for church architecture to maximize its impact on the urban fabric of New Haven as well as to question the role of the primary 'sacred' space. Challenging of the contemporary metaphysical presence of God has led to a range of reactions in the profession. From Modernism to Deconstructivism, attempts to locate the metaphysical presence of architecture in the "sacred" have produced a variety of intellectual movements. Moving beyond the symbolism embedded in religious structures, contemporary architecture necessarily explores a renewed understanding of sacred space when we can no longer go back to the typological traditions.

DAPHNE BINDER

Since their appearance in Jerusalem in the early 1920's, movie theaters have repeatedly given rise to the tension between adherence to Jewish religious traditions and cultural freedom. The recently completed Cinema City complex—part cinema, part amusement park—continued the fraught history of cinemas in Jerusalem, sparking a round of protests surrounding its opening on the Sabbath. The cinema's contradictory identity as an agent of moral corruption and a cultural disseminator has led to verbal and physical attacks by the city's Jewish ultra-orthodox community. A study of the architecture and history of Zion Cinema and Edison Theater, "New" Jerusalem's early cultural centers, makes evident the ways in which the cinema heightened the schism between secular and religious groups in the city. Their unique scale and locations offered Jerusalem's growing secular community an alternative congregation space outside the domain of religious institutions. The cinema thereby constituted a venue for secular transgression in a city predominantly perceived as sacred. The resultant conflict sheds light on the problematic legacy of Jerusalem's modern urban planning that prioritized the city's preservation as a global religious epicenter, and restricted its ability to adapt to the city's changing culture and society.

4011b
Introduction to Urban Design
Alan Plattus with Andrei Harwell

ANNY CHANG & CASEY FURMAN

The earliest evidence of settlement in Copenhagen dates back to the 1100s. The main infrastructure of the early walled city from the 1400s still remains as the spine of the old city center. The city walls were mostly taken down in the 1850s due to siege and plagues, and the city expanded. This expansion occurred along five "fingers" that were derived from the old city gates, and are still named as such—Nørrebrogade, i.e. north gate, Østerbrogade i.e. west gate, and so on. Copenhagen's entire transportation infrastructure belong to these fingers, and the resulting neighborhoods have also been named after the old city gates. [■ 1]

ETHAN FISCHER, CECILIA HUI, ILANA SIMHON

Urban public space is often conceptualized as the physical manifestation of the democratic process. It is in these spaces that citizens can freely gather and express their political beliefs. Rather than the stage in which acts of political contestation play out, the urban public may be the subject of contestation. The renovation of Miyashita Park in Tokyo serves as a case study for the perceived infringement on public space by state and/or corporate entities. In this example, local inhabitants stood firmly in opposition not to the proposed physical changes to a public space, but rather to social and organizational changes. The case of the renovation of Miyashita

Park demonstrates that the defense of public space is the defense of its political potential. [■ 2]

TESS McNAMARA, PAUL RASMUSSEN

Amsterdam is a city defined by and created through its relationship to water. Beginning with a dam across the River Amstel in 1320, now Dam Square, a consistent tradition of space making through water infrastructure is present throughout Amsterdam's history. The city's ring canals, excavated during the 16th and 17th centuries, continued this practice by expanding the city's water infrastructure in order to expand the city itself. The radial roads that push outward across the canals maintain Dam Square as the center of city life and transit throughout the city's history. Manipulating water infrastructure to develop the city is at the core of Amsterdam's urban identity. [■ 3]

2215b
Architecture as Building
Thomas Beeby

This course analyzes the major buildings of this century through detailed dissection of their methods of construction. Graphic display of the major systems that make up a contemporary work of architecture allows for a reconstruction of the design process and reestablishes the thought patterns that formed the design priorities. Emphasis is on the relation of systems of structure and enclosure with the required technical systems.

ELENA BARANES, KIN TAK YU, IAN SPENCER, MICHAEL MILLER
Eames House [■ 4]

HIBA BHATTY, ELVIRA HOXHA, JEANNETTE PENNIMAN, MENGSHI SUN
Farnsworth House [■ 5]

SUNHI CHUNG, STEPHANIE JAZMINES, PHILLIP NAKAMURA, BOYUAN ZHANG
Glass House [■ 6]

■ 1

Sumida River

■ 2

■ 3

■ 6

Park and Connectivity
Structural And Modular Bay
Park and Connectivity

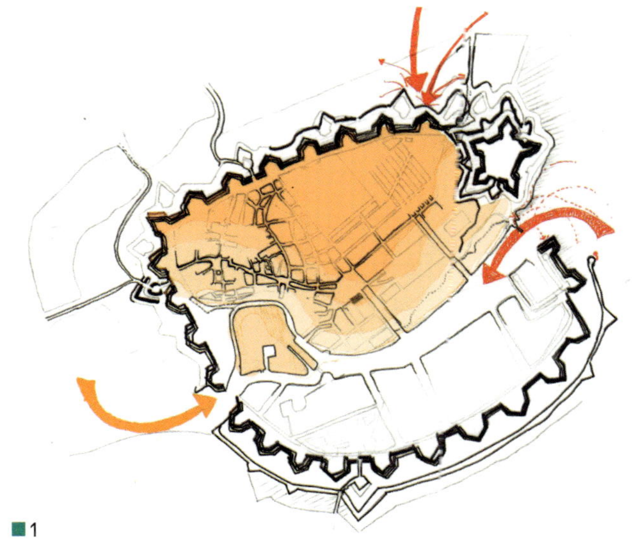

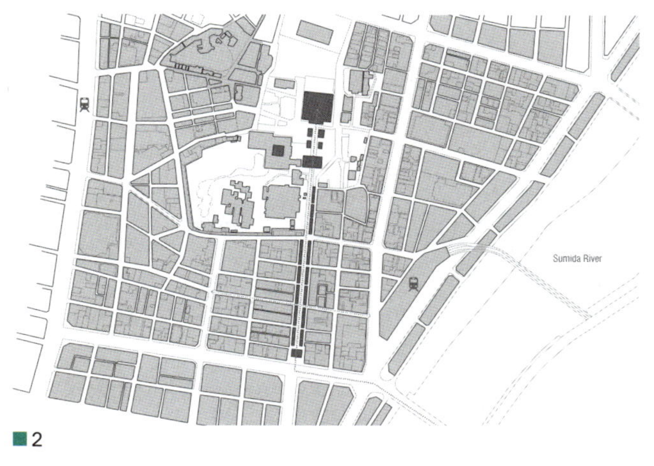

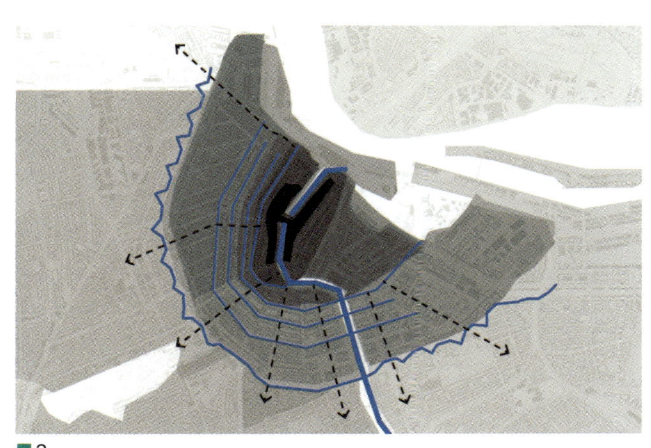

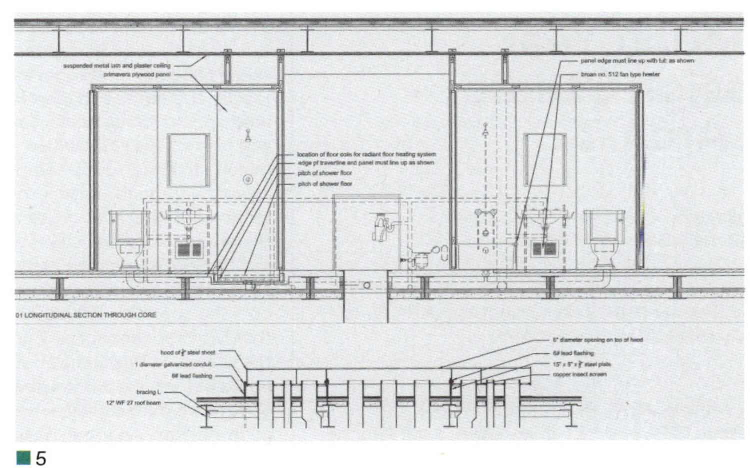

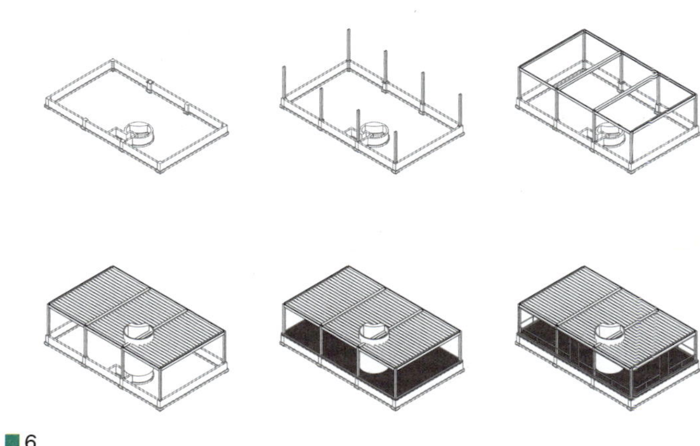

■ 4

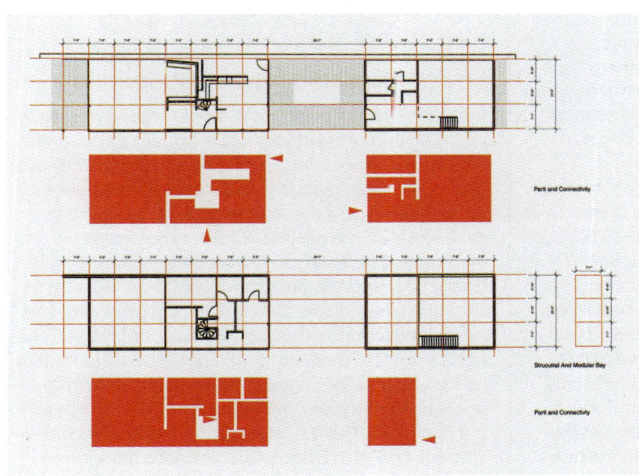

■ 5

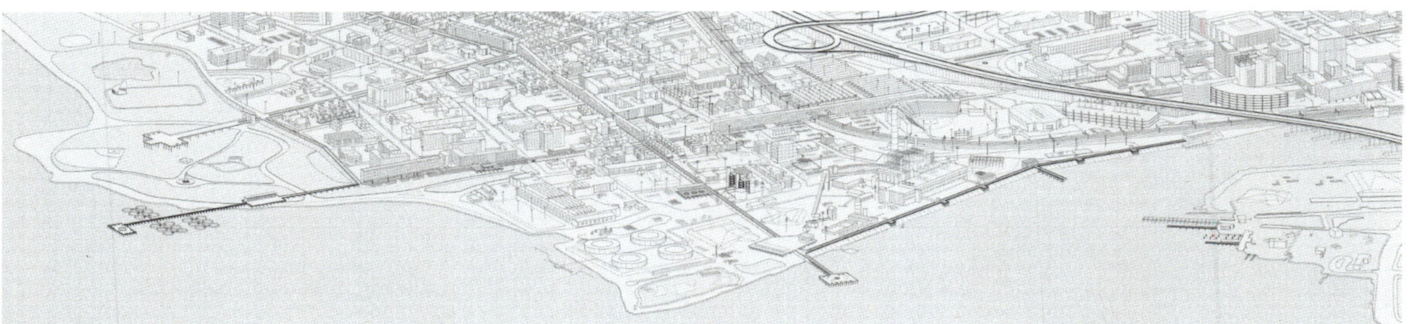

1022b
Second Year Design Studio M.Arch. I

<u>Coordinator</u>
Ed Mitchell {**EM**}

<u>Critics</u>
Peggy Deamer {**PD**}, Keller Easterling {**KE**}, Bimal Mendis {**BM**}, Alan Plattus {**AP**}

<u>Jurors</u>
Emily Abruzzo {**EA**}, Parag Agrawal {**PA**}, Tatiana Bilbao {**TB**}, Matthijs Bouw {**MB**}, April Capone {**AC**}, Alexander Felson {**AF**}, Alexander Garvin {**AG**}, Lorena Gomez {**LG**}, Kevin Gray {**KG**}, Andrei Harwell {**AH**}, Derek Hoeferlin {**DH**}, Denise Hoffman-Brandt {**DHB**}, Alfie Koetter {**AK**}, David Kooris {**DK**}, Andrew Lyon {**AL**}, Chris Marcinkoski {**CM**}, Joeb Moore {**JM**}, Alan Organschi {**AO**}, Todd Reisz {**TR**}, Brent Ryan {**BR**}, Aniket Shahane {**AS**}, Robert A. M. Stern {**RAMS**}, Anthony Vidler {**AV**}, David Waggoner {**DW**}, Edgar Westernot {**EW**}

This fourth core studio, an introduction to the planning and architecture of cities, concerns two distinct scales of operation: that of neighborhood and that of the dwellings and the institutional and commercial building types that typically contribute to neighborhood. Issues of community, group form, and the public realm, as well as the formation of public space, blocks, streets, and squares are emphasized. The studio is organized to follow a distinct design methodology, which begins with the study of context and precedents. It postulates that new architecture can be made as a continuation and extension of normative urban structure and building types. The studio examines how one represents, analyzes, constructs and projects the future design of an urban site focusing on two

competing but at times complementary ways for architects to approach city making. One approach examines the city as a series of distinct physical spaces and generally operates by establishing typological standards and identifies and constructs significant and iconic public spaces—streets, squares, and parks. This establishes the grammar of city making to construct a comprehensible fabric. The second approach is concerned with the city as a technical object that organizes time—the operational aspects of the city—as well as space. This method envisions the city as the performance of both large and small scale infrastructures that support the operative vitality of the city. We could say that the first conceptual method is linguistic while the second is functional, but clearly the two methodologies inform one another. Any design proposal does more than simply solve a given set of immediate problems. An urban design proposal embodies a position about, and has consequences for, urban life and urban form. In urban design the term "program" has a more open-ended meaning than when applied to a single building. Urban design programming involves a process of ascribing value to different needs, demands and desires. These projected urban visions for Bridgeport were the result of negotiating between, and determining the relative value of, various possible urbanisms. At the city scale, the term "site" also has broad implications. Urban design site boundaries are both political and ideological points of contestation. This studio considered how intervening in a specific and limited location in downtown Bridgeport could initiate a larger plan and longer-term vision through urban and architectural scale propositions. This year the studio operated as five distinct sections working as five teams to orchestrate the infrastructure and design of Bridgeport's South End. The project is currently in the design and research phase with the cooperative efforts of a number of offices and agencies. Our work was part of a parallel research project to the actual implementation of the master plan strategy for the city.

Bimal Mendis

DOV FEINMESSER & MEGAN MCDONOUGH

A critique of the linear, visionary standard of urban planning and presentation, this project embraces the unpredictable nature of urban development over time. By focusing on the multitude of variables and individuals involved in changing within the urban environment, the project involves the development of a non-linear, turn-based game. Using South Bridgeport and the projected 2080 sea level rise as a testing ground and time frame prospectively, this game incorporates four key groups of players in the site's potential development, splits the site into five zones and, finally, divides the development timeline into four phases leading up to 2080. The result is a matrix of 1020 possible outcomes for the development of South Bridgeport, reflecting the great number of potential outcomes, over time, in urban development and simultaneously providing the framework for a tool that could help future city planners, architects, politicians, ecologists and the like, anticipate the outcomes of diverse decisions on projected urban development. {● 1–2}

> "Urbanism is not a thing you can rationalize, it's more like a poker game where you're watching people's choices."
> **Keller Easterling**

●**CM:** The thing that fascinates me now, given the specificity of what you've done, is that it seems like what you're trying to design is not a new Bridgeport but actually a new tool for thinking about development. I think that's super essential at the moment. It should be what we're teaching in school; how to design the mechanisms by which certain urban transformations come about. ●**KG:** You really want that optimization algorithm. There are all of these robotic investing websites that have all these algorithms and tell you how much you should have in stocks and bonds and cash. I think you might have something here. You might have a

● 4

● 5

● 6

valuable start-up, if you can create an optimization algorithm for developers. ●KE: I would be careful there. We are artists. We are architects. It's strange in some ways that, to be more practical, you have to be more indeterminate. Urbanism is not a thing you can rationalize, it's more like a poker game where you're watching people's choices. ●KG: Didn't people say the same thing about Google, that it was never going to happen? ●KE: I love that you are illuminating all kinds of options. It's like you're keeping the urban fabric almost fluid while you think about it, and that's really great, but you also don't want to get into a game of hyper-rationalizing it. ●CM: I think you have to be careful—you can't expect to tell this what to do. If you can self-generate, fabulous. ●KG: But then you just run back test, like you do in finance. You can have a predictive algorithm. You back test your results, and your algorithm will self-modify to predict the future. I really do believe you're onto something that has more power than you may believe. ●KE: Someone who is good at gambling can run the numbers. It's a model, just like you all have trained your habit of mind by modeling it. It's pretty useful. But eventually, you have to put your chips down. ●AG: Put your chips down. In the game, the big winners are the ones that know when to put the chips down. That's what I want to see.

JESSICA ANGEL & LUIS SALAS PORRAS

The key elements of a city's composition and preservation are ripe for thought under the threat of global warming, sea level rise and the foreseeable shortage of natural resources. The proposed project develops a series of programmatic "rooms" delineated by infrastructural "walls" which resist or allow the passage water. These walls respond to Bridgeport's current urban predicament—a condition epitomized by sprawling vacant lots and abandoned buildings. These walls are seen as spatial catalysts that frame defined zones in order to control the potential de-growth of the area stretching from downtown to Seaside Park. Like Highway I-95, they are always twofold: they work as enclosures as

well as connective elements. We believe that introducing new boundaries can revitalize some important areas that have sunken in the homogenous landscape of Bridgeport and simultaneously connect different isolated zones of the city. Programmatically, the entire waterfront area is rehabilitated around new forms of local production, from aquaculture to greenhouses agriculture. Wetlands and dry terrains alternate in order to form a diverse landscape. [●3–4]

"Starting with the original Remington factory, the tragic irony is that half the stuff that would make this city has been there already and has been torn down." **Alan Plattus**

●EM: I'm in support of your proposition. What's interesting is that bottom floor. I know people who jack their houses up the first storm and nothing happens, but then get blown out the next year when they don't. But I like the idea that you have this space that's basically a garage that could take a beating. You don't put your mechanical down there, so what would you do with it? And I'm continuously asking students to think about this. You could have a whole city of plastic furniture, and it would just constantly be flooded. It could be an interesting place. ●AP: I've been hugely attracted to this scheme all along in part because it works with the type that is ubiquitous in Bridgeport throughout its history—its infrastructural buildings. Starting with the original Remington factory, the tragic irony is that half the stuff that would make this city has been there already and has been torn down. So I think the rigor in it would be identifying those pieces of surviving infrastructure, which you've sort of done, which would include things like parking garages, power plants, mill buildings, train viaducts, probably also the ball park is peculiar. I think I'm describing your project actually, thinking about how new, strategic intervention starts to link those cognate types together to produce something that is, you know, really just a rereading of the sea levels that are already there. ●AO: The question I

have is that in some cases the proposal is defensive. It's a moat or it's a seawall, a levy. That has one particular characteristic relative to the land, and its value beneath the level of the water. And there's other cases where it's just a frame to demarcate a city district. I think you can't just say sometimes it's this and sometimes it's that. You have to say, at this point, this is a protective dike that's going to give value to this particular area. In another location, we're trying to create definition, and bound it so density can increase, or vice versa.

BEN BOURGOIN & MICHELLE CHEN

Our proposal, JANUS, is a new vision for Bridgeport that leverages the simple and fluid reversal of fronts and backs of buildings to redefine this neighborhood's urban fabric and provide it with viable land above the flood plain for future development. Most properties in this neighborhood remain uninsurable due to their location within the flood plain—during even light rains the streets become flooded to the curb. This proposal shifts the current street grid to occupy the space of backyards, allowing for a re-grading of the street without the need to relocate utilities. The low lying areas that were streets before would be redefined as a system of pedestrian paths whose natural slope and permeable surfaces would help keep adjacent lots dry. Additionally, the vacant and unkempt lots that characterize many of these streets would be used as retention basins during flood events, and provide a recreational amenity connected to the system of pedestrian paths during the rest of the year. What was once the backside of these properties becomes an enlivened street, while the front side opens onto new trails and gardens. [●5–6]

"Developers are venal, but they're not always stupid." **Alan Plattus**

●AP: You may or may not know this, but there are infill projects going on in the lower east end that are not dissimilar to fragments of what you're proposing. Developers are venal, but they're not always stupid. So as they get little pieces of property, there is some house-raising on some remediated sites. What I'm having trouble getting my head around is the quiet, gentle rhetoric of the land itself, and then the vaguely cynical and certainly branded, in a totally non-Bridgeport way, nature of your imagery. You're producing the kind of brand you could bring into the neighborhood and most people would say, "Hmm, I can see the conversion of that." But as soon as they saw that, they would know that they're being set up. ●AF: Part of the strategy is a spine, and part of it is elevated, which is already happening. There's a funny mechanism for that. There are lots of houses that are being elevated in Connecticut at this point, or at least that's a strategy. The idea is that you establish a development spine and other houses see the value in that. They see that there is an investment going on, and they follow suit. ●DW: It's about how a back becomes a front. Are they wood houses? Because if they are wooden houses, it's not that much, we've done a million of them in Louisiana, or at least several hundred thousand. You can lift them, I lifted my own. They're not hard if they're wood. ●AO: I think the matter is it's a cut and fill project, which would be shown really clearly in a section that should have been done. The argument is not about cutting the house in two. It's not really a two-faced Janus house at all. It's really frontal. I think you have to make a clearer argument about that. I'm not saying that this might not be some really great way of creating more displacement area for flood water. I think that would be part of the argument plus the developer sell, but I do think there are basic sectional questions.

Alan Plattus

NICOLAS KEMPER & ANNE MA

Once in the ocean, the average water molecule will spend thousands of years trapped, waiting, saline. To escape requires energy, the proper vector, and above all, a berth on the surface. These factors do not align often: At a given time only one in every 100,000 molecules of water participates in the water cycle. Bands of heat and weather conspire to bring a disproportionate number of those molecules to the skies, hills, and umbrellas of Connecticut. There, they join WASSERGEIST. Reclaiming Bridgeport's intimate relationship with the water, WASSERGEIST raises two roads which then protect the South End neighborhood from the ocean while wrapping a series of lakes. These roads treat, celebrate, and enjoy one of Connecticut's most maligned resources: rainwater. Before plunging back into the salty depths, the water molecule gets one last hurrah. 〔●7–8〕

> "What's paradoxical about this is that it's quite cheerful and ebullient, but essentially the public amenity that you seem to be providing, which you graphically represent in the spirit of the 19th-century picturesque, is actually not a series of recreational ponds." **Brent Ryan**

●PD: This is a fabulous proposal in that it takes advantage of how to make a berm a pleasant place, but I am going to protest your representation. It's all blue with fun sailing and the like, and it's really counter-intuitive to this much more technical, mechanical, water-treatment knowledge that you actually have. I would totally redo your graphics to correspond to the intelligence of the proposal. ●BR: What's paradoxical about this is that it's quite cheerful and ebullient, but essentially the public amenity that you seem to be providing, which you graphically represent in the spirit of the 19th-century picturesque, is actually not a series of recreational ponds. If most of the ponds are actually not publically accessible, that seems to be massively defeating the purpose of creating a chain of ponds in the middle of the city's principal park. I would have loved to have seen these public in the way that they are in Copenhagen and Hamburg. I can imagine a re-urbanization of this part of the city based on the completion of that amenity, which does happen in those places. ●AP: I think the challenge of this project is that we're going to take a much beloved park, not just in Bridgeport but nationally—it's a special seaside Olmsted park and it's going to

change radically. How do you position those needed changes to convince the people to use it in a way that it actually enhances the public dimension of their park? ●JM: This could be part of a history lesson, because if you actually look at Olmsted and Olmsted's travels early in his career through England, he writes the memoirs of his experiences with these newfound parks. In London you'll have a direct connection to Olmsted's own discoveries late in his life. I think there's a perfect way to link this to this project.

JOHN WAN & DIMA SROUJI

This scheme proposes a combination of new mixed use structures, event urbanism, and water resilience as the basis of a culturally referential urban intervention in an underused neighborhood of the city—Cedar Creek. Cedar Creek is a forgotten zone that currently separates the Black Rock neighborhood from the South End. We're proposing a solution for the land to be converted so that it can connect the neighborhoods while solving the flooding issues. Part of our proposal then is to let Cedar Creek breathe by allowing it to return to its natural state as well as using it to attract people, through a series of key event spaces, to the underused spaces surrounding the creek. The key event spaces include a hotel inspired by the Iranistan mansion, a circus berm, and a system of constructed wetlands. Storm water runoff ponds area unified along with the key event spaces under a dazzlingly colorful landscaping scheme, promising an optimistic new urban heart for the troubled city. 〔●9–10〕

> "The circle—it's something you could just do. Go there and it doesn't cost a thing but gives so much. You can almost imagine it's this love child between Burning Man and Ocean Grove." **Keller Easterling**

●AS: Your drawings are really colorful and vibrant and I want to see how that translates to what the surface material is or what the character of the edges might be. What's it like to stand in that space when it's empty? The emptiness of a space can be an event on its own, and that's something to be designed. ●BR: I think the graphic representation is superbly fantastical, but it's also completely pragmatic in terms of the realism of having people come down here. In New England we're so stiff we don't inhabit the ocean in this way, but this is quite common in Britain where people come and they caravan. You get these caravan parks of like ten thousand caravans parked along the sea for the summer, so the whole park could become part of your project. ●KE: The circle—it's something you could just do. Go there and it doesn't cost a thing but gives so much. You can almost imagine it's this love child between Burning Man and Ocean Grove. I'm just sitting here thinking of all these different things it could be. ●BR: This raises a foundational problem in architecture, which is when you look at something like this fun palace that simply acts as a framework for the rest of the activity and program in the building that is made by the inhabitants themselves. In a way this architecture is stepping back and letting people animate it. ●AP: This is sort of the Midway—when you think about world's fairs, most of them since 1893, they've always had this marginal area where the fun stuff happens, but with serious cultural displays of prize hogs, technology, or whatever. Midway was where the action was.

ANNE HOUSEHOLDER & JOHN KLEINSCHMIDT

In a contemporary coastal city, the ground and buildings need to be active performers in the negotiation between water and land. This project envisions the ground as a piece of infrastructure that protects against storm-surge and directs rainwater. Bridgeport's coal-fired power plant is phased out and replaced by a new power plant embedded in a public park built with "spoils" dredged from the softened east bank of the Pequonnock River. The "headland" created by this dramatic new topography amps up Bridgeport's underlying structure as a peninsula. Private investment in the power plant is leveraged to enable a new hardened edge on the Pequonnock's west bank. Swapping of rail and highway creates a previously overlooked site for new residential development, protected by the remnants of the rail line reborn as a recreational greenway. The

result is a reorientation of downtown Bridgeport to its third waterfront, the Pequonnock River. 〔●11–12〕

> "When looking here, it seems that you have an approach to urban planning that exists in a world with unlimited resources." **Edgar Westernot**

●AS: I really appreciate the way you described the space and the site you carved out for yourself, showing the bounds that you'd be working in. I'm clear on what your attitude is on the water edge, but right now I'm not sure what your attitude is towards the city edge, which can inform all kinds of things—from why is a residential district only confined to one zone to why the massing is oriented the way it is, making it waterfront housing. ●JM: Well that seems pragmatic in the big picture, but I also want to say there's some very sensitive, strategic moves here, whether we question them overall is another issue. With the drainage overflow, you've very sensitively thought about how the water from this horizontal sink flows along this edge and reinforces where this becomes a peninsula and then a park. ●EW: You need to show it's a transition, it's something you need to embrace all the time. When looking here, it seems that you have an approach to urban planning that exists in a world with unlimited resources. What I would like to hear is how your project fits into the timeline of both the past and the future. How can you make logical steps when it comes to resiliency? How can you create stepping stones where each action is a driver for the next one? Because you know if you jump straight in, that's where things get slippery, and in our work, we have to deal with these things every single day. ●AP: Well, I think we'll keep worrying about that question. Time has leveled us somewhat. It's a legitimate and pressing question because one of the intriguing things about what you guys have done is that between moving the power plant and the new housing, you could very well get someone else to pay for about a mile or two of protection other than the government.

Ed Mitchell

ANTHONY GAGLIARDI & KRISTIN NOTHWEHR

The site on the Southeast end of Bridgeport is a microcosm of the larger issues afflicting the city. With four disparate zones of program—recreation, industry, residential and institutional—harshly juxtaposed against one another, the Broad Street artery connecting downtown with the waterfront has become an unoccupied line of demarcation with no character or pedestrian presence. The large power plants on the site have proven repellent to pedestrian-oriented development, but their presence there provides the economic lifeblood of the city and looms large as the prevailing image of Bridgeport. This project seeks to learn from these industrial structures, taking formal and operative cues from this type and repurposing their program as a public amenity. 〔●13–14〕

> "Back in the 1930s, 1940s, and 1950s, every architect would scramble for these commissions for power plants and industrial centers. What could these things be like in the future if w became involved in them?" **Alan Plattus**

●TR: This is the one project so far that has really exhibited existential frustration. Yes we all can see in the style a call-back to Ruhrgebiet and other such post-industrial parks that we've seen, but what I've liked in your story, which I wish I could've seen in your visualizations, is that there is a sense that you were trying to avoid making industrial buildings precious. This isn't necessarily a park that is going to be preserved as such to represent Bridgeport of the 19th and 20th centuries, but you're doing damage control. ●EM: It's a real issue looking at the site. It's so toxic, but part of the public land. It's going to be part of this city, and its biggest value is in that first power station. They power all of Fairfield County. They're changing, but they're not going away. ●DW: I think you're still stuck a little bit too much with building a diagram. After you draw the line you can still move the line. The gesture's still there. But I think you're starting to make the connection that no one else is making and that we need to make,

●7

●8

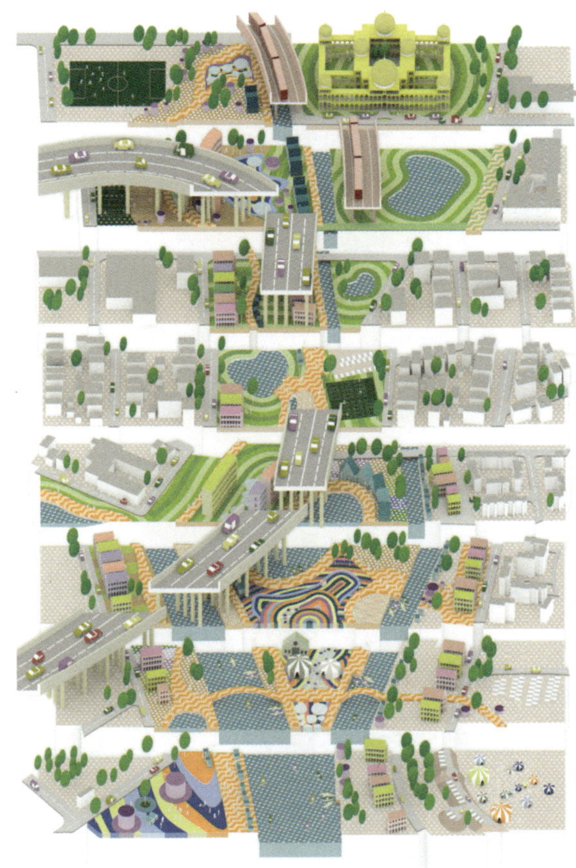

●9

●10

●12

●11

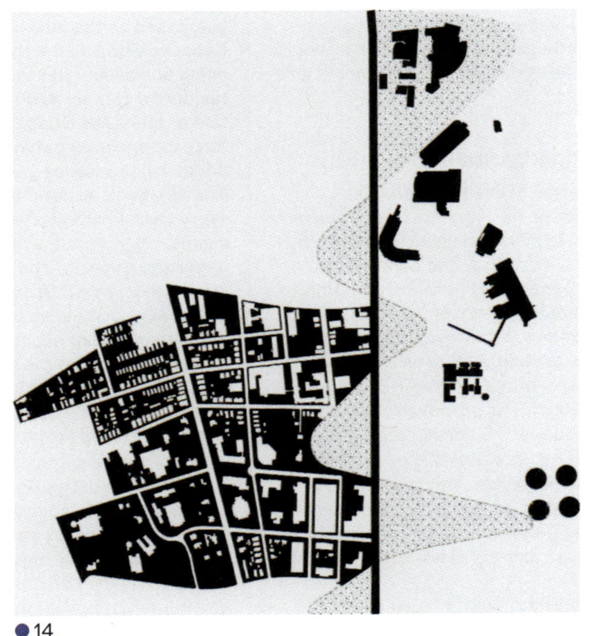

●14

●13

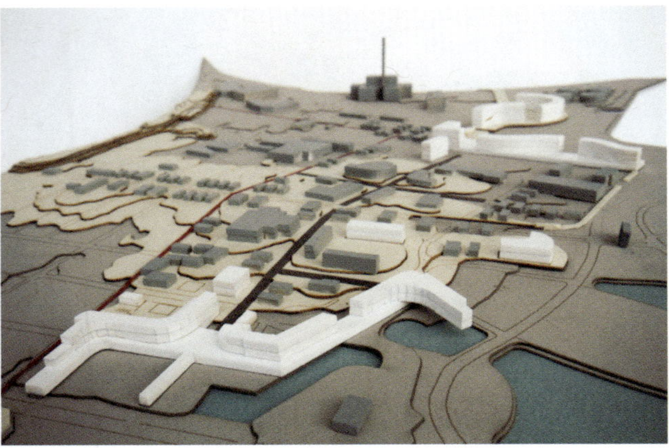

●17

●18

●15

●16

between water and energy, which is competing for value in the future world. I think everything you can capture from everything around this to put into this cycle would make Bridgeport a smarter city, and you actually have the mayor who would engage some of these ideas. ●AP: David and I were talking about this: back in the 1930s, 1940s, and 1950s, every architect would scramble for these commissions for power plants and industrial centers. They were great commissions and we gave that away, along with a lot of other things. And the question is, what could these things be like in the future if we became involved in them?

HUGO FENAUX & LUKE ANDERSON

As a new interpretation of the traditional factory housing, this proposal suggests new types of dwellings that deviate from the usual relationship between residential, industrial, and commercial zones. The deployment of this new housing prototype will act as an economic driver in critical areas and a dry edge against coastal storm surge—its purpose is to stimulate growth. Acting as a new city center, it will ensure continued density and activity within and around itself. The proposal looks at two distinct sites in Bridgeport: Sikorsky, an existing helicopter factory, and Steel Point, a new commercial development. In each case, this project looks at Bridgeport in terms of its scale, isolated building types, and posits an urban prototype for revitalizing and densifying these introverted islands. {●15–16}

> "It's a Bass Pro Shop, what I'll call a late box store, in that it is about the spectacle of being on the interior. I wonder if you could make that a theme for the site—that this is a spectacle of box stores." **Andrei Harwell**

●AK: There are some who would argue that a big box store is responsible for killing a lot of cities in that it puts a lot of businesses out of business. So why is it that you guys are holding onto things like Walmart and Bass Pro Shop? It's a cool project in terms of the big box store being something you drop in that then generates something, kind of in the same way your whole project seems like something that's dropped in. It's almost like a Roman city. ●AH: It's a Bass Pro Shop, what I'll call a late box store, in that it is about the spectacle of being on the interior. I wonder if you could make that a theme for the site—that this is a spectacle of box stores. I know you said "Walmart," so some of the criticism is focused on the idea of that. But I don't think of a Bass Pro Shop as the same as a Walmart. It's about going and seeing the exotic fish in the tanks and the taxidermy zebras. ●AP: One wonders if the ultimate fate of cities like Bridgeport is to create relatively fortified enclaves between which both natural and unnatural processes are allowed to work their way. And what you've done that I want to highlight is in every case where you've found an anchor use that seems, like it or not, worth protecting in the short-run or the mid-run. The University of Bridgeport is probably not going anywhere. Sikorsky may eventually go somewhere, but right now it's a pretty important anchor use for the local industry. The Bass Pro Shop and the future development of Steel Point, you've said that in order to do protection, protection is not a collective project, protection is an individualized project associated with something worth protecting. I think it's very likely that is what we'll see in the kind of political and economic landscape that we occupy—that rather than doing old-style army corps shared infrastructure, we may find ourselves entering an age of protecting those things which can be proven. Where the federal government and the city will effectively pay to have that particular area protected in order to keep the use that is associated with it.

ANDREW STERNAD

Bridgeport is susceptible to storm surge flooding, yet underlying urban issues are the real threat to the city's future development. A new campus plan for the University of Bridgeport, an important South End neighborhood institution, aligns the urban edge with topographic features and coheres university and civic functions around waterfront access points. Publicly-funded flood protection forms the foundation for elevated private development, including new student housing oriented toward Long Island Sound and Olmstead's Seaside Park. The protected edge is thickened with subtle sectional variations that respect historic fabric within while framing views of sea beyond. {●17–18}

> "One wonders if the ultimate fate of cities like Bridgeport is to create relatively fortified enclaves between which both natural and unnatural processes are allowed to work their way." **Alan Plattus**

●RAMS: You know, if you could keep the water up there it would make a nice place for kids to play and maybe even sailboats. ●DH: I think you've figured out the ground plane really well. You've got your hands around how this thing works sectionally as it builds up, but then it's almost like that thing gets put on top of it. So how can that ground strategy and its logic be followed up through. ●RAMS: What I wonder about your scheme is why you've quartered off the campus with a sort of loop road when you're already in a destination area—which means people are not traversing to go somewhere else. So I think you're making something suburban rather than urban. The Yale campus is nice because the streets go through it, even though people once rejected it. It seems to me you've taken the University of Bridgeport out of its context. ●AP: There are a couple really provocative things about this, and one wonders whether the ultimate fate of cities like Bridgeport are to create relatively fortified enclaves between which both natural and unnatural processes are allowed to work their way. And what you've done which I want to highlight is in every case you've found an anchoring use that seems, like it or not, to be worth protecting.

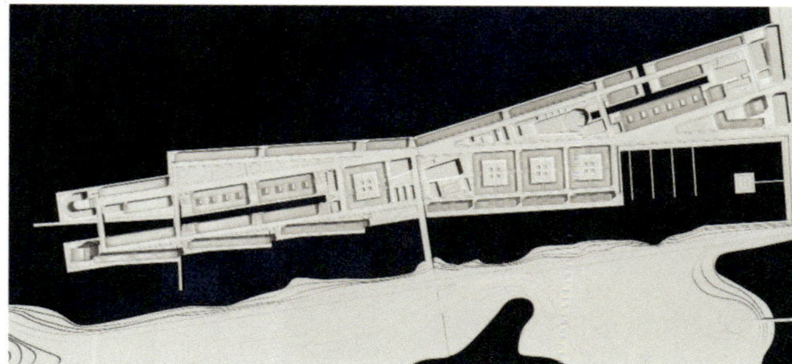

●19. Sarah Kasper & Katie Stege

●22. Kiana Hosseini

●20. James Kehl

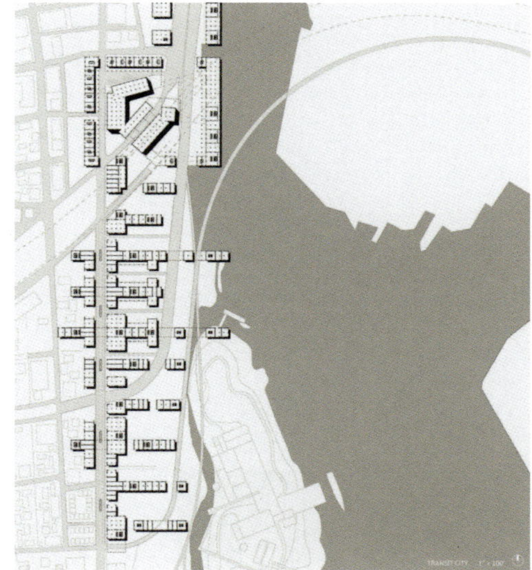

●23. Xiao Wu

●21. Boris Morin-Delfoy

Peggy Deamer

<u>Students</u>
Kiana Hosseni, Cynthia Hsu, Charles Kane, Sarah Kasper, James Kehl, Anna Meloyan, Boris Morin-Defoy, Justin Oh, Madelynn Ringo, Katie Stege, Xiao Wu

This urban intervention in Bridgeport resulted from the work of the entire studio. The plan is set 100 years in the future and considers Bridgeport's threatened economy and shoreline. The project proposes various building stock that coexists with flooding, storm surge, existing fabric, and giant infrastructure. This proposal envisions Bridgeport as a key player in the future development of the northeast due to its transportation potential by both rail and water. Simultaneously, the project focuses on re-stitching the city together through additional transit connections and architectural interventions. This proposal envisions a city that responds to and exists in coordination with a more volatile world. [●19–24]

> "It's not just because we like the future and this is the Jetsons. We're given that date by nature. We didn't choose it."
> **Peggy Deamer**

●PD: At the midterm, we assumed that the 100 year flood plain gave us 100 years to think. We naively thought we had 100 years. So at midterm, there was a big discussion about the fact that the 100 years that ecology is giving us is different from the time frame that urban design, politics, and economics gives us. Nevertheless, we stuck with 100 years, and it seems like, if nothing else, ecology now is giving us a different kind of lesson. For me, teaching this urban design studio is unlike any other urban design studio I've ever taught because of Rebuild by Design and the energy and the logic that has gone into that. This came to us with a whole sense of reality that we haven't had in other

studios; and we have had to live up to that. The reality may fly in the face of having to imagine 100 years, but we let it rip with the students. ●KE: 100 years is working for you guys. It has to do with the palette that you've chosen, the style, the impression that you're giving—it's gorgeous—and it has a gift that you can work back from. It's a different kind of document than we ordinarily operate with in planning. It's like a kit—an impression that you're giving to the city about what could be that's not overly futuristic. Spot on. ●AK: You talked about Bridgeport as a destination. You showed New Haven and Stamford. Those are two very different types of destination cities with different types of characters, and I wonder if there is a cohesive understanding as a studio about what sort of destination Bridgeport is. ●Madelynn Ringo: It's definitely a shared idea. The industry was a way to revitalize the economy of Bridgeport, but we also understood that the eco-industry and some of the research initiatives could themselves become a tourist attraction. Especially as you are coming over the highway, you are going over all of the good stuff. ●AP: I've been fascinated by this all semester. This kind of projection of a future city has gotten so discredited or so commercialized that it's very hard to inject into a real world conversations. But there is something about the water issue that you've identified that might actually authorize this conversation. And if you go far enough out—twenty years is not enough, because people can still imagine themselves in the picture—and challenge people to visualize something dramatically different, it may be an opportunity that we haven't had in a long time to put this back on the table in a constructive and serious way. Then I think that your responsibility as the conveners of that conversation is to give the people that you need to participate in that conversation a place to grab on, and that's what I'm not seeing yet. In all of the renderings, there is a total defamiliarization process—maybe not so much in the models. ●AV: I see the foothold in shadow form underneath the transparency of the model. I think the models are much more successful than the renderings. Right now, I'm involved in trying

to retrace a whole series of utopian projects from Plato on, and what I find fascinating is the project of a hundred year utopia with a contemporary technology. All of the technologies of extraction, ecology, recycling, treatments, and so on you could have on an island. But that island is something that is projected to develop over one hundred years. That would be my foothold. It's a kind of second-best utopia where you can start in one place and then the technologies can transform themselves over a hundred years, but you will still have that island left. ●KE: What if we say it's the most practical? There is something that Peggy mentioned in midterm about changing cycles. What you could be showing us is that those short-sighted cycles of change have been altered because of another kind of issue. You could actually be crunching numbers and showing us the difference between a certain kind of investment that is more short-sighted and the extra growth that comes from being more far-sighted. ●AP: You're trying to make it a twenty-year plan. ●KE: Maybe. I'm just trying to take the ethereal clouds away and ask what if it was practical. ●AV: Nobody is telling us that the 100 year surge isn't coming tomorrow. ●RAMS: There is a quality to this presentation that to me is from the 1950s in American cities. Let's tear down New Haven in the middle, and this will be the future. There would always be a cable car, and there would certainly be some whirling traffic thing, and there are some very tantalizing images, but they're old and, to me, very familiar images. I don't think anybody has dared to propose such a thing in recent times, but I have to ask why they haven't. They become like Jetsons—comic book allure. Not really believable. ●PD: I'll say that the 100 year flood gave us 100 years. It's not just because we like the future and this is the Jetsons. We're given that date by nature. We didn't choose it. Part of what one has to think about when doing urban design is: Are you going to do something that looks twenty years in advance, but prevents what actually needs to happen 100 years in advance?

● 25. Feng Qian

● 26. Winny Tan & Lila Chen

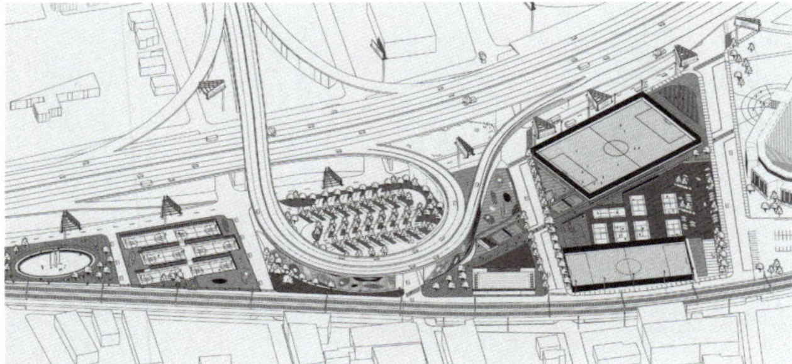

● 27. Pearl Ho & Andrew Dadds

● 28. Jenny Kim & Dorian Booth

● 29. Michelle Gonzalez & Shayari de Silva

● 30. Vittorio Lovato & Eugene Tan

Keller Easterling

Students
Dorian Booth, Lila Chen, Andrew Dadds, Shayari
de Silva, Michelle Gonzalez, Pearl Ho, Jenny Kim,
Vittorio Lovato, Feng Qian, Eugene Tan, Winny Tan

●KE: We started up with some frustration about Bridgeport. We were worried about certain forms of injustice; taxation among them, crime, and so on. We were worried about focusing so much on the resiliency issue, so we started focusing on some other things to see if those other things might leverage the resiliency issue to make a better bargain for the city. These are the six projects that are in ratcheting interplay with each other. We started with the idea, "what if we had nothing times zero?" So we looked at a lot of tools being used in cities all around the country, from creative shrinking to different taxation schemes, and so on. You'll see that we come back around to the resiliency issues—we even come back around to the 100 year idea—but you might not see that in the forefront this time. There's a hand-off between the projects. Each project has made a bargain with another project to get some resource or leverage something. We questioned ourselves, "how do you present things to a difference audience?" One of the things we've been contemplating is making a music video that we could release and leapfrog over certain kinds of planning bureaucracy. What if we could just release an urban idea? Everybody did their own music video that they have released at some point since the midterm. Some of them got some traction. Some of them probably didn't work at all. And some of the groups tried other kinds of documents and other kinds of approaches to release the information. Everyone worked on the architecture muscle document, which is for the architecture school audience, and the music videos are trying to see what a little bit of pop or funk does for these urban ideas. [●25–31]

"Somebody yesterday said 'we don't just want to make pretty pictures.' But you don't understand how powerful pretty pictures can be when given to the right audience." Ed Mitchell

●AS: All of the material is so incredibly convincing—the campus map, the guide, the viewmaster. It's fascinating, but my question is who do you work for and who works for you? What is your role in this? ●JM: What's the strategic plan? I thought that going after the highway and getting the digital screens was proven to be a generator of income. The next question is what of the five or seven proposals gets instigated next? The monies are always being used to be quasi private and public, but you have to track that beyond a generic term. The way you go around and take us through the circus is really powerful and works really well, but it's also pragmatic. It takes on these minor moments and structures that are embedded in the city already and tries to find way to activate them. Let's just be clear. These are not just your audiences. These are your clients. And that's a more proactive engagement than "audience". ●EM: There are a couple of projects that I would call classic public works projects. And then there are the other two projects that have private investment—the eco-park and the billboards. If the city got the revenue that was theirs to take, would the best thing to do with that money be to build a big sports complex, or would it go to the Board of Education? We, as architects, want the tangible, visibility of that thing evident in the thing itself rather than a transfer of some investment. That's really the public game. My guess is that if you put this out for a public vote, the community would reject the project. They don't need another ten basketball courts. They need a pocket community garden. They might vote differently. ●KE: The money boomerangs around. You couldn't sit down and play chess without rehearsing it. Just to get back to Aniket's question, so we're not being coy about this. At the beginning, we just thought: why can't some of the imagery—if urbanism is a confidence game anyway—jump outside of the academy and be shared in a social way? ● EM: That's what I like about the toys and the games. Those are the power of what you are doing. Somebody yesterday said "we don't just want to make pretty pictures." But you don't understand how powerful pretty pictures can be when given to the right audience. ●PD: It's different to say students than to say potential architects with clients. Part of what is great here is that they are students. It says something about education, and it says something about your actions as a group—the fact there wasn't just one video going out to the client, but that somehow Bridgeport got seven of them. The onslaught is part of a strategy. ●KE: Students, yes. But who's to say when your career begins. Couldn't your career begin at any time in here? ●DW: This is not the most efficient aspect of architecture. If you really want to get a return on your time, urban design, in my experience, is not the quickest way. It's a longer force. In terms of the question about how you find a client, well that's always the question. Finding clients by making propositions is like casting. Maybe there's no fish in that water. You don't know. You can't really see. The effort made here in this studio really brought together an earnest intention to find something that would be actionable. ●PD: The things that stick out to me—leveraging the billboard and the meal plan—are such obvious game changers but they don't have an architectural result. What is the status of this? If they are too specific, then they are not appropriate because they may not play out that way. What is the kind of image or video that is seductive that allows for multiple interpretations? ●EM: When is the visibility of a thing that's not there your project? What do you choose to make visible? You could make things seen that hadn't been seen. That's one step to making things public. ●BM: Does it have to result in a design? You probably felt obliged to design because it's a school of architecture, but that's where the projects were the weakest. They were strongest when you were actually brokering or leveraging. Could that be a new role of function for the architect?

● 31. Keller Easterling Studio Master Plan

● 24. Peggy Deamer Studio Master Plan

Systems Integration and Development in Design

<u>Coordinator</u>
Martin Finio

<u>Faculty</u>
Anibal Bellomio, Eric Buckley, Robert Haughney, Kristin Hawkins, Kenneth Gibble, John D. Jacobson, Larry Jones, Laura Pirie, Victoria Ponce de Leon, Craig Razza, Edward M. Stanley, Philip Steiner, Adam Trojanowski

This course is an integrated workshop and lecture series in which students develop the technical systems of preliminary design proposals from earlier studio work. The careful advancement of structural form and detail, environmental systems, and envelope design, as well as an understanding of the constructive processes from which a building emerges, are all approached systematically, as elements of design used not only to achieve technical and performance goals, but also to reinforce and re-inform the conceptual origins of the work. The workshop is complemented by a series of lectures from leading structural, environmental, and envelope consultants.

LILA CHEN, MICHAEL HARRISON, JAMES KEHL, ANNA MELOYAN

This proposal for a high-rise architecture school centralizes gathering areas within the tower at different heights, and connects them to cantilevered glass-box studios that overlook the site. All levels of the tower are made accessible and continuous by contemplative passages in its edge which are screened by a brick curtain wall of varying transparencies. Braced steel frame construction provides lateral resistance and supports the load of the studio cantilevers and their roof terraces. A combination of chilled beams and natural ventilation facilitates heating and cooling. ⟨■1⟩

MICHELLE CHEN, JUSTIN OH, MADELYNN RINGO, EUGENE TAN

The fundamental architectural characteristics of the Cloud are also its jarring structural/mechanical challenges. Quite simply, the entire building is an atrium, is clad entirely in glass, and cantilevers forty feet to one side. To accommodate for this large cantilever, the overhanging portion of the building is hung from a series of twelve-foot trusses located at the uppermost floor. The facade is composed of layered extensions of the primary superstructure to ensure the building can support the large expanses of glass, resist lateral wind loads, while retaining open voids between the edge of each floor plate and the facade itself. The white steel frame unique to this project is assembled and attached to the facade in ten-foot modules utilizing insulated steel sleeve connections to minimize thermal bridging. ⟨■2⟩

BENJAMIN BOURGOIN, JESSICA ELLIOTT, KIANA HOSSEINI, ANDREW STERNAD

Our project is a simple cubic volume characterized by column-free corners at ground level and a deep, variegated facade. We first devised a steel structural system to suspend the corners of the building, including temporary shoring during construction. We then focused on facade details, creating a series of prefabricated panels to accommodate vertical structure at the perimeter and negotiate complex geometries at the slab edge. ⟨■3⟩

■1

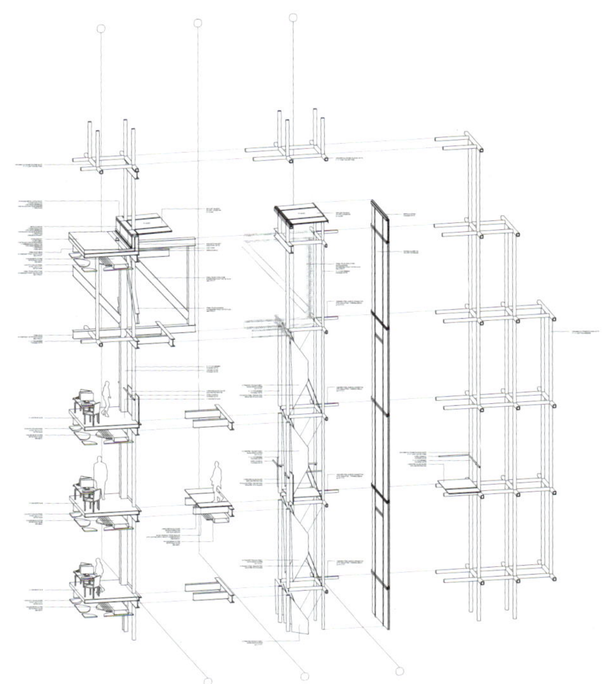

■2

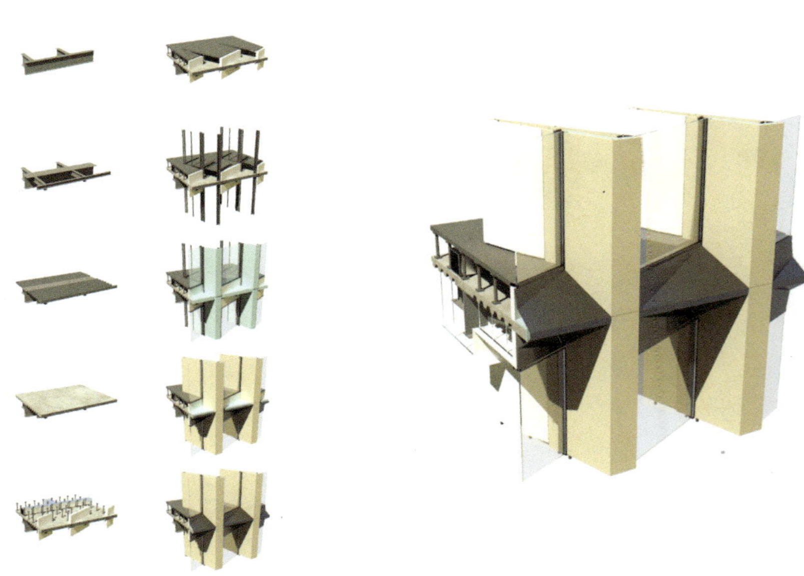

■3

Architectural Theory II: 1968–Present
Anthony Vidler

This course is a survey of theoretical and critical literature on contemporary architecture. It explores the texts of postmodernism, post-structuralism, and critical and post-critical discourses, as well as current debates in globalization, post-humanism, and environmentalism in the architectural discipline from 1960 to the present.

DORIAN BOOTH

A Question of Form: The Algorithm and the Object in Art and Architecture
Algorithmic control in both art and architecture can trace its lineage to early explorations in the Minimalist art movement. While the algorithm has garnered much attention by artists, architects, and theorists since the digital turn, Minimalists such as Sol Lewitt and Donald Judd deployed similar algorithmic techniques as early as the 1950s. The fundamental difference between the use of the algorithm in the case of Judd and Lewitt and in contemporary art lies in the notion of limits. Whereas the algorithm became an operative tool for Minimalist art in the creation of objects and establishment of objecthood, the contemporary algorithm has been transformed to subvert the very singularity and inherent limits of what David Joselit calls "well-defined forms." As illustrated by Joselit in his book *After Art*, contemporary art has effectively developed algorithms and procedures specifically designed to deal with the dissolution of singular, well-defined objects and forms. For architecture, this is a decidedly more difficult task, and one that questions the role of the algorithm within the contemporary practice of architecture. By understanding the evolution of the algorithm and its relationship to objects in art, potentially new understandings can develop to both inform and critique the use of the algorithm in architecture as architects increasingly question the limitations imposed upon the field by traditional and functional concerns.

MEGAN MCDONOUGH

A Landscape of Little Differentiation
While writing for the 1960 edition of *Perspecta*, Charles Moore searched the sprawling suburbs of coastal California for oases of public space. His disheartened findings are detailed in a poetic script of autonomous homes moored to carports—a metaphor that is later picked up by Deleuze and Guattari when defining smooth {as opposed to striated} landscapes. The landscape of little differentiation—and the population that resides within it—generated a terrifying psyche that is picked up in postmodern literature in the 1950's: almost two decades before it is addressed in postmodern architecture. This paper delves into three works of literature, Allen Ginsberg's *Howl*, Thomas Pynchon's *Crying of Lot 49*, and John Cheever's *Bullet Park* scouring them for the resistive language of schizophrenic and disjunctive reactions to a suburban landscape made unvaryingly smooth, as well as linking the writing styles and metaphors to later postmodern texts. Despite the cautionary and, frankly, weird realities woven into these tales, the suburban sprawl that exists and persists across American landscape in a model society continues to produce and buy.

Architecture and Capitalism
Peggy Deamer

Architecture and Capitalism examines the relationship between capitalism and architecture from both a theoretical perspective—Marxism's/neo-Marxism's critique of culture, art, and architecture—and from an architectural perspective—architecture's participation in, resistance to, and speculation about capitalism. The seminar examines different periods of architectural history from the perspective of theorists and what they had to say about cultural/architectural production and from the perspective of architects and what they had to say about their role in capitalism. The theorists examined include Marx, Ruskin, Simmel, thinkers of the Frankfurt School, Tafuri, Jameson, Slavoj Zizek, Naomi Klein, while the architects include Morris, Muthesius, Gropius, Hilberseimer, Peter Eisenman, and Rem Koolhaas.

VITTORIO LOVATO

Trans-Spatial Commoning: A Theoretical Examination of the Alternative Spatial and Economic Practices in Detroit
In his *Unreal Estate Guide to Detroit*, Andrew Herscher posed the question: What can we learn from Detroit? The city is clearly home to a complex and visible urban situation. With over 200,000 vacant or abandoned properties scattered throughout the city, Detroit remains in a situation wedged between future dissolution and past economic solvency. Detroit's problems of valuation seem insurmountable given the vastness of its economic decay and its dependency on extreme economic change for its future salvation. This essay attempts to answer this question and explore how vacancy and disinvestment in seriously blighted communities in Detroit have led to the dissolution of typical capitalist structures and the emergence of a new trans-spatial communing. Detroit is one of the only cities where small practices and large practices have taken on exaggerated and highly visible forms. Detroit provides a fertile ground for the study of the minor and major as they unfold, negotiate each other, and attempt to shape the city into their own image. Events and collective engagement establish spatial meaning through occupation of urban territories. In many cases in Detroit, these alternative practices sacrifice their labor to meet basic needs. What makes them distinct from typical economic forms is that these sacrifices are not for private gains or unproductive activities but the transition toward a spatial commons for the benefit of the collective community. This disassociation of material gains, suggests that these practices trade on the development of knowledge and the immaterial formation of the social. Therefore, Detroit is uniquely positioned to make these hidden events and alternative economies visible by virtue of their quantity and capacity to attract attention within the community and leverage the urban landscape.

CAITLIN THISSEN

Iceland: National Scarcity in Excess
Iceland's recent and rapid modernization, paired with the banking collapse in 2000, have rendered forecasts on its economic stability moot. Currently, the island nation straddles a tourist and manufacturing based economy with a longstanding commercial fishing industry hanging pendent. Industrialization—via aluminum smelting plants such as the American-based company Alcoa—and transnationally targeted tourism are vying for Iceland's non-renewable resources, as well as overall socioeconomic control. Yet marine product caught via the commercial fishing industry remains Iceland's number one Gross Domestic Product and the nation's leading sustainable export. With manufacturing on the rise, Iceland's domestic growth remain questionable. The nation will inevitably pursue the most marketable track, commoditizing and negotiating away its natural resources. The key to its domestic success or failure should and will be realized through conscious and policed policy formation. Recent attempts at regulating the socio-economic landscape by companies like Globe 21 have not effectively regulated existing Icelandic resources and consumption surrounding the tourist industry. Policies preventing the collapse of sustaining food industries in the form of "Total Allowable Catch" and "The Fishing Quota System" has allowed fisherman to sell their national heritage off in the form of quota for cash value to transnational corporations. Nevertheless, while the quota system has failed to safeguard the heritage rights of Icelandic fisherman, it continues to protect fishing stock from imminent collapse due to overfishing. Similar quota could be placed on the number of tourists moving in and out of the country seasonally—a rule aimed at existing resource preservation and environmental consciousness in terms of the impacts reaped by international jet travel. Ultimately, social and physical space are impacted through the codification of values through law and regulation, which have the flexibility to change with social, political, and environmental factors. Thus, economics and policy are the somewhat ethereal human constructs and the key to understanding and eventually realizing effective future development, which reshapes and reforms the Icelandic landscape.

KAROLINA CZECZEK

The Production of Space in Nowa Huta
Nowa Huta {New Steelworks} was the biggest project executed by the Communist Party in Poland. This new industrial city and steelworks plant belonged to a family of "socialist cities" built across the Soviet Block. *Nowa Huta* was built between 1940 and 1950 and had a very clear economic and political agenda. It would generate not only steel but hope for Poland following the destruction of World War II. Rooted in Stalinist ideology, it was promoted as a symbol of national rebirth and social revolution. Built "for people and by people," *Nowa Huta* represented the promise of freedom. The architecture in *Nowa Huta* was an extremely important tool to the creators of a new social order and the role of architect was elevated above merely an engineer to an "engineer of the human soul". The plant dominated the local economy and society. In the same way the steelworks plant was dependent on Communist policies, the city of *Nowa Huta* was dependent on the steel plant. After the fall of the Berlin Wall in 1980 and a rapid shift from the unrealistic state planning system to a Western style market economy, *Nowa Huta* steelworks plant was privatized. Rooted in market principles, a broader connection between the plant and its surroundings was broken. For the first time in its history, the town of Nowa Huta must stand apart from the steel plant. The city is considered as a symbol of change but also a victim. Due to its history and urban structure *Nowa Huta* seems to be a city trapped between two political and economic systems. Twenty-five years after the fall of communism in Poland, it still tries to respond to question of productive transformation that goes beyond total rejection of communism and immersion in the capitalist economy.

Residential Design, Development, and Management

Alexander Garvin & Ryan Salvatore

This seminar examines the creation and evolution of residential housing in the United States over the past century. Individual sessions are devoted to a critical and in-depth review of housing types and their development in both urban and suburban environments and to the exploration of the architectural, financial, legal, marketing, and social issues involved in the creation, management, and maintenance of housing. The seminar includes scheduled visits to specific examples of for-profit, nonprofit, and government-developed residential properties where students meet and speak with the designers and developers responsible for the building's construction and management.

DOV FEINMESSER

In an effort to promote a more inviting and pedestrian-friendly public domain, this policy proposal aims at city street rehabilitation, restoration, and improvement for FAR increases in medium-density zones. According to NYC Department of Transportation (DOT) design guidelines, sidewalks need only run from the right-of-way line of a building site to the existing curb. In many medium density zones, such as large parts of Manhattan, this results in narrow, sparse streets. This policy would offers a square foot bonus to new developments, in medium density commercial and mixed use zones, that provide a wider right-of-way abutting the property along with beautification and public amenity installations, such as benches, trees, or public art. The bonus would be equal to 5,000 square feet per five-foot setback with bonuses only approved after suitable amenities for the setback have been reported and submitted with the application. Maintenance of the setback would be the owner's responsibility, while supervision of the setback would be under the responsibility of the DOT. (■1)

JESSICA ELLIOTT

In order to create a more pedestrian and activated urban street frontage for New York City's new and existing built residential environment, a street revitalization and management policy is being proposed. With successful precedents including 56 Leonard Street, London Terrace, and the Boston row house typology, the valuable and aesthetic characteristics that are intended to be promoted include elements such as façade differentiation, designed fire stairs, multi-transit hubs, park and plaza spaces, permeable ground floor plans, and mixed-use development that are reinforced through design and planning strategies. Following the study of the Tracey Towers social housing project, it was evident that the automobile-oriented site plan design and the building's frontage to the street produced a detrimental effect to the ability of residents to be connected to the urban environment, as well as creating lifeless and potentially unsafe ground floor experience. The policy intends to reconnect existing residential buildings to the street and to the public realm through the addition of site interventions and the management of these and existing street-facing architectural and landscaping elements through the involvement of the residents, building owners and management, and the community. (■2)

JAMES KEHL

New Yorkers live really closely together. Yet, alienation and unfamiliarity among building tenants is the status quo in NYC apartment buildings. An 'in-between' space other than the corridor is needed for informal gathering and socialization. By establishing a threshold place to chat, rest, sit, eat, gather, and shop—in between a resident's building and the street—greater opportunities for social living within the building and the neighborhood emerge. (■3)

■1

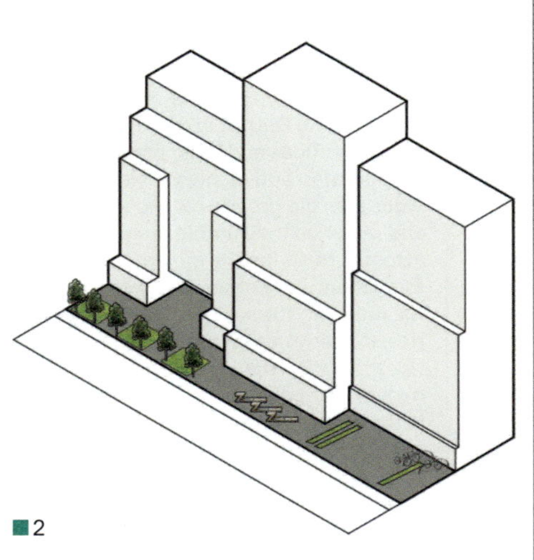

■2

■3

A Different Kind of Architect
{Eero Saarinen Lecture}

Sarah Herda

Organizing the Chicago Architecture Biennale starts with history. We have a hypothesis that, if you were trained as an architect anywhere on the planet, you studied Chicago. Chicago is the canon, so it is a part of what makes you an architect, and it is the perfect backdrop.

We want every aspect of the Biennale to produce new knowledge. We do not want to take for granted that the exhibition catalog is only a document about what may happen. We use all these different platforms—publications, exhibitions, and public programs—to introduce new ideas into the field. We did not choose a theme for the biennale, but a title. "The State of Art & Architecture" references the 1977 Biennale organized by Stanley Tigerman. Tigerman invited a version of the world to Chicago, which was essentially New York and Los Angeles and two interlopers from Europe—James Stirling and Charles Jencks. They were charged with presenting a project that demonstrated the position they were taking on architecture. Stanley often reminds me that it was not necessarily what happened, but we are inviting the scope and spirit of that by inviting the world.

LC After LC: Le Corbusier Translated, Corrected, Completed

Leon Krier
{Robert A.M. Stern Visiting Professor}

Le Corbusier's "Five Points of Architecture", self-proclaimed as revolutionary, were merely a succinct statement of what the building industry had been practicing for a generation. It was only Corb's radical and exclusivist stance which was revolutionary: stating that his "Dom-ino" system had not only to "dominate," but to replace all traditional construction techniques and methods, and that industrial production had to replace all craft production—there was no choice in the matter. Corb's building designs often contradict his stated principles, mixing natural and synthetic materials, craft and industrial methods, and Beaux-Arts *parti* and nautical-style buildings. Some of his most successful examples are inserted in an established urban fabric. Although he was a great writer and polemicist, Le Corbusier was a poor thinker. He was moved by an overpowering artistic impulse little moderated by reason and often contradicting his professed ideological line.

The "Le Corbusier Revision Project" is limited to a critical inspection and development of Corb's architectures. His theories and projects are, with the exception of Crétets, Pessac, and Chandigarh, considered aberrations calling for condemnation—a "page of LC urbanistic horrors," to paraphrase Pietro Maria Bardi.

Ornament
Theory and Design
Kent Bloomer

This seminar begins by reviewing the major writings governing the identities of and distinctions between ornament and decoration in architecture, e.g., Owen Jones, Riegl, Sullivan, Beeby, etc. 20th-century modernist actions against ornament are also examined. After individual student analysis of Victorian, Art Nouveau, and Art Deco production, the focus turns to ornament in 21st-century design.

CYNTHIA HSU

This project explores ornament's relationship with darkness. It combines the deep crevices found in gothic portals with the fluid intensity of Rococo design within an environment that necessitates controlled darkness. In an aquarium exhibit, the light from behind the glass of the tanks penetrates the darkness of the hall. The ornament surrounding the tank enhances the glowing light of the tank by generating its own darkness in the enclosure. A dialogue between ornament and exhibit is generated from simulating creatures inside the tank *Syngnathidae*, the family of fish including seahorses and their close relatives, have the unique capability of blending in with its surroundings. The flexibility of the animal's body is due to the shape of the spiral already embedded into its anatomic structure, generating incredible variety since the animals can hide in or curl around nearly any organic form. There are at least eighteen animals hidden in the drawing. Try to find them all! {■1}

DANIEL MARTY

This ornament project challenges the notion of traditionally modest public amenities, and asks what it would look like if some of society's everyday public spaces were ornamented. The project uses Gaudi and Guimard's figurative and sculptural systems-of-ornament, but brings these systems into the tectonically honest economies of the modern day bus stop. In each of the precedents, the ornament and forms are able to generate an object that is fantastic and something that looks "other-worldly", but architectural elements are still recognizable—such as columns still reading as columns due to their vertical nature and one's ability to read them as supporting the roof. Ornament reads in multiple scales, from the large sculptural main column, to the tendrils which accentuate the intersections of different architectural elements, and to the small interlaced weave pattern of leaf-like elements between the columns. This project attempts to create an equilibrium between the whimsical and the grounded, ornament and utility, and transforms this humble commuter space into an object that is both fantastical and recognizable. {■2}

JUSTIN OH

The Seed Cathedral seeks a language of ornament that is utilitarian—here, ornament is united with structure, thermal enclosure, and building systems—investigating a language of building where architecture and ornament are dependent on one another to exist. The building block of the cathedral is the "seed", a repeated unit that rises to the pinnacle of the cathedral where it becomes the skylight of the sanctuary. From the ceiling are ornamented skylight openings and light fixtures, all of which retain the seed geometry and are generated from the spiraling nature of clustered floral seeds. The Seed Cathedral seeks to revive the forgotten but highly valuable tool of ornament by making it a necessity to the cathedral's existence itself. {■3}

■ 1

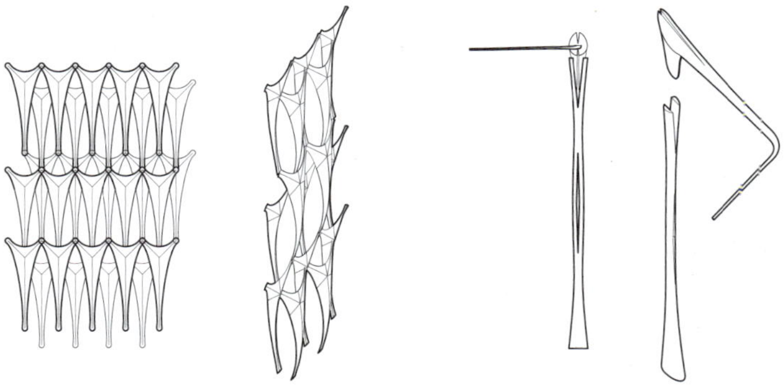

■ 2

■ 3

First Year Design Studio
M.Arch I

Coordinator
Alan Organschi {AO}

Critics
Trattie Davies {TD}, Peter de Bretteville {PDB},
Amy Lelyveld {AL}, Joeb Moore {JM}

Jurors
Adam Hopfner {AH}, Andrei Harwell {AHa}, Aniket
Shahane {AS}, Andy Bernheimer {ABe}, Andrew
Benner {AB}, Beka Sturges {BS}, Bimal Mendis
{BM}, Dana Getman {DG}, Emily Abruzzo {EA}, Ed
Mitchell {EM}, Eero Puurunen {EP}, Eeva-Liisa
Pelkonen {ELP}, John Brown {JB}, Julie Savin {JS},
Julian Bonder {JBo}, Joyce Hsiang {JH}, Karen
Fairbanks {KF}, Kurt Roeloffs {KR}, Kyle Dugdale
{KD}, Michael Szivos {MS}, Peggy Deamer {PD},
Robert A. M. Stern {RAMS}, Seila Mosquera {SM},
Stella Betts {SB}, Surry Schlabs {SS}, Turner Brooks
{TB}, Tessa Kelly {TK}, Thach Pham {TP}, Xiahong
Hua {XH}

This second core studio explores inhabitation
through the design and detail of enclosure, structure, circulation, as well as the habitable space it
produces. The work focuses on the simultaneous
relationship of the body to both interior and exterior environments, and its mediation of the material
assemblies of building. With an initial focus on the
conception and production of a single interior space,
a sequence of projects gives way to increasing physical and spatial complexity by requiring students to
investigate issues of structure, enclosure, organization, circulation, urban site, and climate. This work
forms the conceptual background for the work in
the latter half of the term—the collaborative design
and construction of the Building Project, an affordable house for a nonprofit developer in New Haven.

Minimal Dwelling Code ●
Students examined, documented, and tested the
constituent physical elements, required functions,
and necessary spaces that make up the minimum
dwelling. For the purposes of this initial assignment, the findings of their research did not manifest
themselves as a completed building design. Instead,
they were to develop a series of measured graphic
and physical representations that encode a matrix
of possibilities for dwelling; potentialities dependent
upon {and intermingled with} a series of environmental, social, and economic conditions that might
give rise to specific instances of dwelling. In other
words, to adopt a necessarily limited biological metaphor, they assayed a genotype of basic dwelling so
that they might later track and better understand
its phenotypic manifestations and effects.

Reduction and Recombination ●●
Students speculated further on the nature of dwelling and construction by applying the principles of
their dwelling "code" to the physical conditions of
a stair. Through this necessarily awkward conflation of code and artifact, they produced a kind of
extreme, perhaps even monstrous, phenotype of
the minimal dwelling genotype—one in which the
capacities of their rule-set and the limits of the stair
were tested and distorted. The project was at once
active, deliberate, and reflective—as much a surgical
operation as it was an observation of the effects of
one body on the other. In the end, it might be difficult to discern where the boundaries between them
were, but the dimensional and functional logics of
the students' code and the conceptual and material
conditions of their stair were instrumental to
their process.

New Haven Test ●●●
For the remainder of the semester and into the summer, students worked—first individually and then
collaboratively—to develop a new type of dwelling
for New Haven. Their assignment was the design of
a house. The house will be home to no fewer than
three inhabitants that comprise a "household," a
term used in demographics to describe a group
of individuals that cohabit within a single residential unit. As an architectural proposition, the house
must be materially and procedurally efficient, and
physically compact while spatially expansive. The
research students undertook at the outset of the
semester explored the architecture of the "minimal"
dwelling. Here they were asked to deploy and manage limited material, spatial, financial, and human
resources in the design of an "optimal" dwelling,
drawing maximal utility, economy, comfort, and spatial richness from conditions of constraint.

Trattie Davies

LUCAS BOYD

This exercise explored the relationship between
Architecture and representation. It attempted to
condense an entire set of construction instructions into a single text message and, in turn, limited
itself to very strict rules and eliminated any qualitative value within the dwelling. The text message
was passed on to three unknowing parties who were
able to interpret the instructions almost perfectly.
Conclusion: spend time and effort on instructional
representation, unless boring utility is the goal. The
house design seeks to make a case for an affordable
housing strategy that is already extremely prevalent
in many other cultures and is increasingly popular in
our own—multigenerational living. An organization
strategy was developed that creates three distinct
levels of autonomy for the individual private spaces
of the home but simultaneously uses common programming to emphasize the communal areas. The
form of the house is developed directly from a combination of these planning moves and the existing
housing stock of the neighborhood. {●●●1–2}

"You still want a sense of event and
mobility in your life, even if you can't
move easily." **Robert A.M. Stern**

●**RAMS**: I also have a couple of projects right
now that are dealing with this issue of getting
confined to your home, which often happens when
you get older. You still want a sense of event and
mobility in your life, even if you can't move easily.
The stoop is a longstanding tradition. Being able
to roll or walk out of your home to engage with the
street is critical. This idea is very intelligent and
compelling; it's a really nice way of framing this
project. I actually live in a three story house, and
we have the second story as our main residence.
It's totally beautiful because it's flooded with light
and there is a dappled canopy coming through.
It's fantastic. But there is something, particularly
for seniors, about being on the ground and being
able to get out and engage. ●**EM**: I think this is
really interesting, because when you just accept
the house type, you get so much more freedom to
invent details and other additional elements in the
house. You don't have to solve those elementary
problems; you get to find new ones to tackle
and perfect.

ROB CORNELISSEN

This courtyard house uses exterior space to set up
functional and spatial relationships while dealing
with the limits of space and privacy on an exposed
site. The plan is arranged about a set of openings
and courtyards that mediate between spaces and
intend to capitalize on the exterior as an extension
of the interior. Exploiting the horizontal plane, deep
continuous surfaces and large expanses of glass,
the aim is to dematerialize boundaries between
the two conditions. Around each of the roof openings, functions are arranged into "sets" or "families,"
making sense of related activities and sequences.
Within the pairing of these programs, formal relationships provide the sense of spatial organization,
while enabling a seemingly random arrangement of
openings throughout the house. {●●●3}

ILANA SIMHON

A house is a series of isolated layers with varying lifespans and rates of change. Weathering
and human activity are the overarching forces
that set the elements of a house in motion as the
users alter and reinvent aspects to assert ownership. Simultaneously, exterior forces wear on the
house and render certain layers worn and in need
of replacement. A house is never a finished product. The events within a home customize the layers
and determine what is permanent, ephemeral, and
everything in between. Site, skin, structure, and services seem to be the most static layers; however,
certain objects such as a teapot passed down for
generations can outlive the home. A house responds
to the activity within, like a growing family and
changing tastes, the layers are in constant evolution.
The minimum dwelling code includes the layers that
often transcend time. {●4}

Peter de Bretteville

WES HIATT

This house for New Haven is concerned with providing maximum diversity of identity between the
spaces of a small home. It is made up of two bars,
one housing all the services and vertical circulation,
the other all the living spaces. The sides are separated by a thickened wall containing plumbing and
electrical utilities that also serves as a thick threshold between both parts of the house. A court is
cut between the ends of the bar on the living side,
which makes a side porch to a garden that allows
for views through the entire length of the bar—from
inside, out, and in again. On the second floor, children's and parent's rooms are given their own identity on either wing of the house, each served by their
own bath. Porthole windows and bays in the children's rooms are added for a bit of fun and whimsy,
as well as to become secondary identifiers of place
within a tiny house. {●●●5–6}

"The projects that have to most legible diagram—in some ways the most
simple—have turned out to be the most
flexible and variable." **Peter de Bretteville**

●**EA**: There could be another language to
express this. The diagram is right on. I don't know
how reproducible it is. Some differentiation
between the two languages that relies on the unifying form we are so used to might help the project.
●**KD**: What it has going for it is extraordinary flexibility. Every part of this could be expanded or contracted without damaging it. ●**AO**: The merit of this
project is actually how tough the wall on Scranton
is. I would make it as tough as possible. ●**SB**: I agree.
I love it diagrammatically. The other challenge that
could add to the project is if you could get the hall-
way out of the living bar so you could plug the
rooms in directly. The corridor to me feels like the
only thing that is not working. ●**PDB**: The projects
that have to most legible diagram—in some ways
the most simple—have turned out to be the most
flexible and variable. That has been behind almost
all the comments. You have given us a methodology
here, and that suggests a lot of promise.

STEPHEN MCNAMARA

Although the utilities of the house exist at the
center of domestic activity, they are frequently
designed to their minimal requirements. Conversely, the most trafficked area of the home, the
corridor, is typically seen as secondary space. Here
it is optimized to take on its own character. The
enlarged stair allows for the central circulation zone
to fuse with the most dense program. The procession between floors is heightened when the landing
of the switchback stair breaks the envelope of the
house and nods towards the garden. The kitchen
and bathroom are then centered on this spline to
be accessible from multiple areas of the home and
work with the needs of a contemporary family. By
consolidating these highly specific programs to
a center strip, the primary rooms can be hung on
either side. {●●●7–8}

●**BM**: What does the middle space do? It's
kind of grand. ●**AL**: Yoga. ●**JH**: The detail model
reminds me of a barn. It's this big central thing with
these stalls on the side. When I looked at the plans
it worried me that the dimensions were so equal,
but in the model it really works. ●**RAMS**: I know
this is a strange thing to say, but the house seems
friendly. I think your cubic form with bump-outs that
allow light in and the way it's placed on the site lead
me to believe that you've created something truly

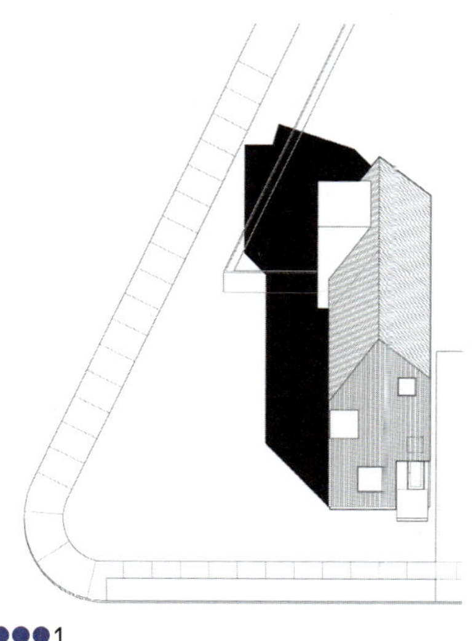

●●●1

●●●2

●●●3

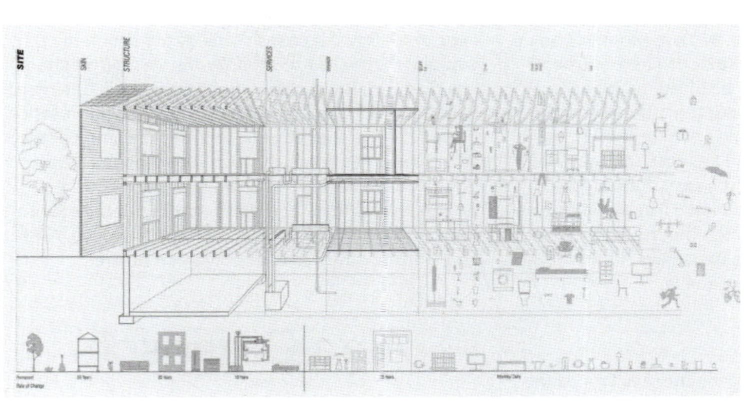

●●4

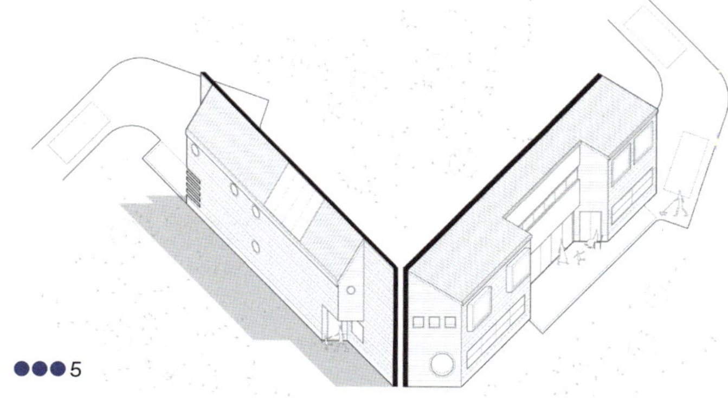

●●●5

●●●6

●●●7

●●●8

reproducible. You have sited it very sensitively and are making use of the adjacencies in an intelligent way. It's got privacy in all the ways you would want it. There's something about the composition and the way you made these spaces that's very friendly. Normally when you deny a window like this, it's really off-putting. But the way you've done it, it's not so. ●EM: I like the clarity of the general parti. I wonder if you might benefit from freeing that stair from the volume and turning it into a mini-Kahn job.

PAUL RASMUSSEN

This project appropriates the circulation strategy of the Salk Institute to organize the domestic needs of an individual. The circulation rises around the programmatic space and serves as the active agent of compression and release. This approach organizes minimal space to compress and release the body, where requisite programming is compacted to create open spaces. This project seeks to explore temporality and permanence by rendering the durable material of concrete in varying state of decay or disruption. The object's unfamiliar origin lends it an air of mystery. {●●9}

Amy Lelyveld

MATTHEW KABALA

Situated within an underserved urban context, this proposal seeks to make explicit the various externally and internally imposed strictures that often divest certain individuals of a requisite degree of second-order agency. By architecturally translating and then amplifying what are otherwise largely metaphysical confines, the house acts as a vehicle for affecting an epistemic clarity. Using anxiety-inducing portents, this clarity, when successfully married to an intimate relationship with one's own moral identity and physical finitude, ontologically frees the individual to begin realizing the volition necessary for "transcending" the deterministic moments found within such circumstances. {●10}

LAURA MEADE

At the nose of this vessel is an open and lofty "event" space where movies are watched, arguments erupt and meals are eaten. Architecture takes a back seat to the activity: a clerestory softly illuminates the airy space that is packed with operable cabinets to stow away the "stuff" of family life. The dense respite areas at the keel of the house are where one can achieve mental clarity as biological and sociological needs are left behind. Architecture then fills in where human activity stops: clerestory windows illuminate the axes where operable windows cross-ventilate air and sound, which allows the house to live and breathe with its occupants. These axes intersect beneath an oculus, where blades pull the air from under the house's low roofline, which enables the house to inhale with those living beneath it. At the center, the threshold between these different spatial conditions is a transcendental cockpit where the family boards, beginning their journey to elsewhere. {●●●11–12}

"The action is all spatial and the energy is within. So you could make an envelope that is disarmingly simple—that's what your diagram loudly says when it speaks." **Peter de Bretteville**

●EP: Are you able to produce something that benefits the site with the shifting of those bedrooms? You suggest that, but I think you could work a little harder and investigate the results. I do like this atypical plan. It could be amazing. ●EA: There's something really nice about this scheme. The diagram that is not quite expressed, though, is a large roof with areas of solid and void underneath. Be more severe. ●DG: I like that you left out the door swings, because it makes the corridor part of the private space. It makes the bedrooms the absolute minimum size, and the corridor, even though it's in the bedrooms, becomes part of that semi-public interior space. It's a beautiful transition. ●AH: This is a very strong scheme; the plan is beautiful. Everything is already doing the work that the diagram expresses, so doors should just pocket away and never swing. ●PDB: The action is all

spatial and the energy is within. So you could make an envelope that is disarmingly simple—that's what your diagram loudly says when it speaks. You've made a lot of really bold moves here. Trusting in them will move you forward.

ROBERT YOOS

A Shaker community is reimagined according to a dwelling code based on Maslow's Hierarchy of Needs. Various elements of a Shaker dwelling are reorganized into an over-scaled megastructure according to parameters of physiology, safety, belonging, esteem, and self-actualization. Sleeping pods, excessive built-ins, and embedded lookouts cluster around an amplified Shaker staircase to collectively conjure a critique of the ritualistic and uncanny architectural tendencies of Shaker life. The final proposal for a house in New Haven echoes these ideas of psychological human needs and the architectural methodology of the Shakers by emphasizing communal space and anchoring it with the stair. An internal volume of social space thrusts through the house and connects internal space with external context, which gestures toward the neighborhood and mediatesthe corner condition of the site. Formal composition is directly linked to the hierarchy of social volumes, connection to the outdoors, and the distribution of natural light. {●●13}

Joeb Moore

ELAINA BERKOWITZ

This proposal maximizes communal space and minimizes the imprint of permanent fixtures, thereby allowing the most user flexibility. The psychological importance of community is paramount to the diagram because the most important space for the psychology of community is the living room, which becomes the largest and most flexible space in this design. This allows the activities of the living space to be determined by the user. In addition, minimizing zones of permanent fixtures allows for efficiency of construction and cost. The idea of opening a corner or edge to the context is adaptable to any site and is an important strategy for creating community in this neighborhood and throughout New Haven. {●●●14}

"That's why we're all excited about it—it's expensive." **John Brown**

●AO: There's a real clarity to what the open space is versus this semi-permanent zone that you move through. Maybe it doesn't follow the same logic, but it's locked in. Then you have this zone, and maybe it's more important than whether things move or not, that is just a container for core space. You can move through and rest there. I think this is where the stair fits. ●ELP: I really like this scheme, but this thickness should not continue into the open space. It looks like this stuff wants to be a new surface, but it's not. ●PD: It shouldn't be conflated with the wall itself. ●ELP: The treatment of all wood stuff here should be lifted up, it has to gain a ritualistic quality. It looks too much like 2x4's at the moment. It has to gain its own ornament or individual identity. This would animate the material. ●JB: It's a beautiful scheme; it's very rigorous and complete. However I don't think it's a scheme for workers' housing. To me, it's too much. That's why we're all excited about it—it's expensive. I think that raises a question of appropriateness.

GRAHAM BRINDLE

This graphic taxonomy examines the dwelling as the bare interface between the inhabitant and the utility networks that connect cities with water, natural gas, sewage, and electricity. The drawing details the minimum kit of parts required to plug into these systems, and transform the volatile raw utilities into consumable products via the sink, the electrical outlet, etc. The dwelling is distilled to a fixed matrix of valves, meters, pipes, and adapters that occupy the space between the water main and the faucet. The design for a compact house is predicated on a contextual massing that distorts the neighboring gable house to meet the corner lot site. The two-story home is enclosed by an outer shell, which is sliced and cut to create entrances and allow light

deep into the space. On the interior, furniture and storage elements are aggregated into compact blocks that are used to subtly partition the open living areas. {●●●15–16}

"Make the steps clearer and more rigorous so that you can love the thing that is more banal or a little less perfect." **Alan Organschi**

●ELP: It's very efficient and there's hardly any wasted space. Spatially, it is a very rich and complex experience. You are almost in a forest-like space where the furniture provides a topography. ●JB: For me, the piece that's not satisfying is the second floor. You have a few options. You could lower the second floor so the ridge line is closer to the shoulder or you could invert the house with the living space on the second floor. Then you could think about the private rooms on the first floor and allow the largess of the architectural move coincide with the public space. ●JBo: We are all playing with what we would propose here. This talks very highly about what you have accomplished. Given the quality of what you have done, what is wrong with it? ●AO: It's really accomplished and in the hands of a less-skilled formalist, it might be dangerous. In your next iteration, think about how you could make the steps clearer and more rigorous so that you can love the thing that is more banal or a little less perfect.

BRITTANY OLIVARI

The Minimal Dwelling is defined in this code as a series of bodily movements over the course of a twenty-four hour cycle. Based on the racial geometry, the drawing is sectioned into a series of rings. The central ring represents the private realm and the outermost ring represents the communal realm beyond the dwelling itself. A range of possibilities can be tested based on each individual's unique daily rituals. When applied to the design of a compact house, the minimal dwelling code is translated into a central utility hub containing plumbing essentials and circulation. Condensing these functions allows the living, sleeping, and social spaces to open up off of the hub and adapt to varied sites through a shift in scale. On the given site, the scheme plays with the formal language of shearing two volumes off of the utility hub to address the corner lot condition and to carve out the exterior spaces of a front porch and rear terrace. {●●●17–18}

●ELP: It's interesting that you did not mention in your presentation that which is the most obvious—this is a riff on the vernacular house. Why would you want to damper that? Your riff is quite brilliant, the way that splitting allows you to fit it into the site and create exterior space is quite brilliant. ●PD: I had the opposite reaction to Eeva, which is that successively as it went massing diagram to a building to a vernacular building, I got less and less interested! And it could be this idea that you have to sell the scheme, but I lose the concept. ●AO: This exposes some of the problems that you're wrestling with, which is the formal/mechanical diagram. Right now, what we've got is this residue of those mechanical operations—shear, rotation, moment—and then it gets 'architected' and detailed. ●JB: This is really good house for someone who's done houses before, much less someone in their first year of school. You don't need to detail every nook and cranny to make a really good house. And I just want to say, this is a really good house.

Alan Organschi

MAGGIE TSANG

Emerging from the study of ergonomic sections of the body, this house investigates how a simple three-foot sectional shift produces both a richly varied and efficient living space. Tested against the site at the corner of Winthrop and Scranton, this simple shift becomes the driving force for both the interior organization of spaces as well as the site around it. The break is not simply a jog in the ground plane; it furnishes the "stuff" of dwelling along its spine. The spine grows and changes from thick seating and cabinetry to small enclosures for storage and bathrooms as well as large enclosures for the bedrooms.

●●9

●●13

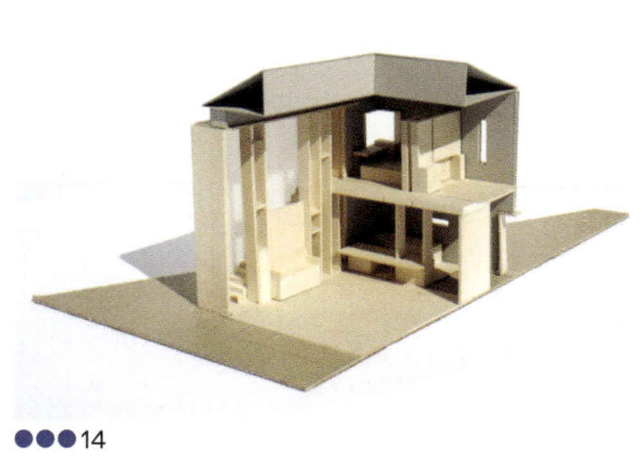

●●●14

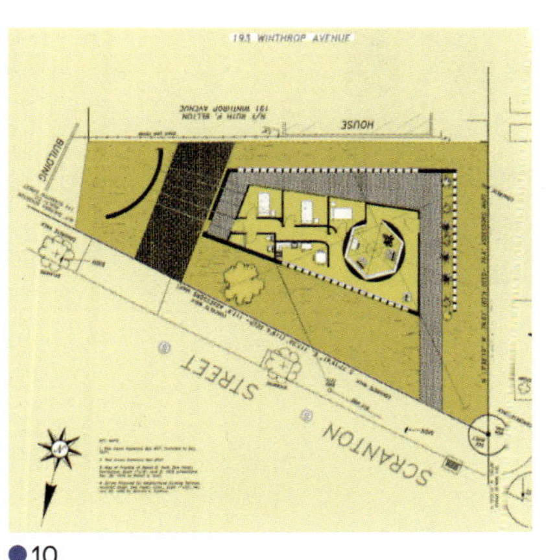

●10

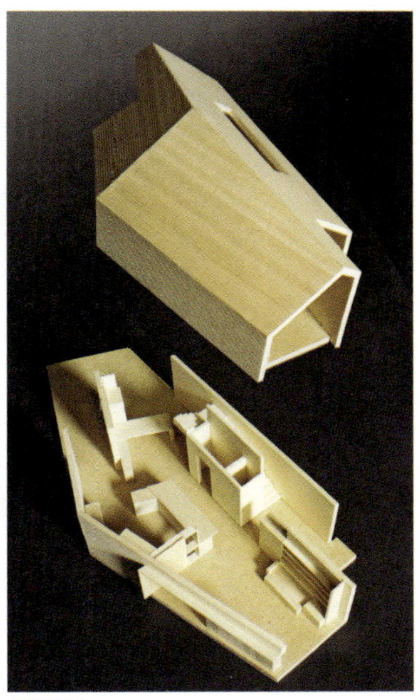

●●●15

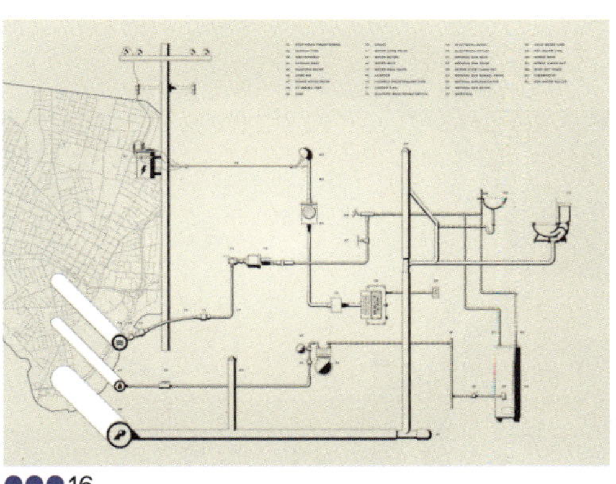

●●●16

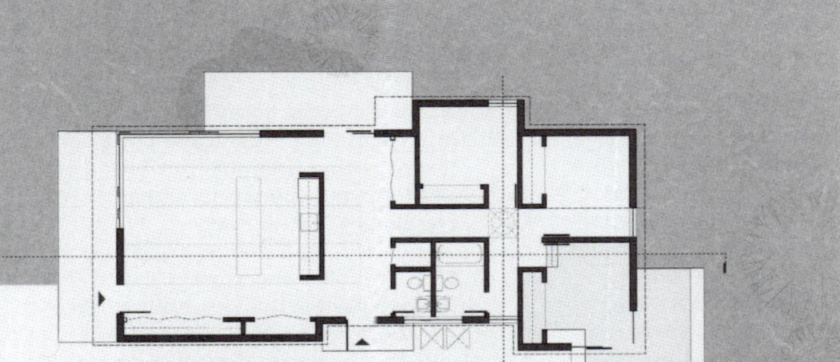

●●●11

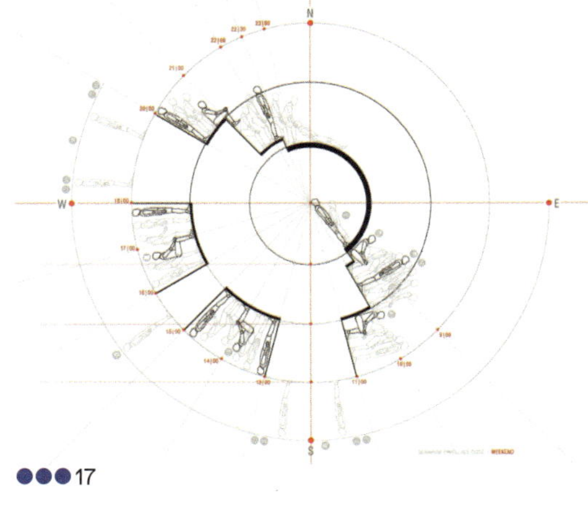

●●●17

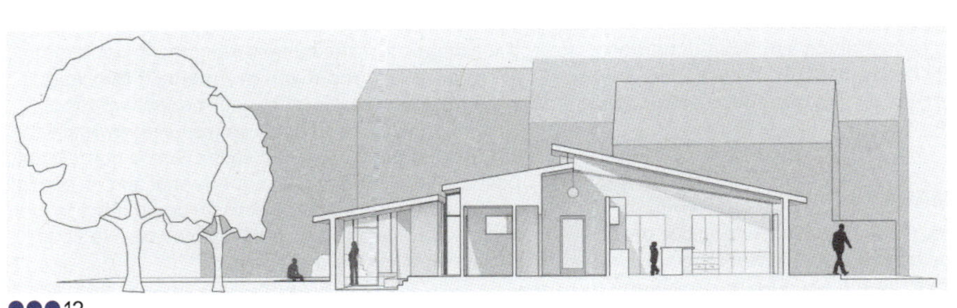

●●●12

●●●18

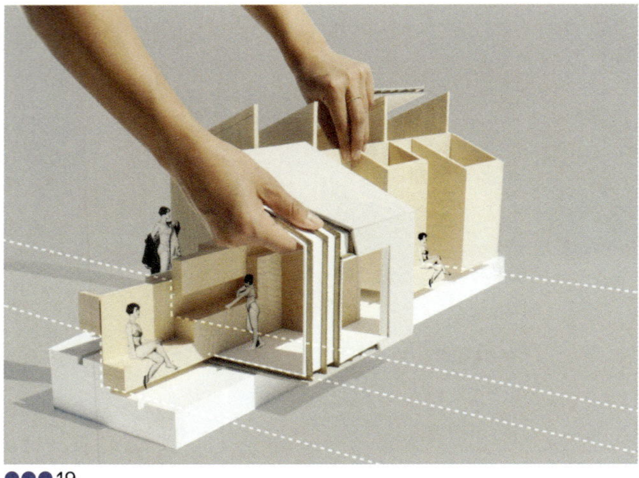

●●●19

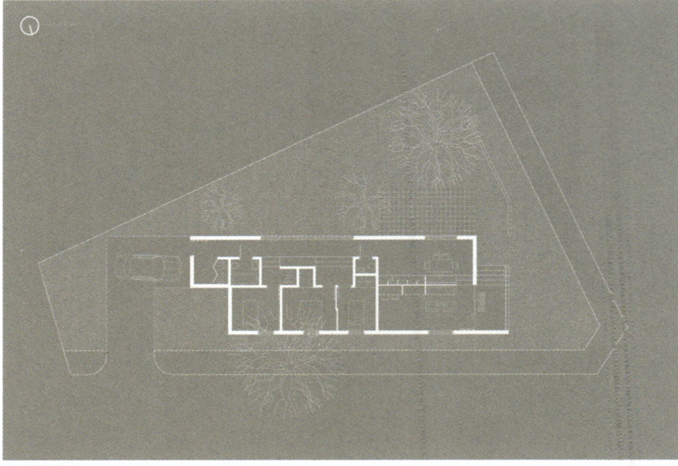

●●●20

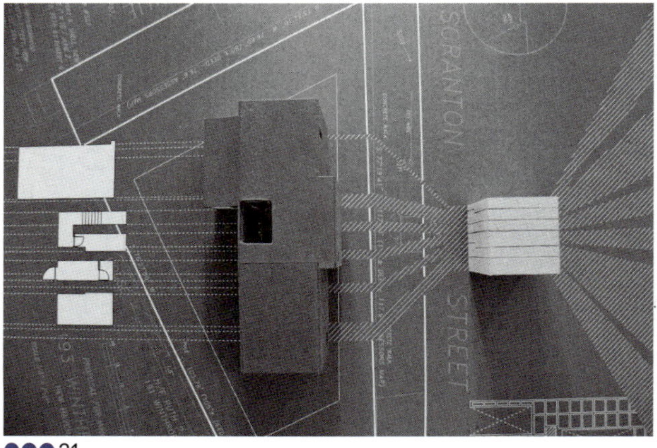

●●●21

●●●22

On the corner site, the three-foot shift provides a high, protected zone along Scranton Street that contains the living space and the bedrooms as well as a low zone that houses the kitchen/dining area that opens out into a side yard where the distinction between public and private continues. As a prototype, the shifted volume is not only appropriate for a variety of sliver lots as a consequence of its mere narrowness and size, but also harnesses the action of shearing to create new possibilities for dwelling. {●●●19–20}

"Having the long form of the house inherently protects the yard—something a lot of the other schemes are having to work quite hard to get." Tessa Kelly

●TK: The site strategy is very convincing. The long edge aligned with the short neighboring building is great, and having the long form of the house inherently protects the yard—something a lot of the other schemes are having to work quite hard to get. ●KB: We all agree that this is a gorgeous and clear scheme. That said I wish that the sectional shift and whatever cabinetry that might produce for you did more for you. I'm surprised that there are walls that here that just divide everything. It would be helpful to test the shift without floor to ceiling walls so you could really sense the big move. ●SS: The presentation and project are both very elegant, but it's all almost too clear. My concern is that, in this neighborhood, a house like this with those windows and at this size might be read as a double wide trailer—and I don't think any of us want to read it as that. There's not enough variation on the exterior between the two halves or how they come together yet to make it look not so off-the-shelf.

PAUL LORENZ

This study is focused on the occupation of a space by its human inhabitants as well as its object inhabitants. An exhaustive cataloguing of the accumulation of things seemingly required for living becomes the primary driver for this system. Here, objects are initially tightly packed into a physically minimal dwelling in which each thing is accommodated, but this leaves no space for the dwelling's human occupants to interact with their possessions. The space given to the object must be displaced in order for people to pry into the domain their paraphernalia. This action produces space for sleeping, hygiene, cooking, and gathering. {●●●21}

●JB: There's a clear diagrammatic strategy here. It works pretty well in the abstract, but I think living here would make me want to get rid of some of it. If you considered the quality of the space that's resulting from the diagram and made some adjustments it would be both a rigorous and enjoyable piece of architecture. ●AH: This makes me think about Thomas Jefferson's bed at Monticello—where if you roll out of bed one way you're in the office, or if you roll the other way you're in the dressing chamber. It just seems to me you're making a taxonomy of different storage types and interactions with different objects, and I'd like to understand better the set of interactions you want to produce. Instead of the kind of Ikea condition there is now, aren't there a whole set of conditions you want to make? ●AO: There are differences—the Monticello bed is describing a difficult condition, and the Murphy bed is just sort of packed up and kind of finicky. How do you give these things some agency and intention?

TESS MCNAMARA

The Phototropic House is a site-responsive prototype for affordable housing in New Haven. It responds to solar conditions on-site, providing direct sunlight and solar heating to spaces at the time they are occupied. It also provides an economy of construction through a clear and straightforward hierarchy of formal and material elements. A series of operations generate the prototype depending on its specific location and orientation. The house begins with a square foundation, then close-packs program within a cubic envelope. Next is a tropic response—cantilevers are pulled over the foundation where light access is needed, which results in a dense, central thermal column. Apertures are created by the shearing of the cantilevers or are punched through the envelope to select views. Outdoor space is defined by the axes of these tropic cantilevers, within which private space is created using excess foundation soil. {●●●22}

"How might this, as a thesis, make us interrogate the organization of a domestic space that is completely based on the sun from an experiential and an energy standpoint?" Stella Betts

●DG: I'm still trying to grapple with what type of effect you want in this space. What types of light are these moves producing? ●EA: You could play with the shifting a lot more and be more aggressive about it. ●EP: Two main things: energy and daylight. I would like to see something more expressive related to daylighting and how that relates to views. From the energy use perspective, while thermal mass will be positive in the winter, it's disadvantageous during the summer. ●SB: It's a great premise for the project and everyone is just wanting more follow through. In a way, with the exception of the sundial diagram, if I looked at the project without you describing it that way, I wouldn't know that's what your project was about. How might this, as a thesis, make us interrogate the organization of a domestic space that is completely based on the sun from an experiential and an energy standpoint? The plan and section could start to look distorted to us but it would be based on a logic of the sun and light and shadow.

Building Technology
Alan Organschi &
Adam Hopfner

This course examines the role of material and procedure in the formation of architecture and the physical, logistical, and environmental constraints and demands that shape the processes of construction. In the first half of the term, a sequence of lectures surveys the conceptual concerns and technological factors of building: the origin and processing of the major classes of building materials; their physical properties, capacities, and vulnerabilities to physical and environmental stressors; the techniques used to work those materials; and the principles, procedures, and details of building assembly. Corresponding construction examples and case studies of mid-scale public buildings introduce students to the exigencies that so often influence decision making in the technical process and inflect (and potentially enrich) design intention—regulatory requirement, physical and environmental stress and constraint, procedural complication, labor and material availability and quality, energy consumption, and ecological impact. After spring recess and in coordination with the studio design phase of the Building Project, the course turns to the detailed study of light wood-frame construction. In both its direct technical application to the work in the studio and its exploration of more general themes in current construction practice, the course seeks to illuminate the ecological considerations as well as the materials, means, and methods that are fundamental to the conception and execution of contemporary building. (■1–3)

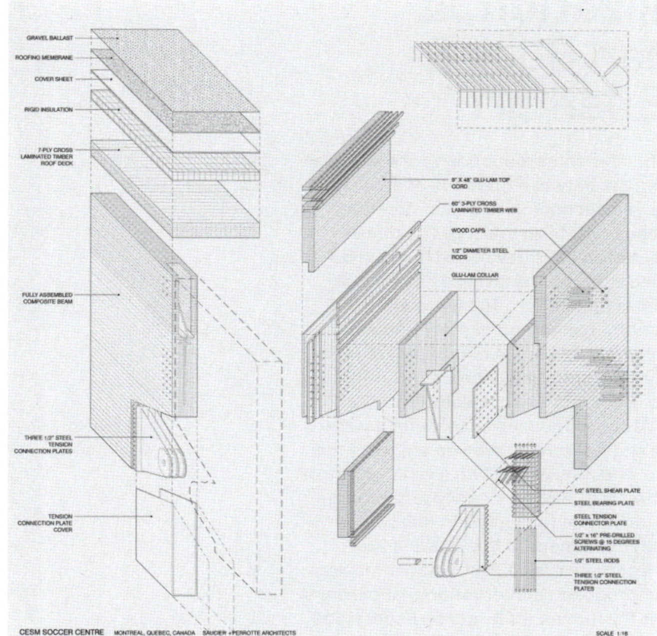

■ 1. Lucas Boyd

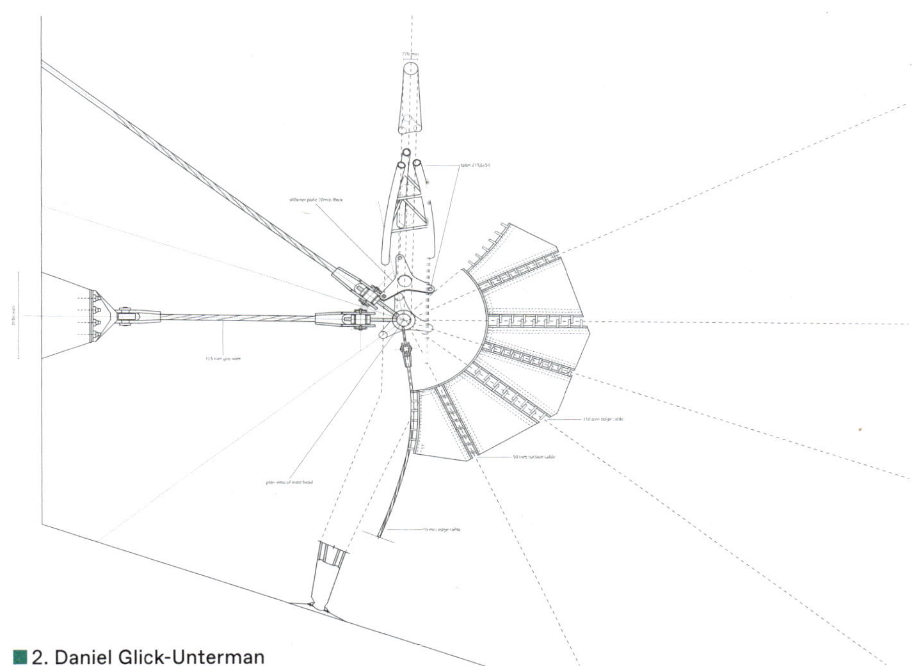

■ 2. Daniel Glick-Unterman

■ 3. Graham Brindle, Chad Greenlee, Lily Hou, Samuel King, Laura Meade, Brittany Olivari

Visualization Ⅲ
Brennan Buck &
John Eberhart

This course provides an introduction to the key relationships that exist between methods of drawing, physical materials, technologies of construction, and three-dimensional form making. The material and formal sensibilities developed in Visualization II are mined to explore drawing as a tool that leads to full-scale fabrication. The generation of form through both manual and digital methods is tested through materials and technologies of fabrication. Additive and subtractive processes, repetition and mass production, and building information modeling {BIM} are introduced as tools for assembly. Exercises and workshops provide students the opportunity to work physically with a wide variety of tools and materials as well as digitally with emerging computer-driven technologies. In this course conceived as a supplement to the Building Project, students integrate drawing and model-making to develop and propose a construction that can be experienced at the human scale and be understood as an integrated architectural element.

CAROLINE ACHEATAL, WILSON CARROLL, ROBERT CORNELISSEN, CECILIA HUI, MICHAEL LOYA, GEORGIA TODD

This project explores the hidden capacities and potentials of a simple, three-axis wooden form. Through use of a modular shape, the project addresses systems of order and chaos via multi-dimensional stacking. The assemblies were displayed via time lapse videos, which served to show the building sequence of the model and also to illustrate the various ways in which the system was tested. Certain tests explored how an ordered system breaks down, while other iterations focused specifically on site, aperture, or the use of formwork. Over time, we realized the small, somewhat unassuming form of the jack was amoebic and expansive, multiplying in size and mass to fill whatever space it occupied. Dashes of color on the ends of each module alluded to the installation's playful qualities, and also further conveyed the layering and clumping patterns of each new form. {■1}

DANIEL MARTY, STEPHEN McNAMARA, MAXWELL MENSCHING, CECILY NG, ROBERT YOOS

The wall is an aggregation of fourteen unique bricks that were CNC carved from foam blocks. The bricks aggregate and nest into each other to form the wall without any nails or glue. The nested bricks are held by friction and connected by 3D-printed clamps that cinch them together. Instead of remaining a static partition, the bricks are interactive and responsive to movement. As people move around the wall, the bricks undulate at their centers. A motor pulls the white fabric stretched over each brick inward to its center—the motion mimics the poking of a belly button. The wall becomes more than a barrier by interacting with its environment. The responsive brick makes it possible to perceive movement on the other side of the wall without having to see it. {■2}

LUCAS BOYD, GRAHAM BRINDLE, RACHEL GAMBLE, CHAD GREENLEE, ALEXANDER STAGGE

This installation combined fifty-two wooden 2x4 studs into a complex tectonic surface. The structure uses the 2x4 as a cheap, easily accessible module, but subverts its common use by kerfing the wood to allow the members to curve and undulate. The geometry of the wall is dictated by the one foot minimum radius permitted by the double-sided kerf, which provides the structure with stability and moments of transparency. {■3}

■1

■2

■3

The Jim Vlock First-Year Building Project
M.Arch I

Coordinator
Alan Organschi {**AO**}

Critics
Adam Hopfner {**AH**}, Amy Lelyveld {**AL**}, Herbert Newman {**HN**}, Joeb Moore {**JM**}, Kyle Bradley {**KB**}, Peter de Bretteville {**PdB**}, Trattie Davies {**TD**}

Jurors
Andy Bernheimer {**AB**}, Beka Sturges {**BS**}, David Lewis {**DL**}, John Jacobson {**JJ**}, Julie Savin {**JS**}, Karen Fairbanks {**KF**}, Kurt Roeloffs {**KR**}, Marta Caldiera {**MC**}, Peggy Deamer {**PD**}, Robert A. M. Stern {**RAMS**}, Seila Mosquera {**SM**}, Thach Pham {**TP**}

Since 1967, the Yale School of Architecture has offered its first-year students the unique chance to design and build a structure as part of their graduate education. Unique among architecture schools, this program is mandatory for all members of the class. The Building Project results in a single-family house in an economically depressed neighborhood. The late Charles W. Moore, who headed Yale's Department of Architecture {later the School of Architecture} from 1960 to 1971, founded the First-year Building Project in collaboration with faculty member Kent Bloomer. Moore saw that getting out of the studio and building something would have several benefits for students. As a believer in simple tectonics and basic technologies, he hoped students would be inspired by the mechanics of building. In the midst of the student unrest in the 1960s, he saw the project as a way for students to commit to positive social action by building for the underserved. The earliest projects were outside of New Haven, and included community centers in Appalachia and a series of camp buildings in Connecticut. Reduced budgets in the 1970s and 80s, as well as increasing pressure on student schedules, led to a scaling back of the program and projects—which included several park pavilions and were confined to the New Haven area. More recently partnerships with Habitat for Humanity and Home, Inc., Neighborhood Housing, Common Ground, and currently NeighborWorks New Horizons, have led to a focus on affordable housing. The houses allow students the experience of working with a client and the opportunity to respond to the challenges of affordable housing and urban infill. Students have shown great enthusiasm for projects that focus on community development and neighborhood improvement. Many of them arrive at school with a desire to include such socially responsible work in their future professional lives. Having the opportunity to participate in the design and construction of such building projects often reinforces their conviction and inspiration to do so.

TEAM A

Students

Garrett Hardee, Robert Hon, Matthew Kabala,
Paul Lorenz, Rashidbek Muydinov, Anna Nasonova

Our proposal defines the house as an agglomeration of systems and paraphernalia of dwelling. Such agglomeration activates spaces around itself for relevant activities—storing and preparing food, cooking, eating, entertaining, resting, washing, bathing, laundering, ironing, dressing—each activity is accommodated within an optimal volume of space. The envelope then assumes the role of mediating between the internal activities of the dwelling and the external forces of the site, such as environmental conditions, cultural and vernacular patterns, or vehicular and pedestrian traffic. While the Winthrop Avenue façade is informed by the continuity of vernacular elements of porches and gable roofs, the lack of this continuity on Scranton Street allows some liberty on this elevation. The plasticity of the envelope allows the building to be replicated virtually for any infill site in New Haven and beyond. Within these new sites, the function and the form of the core remains the same, while the envelope is rearticulated in order to accommodate a new context. {●1–4}

●RAMS: I think your efforts to fit into the neighborhood are entirely admirable. This scheme has its own geometrical impression, but it fits in. The only thing I would fault is on the façade. In that one little window on the second floor, there seems to be a blankness there in the dialogue between the inside and the outside. I think the site is very interesting. Somebody could make a garden at the corner or just keep it as a lawn. You still have space at the back. ●PD: There's a lot to admire here. I wish that the core itself had more logic. I want to see this really clear core draped with these spaces. But the core itself takes on aspects that aren't totally clear. I don't know what its boundaries are, and I don't know what its limits are. For instance I don't know why, sometimes, shelves are considered core. I just wish I understood the core better. ●DL: We've been considering the core to be this highly plastic substance that can morph and become any number of solutions to problems of the micro-dwelling. What if you start thinking about it not as plastic but as a very particular material? Is it stud walls? Is it a masonry chimney to anchor the leaves? All of a sudden you start pushing up against resistance, and I think that's where the project needs to be tighter. I think the project will actually get better when it starts heading in that direction. ●HN: It feels very comfortable on the site, partially because it's zoned so well. It really takes an attitude about defining the public side. How do you deal with the corner, and what are the most efficient gestures you can make to create privacy? The interior zoning really relates very well to the outside. One could do a Nolli Map of this house. This house is very successful in dealing with what is open space and what's not. This one in particular is comfortable, and very unselfconscious. ●RAMS: I think the more you design elements that don't tyrannize the lives of the people that are going to live there, the better your houses you are. That's why those old 19th century four square houses with a central hall or whatever are so easy to live in. You can put your modern furniture in, traditional furniture in, or anything in between. It's not tyrannical. When you design everything, people have to live exactly the way the architect intended, or not at all.

●Original Scheme: Alexander Stagge

●1

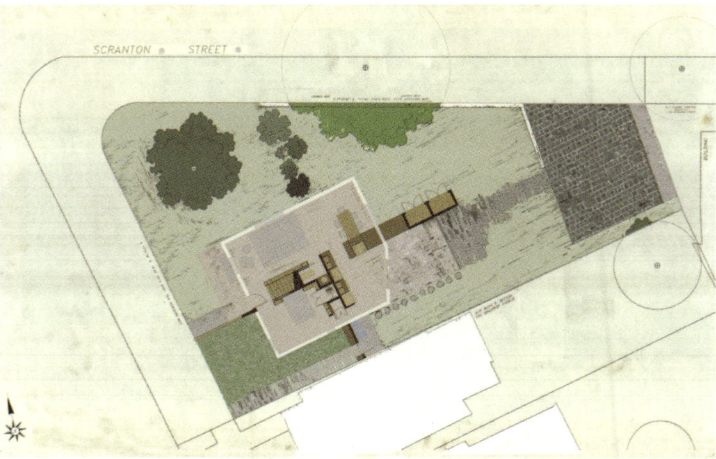

●2

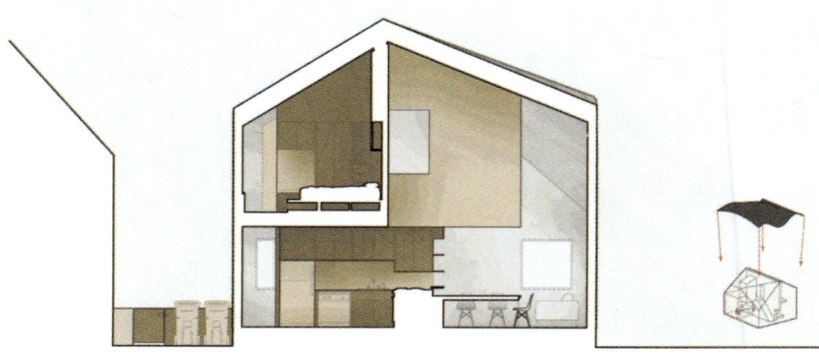

●3

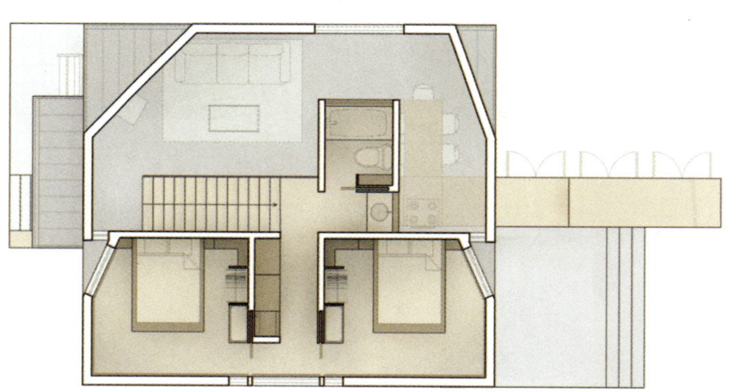

●4

<u>Students</u>
Caroline Acheatel, Tess McNamara, Daniel Marty, Cathryn Garcia-Menocal, Paul Rasmussen, Alexander Stagge, Matthew Zuckerman

Our scheme centers on the idea of a deployable and multi-functional core. The core is efficient—consolidating stairs and utilities to leave the remainder of space open, gracious, and able to connect to the site. The house is a spatial inversion: on the second floor, the core opens into a more private communal space. The density of the first floor is flung to the perimeter of the house on the second floor creating a thickness to hold furniture and fixtures for bedrooms and bath. The core can be shifted within the volume of the house, which can be deployed on different lots around New Haven. The house is able to adapt to site constraints through the positioning of the core, which can both shield and reveal space. {●5–8}

●RAMS: It's a nice, compact plan. It seems fairly logical. I just wonder why the roof doesn't have the logic of the plan. It could have a flat roof, a hipped roof, crossed gables—something that fits in. I mean, Frank Lloyd Wright would've had a gable running this way and a gable running that way. You've got this thing that's sort of a beanie off-kilter, or a mortar board from the graduation you are hoping for. ●JM: The site strategy is so well-resolved and your occupation of the site corner is done really well. It was strong before, and it's gotten even stronger. I like way that you're playing with the porosity of the edges and the visibility over your wall and your fence, which takes advantage of this enormous lot to make it very domestic. It's well-scaled with the proportion of the house so it doesn't feel too small in the neighborhood. I question the fenestration. I like the big window over the entry, but it seems a little parsimonious in an otherwise very generous set of moves. ●HN: The site plan works beautifully, and the plan is great. I like that each bedroom is on a corner so you get cross-ventilation. The idea that this is being thought of from a three-dimensional point of view as an object is its problem. It's not responding to the various geometries of the neighborhood. You have really understood the two-dimensional aspect of the house on this site. By pushing the building to the corner, you've created a really great side yard that is very flexible. These ideas are not generated at all in what we're looking at. ●MC: It's really nice how the lower level opens up on one corner to the landscape, and the upper level opens up in a more protected way to the street, but it would be a really great place to hang out. We may have to worry about what gets put up against the glass but I think that becomes an amazing pull across the house from one living space to the other and I think bringing light down through the stair might help. It seems like it works really well but I'm worried that some of these dimensions might be too tight. It's a really nice circulation space, but can you still circulate? ●RAMS: Given the opportunity, you need to redo that entrance corner. ●MC: I think the whole entry itself and the scale of some of those elements are the place that your site planning is less successful. The scale of arriving at the corner, the porch to step up, those dimensions... It's just a really tight arrival. You come in the front door and you're faced with an equal dimension ahead of you and to your right. You're in a square space.

●Original Scheme: Ava Amirahmadi

●5

●6

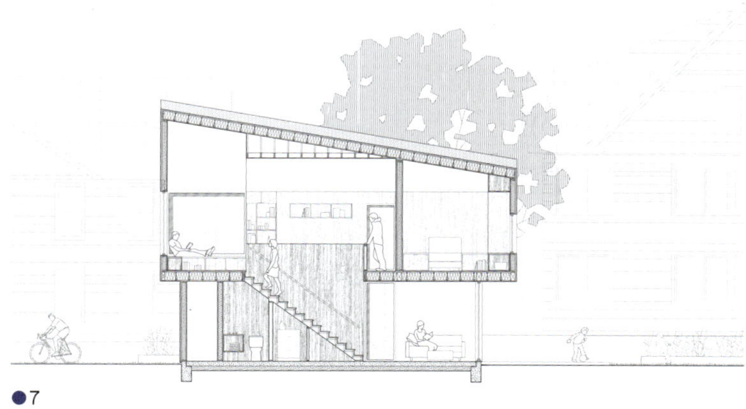

●7

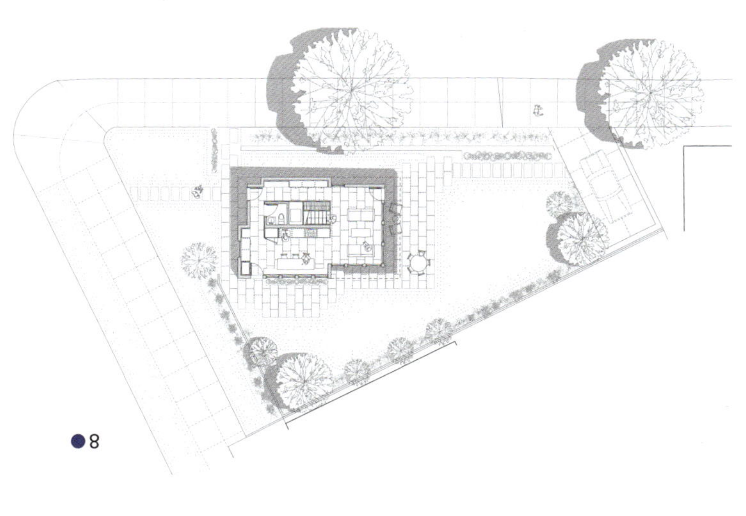

●8

TEAM C

Students
Lucas Boyd, Rachel Gamble, Alexander Kruhly, Maxwell Mensching, Elizabeth Nadai, Nasim Rowshanabadi

A careful consideration and enthusiastic embrace of the unusual corner site informed this design proposal. In order to address the existing urban fabric on both Winthrop Avenue and Scranton Street, a simple bend in plan allows for façades parallel to both sides of the corner lot. The traditional New England gable roof is folded accordingly, to create a contextually sensitive, yet innovative architectural form. On the ground floor, a consolidation of the stair, utilities, storage spaces, and powder room into a single service bar allows for an open floor plan of living, dining, and kitchen spaces. On the second floor, the consolidated service bar transforms into an aggregated set of "utility packs" which fan out along the bend in plan. These packs create partitions between the bedrooms and combine storage units, nightstands, and window seats into uniform strips of millwork. {●9–11}

●RAMS: I think the plan is very ingenious. I think you're timid with those little peanut skylights. They should probably be bold dormers with light coming from different ways, and you could introduce that strategy on both sides of the house—or maybe on the street side, which would enliven it. Because for a very commendable effort to fit in, it's a little dull. You can make it interesting. I like it! Anyone disagree with me? ●PD: I just want to ask about the lack of windows on the ground floor at either end. Is that because you like the ambient light and getting direct windows with direct light is a problem? Or is it a defense thing from the neighborhood? It's not a fortress. ●HN: But those windows could come below that line between the first and second floor. If you did that, the bulk and quality of light coming into the room is linking with the privacy, which responds to Bob's notion of making it more interesting. ●JM: Not just more interesting, but also tied to your conceptual building and site strategy. ●RAMS: You want privacy, and you want places for cubbies, bookshelves, pictures, whatever. People need wall space just as much as they need window space. ●RAMS: I think your site plan needs a lot of strengthening because the power of these moves is derived from that inside/outside connection, and right now it's the weakest point of your presentation. The way you're expressing this corner right now is sort of like a bulwark or a corner of cluttery shrubs. And I don't think that is doing any justice to the beauty of the moves that you're making. ●DL: I'm trying to figure out how you can really do more with the sectional introduction onto the second floor. You've got a motivation that's driven in plan and generates something in section, but when you go and look at what the section is doing for it, that surface is just left as a surface. I'm not sure what the answer is, but you're putting a lot of moves into the project and I don't know how you resolve that yet. ●DL: I'm just saying that if you're going to put something in section, you've got an opportunity there to think about what that moment is and what that space is. It really only is experienced from below, not from the sides, and I think there's an opportunity there to think about that. It's not just a "Hello, Mom" space, where you can experience the relationship between the bedrooms and below. It shouldn't just be a void down to the first floor because, if you need to let light in, there are easier and cheaper ways to get light in a small building.

●Original Scheme: Graham Brindle

●9

●10

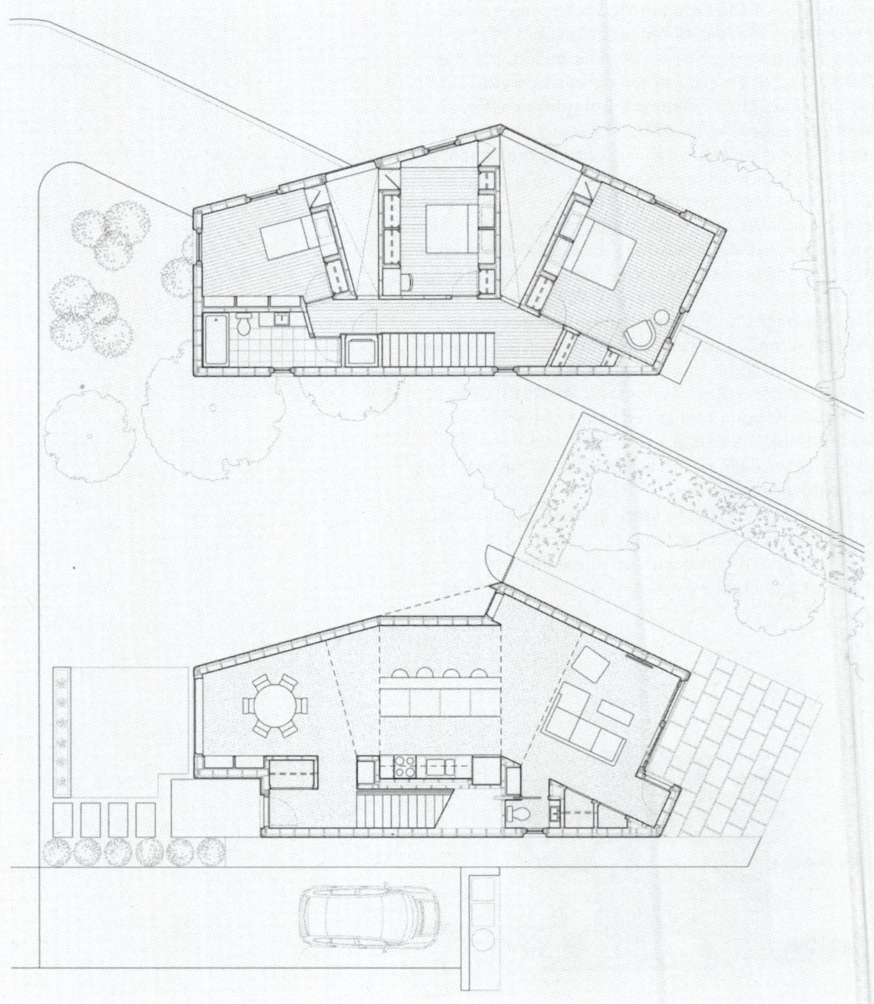

●11

TEAM D

Students
Graham Brindle, Chad Greenlee, Lily Hou, Samuel King, Laura Meade, Brittany Olivari

Envisioned as a house on three stories, our scheme separates the three bedrooms onto their own individual floors. The bedrooms' respective placements allow for a number of varied family or household configurations that would be able to use the space comfortably. Communal spaces are also evenly distributed among the three stories. As users progress through the house, they consequently experience an alternating sequence of communal and personally scaled spaces. The house fits into its contextual fabric, but still establishes its own characterized identity through these architectural gestures. At the corner of the site, we have carved away the "claimed" landscape to dissolve the house's influence to the street corner. We're creating the gesture of making a new communal space and and then offering it to the community. {●12–15}

●RAMS: I think the desire to make the house as tall as many in the neighborhood is commendable, but it comes at a steep price. It's not just the extra square footage—three floors is difficult not only for the old and decrepit like me, but also for people with children. I think it led you to an odd arrangement. I also think the idea of making the walls and roof the same is old and boring. Until water and snow change their nature, this is not going to happen. ●TP: I want to complement your team on your site strategy. This is one of the more elegant schemes we've seen today. Your landscape plan is really quite effective. ●KF: Yes, there are different spatial conditions and the way that you connect them is clever. I find the way that you accommodate different scenarios very commendable. While it might be hard to live on the three floors that you were dealt in this scheme, I really appreciate that variation and the way that it begins to address different parts of the landscape. You've explored how you might live differently in this place over time. ●MC: And that flexibility over time is very convincing. I find the way you appropriated the use of contextual elements {like the dormer of the roof and the proportions of the porch elements}, and the way you've twisted them with your own expression—I think you've done a beautiful job. It connects and relates back to the rooms that are on the site, but you made it something else. ●PD: I admire that you're trying to do something different here. I do worry that the difference is masked by the other motivation you have to blend in with the context. Embrace the weirdness. You're making a better front porch, and you're actually riding the property line, and that says something about the multiple people that live here. It is really describing the difficulty of what you're doing. I also think that your elevations could express the interior more. You guys are so limited and so modest. I think you can go for bizarre and still pay the proper respect to the neighborhood. ●TP: Well done, team. That corner on the site plan truly should belong to the neighborhood. This is a contrast to the more introspective layouts that we've seen so far. I think it's a nice change of pace. ●AO: I just want to say that I think there are a lot of really beautiful things about this project. There is a lot of hermeticism in the way that you've thought about the envelope, and that betrays some of the really sensitive connections to site that are in this project. So, we can quibble about the roof angles, but it's a really nice project, and I want to congratulate you.

●Original Scheme: Lucas Boyd

●12

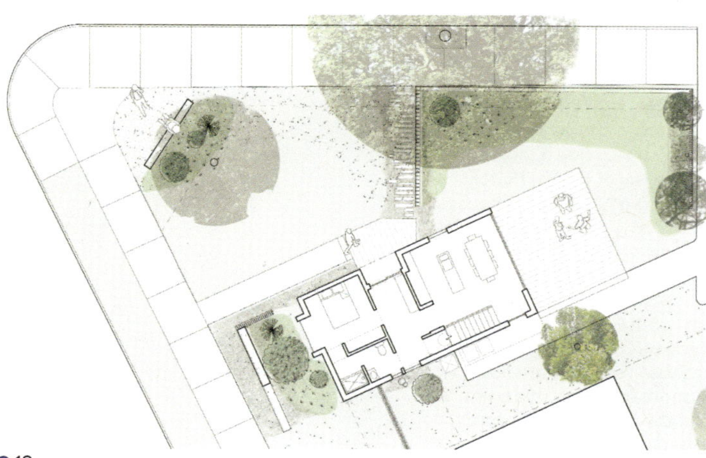

●13

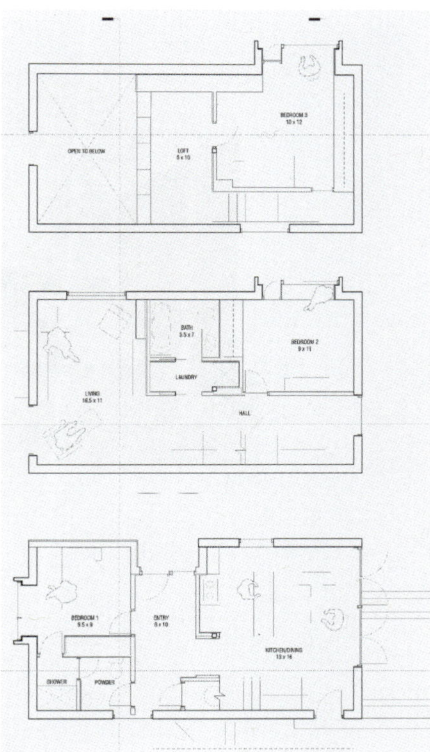

●14

●15

TEAM E

Students
Wilson Carroll, Dakota Cooley, Casey Furman, Cecilia Hui, Hannah Novack, Andrew Padron, Ilana Simhon

The courtyard house adhered to a simple scheme using transparency and an economy of space to expand the minimal footprint beyond the interior and claim a generous patio as additional living space. The unique corner lot configuration led to an L-shaped block of program that presented a buffer to the street and sheltered the resulting social spaces. The concise plan used an orthogonal orientation to imply oblique movement and views. The solid carved entry on the corner opposed the back living space that featured a fully glazed curtain wall opening to views of the yard. The minimal circulation eliminated wasted space and allowed for a flexible third bedroom that could also serve as a study. The form was driven by both the internal conditions and the unique buildings surrounding the site. The mono-pitched roof relieved the excessive volume of the double-height space, while also creating more domestic spaces on the corners. [●16–19]

●PD: I can't believe how clear this is; you make it look so simple. I feel bad that you're going first, because I suspect that, as we go around, the difficulty of the site and the difficulty of square footage with three bedrooms and so on will not make it look as easy as you've made it look. I also really appreciate the analysis of the roof pitch that picks up the scale of the neighboring houses without mimicking the roof typology. ●DL: I think one of the clearest things is that diagram you set up for how you deal with the buffer zone opening up and moving to the back. How do you actually maximize this in terms of the complexities of the diagonal? Where do you put the gutter? It's not an arbitrary thing, because what you are doing is sending all the water more or less to this point. You don't want to obscure the view. In other words, the challenge of the geometry is one in which we are setting up a diagonal movement through a square—in which your actual movement as a person can never move diagonally, but the water will move diagonally. ●RAMS: That mono-pitch roof has nothing to do with giving three-dimensional expression to your client. There are many ways you could have done it. There are many houses by excellent architects, at least during the period of Charles Moore, that use this strategy. It makes for a wonderful house and helps it into the corner of the site. The roof is not simplicity. It is simple mindedness. It's got nothing to do with the way that you come in, including the wrap of the secondary spaces, kitchens, bathrooms, bedrooms, and larger volume of the living room. There's no diagonal involved. You can walk across a square room on a diagonal. That doesn't mean the room is a diagonally oriented room. You've done something really nice, and then your search for "ineffable simplicity" went flying through the neighborhood and landed on the roof. ●AB: Let's dig into that issue of simplicity and whether or not you're actually achieving that. The simplicity of your diagrams is creating quite a bit of complexity. I agree with Peggy and think there's a strong clarity in the planning. The bigger issue is assembling a piece of architecture. For instance, the threshold of material from, say, wood to what might be stone is an issue. All of a sudden the threshold becomes a very complex moment, and your project says nothing of what the threshold means as an architectural experience.

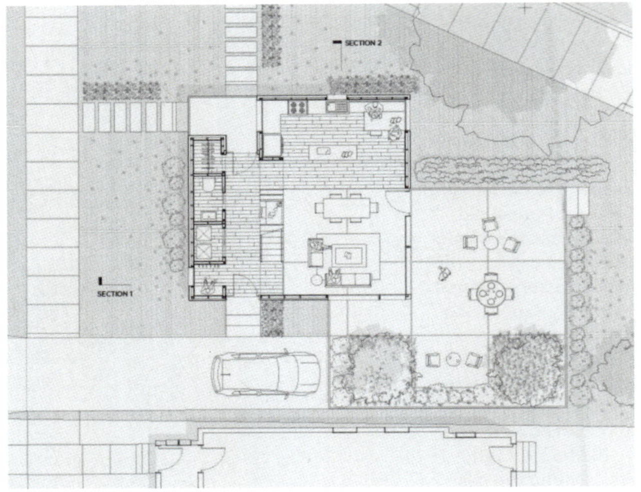

●16

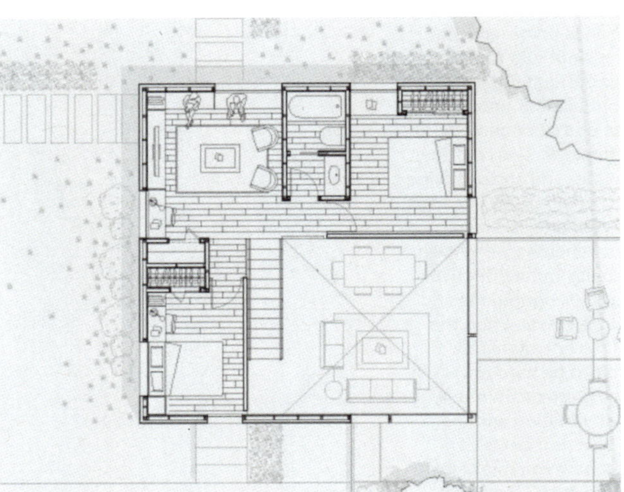

●17

●18

●Original Scheme: Elaina Berkowitz

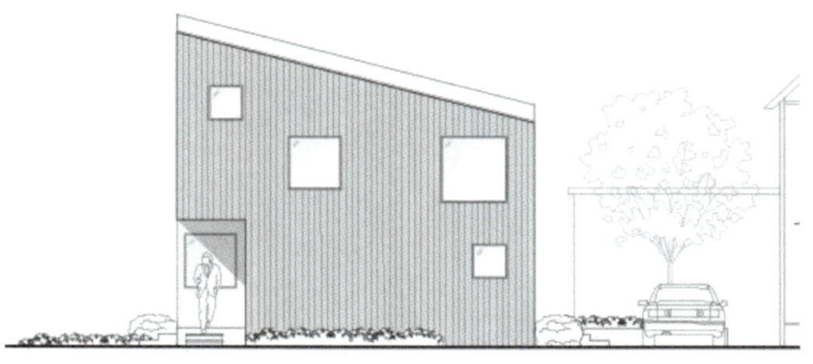

●19

U.S. Secretary of Agriculture Discusses "Timber City" Studio

Tom Vilsack {U.S. Secretary of Agriculture}

On Tuesday, April 14th, US Secretary of Agriculture Tom Vilsack and several guests from Yale School of Forestry visited the School of Architecture for a presentation of the work of an advanced design studio led by Alan Organschi and Lisa Gray. The studio was inspired by Secretary Vilsack's federal initiative to encourage high rise timber construction in American cities as a means to promote rural industry and job creation, improve the resiliency of American forests, and develop a sustainable response to rapidly changing urban demographics. Students had an opportunity to present their research in contemporary timber manufacturing and construction technologies as well as the resultant design work to with the Secretary of Agriculture himself.

The next time I [have an opportunity], I'm going to suggest [less spending] on political campaigns and put a couple million into something like this. They could actually build something that would then create the momentum for this to really take off. — U.S. Secretary of Agriculture, Tom Vilsack

Photo: Vivian Felten

Getting Real {Paul Rudolph Lecture}

Jeanne Gang
Studio Gang, Founder and Principal

In the Industrial Era, different design areas were separated out and became more specialized. This is the time when we see the architect as the lone genius, so I think what we are proposing is a collective of design thinkers—a team which is diverse and able to bring in different perspectives. That has been our strength all along, and it is really something we draw on: all the diversity in our team and groups.

As we have grown as an office, one of the things we've had to deal with is figuring out the structure, and that became a design project in of itself. Consultants came in and told us how to create an org chart: start with a ladder. We didn't really like this idea, but we knew that we needed some structure, so we worked on it together and finally decided that the structure of the office really should be turned upside down. It should be more of a tree. Our organization chart is more of a growing tree that starts with ideas in the ground roots, and then the people are like branches which support other people; that's a more representative metaphor for the way that we work today.

Students
Anny Chang, Jacqueline Hall, Wes Hiatt,
Michael Loya, Cecily Ng, Madison Sembler

This proposal is a long, one-story scheme in which two split bars shift in section, an action which allows the house to maintain some privacy along Scranton Street to which it aligns. This orientation, together with the length and thinness of our scheme, grants us the most generous possible side yard with the house acting as a garden wall, sheltering the yard from passersby. A clerestory window that runs the length of the house brings in southern light. Landscaping is simple but ties outdoor zones into the patterns of scale, intimacy, and utility set out by the interior plan. The character of this scheme recalls midcentury California suburban ranch houses—a natural fit for its plan and section—while making this precedent fresh for the realities of urban life in New Haven. (●20–23)

●DL: One would assume from the renderings that there's either a great affinity for or a desire to somehow associate with Post-World War II advertising structures. That begins to flavor the quality and interpretation of whether this is reinforcing the nuclear family or a more diverse set of residents. The bedroom unit becomes a kind of machine. I think you've done really well to develop a clarity in the plan and produce as much diversity as you can in what is otherwise a single-story project. ●MC: You've set up this house as a way to watch or engage with the outside space almost theatrically—you're always up high looking down on it, and the section is stepping down through there. It would be good to represent that. All your section perspectives show how you have different heights, but they don't show why you have those different heights, except to say that you're creating different zones. I think you've done something interesting in how the house and the outdoor space starts to loop around and connect to each other in a very dynamic way. ●PD: This scheme suffers from a wrapper that's stylistically determined. In your case it's trying to look like a 1950s house, when in fact what's happening is much more interesting than what that style says. All the things you're describing are not actually like a ranch—an object in a neutral field—it's very orchestrated in its section and its connection to outside. When you take off the roof and we actually see the interior, I think that's cool, but it really does emphasize something that works against this wrapped shed and wants to identify itself as an object distinct from its landscape. So if you just looked at what the section is doing, you'd come up with something very different that I think would also give you some more frontality. When you just have this extruded bar, and the front is just the end of that extrusion, you're not doing justice to that street front. You need to come up with something that does. ●RAMS: For me, the issue is character. I think architects should discover not how to express themselves, but how to express the character of the neighborhood or the place. You should be trying to find out how to make something fresh that fits in. So the character of a ranch house from 1950 Marin County or wherever—what does that have to do with this great 19th century neighborhood that's struggling to catch on again and get people here? Why not work with that? It's about the character of the place, and that character is decided by much more than just one building. Character is like pornography: you know it when you see it. ●PD: Gross.

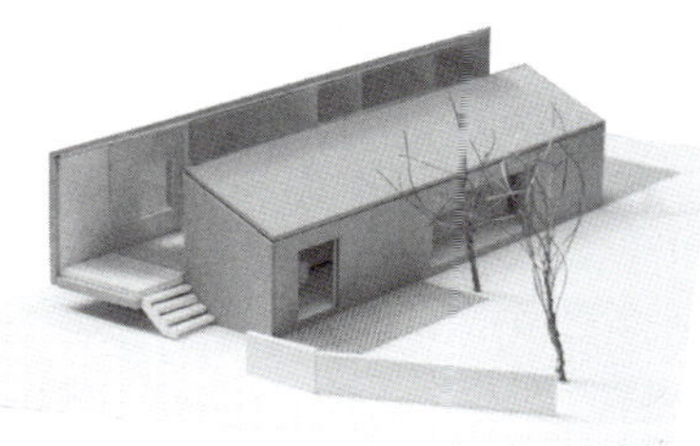

●Original Scheme: Maggie Tsang

●20

●21

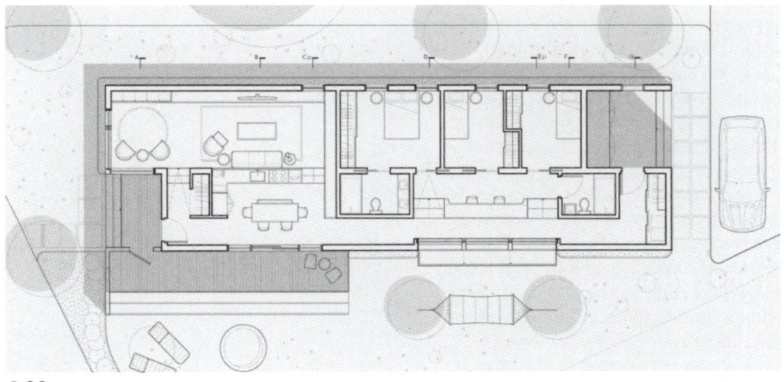

●22

●23

<u>Students</u>
Ava Amirahmadi, Daniel Glick-Unterman, Aary Lee, Christopher Leung, James Schwartz, Georgia Todd

Starting with the bi-nuclear scheme that we inherited, we devised a series of manipulations to the basic diagram that allows our house to both maximize the irregular site and maintain a sense of contextual relevance. The introduction of axes that open all the interior spaces to the outdoors allows for light and cross-ventilation. Though the footprint is small, the immaterial becomes the material of the house, which causes the home to feel larger. By popping up the living room ceiling, light floods into the main communal space. While imbuing the interior of the house with a sense of grandeur, this gesture also serves to give back to the neighborhood at night by creating a glowing beacon on the corner. The living space can open up completely to the backyard so that it becomes a continuation and expansion of the social space. By carving into the house at the end of the main axes, other moments where the garden encroaches into the home are introduced making for a seamless relationship to the outdoors. {●24–27}

●DL: You're really developing this wall as a thick, super-insulated boundary that's going to make a claim about the neighborhood. Once you set up this idea, you can start producing penetrations that are incredibly important in the living room, or incredibly important to the entrance. I think that's really where the project is—trying to figure out how to set up a marker that is really strong, but gives you the opportunity to play that much stronger. I want to figure out how you can turn that wall into more of a generator of the plan, because the plan is of a very different logic. The wall in the plan actually disappears, except for in the living room, so when it goes to the bedrooms or bathrooms it's simply like any other wall as opposed to the place where you circulate. If that wall is a gesture—a dominant piece—then you want to set that up as a circulation zone so that you're reinforcing it. There's a conflict between the organization of the plan and the gesture of the wall. ●KF: I feel like you've spent a lot of time with nuanced interior spaces that have a lot of layers between private and public, and less with how your outermost layers relate to the context of the neighborhood. From site to building, there's no ambiguity in where one starts and ends. In the building you've found yourself a lot of interesting gestures and interesting moments. It would be great if you guys could have figured out how to do that from your building edge to the site itself. Make something—it doesn't have to be a porch—which can engage the outside space in a more open way. I just don't know if that wall needed to turn the corner, or that you needed to make that solid edge. ●AO: I think these comments really picked up on a crisis in your project that you've been trying to sort through. I admire that a lot. The wall was a solution to a site with preponderance of street frontage so much so that it was actually over exposed. It's a really hard question. How do you suddenly see that the diagram you've come to from another set of analyses contradicts the diagram that you started with? That moment is really hard to manage. I appreciate that one solution to the site might be to wall it, just as Bob said, and then that project turns the corner as you consider the rest of the planning.

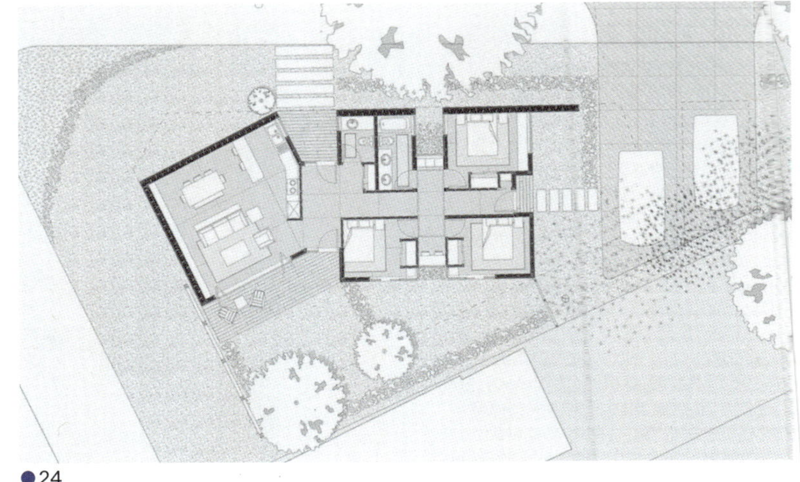

●24

●25

●26

●27

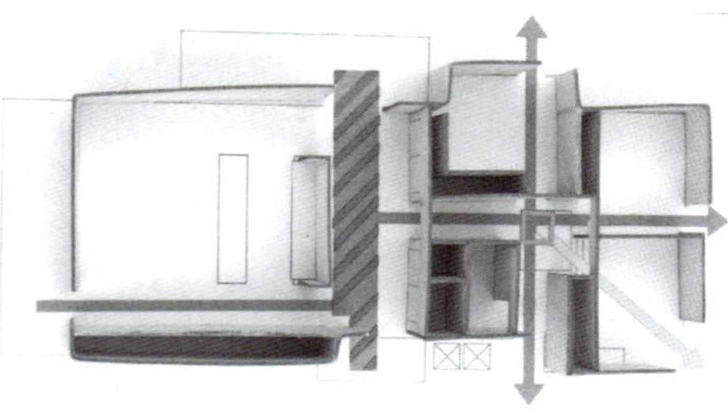

●Original Scheme: Laura Meade

TEAM H

Students
Elaina Berkowitz, Francesca Carney, Robert
Cornelissen, Ethan Fischer, Benjamin Rubenstein,
Maggie Tsang, Robert Yoos

The Mullet House is "business in the front and party
in the back". On the business end: the dense utility
bar. On the party end: large, open living rooms and
bedrooms. The house takes advantage of the awkward geometry of the site by packing all of the necessary utilities within a five-foot core along Scranton Street. Like a single-loaded corridor, the house
leverages extreme efficiency on the street side for
truly open, adaptable, and porous spaces that plug
into the core and face the garden. Designed to be
built with four-foot structurally insulated panels,
the house offers a flexible and simple construction
techniques that could be deployed across variously
sized lots in New Haven. With the utilities of the
house packed into the bar, the Mullet House capitalizes on a building system that grants the inhabitants
not only efficiency and flexibility, but also generous
living spaces. ●28–31

●RAMS: This is a very well-planned house. I
wonder if the decision to separate the living room
and dining room on the ground floor really reflects
how people with small quarters might prefer to
live. I appreciate your wanting to break down the
two tower-like volumes, but if you had closed them
and made it a double-height, glazed conservatory
and you could look down on it from above or look
through it on the bedroom floor, it would have made
the ground floor more flexible. It would have made
the house more affordable, because you would have
had less exterior walls. ●PD: That question points
to the weaker part of your scheme, which is how
it sits on the site. It's not just the choice of making
it parallel to the context; it has to do with the core
space being on the corner. The core itself, or even
the division between the core and the rest of the
house, doesn't say "corner." Your desire for this to
work as a prototype is fabulous. I really appreciate
the flexibility. That is the real asset of the scheme,
but in the case of this specific site, it's not helping
you feel like this house is necessary. ●DL: In order
to make the diagram work between the served and
service spaces—the core and the public—you're
relying upon a circulation corridor. How can this
corridor be much more than a residual space, and
actually activated? If you go to the analogy, the
mullet has the front and the back and then there's
all that middle zone that you're not sure what to do
with. In some ways, the challenge is what to do with
the top. Do you go spiky? Does it become part of
the front? Having witnessed and experienced the
challenge of a mullet myself, I think the challenge
is what to do with moments of pure circulation if
the argument is about efficiency. ●AB: It might just
be a matter of calibration. First of all, I think this
is a beautiful scheme. But I think there are more
opportunities for compaction. I actually quite like
the siting and the way you create a generous side/
rear yard, but then you place this little eating table
in a nook. Why not just make that gap between
the dining room and the living room a transitional
space? The louvers and the clerestory at the
roof—it's like someone put a baseball hat on top
of a mullet. I find them unnecessary. There's a
language that gets undone by this strange, filigreed
clerestory that would be very hard to build. You
should think of the composition of elevations
absent those horizontal clerestories that are mixing
up the message.

●Original Scheme: Wes Hiatt

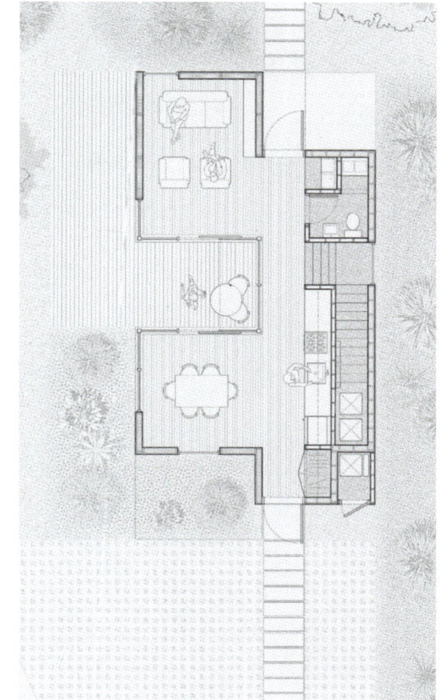

●28

●29

●30

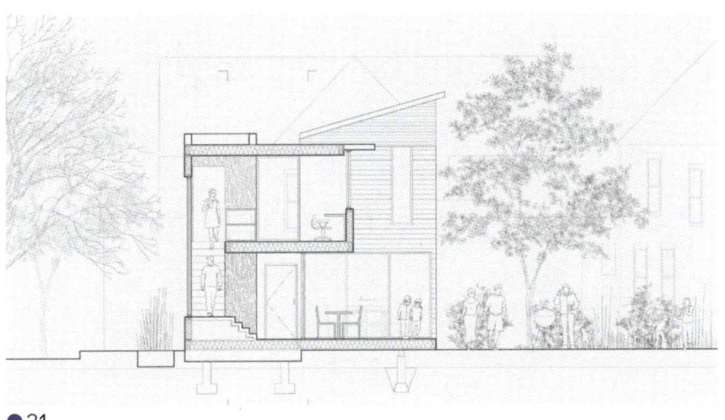

●31

Summer

The Jim Vlock First-Year Building Project: Fieldwork
M.Arch I

Coordinators
Adam Hopfner & Kyle Bradley

This course examines the materialization of a building, whereby students are required to physically participate in the construction of a structure that they have designed. By engaging in the act of building, students are exposed to the material, procedural, and technical demands that shape architecture. Construction documents are generated and subsequently put to the test in the field. Students engage in collaboration with each other and with a client as they reconcile budgetary, scheduling, and labor constraints, and negotiate myriad regulatory, political, and community agencies. The course seeks to demonstrate the multiplicity of forces that come to influence the execution of an architectural intention, all the while fostering an architecture of social responsibility by providing structures for an underserved and marginalized segment of the community.

Visualization IV
John Eberhart & John Blood

This seven-week, intensive course introduces Building Information Modeling (BIM) alongside manual drawing to expand each student's analytical and expressive repertoire. Fundamental techniques are introduced through short exercises and workshops leading toward a sustained study of an exemplary precedent building. Quantitative analysis is pursued through both assembly modeling and visual dissection of both the programmatic spaces and functional elements. Observational and imaginative manual drawings allow for a reconstruction of the design process and reestablish the thought patterns that formed the building's design priorities. These discoveries then are represented through interactive, multimedia presentations to describe the building assembly and its design ambitions.

ELAINA BERKOWITZ, DANIEL MARTY, MAGGIE TSANG

Chapel of the Holy Cross and Crematorium (1–2)

DAKOTA COOLEY, MATTHEW KABALA, NASIM ROWSHANABADI

Dutchess County Guest House (■3–4)

CATHRYN GARCIA-MENOCAL, PAUL RASMUSSEN , MADISON SEMBLER

Villa Stein (■5–6)

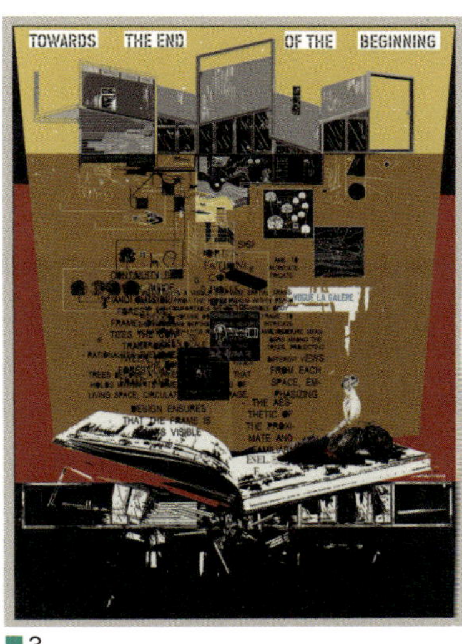

■1

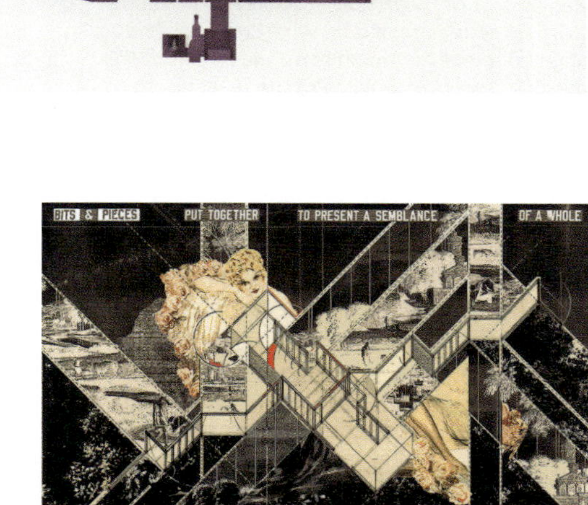

■3

■2

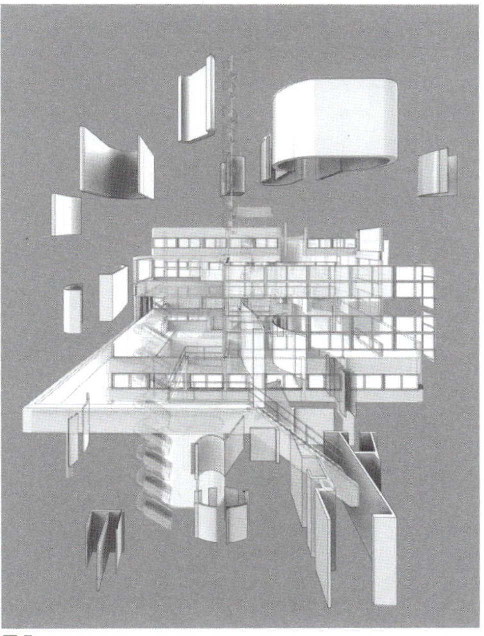

■4

■5

■6

Rome: Continuity and Change

Alexander Purves, Stephen Harby, Bimal Mendis, Bryan Fuermann

This intensive five-week summer workshop takes place in Rome and is designed to provide a broad overview of that city's major architectural sites, topography, and systems of urban organization. Examples from antiquity to the present day are studied as part of the context of an ever-changing city with its sequence of layered accretions. The seminar examines historical continuity and change as well as the ways in which and the reasons why some elements and approaches were maintained over time and others abandoned. Hand drawing is used as a primary tool of discovery during explorations of buildings, landscapes, and gardens, both within and outside the city. Students devote the final week to an intensive independent analysis of a building or place. ▪1–5▸

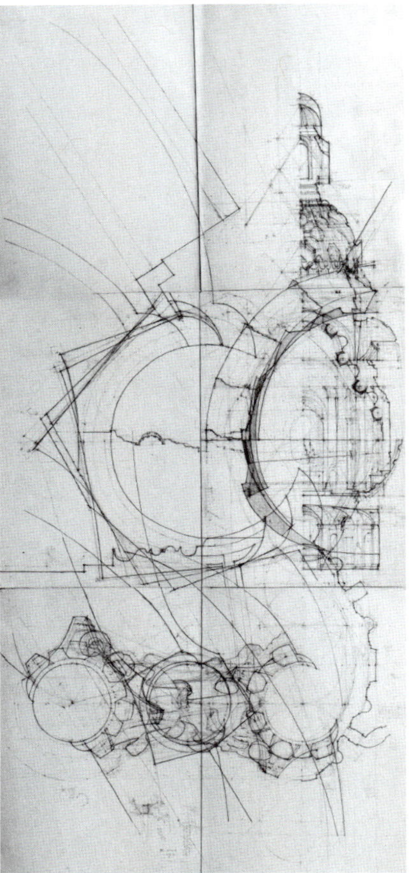

▪ 1. John Kleinschmidt

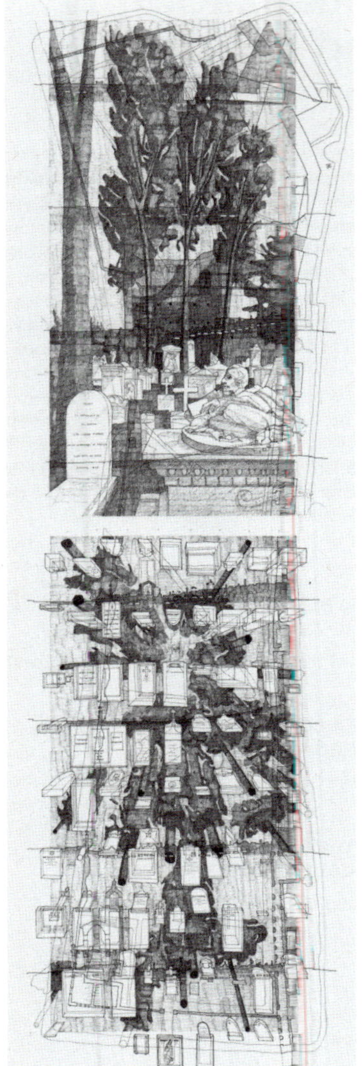

▪ 2. Isaac Southard

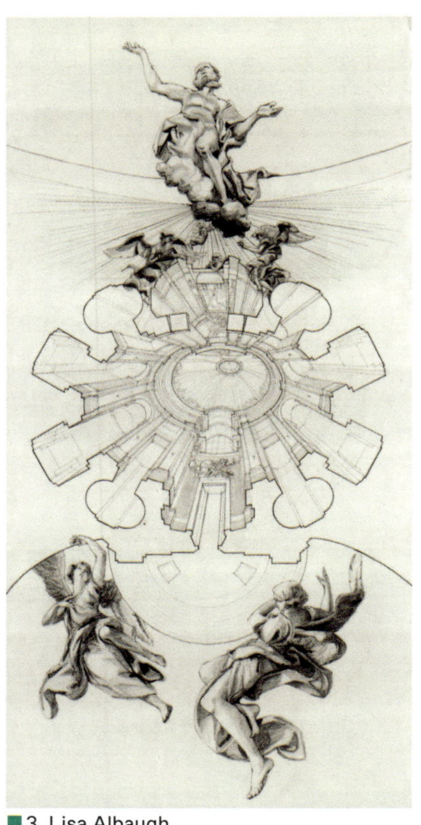

▪ 3. Lisa Albaugh

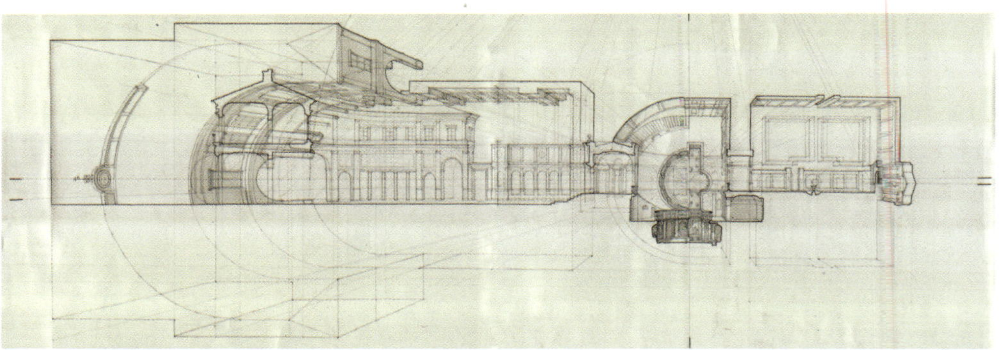

▪ 4. Andrew Sternad

▪ 5. Dima Srouji

TRAVEL AWARDS

KIANA HOSSEINI

David Schwarz Fellowship

**Symbiosis, Adaptation, and Absorption:
A Historical Survey of Islamic Architecture**
The current view towards Islamic architecture is often focused on the superficial and the visual. This misplaced fascination with the exotic, or the alien, when referencing Islamic influences has led to a shallow admiration and uncritical perception towards Islamic architecture. This manifests itself in the majority of contemporary "Islamic" architectural and urban projects, ranging from the conventional commercial buildings in Dubai dipped in a facade of Islamic decoration to entire cities designed by starchitects. A critical exploration of the history of Islamic architecture, and its evolution in different regions of the world is the first step in understanding its core principles and their implication today. Expanding from East Asia, through Europe, and eventually to Northwestern Africa, Islamic Architecture has transformed to adapt to different geographical, cultural and political conditions over the past fourteen centuries. The three major styles that I will be focusing on are Persian, Ottoman, and Moorish architecture. Through studying these styles, I wish to gain a more in-depth understanding of Islamic architecture and its process of symbiosis, adaptation and absorption of form, structure and space into a new cultural climate. {↳1}

ANDREW STERNAD

George Nelson Scholarship

Water World
Rising seas, stronger rain, sinking land. Waterfront cities around the world have banded together to share expertise in fighting these increasingly common threats, with the Dutch at the helm of the international water sector. Over centuries, the Dutch have perfected strategies for living in low, soggy places—sixty percent of the Netherlands GDP is produced below sea level—although they are not alone in the market. As vulnerable coastal cities begin to feel the effects of climate change, a multi-billion-dollar global knowledge economy has sprung up to plug the leaks. Many cities have contracted foreign experts to design flood mitigation projects, many resulting from rapid urban development and complex political relationships. While each site is unique, an examination of recent flood protection proposals reveals many commonalities. They have appear the same: internal "blue-green" networks, ringed by massive, and expensive, pumps and barriers. This research will focus primarily on three cities in Southeast Asia to test satellite-view planning against ground truth: Jakarta, Indonesia; Ho Chi Minh City, Vietnam; and Phnom Penh, Cambodia. Perhaps conceptual similarities the coincidental result of efficient pro forma approaches to familiar water challenges. On the other hand, flood management risks becoming a commodity-driven exchange that undervalues—or overwhelms—local building forms and insight. Does the international business of water planning risk drowning out home-grown innovation? How is local knowledge incorporated, if at all, and who are the real experts? And what form does development ultimately take? The answers will determine if up-and-coming cities sink or swim in the 21st century water world. {↳2}

ANNE MA

Gertraud A. Wood Traveling Fellowship

Megalopolis
The documentation of this expedition stemmed from a growing interest in drawing large dense megalopolises. The similarities and differences in density, city fabric, and iconic monuments was one of the main motivations as I explored a series of large city centers in the Asia-Pacific region. The destinations vary in culture, daily pace, and style but they also overlap in many areas such as density and city planning. Through an amalgamation of traditional photography and on-site hand sketching, I was interested not only in what I saw before me physically, but also the experience as I walked through each city center. The final result is a combination of photograph/drawing collage, and city perspectives in the form of a graphic narrative. The narrative enables me to re-count and represents my personal experiences and thoughts during my travel. Although the ideas and work are raw and itching for refinement, I hope that my experiences are documented in an effective yet entertaining fashion. {↳3}

JEAN CHEN

Takenaka Corporation Summer Internship

Japanese Residential Architecture
During my travels in Japan, I have travelled from Tokyo on the east to Naoshima on the west. My internship at Takenaka not only gives me insight to one of the most renowned, largest architecture design and construction firms, but also gives me opportunity to experience Japanese culture Japanese citizens and workers that hail from all parts of the country. My research focuses on residential architecture and the paradoxical relationship between the old and the new, the traditional and the popular, the ephemeral and the monumental. During my stay in Japan, I was fortunate enough to not only do a homestay in a contemporary house in Tokyo, but also visit a traditional, old Japanese house in Kyoto, and observe how many aspects of traditional Japanese culture have persisted through the architectural stylistic changes and maintained an unequivocally familiar nature. In my research, I seek to understand the cultural mentality underlying these paradoxical phenomena and how they manifest in architecture and everyday life. {↳4}

↳ 1

↳ 2

↳ 3

↳ 4

Friends

Nancy Alexander
'79 B.A., '84 M.B.A.
Anonymous (2)
Autodesk, Inc.
Michael C. Barry
'09 B.A.
Penelope Bellamy
A. Robert Bissell
'72 B.S.
Howard M. Brenner
'54 B.A.
Carl L. Britton, Jr.
'87 B.A.
James C. Childress
William D. Chilton
Douglas Durst
Constance Eiseman
M. Arthur Gensler, Jr.
Graham Foundation for
Advanced Studies in
the Fine Arts
Julia & Seymour Gross
Foundation Inc.
Steven Harris
HBRA Architects
Andrew Philip Heid
'02 B.A.
HOK, Inc.
Thomas C. & Beryl S.
Hsiang
Judith T. Hunt
James L. Iker
Elise Jaffe & Jeffrey
Brown
Jesse Johnston
Joanna Kerns
Ken Kuchin
Wilmoth G. Lewis
'79 B.A.
Anne Kriken Mann
Ann Maurer
Gilbert Maurer
Margaret McCurry
Susan McKenna
Susan Mead
Louis C.S. Ng
Helen W. Nitkin
Michael A. Pearce
'09 B.A.
Richard B. Peiser
'70 B.A.
Cesar Pelli
'76 M.A.H.,
'08 D.F.A.H.
Pickard Chilton
Architects Inc.
William L. Rawn III
'65 B.A.
William K. Reilly
'62 B.A., '94 M.A.H.
Eve Hart Rice
Robert Rosenkranz
'62 B.A.
Carolyn Greenspan &
Marshall S. Ruben
'82 B.A.
Melissa G. Vail '74 B.A.
& Norman C. Selby
'74 B.A.
Brenda Shapiro
Simon B. & Linda M. Sobo
Jon Stryker
Oscar Tang
'60 B.E.
The BPB & HBB
Foundation
The Mari Souval
Spacedrafting
Foundation, Inc.
The Maurer Family
Foundation, Inc.
Janie M. Vanpee
'75 M.A., '77 M.Phil.,
'82 Ph.D.
Betty L. Wagner
Anne C. Weisberg
Winston Family
Ann E. Wolf
Mathew D. Wolf
Ben Wood Studio
Shanghai
Pei-Tse Wu
'89 B.A.

Yale Club of New Haven
Arthur W. Zeckendorf

1949

Frank S. Alschuler
Theodore F. Babbitt
Charles H. Brewer, Jr.
George A. Hinds
Augustine J. Palmieri*
George D. Waltz

1951

Phelps H. Bultman*
Ross H. De Young
Martha Cantwell Meeker

1952

Frank C. Boyer, Jr.
James A. Evans
George C. Holm
Donald C. Mallow
Lawrence Frederick
Nulty
James E. Palmer

1953

Duncan W. Buell*
Milton Klein
John V. Sheoris

1954

Charles G. Brickbauer
George R. Brunjes, Jr.
James D. Gibans
John F. Lee, Jr.
Boris S. Pushkarev
Roger L. Strassman
Thomas R. Vreeland

1955

Vica S. Emery
John L. Field
Thomas F. Graves
James Leslie

1956

Walter D. Ramberg

1957

Ernest L. Ames
Edwin William de Cossy
James H. Handley
Clovis B. Heimsath
Richard A. Nininger
William L. Porter
Richard Elliott Wagner
Mary S. Winder

1958

James S. Dudley
Harold D. Fredenburgh
Mark H. Hardenbergh
Allen Moore, Jr.
Malcolm Strachan, 2d
Michael W. Stuhldreher
Harold F. VanDine, Jr.

1959

Bernard M. Boyle
Frank C. Chapman
Louis P. Inserra
Robert M. Kliment
Earl A. Quenneville
Bruce W. Sielaff
Terry G. Twitchell
Donald W. Velsey
Carolyn H. Westerfield
Andrew C. Wheeler

1960

Lawrence N. Argraves
James B. Baker
Thomas L. Bosworth
Richard S. Chafee
Bryant L. Conant
John K. Copelin
Michael Gruenbaum
Louis B. Joline
Julia H. Keydel
James D. McNeely
Oscar E. Menzer
Robert A. Mitchell
Konrad J. Perlman
Walter Rosenfeld

1961

Edward R. Baldwin
Paul B. Brouard
Robert W. Carington
Peter Cooke
Warren Jacob Cox
Francis W. Gencorelli
Charles T. Haddad
William J. Hawkins
Lewis S. Roscoe
W. Eugene Sage
Stanley Tigerman
Yung G. Wang

1962

James L. Alcorn
George E. Buchanan
David W. Fix
Richard A. Hansen
Tai Soo Kim
Keith R. Kroeger
James Morganstern
Leonard P. Perfido
Renato Rossi-Loureiro
Meredith M. Seikel
Ming-Hsien Wang
Donald R. Watson
Myles Weintraub

1963

Austin Church III
Howard H. Foster, Jr.
Ward Joseph Miles
F. Kempton Mooney
Louis H. Skidmore, Jr.
William A. Werner, Jr.
John V. Yanik

1964

Philip Allen
Charles D. Hosford
Augustus G. Kellogg
Judith A. Lawler
Charles L W. Leider
Robert J. Mittelstadt
Elizabeth B. Rogers
Joan F. Stogis

1965

Michael J. Altschuler
Thomas Hall Beeby
H. Calvin Cook
Richard C. Fogelson
Peter L. Gluck
Neil Goodwin
Norman E. Jackson, Jr.
Isidoro Korngold
Thai Ker Liu
Gary L. Michael
John I. Pearce, Jr.
Alexander Purves
Elliot A. Segal
Robert A.M. Stern
Frederick C. Terzo
Leonard M. Todd, Jr.
Jeremy A. Walsh
Arnold N. Wile

1966

Andrew Andersons
Emily Nugent Carrier
Richard C. Carroll, Jr.
James Scott Cook
John J. Damico
Loren Ghiglione
Frank S. Grosso
John S. Hagmann
Michael Hollander
William F. Moore
Myron B. Silberman
W. Mason Smith III
Lester R. Walker

1967

William H. Albinson
Edward A. Arens
Robert A. Bell
R. Caswell Cooke
Alexander D. Garvin
Howard E. Goldstein
Glenn H. Gregg
Walter A. Hunt, Jr.
Chung Nung Lee
John W. Mullen III

Annette B. Ramirez
de Arellano
Charles S. Rotenberg
Theodore Paul Streibert
Darius Toraby

1968

Frederick S. Andreae
Robert A. Busser
Gail H. Cooke
Peter de Bretteville
David M. Dickson
Richard M. Donnelly
John Fulop, Jr.
Christopher C. Glass
John Holbrook, Jr.
Gerard Ives
Erno Kolodny-Nagy
Peter C. Mayer
Peter Papademetriou
Franklin Satterthwaite
Donald R. Spivack
Salvatore F. Vasi
John J. Vosmek, Jr.
James C. Whitney

1969

John Badman
James E. Caldwell, Jr.
Robert J. Cassidy
David B. Decker
George B. Dudley
James M. Gage
George T. Gardner
Harvey R. Geiger
Jane L. Gilbert
Edward J. Gotgart
William H. Grover
Eric R. Hansen, Jr.
Roderick C. Johnson
Raymond J. Kaskey, Jr.
David H. Lessig
William B. Richardson
John H. Shoaff
Kermit D. Thompson

1970

Judith L. Aronson
Richard F. Barrett
Roland F. Bedford
Paul F. Bloom
F. Andrus Burr
Roc R. Caivano
Thomas Carey
Michael G. Curtis
Brin R. Ford
Morgan H. Grace
Peter Van W. Hoyt
David C. Jamison
Joseph A. Middlebrooks
Kathrin S. Moore
James V. Righter
Steven G. Rockmore
Laurence A. Rosen
Daniel V. Scully
Robert F. Shannon
Marilyn Swartz Lloyd
Walter C. Upton
William L. Yuen
F. Anthony Zunino

1971

John R. Benson
William A. Brenner
Rockwell J. Chin
Edward F. Cox
Anita Holland-Moritz
John Jayner
Humberto L.
Rodriguez-Camilloni
Susan St. John
Peter J. Wood*

1972

Marc F. Appleton
Paul B. Bailey
Edward P. Bass
Richard F. Benedetto
Frederick Bland
Stephen J. Blatt
Philip Mack Caldwell
Roberta Carlson
Carnwath
Heather Willson Cass

William A. Davis
John H. T. Dow, Jr.
Joseph A. Ford III
Coleman A. Harwell
Mark L. Hildebrand
Roberta D. Lawrence
William H. Maxfield
David B. Peck, Jr.
Barton Phelps
Jefferson B. Riley
Paul W. Scovill III
Mark Simon
Carl H. Wies
Roger Hung Tuan Yee

1973

Russell E. Bloodworth, Jr.
Hobart Fairbank
J.P. Chadwick Floyd
John C. Foley
Robert P. Hoffman
Stephen R. Holt
James O. Kruhly
Nancy Brooks Monroe
Robert D. Orr
Robert S. Page
Steven C. Robinson
Michael J. Stanton
William A. Sterling
J. Lawrence Thomas
Stephen C. Thomson
R. Jerome Wagner
John W. Whipple
Robert J. Yudell

1974

Gordon M. Black
Jonathan G. Boyer
Sara E. Caples
Andres M. Duany
William E. Odell
Thomas C. Payne
Patrick L. Pinnell
Elizabeth M.
Plater-Zyberk
Barbara W. Ratner
Barbara J. Resnicow
David M. Schwarz
Richard A. Senechal
George E. Turnbull

1975

Tullio A. Bertoli
Douglas J. Gardner
Karyn M. Gilvarg
Susan E. Godshall
Keith B. Gross
Edwin R. Kimsey, Jr.
Francis C. Klein
Larry W. Richards
Hervin A. Romney
Andrew K. Stevenson
J. David Waggonner III

1976

Benjamin M. Baker III
Henry H. Benedict III
Barbara R. Feibelman
Daniel F. Kallenbach
James R. Kessler
Roy T. Lydon, Jr.
Eric Jay Oliner
Herschel L. Parnes
Adrienne K. Paskind
John K. Spear
Barbara Sundheimer-
Extein

1977

Yeshaya D. Ballon
Louise M. Braverman
Peter D. Clark
Bradley B. Cruickshank
W.J. Patrick Curley
Barry G. Donaldson
Eric W. Epstein
Barbara Fabiani
Barbara Flanagan
Carl M. Geupel
Jeff G. Gold
Jonathan S. Kammel
James Hirsch Liberman
Kevin P. Lichten
Randall T. Mudge

Paul J. Pugliese
Andrew K. Robinson
Charles B. Swanson
Alexander C. Twining

1978

Philip H. Babb
Frederic M. Ball, Jr.
Judith M. Capen
Shiao-Ling Chang
Kenneth H. Colburn
Kathleen A. Dunne
Lisa J. Gelfand
Cynthia N. Hamilton
Kaspar A. Kraemer
John W. Kuipers
Kevin R. O'Connor
William H. Paxson
Daniel Arthur Rosenfeld
Julia Ruch
David Spiker
Leonard Taylor
Margaret T. Weidlein

1979

Steven W. Ansel
Jack Alan Bialosky, Jr.
James Leslie Bodnar
Richard H. Clarke
Daniel Dolan
Bradford W. Fiske
John Charles Hall
Kevin E. Hart
Michele Lew s
Gavin A. Macrae-Gibson
Richard L. McElhiney
George R. Mitchell
Thomas N. Patch
Jon K. Pickard

1980

Jacob D. Albert
J. Scott Finn
Robert S. Kahn
Mariko Masuoka
Ann K. McCallum
Reese T. Owens
William A. Paquette
Beverly F. Pierz
Joseph F. Pierz

1981

Richard L. Brown
Michael B. Cadwell
Douglass W. Cooper
Eric W. Haesloop
Brian E. Healy
Mitchell A. Hirsch
T. Whitcomb Iglehart
Michael G. Kostow
Jonathan Levi
Frances H. Roosevelt
Daniela N. Voith
Spencer Warncke
Diane L. Wilk

1982

John A. Boecker
Michael B. Burch
Domenic Carbone, Jr.
Bruce H. Donnally
Eric J. Gering
Raymond R. Glover
Kay Bea Jones
Thomas A. Kligerman
John C. Locke
Charles F. Lowrey, Jr.
Theodore John Mahl
R. Stephen McDaniel
Paul W. Reiss
Janet S. Roseff
William H. Sherman
Constance A. Spencer
R. Anthony Terry

1983

Maynard M. Ball
Phillip G. Bernstein
Carol J. Burns
Ignacio Dahl-Rocha
Erica N. Ling
Elisabeth Nan Martin
Elizabeth Ann Murrell
Nicholas J. Rehnberg

Jacques M. Richter
Gary Schilling
Brent Sherwood
Sonya R. Sofield
Robert J. Taylor
Nell W. Twining
Michael R. Winstanley

1984
Kenneth A. Boroson
Paul F. Carr, Jr.
Michael J. Chren
Marti M. Cowan
Teresa Ann Dwan
Blair D. Kamin
Elizabeth M. Mahon
Michael L. Marshall
David Chase Martin
Kenneth E. McKently
Scott Merrill
Lawrence S. Ng
David L. Pearce
John R. Perkins
Jennifer C. Sage
Kevin M. Smith
Mary E. Stockton
Marion G. Weiss
Sarah E. Willmer

1985
Barbara A. Ball
Rasa Joana Bauza
Bruce R. Becker
William Robert Bingham
Robert L. Bostwick
M. Virginia Chapman
Michael Coleman Duddy
Jonathan M. Fishman
Lucile S. Irwin
Andrew M. Koglin
Charles H. Loomis
Chariss McAfee
Richard G. Munday
Joseph A. Pasquinelli
Roger O. Schickedantz
R. David Thompson

1986
William Bartow Bialosky
Timothy Burnett
Margaret J. Chambers
Carey Feierabend
David J. Levitt
Jeffrey P. Miles
Nicholas L. Petschek
Aaron E. Rumple
Warren Temple Smith
J. Gilbert Strickler
John B. Tittmann

1987
John P. Blood
Mary Buttrick Burnham
William D. Egan
R A. Garthwaite
Elizabeth P. Gray
Andrew B. Knox
David G. Leary
Douglas S. Marshall
Craig D. Newick
Lilla J. Smith
Duncan Gregory Stroik
Jennifer Tate
William L. Vandeventer
Lester Y. Yuen

1988
Hans Baldauf
Andrew D. Berman
Cary Suzanne Bernstein
John David Butterworth
Aubrey L. Carter
Allison Ewing
Stephen C. Fritzinger
Natalie C. Gray-Miniutti
Drew H. Kepley
Ann Lisa Krsul
Oscar E. Mertz III
Kathryn B. Nesbitt
Kevin V. O'Brien
Alan W. Organschi
Elaine M.
    Rene-Weissman

William Taggart Ruhl
Gilbert P. Schafer III
Matthew Viederman
Li T. Wen
Robert D. Young

1989
Larry G. Chang
Darin C. Cook
John DaSilva
Steve Dumez
Thomas J. Frechette
Jennifer A. Huestis
Timothy C. Joslin
Kevin S. Killen
Frank Koumantaris
Amy H. Lelyveld
Aari B. Ludvigsen
Stephen D. Luoni
Cherie H. Santos-Wuest
Robert Ingram Tucker
Paul K. Watase
Randy Wilmot

1990
Charles S. Bergen
Stephen Brockman
Elizabeth A. Danze
Stancliff C. Elmore
Kristen L. Hodess
David E. Houston
Jeffrey E. Karer
Marc D. L'Italien
David Clayton Miller
Robin E. Osler
Deborah R. Robinson
Mildred I. Sung
Marie B. Wilkinson
Scott Wood

1991
David M. Becker
John C. Gilmer
Dominic L. LaPierre
Joseph W. Moore
Linda Stabler-Talty
Alexander M. Stuart
Claire E. Theobald
Michael W. Wetstone
Kevin Wilkes
Heather H. Young

1992
Andrew James Abraham
Kelly Jean
Carlson-Reddig
Betty Y. Chen
Larry G. Cohen
Frances Douglas Corzine
Perla Jeanne Delson
Frederick Adams
    Farrar, II
Morgan Hare
Maitland Jones II
Douglas Neal Kozel
James A. Langley
Daniel A. Sagar
Daniel P. Towle-Weese
Lynn Waskelis
Marion C. Winkler

1993
Benyamin Ber
Sari Chang
George Andrew Clemens
Richard G. Grisaru
Louise J. Harpman
Michael A. Harshman
Jordan J. Levin
Gitta Robinson
Allen D. Ross
Evan Michael Supcoff

1994
Brendan Russell Coburn
Mark C. Dixon
Pamela J. Fischer
Benjamin J. Horten
Paul W. Jackson
Mark R. Johnson
William J. Massey
Tania K. Mir
Sergey Olhovsky
Edward B. Samuel

Albert J. Tinson, Jr.
Mimi H. Tsai
Andrew C. Winters

1995
Matthew K. Bremer
Carolyn A. Foug
George C. Knight
Aaron M. Lamport
Michael Henry
    Levendusky
Todd Thomas Stodolski
John Christopher Woell

1996
Don M. Dimster-Denk
Russell S. Katz
Michael V. Knopoff
Chung Yin J. Lau
Arthur J. Lee
Alexander F. Levi
Thomas A. Lumikko
Nancy Nienberg
David A. Thurman
Mai-Tse Wu

1997
Victor E. Agran
Richard Kasemsarn
Drew Lang
Peter D. Mullan
Samuel E. Parker
David J. Pascu
Jeffery Ryan Povero
Ian M. Smith
Catherine M. Truman
William James Voulgaris
Shawn Michael Watts
Andrew Paul Wolff

1998
Paul J. Boulifard
Holly M. Chacon
Thalassa A. Curtis
Marjorie K. Dickstein
Edward B. Gulick
Karl A. Krueger
Ceu G. Martinez
Marc A. Roehrle
Elizabeth P. Rutherfurd
Maureen R. Zell

1999
Kimberly Ann Brown
Mark A. Crew
Martha Jane Foss
Bruce D. Kinlin
Moshik S. Mah
Elizabeth R. Manegold
Aaron W. Pine

2000
Benjamin Jon Bischoff
Joseph Shek Yuen Fong
Donald W. Johnson
Thomas Matthew
    Morbitzer
Byung Taek Park
Ron M. Stelmarski
Cheng-Hsun Wu

2001
Ghiora Aharoni
Natalie S. Cheng
Mark Foster Gage
Christopher M. Pizzi
Adam J. Ruedig
Timothy A. Sullivan
Juliana Chittick Tiryaki

2002
Noah K. Biklen
Pengzhan Du
Joseph P. Ferrucci
Sarah Marie Lavery
Yansong Ma
Rashid Jamal Saxton

2003
Andrew William Benner
Marcos Diaz Gonzalez
Li-Yu Hsu
Dongyeop Lee

2004
Valerie Anne Casey
Pu Chen
Leejung Hong
Matthew M. Jogan
James C. Nelson III
Adam Sokol
Na Wei
Damian D. Zunino

2005
Ralph C. Bagley
Ruth Shinenge Gyuse
Diala Salam Hanna
Derek J. Hoeferlin
Brandon F. Pace
Noah Riley
Brett Dalton Spearman
Nicholas Martin Stoutt

2006
Angel Paolo Campos
Michael J. Grogan
Sean A. Khorsandi
David Nam

2007
Brook G. Denison
Geoffrey R. Lawson

2008
Michael B. Crockett
Jennifer J. Dubon
Marc Charles Guberman
Kathleen L. John-Alder
Whitney M. Kraus
Yichen Lu
Maria C. Melniciuc
Jacob I. Reidel
Leo Rowling Stevens IV

2009
Rebecca B. Winik

2010
Brett Patrick Appel
Helen P. Brown
Daniel D. Colvard
Gregory K. Melitonov
Scott Brandon O'Daniel

2011
William Grandison
    Gridley

2012
Christos C. Bolos
Erin C. Dwyer
Clay C. Hayles
Laura C. Wagner

2013
Antonia M. Devine
Altair L. Peterson
Ryan Salvatore

2014
C. Chessin Gertler
Charles M. Hickox
Alexander J. Sassaroli
Kathleen B. Stranix

*Deceased

Retrospecta 38
2014 – 2015

Published by the Yale School of Architecture
Dean Robert A.M. Stern

Editors
Cat Garcia-Menocal, M.Arch. 2017
Wes Hiatt, M.Arch. 2017
Laura Meade, M.Arch. 2017
Maggie Tsang, M.Arch. 2017

Graphic Designers
Laura Foxgrover, MFA 2016
Moonsick Gang, MFA 2016

Editorial Assistants
Caroline Acheatel, M.Arch. 2017
Elaina Berkowitz, M.Arch. 2017
Jack Bian, M.Arch. 2016
Graham Brindle, M.Arch. 2017
Francesca Carney, M.Arch. 2017
Anny Chang, M.Arch. 2017
Rob Cornelissen, M.Arch. 2017
Casey Furman, M.Arch. 2017
Jacqueline Hall, M.Arch. 2017
Lily Hou, M.Arch. 2017
Charles Kane, M.Arch. 2016
Harper Keehn, YC 2017
Sam King, M.Arch. 2017
Richard Mandimika, M.Arch. 2016
Dan Marty, M.Arch. 2017
Tess McNamara, M.Arch. 2017
Rashid Muydinov, M.Arch. 2017
Cecily Ng, M.Arch. 2017
Paul Rasmussen, M.Arch. 2017
Maddy Sembler, M.Arch. 2017
Ilana Simhon, M.Arch. 2017
Alex Stagge, M.Arch. 2017
Isaac Southard, M.Arch. II 2016
Caitlin Thissen, M.Arch. 2016
Rob Yoos, M.Arch. 2017

Photography
Francesca Carney, M.Arch. 2017
Kiana Hosseini, M.Arch. 2016
John Jacobson
Richard Mandimika, M.Arch. 2016
Harold Shapiro
Isaac Southard, M.Arch. II 2016
    {Travel photos by respective studios}

Design Consultant
Pentagram; New York

Printer
Allied Printing Services; Manchester, CT

Typeface
Favorit Favorit Regular, Bold, Underline by
    DINAMO: Fabian Harb and Johannes Breyer;
    Heiden, Switzerland

Paper
Cascades 60lb Rolland Opaque Smooth Text
International Paper 60lb Springhill Opaque
    Canary Text
Mohawk 14pt Kromekote C1S Cast Coated

**We would like to extend our most
sincere gratitude to**

Dean Robert A.M. Stern
Sheila Levrant deBretteville
Richard DeFlumeri
Richard Kaplan, Allied Printing
Michael Bierut, Pentagram
John Jacobson
Jean Sielaff

Dov Feinmesser, M.Arch. 2016
Anthony Gagliardi, M.Arch. 2016
Jenny Kim, M.Arch. 2016
Andrew Sternad, M.Arch. 2016
    {Former editors of Retrospecta }

Rosalie Bernardi
John Eberhart
Francesca Carney, M.Arch. 2017
Vincent Guerrero
Dan Hammond
Robie-Lyn Harnois
Maria Huling

Nicolas Kemper, M.Arch. 2016
Josh Levinson
David Liston
Anne Ma, M.Arch. 2016
Nina Rappaport
Monica Robinson
Lillian Smith
Isaac Southard, M.Arch. II 2016
Rosemary Watts
Marilyn Weiss
Donna Wetmore
Trevor Williams
Doug White

The faculty, staff and students of YSoA

Moms and Dads
Narragansett

We would also like to acknowledge the invaluable
support of the Rutherford Trowbridge Memorial
Publication Fund and the Paul Rudolph Publication
Fund, established by Claire and Maurits Edersheim.

For more information and copies of this book, please
write, call or visit us at:
    Yale School of Architecture
    180 York Street
    New Haven, CT 06511
    {203} 432-2288
    www.architecture.yale.edu

Retrospecta 38